D0234541

"If you still question the emergence of a new non-megachurch tradition among the evangelical younger sorts, you need to read *Emerging Churches*. Not only do Gibbs and Bolger write careful firsthand accounts of new ministries, but they also clearly delineate nine missiological convictions and set forth a vision for the application of the gospel to a postmodern culture."

Robert Webber, Myers Professor of Ministry, Northern Seminary

"Too many books on the emerging church I've come across have been a mile wide and an inch deep (focusing on the 'coffee, candles, and cool videos' veneer of emerging church), but not this book. *Emerging Churches* is a thoroughly researched snapshot of the worldwide emerging church movement and includes extensive interviews with the practitioners who are truly engaged in the emergence of the twenty-first century church."

Karen Ward, Church of the Apostles, Seattle

"Based on extensive research and study, Eddie Gibbs and Ryan Bolger have helpfully identified common patterns of belief and practice in churches that are seriously engaged with postmodern culture. The result is the best book available on the emerging church. It is important reading for all those who are concerned with the future of the church in our culture and the viability of Christian faith for the next generation and the generations to follow."

John R. Franke, professor of theology, Biblical Seminary

"There are many books about and from the emerging church, but no one has done, as of yet, what Gibbs and Bolger have done—to take an honest, missiological, and thoughtful look at the movement as a whole. Gibbs and Bolger don't do this as disengaged theorists, but they put themselves inside the churches and the minds of the pastors and leaders of the movement. They tell the story of its development and offer helpful reflection on its implications. All who are interested in the conversation of the emerging church will find this book a must-have and anchor to their library. We should all be thankful for this unique and well-informed look at the emerging church."

Doug Pagitt, pastor, Solomon's Porch, Minneapolis; Emergent Organizing Group

"No one can question that the churches in the West are in the midst of massive transitions. Wherever one turns there are critiques, experiments, research projects, and conversations of all kinds about the church and its emerging shapes. Clearly, there are many kinds of emergence going on right now, and we aren't going to know for some time what might take form out of these experiments. In this book Eddie Gibbs and Ryan Bolger provide an important reading of some of the creative edges and directions of various groups that are struggling to discern the forms that the Spirit is calling forth. This readable and helpful guide shows us the emergence of churches seeking to engage the changing cultures in which we find ourselves."

Alan Roxburgh, president, Missional Leadership Institute

"Gibbs and Bolger have produced a very welcome and comprehensive piece of research into U.K. and U.S. emerging churches. The book captures the spirit of the emerging church movement wonderfully well from the underside. I love the way it gives voice to leaders from within the movement and helpfully draws out and gives shape to the practices of emerging churches. It is a refreshingly sympathetic and positive critique from two researchers who have clearly been inspired and filled with hope as they have sensed the Spirit at work, beckoning the church into the future."

Jonny Baker, national advisor on youth and emerging church,
Church Mission Society (U.K.)

EMERGING
CHURCHES

CREATING CHRISTIAN COMMUNITY
IN POSTMODERN CULTURES

Eddie Gibbs and Ryan K. Bolger

Published in Great Britain in 2006

Society for Promoting Christian Knowledge
36 Causton Street
London SW1P 4ST

Copyright © Eddie Gibbs and Ryan K. Bolger 2006

Original edition published in the United States of America in 2006
by Baker Academic
a division of Baker Publishing Group
P.O. Box 6287, Grand Rapids, MI 49516-6287
www.bakeracademic.com

All rights reserved. No part of this book may be reproduced or
transmitted in any form or by any means, electronic or mechanical,
including photocopying, recording, or by any information storage or
retrieval system, without permission in writing from the publisher.

SPCK does not necessarily endorse the individual
views contained in its publications.

British Library Cataloguing-in-Publication Data
A catalogue record for this book is available from
the British Library

ISBN-13: 978-0-281-05791-7
ISBN-10: 0-281-05791-5

3 5 7 9 10 8 6 4

Reprinted in Great Britain by
Ashford Colour Press

Contents

Preface

Common needs often create strange alliances. Let us explain. Ryan Bolger was into his second year of a Ph.D., and he needed to undertake field research to fulfill the requirements for his degree. Eddie Gibbs, after completing his book *ChurchNext,* needed to follow up his more theoretical work with one of a more practical or experiential nature. Ryan required Eddie's long-time church expertise for his project. Eddie desired Ryan's help with understanding the emerging cultures. After briefly joking about the implausibility of joining forces, we started to realize it was not such a preposterous idea, and in the spring of 2000, we started research on what was to become this book. Now, in the early part of 2005, we are completing the write-up of the research after numerous driving and lodging adventures, various mishaps, myriad discussions, including the differences between English and American profanity, and our quite dissimilar approaches to writing texts. Remarkably, we are still good friends after all this.

As it turns out, the delay has provided new opportunities for deeper understanding due to the fact that the emerging church movement represents a rapidly evolving scenario. The numerous delays in our deadline did not represent our own procrastination. Rather, they were filled with feverish interviews with emerging church leaders. This book now incorporates over one hundred interviews representing several hundred hours of interview time, either face-to-face, over the phone, or through email. We both want to express our gratitude to Robert N. Hosack, the senior editor of acquisitions for Baker Academic, for his enduring patience with us.

Ryan is a native Angeleno (resident of Los Angeles). Both he and his wife were members of several of the new paradigm churches emerging out of Southern California in the 1970s and 1980s and until recently were part of a leadership team of an emerging church in Pasadena. While working on this project, Ryan joined the faculty at Fuller Theological Seminary as assistant professor of church in contemporary culture.

Eddie has been involved in researching church renewal, leadership, and evangelization in the United Kingdom and the United States for over thirty years. He is a U.K. citizen and was ordained in the Church of England over forty years ago, served as a missionary in Chile, worked on the home staff of the South American Missionary Society in the U.K., served with the British and Foreign Bible Society, served as training director for six Billy Graham missions around the U.K., and since 1984 has been a faculty member at Fuller Theological Seminary. He is currently the Donald A. McGavran Professor of Church Growth in the School of Intercultural Studies.

As we began our research, we realized that we embrace many of the same convictions about the present plight of the church. We both believe the current situation is dire. If the church does not embody its message and life within postmodern culture, it will become increasingly marginalized. Consequently, the church will continue to dwindle in numbers throughout the Western world. We share a common vision to see culturally engaged churches emerge throughout the West as well as in other parts of the world influenced by Western culture.

The Format of the Book

As we plotted these emerging churches around the world (in appendix B, we explain how we identified, collected, and analyzed data on emerging churches between 2000 and 2005), we observed that the U.K. and the U.S. seemed to have the most in terms of numbers, and so we chose our case studies from these countries. Through careful selection, we hoped to pick cases that also typified those outside the U.K. and the U.S., such as in Australia, New Zealand, and continental Europe.

Our limited budget barely allowed for U.K. and U.S. travel, and we felt that our research would lack integrity if we wrote about trends in countries in which we had not conducted direct research. Consequently, this book analyzes emerging church trends in the U.K. and the U.S. exclusively, and we have no data to confirm or deny whether these patterns will hold up in other Western countries or those countries influenced by the West. We suspect that these patterns may be useful measures in these other locales, given our common Western orientation, but that simply remains our educated guess. Verification of that assumption must wait for another day.

Our hope is that the nine patterns yielded (see chap. 2) are rooted in the practices of the emerging churches themselves. We identified these areas after almost five years of research into the characteristics of these communities. We listened to the stories and then formed the categories based on the repeated patterns. But we are not so naive as to believe that any researcher comes to a piece of data as an objective observer. The researcher interacts with the results and sees things given his or her particular background. We came to this process as missiologists, and thus we gave input to the categorizations. For example, if a pattern seemed to repeat something from modernity or Christendom, we did not note it as an emerging pattern. We saw a multitude of patterns beyond the nine listed in this text. However, the nine patterns we identify are those we observed as missiologically significant (i.e., emerging church practices that engage our postmodern context with a gospel native to that same culture).

After three years of research, the approach we took to writing the book was as follows (again, see appendix B for more details). After grouping all the interviews by the nine patterns, we commented on these patterns. At some point, these quotes and comments resembled paragraphs, then sections, then chapters, until the book had some semblance of order. Each of the following chapters was jointly written, and we passed each of the chapters back and forth many times. We reviewed the work performed by the other, made necessary corrections, added supplementary material, and repeated the process.

We see this work as a conversational text. We tell many of these same stories in our classes. Before the telling, however, we are not aware of which story will communicate most powerfully with which students. For that reason, we tell many stories, adding layer upon layer, hoping that one story or another will connect and that the learning process will take hold. The strength of this approach is that listeners often hear their own stories reflected within the stories of others. The downside is that the hearer may feel that some stories are redundant or that we illustrate the same pattern with too many of the same type of stories. That is the risk of this work. We decided, however, in the interest of reinforcement, not to edit out all the redundancies, as they reflect how widely held are some of the views as well as the strength of the convictions expressed. Throughout the book, we have included much of the original interview material so that the conversations and observations speak for themselves. It is primarily in the last part of each section of a chapter that we offer any kind of synthesis and evaluative commentary.

A word about our use of quoting and references. The interviews were conducted through face-to-face contact (both individually and in groups), by telephone, and by email. We use quotation marks when we quote a person directly. At times, we deemed it necessary to correct grammar or to use words that would make sense on both sides of the Atlantic. At all times did we seek to be as true to the heart of the speaker as possible. Each speaker had the opportunity to verify that what we wrote is indeed what he or she said. In the rare case that we quote someone secondarily (e.g., through a website, article, or book), we footnote that source.

When we quote speakers, we provide their name, current ministry, and city. Some of our interviewees live in several contexts and participate in several ministries. This presented us with a problem. After much discussion, we decided to list the ministry about which we queried primarily. In addition, if a person is a part of multiple ministries but the quotation has to do with a particular ministry, we list that particular ministry. If the ministry does not have a name, then we simply list the city in which the person lives. Conversely, if the ministry has no home but is trans-local, we simply list the ministry.

Regarding language, when we say emerging churches do such and such a practice, invariably we are saying that these activities are patterns in emerging churches. Because we are casting the net wide—a church needs to demonstrate only the three core practices to be emerging (see chap. 2)—it follows that many emerging churches do not do all nine practices. We recognize that churches emerge differently. What we intend to say but do not want to qualify each time is that exemplary emerging churches participate in the particular pattern under discussion, a practice that is missiologically significant.

Our Sources

We list the biographies of fifty of our interviewees in appendix A. We quote from these leaders throughout the book. We hope readers will take the time to read their engaging stories so as to understand the "who" of emerging churches.

We are aware of the delimitations in our study. Our research identified that many emerging churches are led by white, anglo, middle-class males. Consequently, some may judge the movement to be deficient multiculturally. At this point in time, the detractors may be right. Part of the reason this particular culture predominates is that many of the pioneering emerging churches arose out of the evangelical charismatic subculture, which has these same characteristics.

We must say, however, that in our interviews we were deeply impressed by what we found in regard to the social and cultural practices of emerging churches. Virtually all these communities support women at all levels of ministry, prioritize the urban over the suburban, speak out politically for justice, serve the poor, and practice fair trade (especially in the U.K.). In addition, because these emerging churches are urban in orientation, and to be urban means to be multicultural, we anticipate that as these missional[1] groups become increasingly rooted in their context, they will increasingly represent its cultural mosaic.

Are We Critical Enough?

We are not starry-eyed about emerging churches, meaning we do not believe all emerging churches perform extraordinary activities at all times. Our primary concern throughout this book is to listen to the concerns of emerging church leaders and to appreciate their insights, recognizing that they do not claim to have the answers but are prepared to embark on a journey of faith, trusting God to give them insight and strength in the course of their pilgrimage. They demonstrate a strong commitment to the Bible as their guide for the journey but are seeking to read it with fresh eyes as they shed the constrictions of modernity and endeavor to apply the story of God's redemptive engagement with humankind in a cultural context that raises new questions and poses fresh challenges.

It is important that their voices be heard with a minimum of intrusive comment. Our main purpose as authors is to indicate the missional significance of their faith journeys. As with any cross-cultural mission enterprise, it is a journey with hazards. From time to time, we indicate some of the potential pitfalls. The contributors are themselves aware of some of these. We are impressed by the breadth of their reading and the

---

1. *Missional* refers to those congregations who see Western culture as a field ripe for mission engagement, thus acknowledging that the period known as Christendom is over.

depth of their insights. Yet in company with the vast majority of church leaders in the West, they are hampered by the lack of available cross-cultural training for missionaries within Western culture. This arises from the fact that most of our training for ministry and mission still assumes a Constantinian, Christendom, and modernist cultural context. In a brief look at culture, we explain this dynamic further.

Acknowledgments

This project would not have been achievable without the enthusiastic support of many people. We express our deep gratitude to our esteemed senior colleague Hoover Wong, who provided a grant for faculty development that funded our field research in the United Kingdom and the United States. We also express our thanks to our provost Sherwood Lingenfelter, our dean C. Douglas McConnell, associate provost Robert Freeman, and director of distance learning Ron Hannaford for their generous support of the project.

In the course of our travels, a number of people provided generous and warm hospitality, which made so many of our stays "home away from home." Mary and John Foote, Eddie's friends of more than fifty years, welcomed him into their home during his stay in Sheffield. Ryan was welcomed "sight unseen" by Paul Williams, Chris Matthews and family, Peter and Caroline Harris, Brian and Linda Auten, and Stuart and Caroline Townend.

As will be evident, this book consists in large part of the contributions of people on the front lines whose names appear throughout the text and are alphabetically listed in appendix A. We appreciate, more than we can tell, their openness, honesty, vulnerability, and patience as they answered our questions and shared their stories. Not a few gave over ten hours of their time to this effort. Their many insights gave rise to the thoughts expressed here.

Thanks also goes to those who read and gave feedback on the manuscript—too many to name here. A big thanks to those who gave extensive feedback: Bob Carlton, Olive Drane, Shane Hipps, Aaron Peterson, and Paul Roberts.

Ryan thanks the Junction leadership team for meals and sustaining prayer throughout the first part of the project. Ryan also thanks Eddie for being his great advocate, for including him in his emerging church research, and for his enduring patience with a slightly different writing style. Ryan hopes he did not drive Eddie to an early retirement.

Last, but by no means least, we thank our spouses and families for the sacrifices they bore during our absences and our preoccupation with researching and writing. Ryan thanks his wife, Julie, and their children, Mackenzie and Luke. Eddie expresses his ongoing appreciation to Renee for enduring yet another writing project.

1

A Brief Look at Culture

There is a lot of money for the postmodern game. Anything can be sponsored and fed money to. The modern church will pump money into church planting, books, and movies. But the sun burns brightest before it sets. They are trying to reach young people. However, they will realize that they were wasting their money and walk away. After this, there will be people who apply the gospel in postmodern cultures.

Spencer Burke, Newport Beach, CA

Churches in the United Kingdom and the United States seriously underestimate the need for cross-cultural training for those in their respective congregations. Consequently, churches misread the culture, thereby undermining the church's overall mission. While we recognize the urgency of the situation, we are filled with hope by communities that are discovering culturally appropriate church practices. Furthermore, senior leaders in traditional denominations have also recognized the great need of our times, and they look to emerging churches as signs of the future. Before examining these emerging churches in the next chapter, we address why cultural study is so critical for the Western church today and discuss the differences between British and American culture.

Why Must the Western Church Today Study Culture?

The study of culture is a highly significant issue that addresses the relationship among Christ, the gospel, the church, and culture. For many years, the standard textbook on this issue was H. Richard Niebuhr's *Christ and Culture*.[1] In recent years, Niebuhr's work has come under severe criticism.[2] Rodney Clapp comments, "*Christ and Culture* was the creature of a time when few Christians could conceive of the church as itself a culture."[3] This raises the missional question as to whether the church exists simply as a subculture or a counterculture or whether it can become truly cross-cultural in the sense of crossing into the broader culture through proclaiming the good news within that cultural context.

There has been a great deal of debate in recent decades over the relationship between the gospel and culture. However, the relationship between the church and culture has not been given the same attention, at least in those parts of the world where Christendom prevailed. There is now a growing realization that churches in the West face a missional challenge, one that is increasingly cross-cultural in nature. This chasm widens as the mainstream culture diverts from its spiritual heritage and society becomes increasingly pluralistic. The following points identify key reasons why the church must seriously study culture.

Because of the Incarnation

Those who call themselves Christian must take seriously the incarnation of Jesus Christ. He took on our culture and our practices; he became one of us. He participated in the local life of the Jews in all their cultural variety. He made himself accessible. "The Word became flesh and made his dwelling [literally, 'pitched his tent'] among us" (John 1:14 NIV). As Jesus did, we must immerse ourselves in the local cultures of our time. As Jesus did, we must provide a critique, but that evaluation must come from within rather than be imposed from outside the cultural context.

1. H. Richard Niebuhr, *Christ and Culture* (New York: Harper Torchbooks, 1951).
2. Stanley Hauerwas and William Willimon, *Resident Aliens* (Nashville: Abingdon, 1989), 40; David Wells (address at the Wheaton Theology Conference, Wheaton, April 21, 1994); and Rodney Clapp, *A Peculiar People* (Downers Grove, IL: InterVarsity, 1996), to name but a few.
3. Clapp, *Peculiar People*, 59.

Because Cultural Understanding Has Always Been Essential to Good Mission Practice

Questions regarding the relationship between church and culture are critical to the mission of the church. Faithful mission practice requires an understanding of the culture in which one is serving. Historically, discerning missionaries have engaged the culture, seeking to communicate the gospel in indigenous forms while remaining faithful to Scripture. Unfortunately, in the West, we often make the mistake of giving culture short shrift, convinced that we understand the various cultures within Western countries.

The church must recognize that we are in the midst of a cultural revolution and that nineteenth-century (or older) forms of church do ??
not communicate clearly to twenty-first-century cultures. A major transformation in the way the church understands culture must occur for the church to negotiate the changed ministry environment of the twenty-first century. The church is a modern institution in a postmodern world, a fact that is often widely overlooked. The church must embody the gospel within the culture of postmodernity for the Western church to survive the twenty-first century.

Relationship with others isr the way!

Because Christendom and Modernity Are in Rapid Decline

Since the conversion of the Roman emperor Constantine in AD 313 until approximately the midpoint of the twentieth century, the church occupied a central position within Western societies. This extensive period is referred to as Christendom, during which the church provided both stability and security as a key social institution. A more recent cultural and social element was the emergence of modernity. It began prior to the Renaissance and survived until it too began to fall apart in the twentieth century. Whereas Christendom provided institutional confidence, modernity provided an epistemological certainty based on foundationalism.

Since the 1950s, two cultural shifts affected the whole of society, embroiling the church at the same time. The first is the transition from Christendom to post-Christendom, with the latter exemplified by pluralism and a radical relativism. Religion is understood in terms of its sociological and psychological significance, discounting any claims to divine revelation and absolute truth. Furthermore, the church as an institution has lost its privileged position and increasingly occupies a place on the margins of society alongside other recreational and non-profit organizations.

The second is the transition from modernity to postmodernity. This shift represents a challenge to the main assertions of modernity, with its pursuit of order, the loss of tradition, and the separation of the different spheres of reality, expressed, for example, in the separation of the sacred and the profane at every level. More often than not, the church has found itself taking the side of modernity, defending its project against all viewpoints.

The combined impact of the challenges to Christendom and modernity has profound implications for the church, the nature of its ministry, mission in the postmodern world, and the ways in which the next generation of leaders needs to be equipped for these new challenges. In response, churches can live in denial, set up a protective perimeter that they will defend against all they define as outsiders, or venture forth in mission.

Because the West Is in the Midst of Huge Cultural Shifts

When a culture is static, as the West was for many years, an understanding of outside culture is not as critical. The culture one imbibed as a baby often lasted a lifetime, and with church culture, the time span was far greater. In a time of immense cultural change, however, the church's ignorance of the wider culture becomes problematic. Due to its cultural entrenchment, the church no longer relates to the surrounding culture, hence its increasing marginalization and perceived irrelevance.

What are these cultural changes that have contributed to the marginalization of the church? First, we are in the midst of a shift from modernity to postmodernity, with the caveats explained above. Second, we are embroiled in a shift from Westernization to globalization. Third, we are engaged in a communication revolution, as we shift from a print culture to an electronic-based culture. Fourth, we are in the midst of a dramatic shift in our economic mode of production, as we transition from national and industrial-based economies to economies that are international, information based, and consumer driven. Fifth, we are on the verge of significant breakthroughs in understanding the human at a biological level. Sixth, we are seeing a convergence of science and religion that has not been seen in centuries.

Any one of these shifts requires significant theological reflection. Pastoral leaders must listen carefully to culture and be prepared to abandon cherished church forms if necessary. To pastor missionally, church leaders must understand the cultural changes that have occurred *outside* its doors.

For the church to be able to situate itself in culture, an understanding of these social processes must be pursued.

Because the Church Is in Decline

Both in the U.K. and the U.S., the decline of the major traditional denominations has been well documented. This decline began in the mid-1960s and continues unabated in most cases to the present time.[4] The reported weekly church attendance in the U.S. is 40 percent, while in the U.K. it is 8 percent. This figure includes all traditions—Anglican, Catholic, and so-called free churches. The decline in church attendance has been occurring for several decades longer in the U.K., which means that churches, new and old, are now seeking to reestablish contact with people three or four generations removed. In the U.S., the bulk of ministry to the "unchurched" is more accurately described as reaching out to welcome back the "previously churched." However, the picture is not rosy for the U.S. either. Even though the U.S. boasts higher figures (a reported 40 percent of the population since World War II), it may be an exaggerated number based on intentions rather than on actions, possibly reducing the number 15 to 20 percent.[5] In addition, as one moves to blue states, as opposed to red states,[6] and interviews the younger generations, the number of people attending church approaches the British counterpart.

Because the Majority of Current Church Practices Are Cultural Accommodations to a Society That No Longer Exists

Just as it is important to understand the culture at large, today's Christians must also understand the culture that exists *inside* the church's doors. Much of what we understand as historical church practices is simply cultural adaptations that occurred at other times and places in church history. The church must "de-absolutize" many of its sacred cows in order to communicate afresh the good news to a new world.

---

4. Peter Brierley, *The Tide Is Running Out* (London: Christian Research, 2000); George Gallup Jr. and D. Michael Lindsey, *Surveying the Religious Landscape* (Harrisburg, PA: Morehouse, 2000); and Dean R. Hoge, Benton Johnson, and Donald A. Luidens, *Vanishing Boundaries: The Religion of Mainline Protestant Baby Boomers* (Louisville: Westminster, 1994).

5. This figure is based on telephone surveys and has been questioned by those who believe it is inflated when compared with data gathered from counts of people in church. The inflation factors, called "the halo effect," may be as high as 100 percent.

6. The division based on the presidential election in the fall of 2004. The red states (on the television maps) voted for George W. Bush, and the blue states voted for John Kerry.

The Protestant Reformation created a church that was closely aligned with the newly literate culture. Linear progression of thought, highly reasoned exegesis, and expository preaching illustrated the new culture's focus on the written word. According to different timetables and different degrees in the various traditions, the church removed the symbolic, the mystical, and the experiential to make a space for logical and linear ways of thinking and living. Church leaders must be aware of the ways in which the church has venerated written culture at the expense of oral, aural, and visual worlds.

Because the Primary Mode and Style of Communication in Western Culture Have Changed

Faithful mission practice requires an understanding of the *language* of culture. Unfortunately, the church has been slow to adopt new communication technologies. Far from being faddish, these technologies are the very essence of how people today construct their worlds. It is here that the church may be most out of step with culture. The Reformation contextualized the gospel for the print era, but there has been no corresponding reformation to bring the gospel to our image-based era. The church continues to communicate a verbal, linear, and abstract message to a culture whose primary language consists of sound, visual images, and experience, in addition to words.[7] Meaningful activity assumes the convergence of sound, sight, and touch through activities, rituals, and stories. Current patterns and styles of preaching communicate with diminishing impact. Pastors must understand the comprehensive nature of language to be heard by the culture.

Because a New Culture Means That New Organizational Structures Are Required

What organizational structures did modernity hand to today's church leaders and members? During the twentieth century, the church, already hierarchical and rationalized, became even more so as it mimicked Henry Ford's hierarchical, assembly-line construction to maximize productivity, resulting in dehumanization and disempowerment. As the twentieth century progressed, characteristics of a McDonaldized

7. Tex Sample, *The Spectacle of Worship in a Wired World: Electronic Culture and the People of God* (Nashville: Abingdon, 1998).

society[8] reigned inside newer forms of church as well. It does not take long to identify the predictable, the calculated, the efficient, and the controlling aspects of McDonald's that are mirrored in today's church. As church leaders in the Western world recognize their role as missionaries, they must rethink many of the inherited ways of administering church in our times.

Because Boomers Are the Last Generation That Is Happy with Modern Churches

The wave of Boomer returnees to church had no parallel in Europe, Canada, Australia, or New Zealand. Experience in those countries suggests that the longer emerging generations remain outside the church the less likely it is that they will return. Furthermore, they are disillusioned with institutionalism and see the church itself as an obstacle to faith. Many churches fail to live out the faith they profess, at least in the estimation of those who taunt them. Consequently, postmodern generations have simply chosen to ignore the organized church as irrelevant to their spiritual quest.

Church leaders often reduce the postmodern shift to that of a generation gap. To be fair, there is benefit to generational theory, even though it tends to oversimplify complex issues. For many cultural theorists, the modern period ended in the U.S. in the 1950s. In the U.S., the Boomer generation, born between 1946 and 1964, was the last generation formed primarily during the cultural period of modernity. As an example of their standardized religious approach, many Boomer churches removed the last remaining symbols, images, and rituals from the church as they built new suburban churches that reflected the corporate culture of affluent functionality. They built churches for one cultural subtype of Boomer, the suburban consumer of religion who is also a corporate achiever in his or her vocational life. This corresponded to a gospel of personal fulfillment and megachurch identification.

Conversely, sociological insights concerning Gen-Xers reveal that when the mystery, the visual, the ritual, the touch, and the beauty are removed, little is left. Thus, the modern church of their Boomer parents does not satisfy the yearnings of the under-forties, and that is why Gen-Xers increas-

---

8. George Ritzer, *The McDonaldization of Society: An Investigation into the Changing Character of Contemporary Social Life* (Thousand Oaks, CA: Pine Forge Press, 1996); and John Drane, *The McDonaldization of the Church: Consumer Culture and the Church's Future* (Macon, GA: Smyth & Helwys, 2002).

ingly participate in churches with pre-Reformation histories. Moreover, new forms of churches have restored an atmosphere of mystery and awe enhanced by the use of incense, candles, and prayer rituals. Local church leaders must seek to communicate the Christian message using ritual and the five senses to lead effectively in the twenty-first century.

Generational analysis may be helpful in revealing that Boomers are the last generation that may be satisfied with a modern church service that is linear, word based, and abstract, whereas Gen-Xers desire rituals, visuals, and touch. However, even in a brief treatment, there are many exceptions to these rules. Looking at Boomers, Gen-Xers, and Millenials has done much more harm than good for those churches that believe the church's main problem is a generational one. Generational issues are imbedded in the much deeper cultural and philosophical shift from modernity to postmodernity.

Because of the Increasing Appeal of Spirituality Derived from Other Religions

A drastic falling away from institutional Christianity should not be seen as conclusive evidence of the triumph of secularization. Spirituality, however vaguely defined, is still prevalent, with indications that it has assumed greater significance in recent years. Popular spirituality surfaced to an unprecedented degree with the death of Princess Diana and the outpouring of grief and prayers from the crowds gathered outside Westminster Abbey that flooded through the open doors of the church to overwhelm the official ceremony inside. On both sides of the Atlantic, the segment of the population that sees reality holistically and spiritually presents a major challenge. Such people are the cultural creatives[9] within society.

In reaction to the Western church's identification with the rationalism of modernity, a significant number of believers are either practicing a smorgasbord form of spirituality or abandoning the Christian faith entirely. They are creating Westernized forms of historic religion that provide immediate access to transcendental reality, offer the means to self-realization, and deemphasize self-discipline and the place of legitimate suffering.[10] The church is sending spiritually minded people to strive after other religions because it has become secularized.

---

9. Paul Ray and Sherry Anderson, *The Cultural Creatives: How Fifty Million People Are Changing the World* (New York: Harmony Books, 2000).

10. Vishal Mangalwadi, *When the New Age Gets Old: Looking for a Greater Spirituality* (Downers Grove, IL: InterVarsity, 1992).

Because Many Christians No Longer Follow the Religion of Their Parents

Religious behavior is not a given, unlike ethnicity, family, or neighborhood.[11] Thus, religious practice transcends primary ties, and no longer does one adopt the traditions of one's parents.[12] Individuals make their own religious choices; the "emancipation of the self" is manifested through the abandoning of all ascriptive barriers and the embracing of subjectivity and individual expression.[13]

It is not that people are less religious but that their religious beliefs are rooted in personal experience rather than in community identity or loyalty to historic institutions. For the first time, at least in American history, religion is chosen rather than received.[14] Religion is now the burden of the solitary individual. He or she must work out his or her own solutions to the spiritual quest.[15] *Consumer approach*

In religion, authority shifted from external sources to internal ones.[16] "For the great mass of American Christians other than Evangelicals, including Roman Catholics, religious authority lies to a considerable extent in the individual believer—rather than in the church or the Bible."[17] *No* External authorities are not shunned; they just need to be confirmed.[18] No longer does one give unwavering support to institutions. Instead, institutions are required to serve the individual and not the other way around.[19]

11. Penny Edgell Becker, *Congregations in Conflict: Cultural Models of Local Religious Life* (New York: Cambridge University Press, 1999), 212.

12. "Families play less of a role than they once did in transmitting religious beliefs and values; there is less of a coherent tradition to inherit" (Wade C. Roof and William McKinney, *American Mainline Religion* [New Brunswick: Rutgers University Press, 1987], 68).

13. Ibid., 49.

14. Wade Clark Roof, *A Generation of Seekers: The Spiritual Journeys of the Baby Boom Generation* (San Francisco: HarperCollins, 1994).

15. According to Robert Bellah, in most denominations, church members must solve their own problems. Churches can provide resources, but ultimately each person must rely on himself or herself for answers (Linda Woodhead and Paul Heelas, eds., *Religion in Modern Times* [Oxford: Blackwell, 2000], 351–52).

16. The individual has internalized religious structures. "In our survey we found that high levels of religious individualism are associated with declining religiosity but are positively related to interest in personal spirituality. If it undermines one, it intensifies the other" (Roof and McKinney, *American Mainline Religion*, 159). Thus, the overall interest in religious activity has not decreased.

17. Ibid., 155–56. By making salvation an individual responsibility, the church added to the growing sense of individualism (Steve Bruce, *Religion in the Modern World: From Cathedrals to Cults* [Oxford: Oxford University Press, 1996], 22–23). Bruce sees the individualism fostered by the Reformation, combined with the printing press, as the source of rationalization, science, and the breakup of a united Christendom.

18. Roof and McKinney, *American Mainline Religion*, 49.

19. Ibid., 50.

Cultural Differences between the United Kingdom and the United States

A few cultural differences between the U.K. and the U.S. influence emerging churches. First, the U.K. is a much-less-churched context than the U.S. As Paul Roberts (Resonance, Bristol, U.K.) explains:

> In the U.K., an average of only 10 percent of people attend church at least once per month. In urban contexts, it is a good deal less, and among the twenty to thirty age range, it is also far less—roughly 2 or 3 percent. So the need and the opportunity are huge—but the post-Christian hangover is also big. There is also a huge amount of hedonistic apathy to religion. The church and religion are just off people's radar screens among that age range. Things are demographically not as bad as this in the United States. But in Europe, Christians under the age of forty are a minority in the churches, and a very small minority among their peers. This has a big effect on what they think is possible and the scale of their ideas. There is therefore a big need for envisioning leadership among this church group, but it also needs to take seriously the cultural challenges in the modes of church that emerge.

Second, there is a marked contrast between urban centers in the U.K. and the U.S. The cities and conurbations of North America, especially on the West Coast, are recent and growing. This is in marked contrast to the cities of Britain, which are either old industrial centers seeking a new identity or ancient cities sustained by their tourism, old-money families, and the ever-growing ranks of commuters. Consequently, in the U.S., emerging churches can capitalize on the mobility of previously churched populations and the expansion of suburban development. In the U.K., emerging churches must be more intentionally missional in establishing a presence and in building indigenous faith communities.

Third, in America, unlike in Britain, there are still social incentives to stay in church that vary greatly by region. In addition, there is an evangelical subculture in the U.S. that enables the church to draw numbers simply by advertising a compelling event to those in the church or to those who were raised in the church. Because of the lack of a Christian subculture and the high social cost of joining the church, Christians in the U.K. must be much more creative to draw those outside the church into the life of the church community.

For our research interests, the biggest difference between the cultures of the U.K. and the U.S. is the prevalence of club culture in the U.K.

Our visit to the U.K. in 2001 alerted us to the significance of club culture in England as well as throughout Europe. The city centers attract crowds on the weekends, especially to the districts that have become the center for clubs. Steve Cockram, who at the time was the leader of Ascension (Manchester, U.K.), a high-profile outreach ministry within club culture initiated by Christians, estimates that more than 60 percent of people between the ages of eighteen and thirty-five identify with the club culture to a greater or lesser extent. This cultural expression is an urban phenomenon that was birthed in the old industrial centers of the north of England. The clubs are a significant expression of popular culture, and the city of Manchester, in northern England, is acknowledged to be the world center of club culture.[20]

These clubs are characterized by loud DJ-led music with sophisticated sound systems. It is important to realize that a DJ within club culture is not the disc jockey of the 1970s who played a selection of music tracks. Rather, he or she is a creative artist who takes segments from songs and arrangements and mixes them together to create new music. The clientele dance into the late hours and sometimes throughout the night. Alcohol is served, and Ecstasy is the most prevalent drug. Many dedicated clubbers get little sleep during the weekends and rely on stimulants to face work on Monday morning. During a typical weekend, a clubber takes over one and a quarter Ecstasy pills.

Despite the fact that many of the leading figures in club culture acquire rock star status, their onstage presence is minimal. They are lost behind record decks and computer banks. The real star is the music they make. These artists create an immediate musical experience, often mixing their songs differently each time they perform.

Currently, club culture is much more prevalent in the U.K. than in the U.S. because it arises out of the urban context. European cities are far more compact than is the case in North America, and people congregate in the city center to a much greater extent, especially on the weekend. The club culture in England is a part of the larger common culture, evidenced by the extensive use of dance music in advertising and on television, much more than in the U.S., where dance club music is only just making forays into the market (Barry Taylor, Sanctuary, Santa Monica, CA).

Club culture affects expressions of church life in the U.K., while in the U.S. it has only a limited presence. Barry Taylor states, "In Brit-

20. Dave Haslam, *Manchester, U.K.: The Story of the Pop Cult City* (London: Fourth Estate, 1999).

ain, there is a lot more engagement with the clubbing culture, mostly because Christians have links, both personally and relationally, to this world." Andrew Jones (Boaz, U.K.) has a two-word explanation for why American churches have few club culture churches: the guitar. "Americans love their guitars. They make the best ones, and they make them sound good. The sound of the Jesus revolution was guitar driven. The emerging church in the U.S. was strummed into being in the 1960s and is far more resistant to the DJ's needle than the church in the U.K. America's commitment to the guitar, and its bias toward live culture over disc culture, prevented dance music from entering the mainstream until the 1990s." Christians producing alternative music in the U.S. were interested in different forms of music, "producing grunge bands in hard core clubs, while their U.K. counterparts were layering electronic sounds in multisensory environments without stages and without bands. The rave scene in the U.K. was probably the dominant youth culture at the time, while in the U.S., rave culture (despite having started in Detroit and Chicago) remained an underground culture until the 1990s" (Jones, Boaz, U.K.).

Those Christians who were wired for club culture in the U.S. had little support from the church; they were on their own. Jones (Boaz, U.K.) says, "Where were the Christian ravers and dance scene DJs? Not in churches. They went around the church and took their worship straight to the clubs, coffee shops, poetry slams, concerts, raves, and galleries and to whatever environment would accept it. It really wasn't until the mid to late 1990s that some of the postmodern forms were integrated back into the faith community."

Ultimately, Christians who want to serve within Western culture must be trained as missionaries. They must understand both the incarnational demands of the gospel and the surrounding context. Because the U.K. has lower church attendance, more aging urban centers, a higher social cost of Christian adherence, a lack of an evangelical subculture, and a preference for club culture over guitar culture, the missional encounter will take different forms in the U.K. than in the U.S.

2

What Is the Emerging Church?

The emerging church is being willing to take the red pill, going down the rabbit hole, and enjoying the ride. It is Dorothy not in Kansas anymore yet finding her way home. It is Superman braving kryptonite to embrace Krypton. It is sight seeking wider vision, relationships seeking expanded embrace, and spirituality seeking holistic practice. It is a "road of destination" where Christ followers, formerly of divergent pasts, are meeting up in the missional present and moving together toward God's future.

Karen Ward, Church of the Apostles, Seattle

People talk of revival but fail to see that what needs reviving must be by definition dying—and we are serious about not wanting that to happen, not standing by to let it all just wilt. But we are also pragmatic. We cannot undertake a revolution—this is not God's style. We worship a God of evolving change. It will take time and generations and mistakes and strange beasts. But we will keep at it, not because we think we are somehow the "salvation" of the church—far from it—but because now we have tasted something of this reconfigured body and we simply cannot go back to pews and song sandwiches.

Kester Brewin, Vaux, London

In recent years, a stream of books has appeared tracing the current trends in church attendance and styles of church. Eddie Gibbs contributed to this discussion in 2000 with *ChurchNext,* published in both the U.S. and the U.K. To some extent, this present volume is an extension of that

27

discussion, yet in another, it represents a significant new phase. We both became aware that the emerging church conversation was generating increasing interest and was making an impact far beyond those groups seeking to embody their insights in new forms of church. Owing to the facts that the emerging church spans a range of church traditions and is geographically dispersed throughout Europe, North America, Australia, and New Zealand, we believed the time had come to invite key leaders to contribute their thinking on the nature and mission of the church.

We were also concerned to dispel the myths that the emerging church is simply a passing fad representing an avant-guard style of worship, a movement seeking to recoup its losses among young people by developing contemporary worship styles, or a new and improved brand or marketing strategy. Neither do we believe emerging churches to be halfway houses of a parent church, established to provide a holding tank for younger members until they emerge from their adolescent years or "worldly ways." Identifying the emerging church with youth church is to miss the point. As will be evident throughout the book, emerging churches are missional communities arising from within postmodern culture and consisting of followers of Jesus who are seeking to be faithful in their place and time.

During this liminal[1] time of change, emerging church leaders sometimes struggle when asked to identify themselves. They may look back to what they are emerging *from* more than they look forward to what they are emerging *into*. That is to be expected. One must dismantle the old, clear the way, before one can build something truly new. Looking back helps these leaders see what must be discarded and what must be retained. In this process, emerging leaders first speak in terms of being "post" something, either in reference to various traditions of the church or in reference to the broader culture. However, we have found that the "post" phase, which may last two to four years, is not the final destination of emerging church leaders but simply a necessary stop along the journey. Rebuilding will come, but it cannot be rushed.

Because of this essential dismantling work, some outside the movement have said that those in emerging churches do not love the church or that they are full of negativity because of their propensity for dismantling church structures. This is to misread the movement entirely. What to some may appear to be pointless complaining is part of a larger process of dismantling ideas of church that simply are not viable in

---

1. Alan J. Roxburgh, *The Missionary Congregation, Leadership, and Liminality* (Harrisburg, PA: Trinity Press International, 1997).

postmodern culture. Neither the gospel nor the culture demands these expressions of the faith. Emerging churches remove modern practices of Christianity, not the faith itself. Western Christianity has wed itself to a culture, the modern culture, which is now in decline. Many of us do not know what a postmodern or post-Christendom expression of faith looks like. Perhaps nobody does. But we need to give these leaders space to have this conversation, for this dismantling needs to occur if we are to see the gospel translated for and embodied in twenty-first-century Western culture. In many ways, this is a fragile movement that can be marginalized by denominational leaders and killed with criticism by theological power brokers. Whatever reservations people may have, these new voices need to be heard. Many of these innovative leaders are looking for mentors rather than critics.

This study of emerging churches represents a determined attempt to identify the key practices of this disparate movement, which is so diverse and fragmented that some observers and insiders do not like to think of it as a movement at all. For insiders, it is more of a conversation. The challenge is to identify these communities and to clarify the concerns that motivate these ground-level leaders to reshape and redirect the church in all aspects of its life. Although the communities they lead may be small in number, the numbers are growing rapidly as their influence spreads through websites, blogs,[2] chat rooms, and conference interactions.

This present work seeks to present the key tenets of emerging churches to a wider audience, to those who may be unaware of its development as well as to those who have some notion of significant changes afoot and are seeking further information and clarification. To those who are aware of, or count themselves a part of, the emerging church, it is our hope that this work will illuminate the familiar, giving words to those who have an intuitive understanding that has yet to mature into critical reflection.

A significant and growing number of churches are moving to the front lines of mission in Europe, North America, and Australia. Most of these emerging churches are new, while others represent the rejuvenation of long-standing congregations and ancient traditions. Some of these frontline churches are large, the biggest attracting crowds of several hundreds or even thousands, but the majority are small, consisting of independent groups of less than thirty or clusters of house groups totaling less than one hundred. To better understand the emerging church,

---

2. A blog is a shortened name for a weblog, an online personal diary or journal that allows for comments and discussion with online visitors. The "posts" appear in reverse chronological order.

it is necessary to give a brief history of the church forms that preceded and exist alongside emerging churches.

Is the Emerging Church about Generational Approaches to Church Life?

Karen Ward (Church of the Apostles, Seattle) initially saw the church challenges as generational in scope. In 1999, she worked at the Evangelical Lutheran Church of America (ELCA) headquarters in Chicago as a self-described "church bureaucrat." While reading about the post-Boomer generation on an Episcopal website, Ward saw her frustrations described perfectly. During the next year, she created a website (www.EmergingChurch.org) to help her work through her questions about church. She had no idea that "emerging church" would become the accepted designation of an international church movement. "I aimed my website at mainline folks who did not know about Gen-Xers. I added other churches, and now evangelicals use it too."

Gen-X churches in the U.S. began in 1986 with Dieter Zander and NewSong in Pomona, California. Over the years, other churches followed suit, with notable leaders and communities such as Chris Seay and University Baptist in Waco, Mark Driscoll and Mars Hill in Seattle, and later Erwin McManus and Mosaic in Los Angeles. To generalize, the church services were characterized by loud, passionate worship music directed toward God and the believer (not the seeker); David Letterman–style, irreverent banter; raw, narrative preaching; *Friends* (the popular TV series) type relationships; and later, candles and the arts. The bulk of church practice remained the same as their conservative Baptist, seeker,[3] new paradigm,[4] purpose-driven[5] predecessors; only the surface techniques changed. In 1993, a second version came on the scene, the "church-within-a-church." Everything about the service was the same as the Gen-X stand-alone church, but it was financially supported by a megachurch. There was Tuesday Night Live, which later became the

3. Seeker churches identify with the seeker approach to ministry as characterized by the Willow Creek Association.

4. New paradigm churches are part of the Southern California church movements that were rooted in the Jesus movement of the 1960s, most specifically the Vineyard, Calvary Chapel, and Hope Chapel. These were identified by Donald E. Miller in *Reinventing American Protestantism: Christianity in the New Millennium* (Berkeley: University of California Press, 1997).

5. Purpose-driven churches form their church life around the purpose-driven principles set forth by Rick Warren of Saddleback Community Church, Lake Forest, California.

Next Level, in Denver with Trevor Bron; Axis in Barrington, Illinois, with Dieter Zander; Graceland in Santa Cruz, California, with Dan Kimball; and Warehouse 242 in Charlotte with Todd Hahn, among many others. These quickly outnumbered the stand-alone Gen-X churches.

Probably the closest U.K. equivalent to the American Gen-X church or church-within-a-church are the youth congregations that began in the southern half of England in the early 1990s. In 1991, New Generation Ministries (NGM) out of Bristol sent its first team to begin a church among twelve- to eighteen-year-olds in coordination with five churches in Swindon. Mike Pilavachi and Matt Redman began Soul Survivor (1993) in London as a youth church plant by St. Andrews, Chorley-wood; Mark Meardon began Eternity (1994) as part of St. Michaels in Bracknell; Billy Kennedy, after a series of Cutting Edge events (1994) with Martin Smith (founder of Delirious?), began Sublime (1995) as part of Southampton Community Church; and Pete Greig, with the help of Brooklyn DJ/missionary Kenny Mitchell and others, began Warehouse (1996) as part of Revelation Church[6] in Chichester. In addition, what was to become the Cultural Shift network (primarily the church-planting networks connected to NGM in Bristol, Sublime in Southampton, and Revelation Church in Chichester) began its Remix conferences (1995). The World Wide Message Tribe began performing their dance music for students in schools in 1993, and in 1997, they created teams of young Christians who moved to the most economically and socially deprived areas of Manchester. They befriended the people of the communities, especially the roaming gangs of young people, as they sought to establish faith communities that would have a transformative effect on the neighborhoods. These were called Eden Projects.

The U.K. youth congregations differ from their American counterparts in the following ways: They are much younger, with the average age ranging from fourteen to eighteen years (and sometimes younger); their leaders are more empowered (i.e., they can do "church" how they see fit; the tradition of autonomous congregations within churches is an accepted practice in the U.K.); they became cell based early on (in 1996 or so); and to different extents they are further along in the shift to postmodernity.

6. In 1983, Roger Ellis started Revelation Church in Chichester with goths and punks. Revelation joined Pioneer, a stream within the new church movement. With his book (with Chris Seaton) *New Celts: Following Jesus into Millennium 3* (Brighton, U.K.: Kingsway, 1998), Ellis moves toward a holistic and contemplative expression of the Christian faith. It expresses a care for the poor, plural leadership, and gender equality, and creativity is front and center. Revelation Church is a source for innovative ministries, with 24-7 Prayer, Fusion, and Cultural Shift receiving much of their initial impetus from this community.

On the U.S. side, in the early 1990s, conferences and books began to notice Generation X as well. In 1993, Leighton Ford Ministries and InterVarsity Christian Fellowship jointly held a Consultation on Evangelizing Generation X, the first conference on Gen-X ministry in the U.S. Influential ministry books by George Barna,[7] Kevin Ford,[8] and Tim Celek and Dieter Zander[9] focused on reaching Busters, or Gen-Xers, through ministry strategy and tactics, just as the conferences did.

In the mid to late 1990s, a shift began to occur that directed the focus away from generational ministries. At Gen-X 2.0 in 1997, the second annual conference on Gen-X put on by the Young Leaders Network (YLN), conversations grew around the topic of postmodernity. Although the conference touted the Gen-X theme, the buzz was about moving beyond generational ministry techniques. By the third conference, in the fall of 1998, postmodernity was a main topic of the Re-evaluation Forum planned by Doug Pagitt for YLN. Discussions at that time revolved around whether postmodernity was good or bad.[10] The consensus was that the evangelistic challenge for the church was not generational angst but a philosophical disconnect with the wider culture. Thus, attendees questioned many of the assumptions they had previously held about ministry. For the next three years, postmodernity continued to be a main topic for the Young Leaders Network, which morphed into the Terra Nova Theological Project and which later became Emergent.

Others were also feeling that the challenges facing the church were not generational in scope. Todd Hunter, former national director of the Association of Vineyard Churches (Yorba Linda, CA), felt this way. "During this time, I found the Gen-X church conversation only marginally interesting. To me, it just seemed like the latest iteration of a sociological approach to church. My big 'aha' moment was when it hit me: Everything I know about church is about Christendom and modernity and the baby boom, and all three of these are going away. These were the three eggs in my basket. So the issues were much deeper than adjusting services for Gen-X." Dan Kimball (author of *The Emerg-*

7. George Barna, *Baby Busters: The Disillusioned Generation* (Chicago: Northfield Publishing, 1994).

8. Kevin Graham Ford, *Jesus for a New Generation: Putting the Gospel in the Language of Gen-Xers* (Downers Grove, IL: InterVarsity, 1995).

9. Tim Celek and Dieter Zander, *Inside the Soul of a New Generation* (Grand Rapids: Zondervan, 1996).

10. This conference marks Brian D. McLaren's first involvement with this group. It was in relation to the Young Leaders/Terra Nova/Emergent community that *A New Kind of Christian: A Tale of Two Friends on a Spiritual Journey* (San Francisco: Jossey-Bass, 2001), was born.

ing Church and founder of Graceland, Santa Cruz, CA) agrees. "The young-adult-service approach to church doesn't really work." According to Kimball, "It lasts about four years and then gets taken over, blows up, or the emerging pastor gets fired due to conflict in values and philosophy of ministry. But this is to be expected if it is a true emerging ministry that is going beyond just changing the style of music and adding candles." Kimball views most churches-within-a-church and young adult services as "preservationist, youth-church models aimed at retaining young adults in the life of the mother church." For this reason, Kimball eventually ended the well-known Gen-X church-within-a-church Graceland and worked with the mother church to start a new church, Vintage Faith.

As already mentioned, Karen Ward of Church of the Apostles (Seattle) first understood the issue as a generational problem, but she then realized it was about something much bigger: the shift from modern to postmodern culture. "I realized that the changes were much bigger than generational grouping. Regarding postmodernity, the Gen-Xers are the first marines on the beach. Every generation hereafter will be postmodern." Ward agrees that the shift from Gen-X ministry needed to occur. "The denominational plans to reach out to Generation X seemed ridiculous to me."

Brad Cecil, leader of Axxess in Arlington, Texas, rejected a generational identification as too shallow in its analysis. "As I listened to others, I realized that our ministry philosophy was quite different. I thought that perhaps everyone was thinking the same way we were, but that was not the case. I would go to conferences eager to learn, because I wanted to learn of the different ministry philosophies that existed. I grew really weary of hearing stuff like 'Gen-Xers are the most disillusioned generation in history'; 'Gen-Xers are all cynical'; 'Gen-Xers can't trust because of the high divorce rate among their parents,' etc. This generational stuff really annoyed me, as I felt it was very shortsighted. I couldn't really figure out why people were obsessing about a subgroup when an enormous epistemological shift was occurring. I never really trust broad generalizations regarding a demographic subgroup anyway."

Postmodernity came on the scene for many U.S. church leaders with J. Richard Middleton and Brian Walsh's *Truth Is Stranger than It Used to Be,* published in 1995.[11] Brian McLaren, whose book *New Kind of Christian* (2001) touted a postmodern form of Christianity, described

---

11. J. Richard Middleton and Brian J. Walsh, *Truth Is Stranger than It Used to Be: Biblical Faith in a Postmodern Age* (Downers Grove, IL: InterVarsity, 1995).

Middleton and Walsh's book as a book that came at a critical juncture for him. "As a graduate student at the University of Maryland, I remember hearing postmodernity discussed for the first time. I remember thinking, if this thinking gets out into the public domain, we Christians are in big trouble because we don't have good enough answers to these questions." Thirteen years later, in 1994, those same questions became McLaren's questions, and he struggled to find the answers. "During this time, I learned I needed to trust God more than my theology about God. I tried to imagine a faith that was not so mechanistic, simplistic, and systematic. I said to myself, one year from now [in 1995], I will be out of the ministry. One year from now I'm not sure I will attend church anywhere." Pete Rollins (ikon, Belfast, U.K.) compares such questioning to that done by the cynics in ancient Greece. "The original cynics were a dusty group of people who questioned ethics, not because they hated ethics but because they loved ethics so much. They questioned God and religion, not because they were skeptical but because they were obsessed with God and religion. Questioning God is not questioning God but only questioning 'God'—in other words, our understanding of God." McLaren needed answers, and in many ways, his first book[12] was his therapy, along with the spiritual disciplines he learned from a charismatic Episcopal church nearby.

Taking postmodernity seriously requires that all church practices come into question. In contrast, Gen-X churches involve simply changes in strategy from what came before (e.g., adding stories, video, raw music, vulnerable preaching, art, and candles). However, to be missional is to go way beyond strategy. It is to look for church practices that can be embodied within a particular culture. In other words, theologies given birth within modernity will not transfer to postmodern cultures.

The Emerging Church and Labels

In the mid-1990s, a conversation began as to whether postmodern Christians could still be considered evangelicals, as evangelicalism was born and given its primary expression within modernity. This discussion was significant in determining whether the movement would become increasingly ostracized or regarded as a legitimate expression of evangelical missional theology and praxis. Perhaps the first church leader to discuss the possibility of a postmodern evangelical was Dave Tomlinson (Holy

12. Brian D. McLaren, *Reinventing Your Church* (Grand Rapids: Zondervan, 1998).

Joes, London) with his book *The Post-Evangelical*, published in the U.K. in 1995.[13] In this work, Tomlinson questioned many of the presuppositions of his own new church (house church) background. The book created quite a stir in the U.K. at the time and served as a catalyst for describing the postmodern phenomenon. Although the controversy waned in the U.K., some in the U.S. have found the description postevangelical helpful in describing their spiritual quests.

Jonny Baker (Grace, London) explains the reception of the term *postevangelical* in the U.K. "The thing about Dave Tomlinson's *The Post-Evangelical* was that it caught a moment. You didn't even have to read the book for the title to produce a wry smile on your face, and you knew what it was about!" Anna Dodridge (Bournemouth, U.K.) reflects on the benefits she received from reading *The Post-Evangelical*.

> I read Tomlinson's *Post-Evangelical* and found it to be very helpful. I realized just how evangelical I was and how much I had been stuck in a type of Christianity, without even realizing it was just that—a type, one way of doing things. The book rather shocked me, I'm ashamed to admit, and made me question some pretty basic evangelical principles. At first I saw it as simply a challenging point but still believed all that was evangelical, but as I have developed and grown away from the evangelical position, I have realized that many of my thoughts are reflected in that book. Certainly, many of the experiences my friends and I have had resonate with his book. *The Post-Evangelical* helped me see what I was going through as I came out of the evangelical tradition. It helped me see that there were lots of other people feeling as disillusioned as I was by evangelicalism and that there were other options other than just giving up. At the time, it was a very challenging read and really got me thinking on some big questions.

The Post-Evangelical put a name to experiences that many shared.

Yet *The Post-Evangelical* stirred up more questions than it answered. Kester Brewin (Vaux, London) states, "I read *The Post-Evangelical* years back and recently have gotten to know Dave Tomlinson. In chatting to him about it, I told him I remember having to read it out of a brown paper bag, like bootleg alcohol, in the church I was in! We both agreed that it provided an excellent set of questions but not a substantial set of answers."

Chris Matthews (Linden Church, Swansea, U.K.) still considers himself an evangelical, with some caveats. "The sort of influences that shape

13. Dave Tomlinson, *The Post-Evangelical* (London: Triangle, 1995).

us continue to be evangelicalism, as this is the tradition we have come from, although in many ways we no longer fit neatly into its boundaries." Doug Pagitt (Solomon's Porch, Minneapolis) agrees. He isn't sure if he is an evangelical theologically; perhaps only culturally. "I can't 'undo' being an evangelical. It's not like I can deny it. For me, it's like when people say they are Catholic. They always are, whether they continue to go to mass or not." Debbie Blue (St. Paul) adds:

> I guess I don't define myself primarily as evangelical or Protestant, but they are certainly a big part of the mix. Those things don't seem to matter too much to me as definitions. But neither would I want to say I am "post" those things, as if we had moved beyond them or as if they did not contribute enormously to the formation of my theology and being in the world and the existence of House of Mercy. I am postevangelical if evangelical means American revivalism but not if it means witnessing to the good news of Jesus Christ.

Emerging church leaders may find congruence with the term *evangelical* in the broad historical sense, but the label does not define these leaders as it has for evangelical leaders in the past.

Many in the U.K. have moved beyond the postevangelical debate. Roger Ellis (Revelation Church, Chichester, U.K.), when asked about the "post" conversation, said, "A lot of people here think whether or not we are postevangelical is a boring discussion. However, many of the things Dave Tomlinson is concerned about I have a great sympathy for." Going even further, Ellis said, "But are we really Protestants? I'm post-Protestant. In many ways, I feel post-charismatic as well. By this I mean that I'm confused. I connect with orthodox belief but often feel a disconnect with parts of contemporary Protestant and charismatic culture." But Ellis feels that a focus on "posts" is missing the point. "Yes, I am *post,* but out of principle I am *pre.* I focus on people out there in Ibiza [Spanish island known for the club scene] and other places." Anna Dodridge (Bournemouth, U.K.) goes further still. "Actually, I don't think I am particularly postevangelical. Perhaps I am more post-postevangelical, as I feel we have moved on even farther from what being postevangelical is about."

While the question of whether one is an evangelical is a nonissue for many emerging church leaders, whether one is a Protestant is a non-issue as well. Si Johnston (headspace, London) addresses this issue in the following terms. "To be honest, not very many in my church would have a clue what they are. 'Becoming Christian' is probably the answer that 50 percent would give you, and those aware of their past or place in history might say 'Protestant' or 'Catholic.' It seems that many have moved beyond here but aren't self-conscious enough to articulate it." Debbie Blue agrees. "We have talked about House of Mercy (St. Paul) as postdenominational. That seems really true. Hardly anyone knows what denomination we are or seems to care. It is really important to us to be tied to a larger and historical church, however. The church universal is more fitting for us than the Baptist Church, though there really are some ways in which we are still very Baptist."

Ben Edson of Sanctus1 (Manchester, U.K.) describes his congregation as a mixture. "Some would definitely see themselves as postevangelical, while others would be more open-evangelical and some are more liberal-Catholic. The issue of denomination is fairly interesting, as we have a mix of people from Plymouth Brethren to Roman Catholic. I sometimes wonder whether we would be better described as postdenominational." Just as with the label *evangelical*, the label *Protestant* means little to many emerging church leaders.

Emerging church leaders believe that to define oneself against something is not helpful either. "When people describe themselves as post-X, they are defining themselves as (in mathematical notation) everything that X isn't" (Kester Brewin, Vaux, London). Paul Roberts (Resonance, Bristol, U.K.) also has reservations about the designation postevangelical. He declares, "I've always been a bit skeptical of the usefulness of Dave's postevangelical concept, as it tends, despite his protestations, to fall into the trap of defining yourself against something, which is an old game and seldom a fruitful one." Kester Brewin shares the same conviction. "I suppose Vaux (London) is trying not to be defined by negatives, by what we are supposedly reacting against, as that gives too much power to the old, to what we have come from, as if we are all sitting around moaning about it and getting angry. We want to be defined by what we are. So 'posts' aren't very helpful in that respect." Andrew Jones (Boaz, U.K.) agrees.

> Those terms are not very helpful at all. I like the idea of moving beyond the horizons of old terms and labels, but at the same time, I cannot remove their influence from me. I would like to be more convergent in terms of connecting with the wider body of Christ, but I don't wish to do so by denying the journey of my past—something that is unique and precious. I feel comfortable adding new things to my identity but not letting those things replace or supercede the old. The goal is for us to put away labels that exclude, to become more like Jesus and less evangelical,

or become more like Jesus and less Protestant. Labels and terms will always come back and bite us.

Putting oneself in a particular camp is difficult for emerging church leaders. Simon Hall (Revive, Leeds, U.K.) states:

> Personally, I think I have to recognize that while I could sign various doctrinal statements (although not all), most evangelicals would consider me to be a little far out. The U.K. is unhelpfully polarized between evangelicals and liberals, with both camps seemingly keen to ensure that there remains clear blue water between them. For as long as I can remember, I haven't really belonged to a particular camp. I'm always "the evangelical who's okay," or "the liberal who's okay," or "the charismatic who thinks," or "the denominational guy who loves the Spirit." The alternative worship thing in Britain has just provided me with another group that I don't completely belong to.

Sue Wallace (Visions, York, U.K.) describes her reluctance to be labeled. "I'm not sure we'd agree on a label. None of them seems to fit us as a group. As has been said on our website, 'Let the world be free of labels!'" Debbie Blue (House of Mercy, St. Paul) is of the same opinion. "I think this is a sort of different era in which some of the old categories matter much less than they used to, and we are very comfortable in this era. Maybe that makes us postevangelical and post-Protestant, but I wouldn't use those terms to describe us."

Brian McLaren has given a great deal of thought to the issue of how one defines oneself. He has come to the conclusion, "In many ways, I have more in common with Catholics than I do with Protestants." Indeed, once one embraces many non-modern forms of Christianity, one may find that one feels more Catholic than Protestant. Doug Pagitt also considers himself post-Protestant in the sense that the Catholic and Reformed battles are not his. McLaren adds, "I advocate the term *post-Protestant* as a move from Protestant to pro-testify. We must testify for some things. Our identity ought to consist in what we are for rather than in what we are against." Jonny Baker (Grace, London) expresses his desire for an inclusive faith. "The danger with the church is that it all gets too tribal. I'm not interested in that. I want to be connected to Christ and the body of Christ, both through history (the communion of saints) and globally (the worldwide church), so it is enough for me to be Christian, a follower of Christ." Simon Hall (Revive, Leeds, U.K.) also favors an inclusive approach. "My main aim for the community is not to be 'post' anything but to be 'and' everything. We are evangelical *and* charismatic *and* liberal *and* orthodox *and* contemplative *and* into social justice *and* into alternative worship."

Anna Dodridge (Bournemouth, U.K.) explains that the postevangelical debate loses importance as we move from a churched to an unchurched culture. "Of course, not all of us come from any Christian background at all, so we don't really fall into the post-anything category." Pete Rollins (ikon, Belfast, U.K.) agrees. "Postevangelical is a title we use loosely. As more people from outside the evangelical community and the church join us, the term *postevangelical* becomes less useful. But for now it is apt."

So can an evangelical be postmodern? A brief answer is yes, if evangelical is used in a broad sense, but no if it means that other designations are not viable as well. From a postmodern perspective, the ultimate question is, Why is it important to label oneself as evangelical? Aren't labels simply artificial divisions that make us feel safe or help us exert control? Why not mine the riches of many traditions? What is obvious is that the ecclesiastical or theological label one decides to wear is of far less concern to emerging churches than how one relates to the gospel and culture.

Can Modern and Postmodern Congregations Exist within a Local Church?

When evangelicals and postevangelicals share leadership in a local congregation, the postevangelical debate comes to the fore. Jonny Baker of Grace (London) believes that there is space for both evangelical and postevangelical leaders to work side by side. "In the U.K., there is a culture of permission for new things at the moment, and the Anglican Church has been running churches with several congregations for years anyway. So adding other congregations into the model isn't too complicated to get your head around." Sue Wallace of Visions (York, U.K.) adds, "The freedom that the charismatic churches negotiated with the Church of England paved the way for alternative worship[14] to be born. The Anglican leadership in the late 1980s was flexible and supportive enough to

14. A movement of alternative worship services within the Church of England began in the late 1980s and may number fifty communities in the U.K. Most congregations number twenty-five or less. If not online, they connect at least yearly at the Greenbelt Festival. Alternative worship groups are highly participatory communities that celebrate the Eucharist; utilize popular culture in worship; have no identified or paid leadership; and have a strong working understanding of postmodernity, an appreciation of the visual arts, and nonlinear worship. Their primary missiological contribution is their method of making worship for themselves in ways that are native to their own culture.

nurture these fledgling communities, which helped new groups to feel they could experiment with worship structure."

Not only alternative services but also youth congregations are accepted as regular congregations in the U.K. The young people own the service and are empowered to run it themselves. They are treated as a separate congregation within the church, fully empowered to create a community in the way they see fit. Phil Ball of NGM (Bristol, U.K.) comments, "We are *not* into running a youth event. Instead, we're talking about an expression of church that reaches the unchurched, and we provide environments for that. Although we have oversight, what we want is meaningful ownership for kids. Sometimes we are behind the scenes, and sometimes we are up front. We serve the youth and help them preach and host. We also have accountable relationships with them."

Others, such as Doug Pagitt of Solomon's Porch (Minneapolis), believe that evangelicals and postevangelicals cannot share leadership, stating that postevangelicals must start new communities outside existing church structures. The difference in perspective between Baker and Pagitt may arise from cultural differences between the Anglican and the free church tradition as well as differences between British and American church culture. American churches do not have a successful track record with evangelicals and postevangelicals on the same staff. Dan Kimball (Vintage Faith Church, Santa Cruz, CA) elaborates: "The church-within-a-church in America doesn't work because the senior pastor cannot handle a congregation in the church that may do things differently. It totally goes against how senior pastors have been trained to think of a church and their role as a senior pastor. It is an issue of control, and Anglicans are able to handle that diversity while Americans struggle with it."

Young adult services in the U.S. are also often doomed to fail. As Kimball adds:

> Churches-within-a-church and young adult services usually start out great, but the reality is they can be successful only if they *don't* work. If they work, and lots of young people go there instead of to the worship service the senior pastor leads, the senior pastor will seek to control them. The direction of these young adult services with different leadership goes against the nature of how most churches are structured around a solo senior leader. This messes everything up. Plus, if the new community is truly rethinking church and messing with other values and philosophical issues, it is dynamite waiting to explode. After the explosion, the senior leadership exerts control and the vitality and viability of the younger congregation ceases.

"One day evangelical seeker pastors and postevangelical emerging church pastors will work together under the same roof," hopes Kimball, but he has yet to see it happen. The only young adult services he observes are "mini-me's[15] of the main church that do not really rethink the nature of church." Postevangelical communities have arisen in the U.K. as separate congregations of a church community. At this point in time in the U.S., however, such arrangements have proven to be untenable.

What Are Emerging Churches?

References to emerging churches abound in recent books, seminar topics on trends in the contemporary church, and the vast blogosphere of the Internet, so much so that the emerging church is in danger of becoming the latest fad to share the fate of so many previous passing interests. As the term becomes more widely used, it is in increasing danger of losing its significance. Popularly, the term *emerging church* has been applied to high-profile, youth-oriented congregations that have gained attention on account of their rapid numerical growth; their ability to attract (or retain) twentysomethings; their contemporary worship, which draws from popular music styles; and their ability to promote themselves to the Christian subculture through websites and by word of mouth.

For many within the movement, the emerging church is an umbrella that covers many diverse movements. In Jonny Baker's (Grace, London) opinion, *emerging church* is a catchall term. "I quite like it for that. Church, as we have inherited it, is no longer working for vast groups of people. The world has changed so much. So I think the term *emerging church* is nothing more than a way of expressing that we need new forms of church that relate to the emerging culture."

Ben Edson of Sanctus1 (Manchester, U.K.) agrees that it is a catchall term but expresses some ambivalence regarding his degree of comfort with it.

We are part of the emerging church scene. The phrase is helpful but lacks a sense of urgency. Existing churches may relax and see what emerges rather than engaging with the serious missional task. Also, we are not an emerging church; we are a church. Within the Anglican Church, the current language is "fresh expressions of church," which suggests a sense

15. In reference to the movie *Austin Powers: The Spy Who Shagged Me* (New Line Cinema, 1999).

of being rooted with a tradition but that something lively and new is happening within that. Again, there are problems with this phrase, as it does not easily differentiate between the old and the new. So emerging church for me is quite simply a church that is rooted in the emerging context and is exploring worship, mission, and community within that context.

Others see the emerging church as a type of church that is coming but has not yet arrived. Spencer Burke (Newport Beach, CA) states that emerging churches are nonexistent at this point. He points out that new forms of church cannot divorce themselves from what has come before. They react, and thus, they are not entirely new. "I love the word *emergence*. But does anyone understand what *emergence* means? You can't emerge without first submerging! What we have today is dead. We need much more than a reformation. We are not just a new strain. The question is, How do we get back to the seed? It is very difficult for a hybrid to multiply, and what we see today are hybrids." Like Burke, Karen Ward (Church of the Apostles, Seattle) sees the emerging church as a process that is just beginning. She defines the emerging church as what is "coming to the surface that is new, unformed, still happening, emerging."

Mark Scandrette (ReIMAGINE! San Francisco) falls somewhere in between the inclusive umbrella of Baker and the exclusive prescription of Burke. Scandrette defines particular aspects of emerging churches. "The emerging church is a quest for a more integrated and whole life of faith. There is a bit of theological questioning going on, focusing more on kingdom theology, the inner life, friendship/community, justice, earth keeping, inclusivity, and inspirational leadership. In addition, the arts are in a renaissance, as are the classical spiritual disciplines. Overall, it is a quest for a holistic spirituality."

Like Scandrette, Doug Pagitt (Solomon's Porch, Minneapolis) looks to define key characteristics of emerging churches. He sees three types of responses to the current context: (1) a return to the Reformation (e.g., Mars Hill in Seattle); (2) deep systemic changes, but Christianity and the church are still in the center and theological changes are not needed (e.g., University Baptist in Waco and Mosaic in Los Angeles); and (3) seeing the church as not necessarily the center of God's intentions. God is working in the world, and the church has the option to join God or not. This third approach focuses more on the kingdom than on the church, and it reflects the perspective of Solomon's Porch in Minneapolis and characterizes what Pagitt would classify as emerging.

There is validity in inclusive, exclusive, and itemized definitions of the emerging church. Emerging churches are physically present today—they exist in the here and now. However, the emerging church is a goal or a process, and it has not yet completely arrived. If anything, it is in its infant stage. Emerging churches also contain various patterns. Finally, the emerging church must be understood in light of the kingdom, for without the kingdom, the church forgets its primary calling. The definition offered in this book contains elements of each of these perspectives.

The church universal is an emerging church, for as the body of Christ here on earth, it awaits with eager anticipation the return of its Lord. As such, it is a church always in the process of becoming. It has never arrived in any final way. It is a pilgrim church, living the present reality of the reign of God in its provisional form until its consummation. It "emerges" as it engages the complex mosaic of cultures represented by the peoples of the earth. In so doing, it is morphed in those cultures and exerts a redemptive influence within them.

Yet some specific churches more clearly fit the emerging church label. After our extensive interviews and research, we identified patterns most prevalent in churches that take culture, specifically postmodern culture, seriously. Nine practices are common to these innovative churches, though not all nine are common to each emerging church. Each emerging church, however, does possess three core practices. The other six practices are derivative of these three core practices.

We use the word *practice* here in a particular way, similar to the way it is used for a medical or a legal practice or the business concept of "communities of practice." Whether involved in a medical, legal, or business practice, one displays a competence in a particular domain and perfects it over a lifetime, often through contact with others who display the same skills. Within these practices, members set standards both for themselves and for others who would like to join the same profession. Like the artisan of old, these practitioners mentor their young apprentices, most often implicitly, in the ways of the craft. Much of this is accomplished by spending time together as they participate in their embodied set of skills. At an intuitive level, the apprentice begins to think like his or her mentor. In a similar way, we often learn Christian activities implicitly, we never arrive at a full understanding, we learn them with our bodies as well as with our minds, we learn in community, and we train others just as we are trained.

The three core practices that combine to create the other practices are (1) identifying with the life of Jesus, (2) transforming secular space, and (3) living as community. To clarify, let us flesh out a bit more what we mean by kingdom, the end of modernity, and community.

We will spend an entire chapter on Jesus, the gospel, and the kingdom, and much of the rest of the book fleshes out the way of Jesus for emerging churches. What do we mean by "the way of Jesus"? Simply, the life of Jesus and his engagement with his culture, as embodied in community and given verbal expression in the Sermon on the Mount, is prescriptive for Christians. Modern readings of Jesus are prone to dismiss his life and focus on his death and resurrection and are preoccupied with a believer's interior experience of Christ. In contrast, Jesus welcomed the outcast, hosted the stranger, and challenged the political authorities by creating an alternative community. Jesus' entire life, including his words, established the way of Jesus, and it is this way that has greatly influenced emerging churches.

Modernity and postmodernity have many definitions, as many as there are different spheres of study. The description changes depending on whether one is discussing architecture, dance, philosophy, or literature. We are concerned with modernity within the field of social theory (i.e., how cultural shifts affect the lives of people as a whole in society). Modernity began with the creation of secular space in the fourteenth century. This sacred/secular split led to fragmentation in society simultaneously with the pursuit of control and order. Postmodernity marks the time when secular space was called into question concurrent with the pursuit of holism and the welcoming of pluralization in Western societies. Emerging churches embody their way of life within postmodern culture.

Like the other core practices, community cannot be understood by itself. The type of community seen in the emerging church pursues the kingdom in all spheres of reality, overcoming all sacred/secular divisions. Kingdom communities do not function as affinity groups but more like extended families. In Christendom, the Sunday meeting was the center of corporate spiritual expression for the community. In a post-Christendom context, a church-meeting focus ceases to be indigenous to the culture or necessary to be faithful to the gospel. Instead, the practice of community formation itself is more central than the church meeting. Thus, an emerging church community seeks the kingdom in all realms as it serves as a way of life for its people.

Having offered tentative descriptions of practice, Jesus, postmodernity, and community, we are now ready to offer our definition of emerging churches: Emerging churches are communities that practice the way of Jesus within postmodern cultures. This definition encompasses the nine practices. Emerging churches (1) identify with the life of Jesus, (2) transform the secular realm, and (3) live highly communal lives. Because of these three activities, they (4) welcome the stranger, (5) serve with generosity, (6) participate as producers, (7) create as created beings, (8) lead as a body, and (9) take part in spiritual activities.

Emerging Churches and Other Forms of Church

At the risk of creating more questions than offering answers, it may be helpful to compare emerging churches (as defined above) with existing forms of church. Against all stereotypes, coffee and candles do not an emerging church make. As already mentioned, Gen-X megachurches are not emerging churches, and neither are Gen-X/young adult services. Indeed, they may meet the criteria for creativity, but they fall short in regard to the other eight categories. Their approach to ministry is modern, with their dualistic/spiritualized/interiorized understanding of Jesus, their embrace of the sacred/secular split, and their focus on the church meeting as opposed to community life. The same is true for their parents, seeker churches that may feature a creative service but do not display the other eight categories. Purpose-driven churches may meet the creativity aspect as well, but that is all. The Vineyard might meet one category, that of Jesus, but it is a spiritualized and powerful Jesus—not a social/political one. Calvary Chapel does not meet any of the categories as defined in this book (with Calvary Chapel Dana Point as an exception).

We do not exclude the possibility that churches within these movements could become emerging churches or that some indeed are. However, at this time, we see little evidence of the nine patterns. Because Gen-X, seeker, new paradigm, and purpose-driven churches are forms that are imbedded in particular cultures, these churches would need to change their practices dramatically (i.e., their church culture) to communicate clearly within a postmodern world. The question is whether these movements could remain true to their tradition while making the transition to an emerging church.

Both fundamentalist and mainline churches will also face numerous challenges in becoming emerging churches, as both of these forms of church are imbedded in modern culture as well. Those churches that preceded the Reformation (Catholic and Orthodox), and to a large extent Anglicanism, have many practices that resonate with those of emerging churches. Likewise, churches outside mainstream culture, such as the various minority and a few free church traditions, strongly resemble emerging churches (modernity was no friend to communities outside the mainstream, and therefore these more marginal communities have lived in opposition to aspects of modernity during their entire existence). Similar to their fundamentalist and liberal counterparts, evangelical churches, also born in modernity, face numerous challenges if they are to embody their way of life within postmodern culture.

The kingdom of God offers a reference point for emerging churches as they dismantle church practices that are no longer culturally viable. A problem with emphasizing deconstruction is that it can too readily result in destruction. However, in the minds of emerging church leaders, it is worth the risk, for to do nothing is to let the church exist without the kingdom, without Jesus, and thus without its proper identity as the people of God. For some, this epistemological journey has led to a comprehensive deconstructionism.[16] At the very least, those within the emerging church regard church as a safe place in which to ask the difficult questions. Pete Rollins (ikon, Belfast, U.K.) explains, "Deconstruction doesn't destroy but always deconstructs (i.e., takes apart) our valuable constructions."

The chapters in the book are full of stories about dismantling and re-building rooted in the kingdom of God. Any non-kingdom reconstruction, after the tearing down process, will prove dehumanizing and fruitless. We share common cause with the postmodern philosophers who revealed the oppressive nature of the master stories (metanarratives) of modernity. But our shared journey ends once the deconstruction is complete, for we *do* believe there is one metanarrative, one master story that redeems our material reality, welcomes the outsider, shares generously, empowers, listens, gives space, and offers true freedom. This metanarrative, even though it manifests in a myriad of local expressions, remains the singular *missio Dei,* the kingdom of God, the gospel. With this in mind, we do well to follow Pete Rollins's (ikon, Belfast, U.K.) advice to hold loosely our reconstructions, for "whatever we put in the void of the divine darkness will end up as a grand conceptual idol if we do not view it with humility." Let us now look at what is built after the dismantling process is complete.

16. This critical movement in philosophy and literary theory looks to uncover contradictions or oppositions within dominant stories, often by listening to those marginalized in the text.

3

Identifying with Jesus

We have come to see that it is all about Jesus and not just a methodology. It is not about mission, not about church, but it's about Jesus and his glory, his life. To know Jesus is not an event, a ritual, a creed, or a religion. It is a journey of trust and adventure. We don't believe in any religion anymore—including Christianity—but we do believe in following Jesus. We no longer need religion with its special buildings, dogmas, programs, clergy, or any other human inventions that displace genuine spirituality. Why do we need a name and address to be church? We've come out of religion and back to God.

Jonathan Campbell, Seattle

I read the Gospels over and over. Nothing I was doing on Sunday was what I thought Jesus would be doing if he were here.

Joe Boyd, Apex, Las Vegas

There is a strong and indissoluble link between the teaching of Jesus and the good news he embodied and proclaimed. His message both announced and inaugurated the reign of God on earth. The long-promised kingdom, spoken of by the Hebrew prophets, was established in provisional form with the coming of Jesus and the outpouring of his Spirit. It is this kingdom hope that inspires emerging church leaders as they seek to realize that promise within their communities, striving for them to become servants and signs of that kingdom as they live God's future, which is both already here and remains to come. In concrete terms, emerging church leaders look to Jesus as the one who initiated the work of the kingdom in Israel, and their hope is to point to the kingdom through their communal practices in postmodern culture today.

It is strange how the church for so long missed the kingdom emphasis in the witness of the authors of the Gospels. The gospel, as proclaimed by Jesus Christ and as understood by the early church, was always more than simply a message of personal salvation and, even more narrowly, the way to get to heaven when one dies. Beginning about midway in the twentieth century, theologians such as George Eldon Ladd began to examine the nature of the gospel of the kingdom. The Reformed and Anabaptist traditions have consistently maintained a clear kingdom perspective. Beginning in the late 1970s, this new understanding found its way to other churches as well, influencing not only the traditional denominations but also the Vineyard. Quite dramatically, emerging churches stress the kingdom of God much more than their new paradigm/purpose-driven/seeker parents ever did.

The Mission of the Emerging Church

How did emerging churches come to emphasize the gospel of the kingdom? It began as a change of focus from the Epistles to the Gospels as a way to understand Jesus more profoundly. With a growing conviction that something was seriously wrong with the church, these emerging leaders felt they needed a fresh understanding of the gospel to proceed any further. As Barry Taylor of Sanctuary (Santa Monica, CA) confides, "I needed to stop reading Paul for a while and instead focus on Jesus." However, not any Jesus would do. Sanctuary adopted the Jesus of popular culture, not the church, as they felt the church's view ignored the life of Jesus. "We focused on the humanity of Jesus and lost all the categories from church history." Karen Ward, of Church of the Apostles (Seattle), agrees. "The cultural view 'gets' that Jesus was for the marginalized and the oppressed. It is only the church that needs to be trained to look at Jesus again. They took a poll here in my area of Seattle and found that 95 percent of the nonchurched have a favorable view of Jesus, so Jesus is not the problem. It is the church they dislike, because they do not readily see the church living out his teachings." In a time of immense cultural change and disconnect with the church, emerging churches retrieved the Jesus of the Gospels but not necessarily the Christ of history.

Although the works of N. T. Wright, Dallas Willard, and Brian McLaren are great influences in emerging churches, their words were not written in isolation. They were delivered at a time when there was growing ferment that not only the *methods* but also the *message* needed to change. Todd Hunter, former national director of the Association of Vineyard Churches (Yorba Linda, CA), confesses, "We got the gospel wrong; we were living in the wrong story. We were telling the story of modernity and Baby Boom aspirations rather than the radical message of the kingdom." Mark Scandrette (ReIMAGINE! San Francisco) explains that Gen-X megachurches missed the point as well. "We got the questions wrong. We started out thinking about what *form* the church should take, as opposed to what the life of Jesus means in this time and place. Now, instead of being preoccupied with new forms of church, we focus on seeking the kingdom as the people of God." Emerging churches not only focus on the life of Jesus but are also taking a fresh look at a gospel they thought they always knew.

Who is the Jesus of the emerging church? The emerging church relies heavily on the New Testament scholarship of N. T. Wright[1] and to a lesser extent the work of Mennonite scholar John Howard Yoder and missiologists David Bosch and Lesslie Newbigin, among others, for its understanding of Jesus, the gospel, the kingdom, and the *missio Dei*. The following discussion sheds light on the Jesus of emerging churches.

How Does Jesus Serve as a Model?

Jesus provides a model for emerging churches through the way of life he formed among his followers. However, because Jesus lived in a different time and place, deciding which of his activities were purely cultural expressions and which were inspired by the gospel of the kingdom is a complex task. Doug Pagitt (Solomon's Porch, Minneapolis) says, "Our twenty-first-century life looks completely different from Jesus' life. He never brushed his teeth, for example. Even so, we are captured by his way of life. He was a practitioner of living in harmony with God, and he proclaimed that life. Jesus was faithful in his day. How can we live in the hope-filled way in which he lived? What would Jesus do? is a really difficult question. In other words, how do we select what to copy?" In essence, what aspects of Jesus' life were simply his participation in culture and what activities were to be translated into other cultures as expressions of the kingdom?

---

1. It has been popularized in Steve Chalke and Alan Mann, *The Lost Message of Jesus* (Grand Rapids: Zondervan, 2004).

Fortunately, the remainder of the New Testament offers some clues as to what Christians are to emulate and what they are to lay aside from the life of Jesus. John Howard Yoder offers help here as he points out that the early church was not encouraged to imitate Jesus in the ways of celibacy, manual labor, itinerancy, desert or mountaintop dwelling, the adoption of small groups, an isolated prayer life, or long periods of fasting. However, these practices were the means of and formed the context for the redemptive activities that were intended to be transcultural. What transcultural practices did the early church copy and that we, by implication, are to copy as well? According to Yoder:

> There is thus but one realm in which the concept of imitation holds—but there it holds in every strand of New Testament literature and all the more strikingly by virtue of the absence of parallels in other realms. This is at the point of the concrete social meaning of the cross in its relation to enmity and power. Servanthood replaces dominion, forgiveness absorbs hostility. Thus—and only thus—are we bound by New Testament thought to "be like Jesus."[2]

Jesus served and forgave others, and the early church was encouraged to do likewise. In doing so, they participated fully in God's redemptive activities. Serving and hospitality are extensively practiced by emerging churches, as we will show in later chapters.

Missio Dei *Replaces "Come to Us" Invitations with "Go" Motivation*

To understand the Jesus of emerging churches, we must first look at how they understand God's mission to all creation. Prior to any missionary activity in the Old or New Testaments lies God's mission, the *missio Dei.* God is a God who redeems, a God who seeks and saves. Adam, Abraham, Israel, Jesus, Paul, the early church, the church in history, and emerging churches today do not have separate missions, for there is only one mission—God's mission. The various individuals and groups represented in Scripture resemble one another only to the extent that they participate fully in God's redemptive activity in the world.

A perspective rooted in the *missio Dei* changes the functional direction of church. In emerging churches, for example, the direction of church changed from a centripetal (flowing in) to a centrifugal (flowing out) dynamic. This in turn led to a shift in emphasis from attracting crowds

2. John Howard Yoder, *The Politics of Jesus* (Grand Rapids: Eerdmans, 1994), 131.

to equipping, dispersing, and multiplying Christ followers as a central function of the church. Andrew Jones (Boaz, U.K.) states, "Emerging churches should be missional. And by missional, I understand that the emerging church will take shape inside the new culture as a redeeming prophetic influence. The church follows the kingdom, the church happens in *their* house rather than *our* house, just as it did in Matthew's house, and in Lydia's house, or the home of Priscilla and Aquila. The motion is always centrifugal, flowing outward to bring reconciliation and blessing to where it is needed. We are people flowing in the stream of God's go, participating with God, who is aggregating for himself a people, a bride."

Conversely, when Christians focus on a "come structure" for church, they cease to be missional in that they are asking those outside the Christian faith to come into their world instead of serving in the world of those outside. "In the U.K., people would no more drop into a church for a casual visit than an outsider might drop into a mosque or a gay bar for a casual visit. It is a big deal to take the initiative to discover an alternative way of life. One wouldn't quite know how to behave and may wonder what other people think" (Steve Collins, Grace, London). As shown by Jesus and his interaction with the temple authorities, the kingdom typically lies outside existing religious structures. Christians need to find God "out there."

Emerging Church Leaders Redefine "Mission"

Dieter Zander (Quest, Novato, CA) labored in two high-profile ministries where the emphasis was "come to us." Having struggled under these high-pressure, quantifiable, results-oriented approaches to ministry, Zander underwent a radical change of emphasis when he moved to San Francisco. On arriving in the city, he and his group prayed for others in their neighborhoods, but they had no desire for these neighbors to come to their group or meeting. Zander's community was completely outward focused. Zander and company seek to be "out there," leaning into their neighborhoods.

Zander uses an expandable rubber band and a ring to compare traditional and missional models of mission. The traditional model works like a rubber band encircling the perimeter. Such Christians look to attract more people, and when they do, they "stuff" them into the middle of the rubber band. As more come, the rubber band stretches. The goal is to get the rubber band to stretch as far as possible. Zander's ring model works much differently. Zander envisions a ring that maybe ten to twenty people can hold around the perimeter. With one hand, they hold on to the ring, and with the other hand, they reach out as far as they can, each one holding another ring for yet another to hold on to. Because of the inner ring, they are able to reach out farther than they could without a ring for support. The inner ring is a supportive accountability group, which asks each person if he or she has been good news (served in the kingdom) that week. The goal is not to bring new people into the small group but to add groups for those who respond to the kingdom. Each new believer joins the contact person's outer ring, which in turn becomes the new believer's inner ring.

By emphasizing church as relationships, emerging church thinkers are advocating not inwardly focused huddles but rather multiple circles of relationships lived out in the wider community. Each circle both reaches out and offers an open door into the circle. "Many of us have pulls in many directions. That is why church can't be a single portal. We have different associations" (Mark Scandrette, ReIMAGINE! San Francisco).

The *missio Dei* is in the world, and Christians have the opportunity to participate with God in those redemptive tasks. Simon Hall roots the work of Revive (Leeds, U.K.) in God's mission. "I definitely see Revive as missional, although that's in terms of participating in the *missio Dei*, which I consider to be broader, wider, higher than our usual understanding of that term." Clearly, mission is much more than simply a statement of purpose or a vision statement. "Mission statements are helpful insofar as they bring clarity, but more important is that we see ourselves *on* a mission. It is God's mission we are participating in, and it is not something we can come up with on our own. It is about participating and cooperating with God's mission, not building our own mission statement" (Joel McClure, Water's Edge, Hudsonville, MI). The church has no separate mission of its own. God already has a mission, and the church has the opportunity of participating in God's mission.

The *missio Dei* precedes the church, and so the issue is not where to bring or take God but to find God where he is working and to participate in redemption according to God-given skills and abilities. "The starting point for mission is that God is a missionary God who is active in the world. God invites and beckons us to join his mission. So in this sense, we join in with what God is doing rather than taking God with us" (Jonny Baker, Grace, London). Ben Edson (Sanctus1, Manchester, U.K.) agrees. "Sanctus's understanding of mission is that God is already working in the world. Our role is to discover where and then to stand alongside God. Many evangelicals believe they are taking God to the world. I do not like the dualism associated with that kind of theology." God leads, and we follow behind as best we can. As Andrew Jones (Boaz, U.K.) aptly states, "We find what God is planting, and we water it."

When Christians join together with God, they may find themselves connecting with those outside their typical church or theological circles. According to Holly Rankin Zaher (Three Nails, Pittsburgh), "We partner with others who seem to embody kingdom values and are doing kingdom work, even if they are not 'orthodox' Christians. We collect cans with Unitarians, work at blues festivals, and work with secular organizations in Pittsburgh. The urban challenges are so great that groups need to work together wherever possible."

When God is in the lead, evangelism changes as well. For leaders such as Dave Sutton (New Duffryn Community Church, Newport, U.K.), evangelism is not about bringing people out of their world but rather identifying with them in their world to discover in what ways God may already be at work in their lives. "I don't take God into somewhere but find God where he is and join him." Sutton encourages his fellow workers with the possibility that they may find God in the process of evangelism. "You might meet God in some of the people you work with."

The *missio Dei* represents God's active participation in the redemption of the world. God pursues everything in creation in need of direction and repair. Christians do not bring the *missio Dei*, nor is there more than one *missio Dei*. The *missio Dei* respects all recipients of the gospel as it identifies with them in their world. Emerging churches seek to embrace this comprehensive understanding of the *missio Dei*.

The Gospel of the Kingdom

Primarily through the work of Anglican theologian N. T. Wright,[3] emerging churches retrieved an ancient understanding of the gospel that dramatically transformed church practice. What is this gospel? Simply put, Jesus announced that the kingdom of God was arriving. Even though the Jews were living in exile, as they were still under Roman occupation and thus overrun by evil, nevertheless YHWH was returning, and *now* was the time of God's work, evidenced in the person of Jesus and in the

3. N. T. Wright, *Jesus and the Victory of God*, vol. 2 of *Christian Origins and the Question of God* (Minneapolis: Fortress, 1996).

signs that accompanied his ministry. Jesus urged his hearers to forget all that they were convinced had to occur to herald God's return and the nature of the reign he would usher in and to believe his reinterpretation of the Torah. He warned them that to oppose the coming kingdom was to oppose the work of God. However, it was good news (the gospel) that he proclaimed. Exile was over and a time of forgiveness had come!

Identifying with Jesus

Rooted in the work of N. T. Wright, emerging churches embrace the gospel of the kingdom as revealed in Mark 1:15–16. At the outset of the Gospel narrative, the good news was not that Jesus was to die on the cross to forgive sins but that God had returned and all were invited to participate with him in this new way of life, in this redemption of the world. It is this gospel that the emerging church seeks to recover. As one leader confided privately, "We have totally reprogrammed ourselves to recognize the good news as a *means* to an end—that the kingdom of God is here. We try to live into that reality and hope. We don't dismiss the cross; it is still a central part. But the good news is not that he died but that the kingdom has come."

The kingdom is present wherever Jesus is present. Each person experiences the kingdom through God's invitation, healing, and restoration. The cross of Christ provides the supreme demonstration of the sacrificial love of both the Son and his heavenly Father as well as the God-provided means to reconciliation. The kingdom is both the pathway *to* the cross and the pathway Christians walk throughout their lives *with* the cross as those who have died to self with Christ in order that they might live in his grace and power.

Clearly, the gospel is not restricted to a message giving an individual assurance about eternal destiny. It is minimally that, but it is much more, being concerned as much with life before death as with life after death. When people are reconciled to God through Christ, they become a "new creation" (2 Cor. 5:17). They first experience God's reconciliation, often in community, which results in a life of radical transformation. The primary reference point is no longer their former alienation but their present and future identification as part of God's new order, which was inaugurated with the first coming of Christ.

Dieter Zander (Quest, Novato, CA) is part of a growing throng of emerging church leaders who have retrieved this understanding of gospel. Zander began his ministry in Southern California as founder of the first Gen-X church, NewSong, in Pomona, California. He then moved to pioneer one of the first churches-within-a-church, Axis, at Willow Creek (Barrington, IL). In 1998, Dallas Willard's *Divine Conspiracy*[4] deeply affected Zander, dramatically altering his understanding of the gospel. "All my Christian life I had been abducted by an alien gospel," he confesses. Building on his newfound understanding, Dieter, his wife, Val, and their three boys moved to San Francisco in 1999. After some experimentation, they tried a different model of church planting, building relationships without even thinking about church locations or meetings. He now has no desire to return to his former understanding of gospel or church planting.

Zander explains his newfound calling: "This is the work of the rest of my life: to form communities of people that produce apprentices of Jesus who live in the gospel and communicate and draw others in a matter of course to the way they live. This is my lifelong quest." More recently, Zander joined Quest in Novato, north of San Francisco. They have five community groups that meet weekly. Every two weeks, they meet as a large group, and once a month, they serve the neighborhood. Zander speaks honestly of his vision for churches: "I want to form apprentices in the life of the kingdom, but it is hard work." Zander finds that, for most Christians, to live like Jesus is foreign to their ears. Instead, most have a church club checklist:

- give a little
- do a little
- pay membership dues
- get a "going to heaven" ticket (through accepting the gospel)

Rooted in the work of Dallas Willard,[5] Zander identifies the key distinction. "In this scenario, the gospel is informing how we die. Instead, the gospel ought to be about how we live! A lot of church people don't know the relationship between the gospel of Jesus and how we are to live. They are threatened by reevaluating that. Their belief is that they try to believe in Jesus so that when they die they get to go to heaven. Populating heaven is the main part of the gospel. Instead, the gospel is about being increasingly alive to God in the world. It is concerned with bringing heaven to earth. This really throws people off."

4. Dallas Willard, *The Divine Conspiracy: Rediscovering Our Hidden Life in God* (San Francisco: HarperSanFrancisco, 1998).
5. Ibid.

Like Zander, Joel McClure (Water's Edge, Hudsonville, MI) sees his primary task as helping Christians understand the gospel, "and they are getting it. They are looking for ways to cooperate with God in their lives, to see Christianity as a way of life. It is not just a brand-name garment I put on, or rules to follow, but an all-encompassing holistic way of life participating with God. It is strangely new to people, but they catch on, and they are talking in different ways as to what it means to be a disciple of Jesus."

In reevaluating evangelism, Joel McClure and Randy Buist asked if it was truly good news they shared or whether they presented a distorted gospel message. Unlike Dieter Zander (Quest, Novato, CA) and Mark Scandrette (ReIMAGINE! San Francisco), Water's Edge is located in suburban Michigan, so they are not likely to find Buddhists living next door. Who they do find as neighbors are those who are disenfranchised from church because of negative experiences or people who think church is only a good thing for children. As McClure talks with these former churchgoers, he asks them what they believe is wrong with the world. After hearing their response, McClure says that God agrees with them. "The gospel is that God wants you to help solve that problem, to participate with God through redeeming acts." McClure reflects on his experience. "The gospel is not that we agree with some abstract propositions in order to qualify to go to heaven when we die but an invitation to live in a new way of life. Sharing the good news is not only about conversion. It is about inviting someone to walk with you relationally, and it takes a while to demonstrate *this* gospel!"

Non-Christians resonate with this participative gospel message. When Zander shared the four spiritual laws with his neighbor, his neighbor replied that it indeed was news, but it was not *good* news. "What difference does this make in my life?" his neighbor asked. When Zander shared with him that we are to participate in God's goodness, that message, for his neighbor, *was* good news. "It had substance." This gospel is for Christians and non-Christians alike, as it is an invitation to participate in God's redemptive activities.

Jesus proclaimed the good news that his hearers could join him in a new way of life. More than simply offering a message of personal salvation, Jesus invited his followers to participate in God's redemption of the world. Emerging churches have adopted this restored understanding of the gospel, and it has dramatically transformed the way they train both new and not-so-new Christians in the faith.

The Costly Nature of the Message of "Free" Grace

Emerging churches understand a Jesus who presented a welcoming yet challenging message that invited his followers to live distinctively in the world. Such an up-front missional challenge, as Jesus issued to his followers, presents quite a contrast to seeker approaches to ministry. Mark Palmer (Landing Place, Columbus, OH) says:

> In 1998, I thought it was the church's responsibility to make church services accessible for everyone. Do the seeker-sensitive thing. Make it completely inoffensive. Make sure everyone was comfortable. By 2001, I had done an about-face. I began to think, maybe, in order to be true to what God called us to be committed to, we need to make it as difficult as we possibly can to follow Jesus, and go from there. Instead of trying to remove the difficult aspects of Christianity, what we did in Landing Place was to put those challenging parts front and center.
>
> When someone makes a decision to come to Landing Place, they know what they are getting into. The American church participates in bait and switch:[6] They get new people to come in the door and make a commitment, and after they make it, they show them what it is really about. It is offensive. It is not honest! When businesses bait and switch, they get shut down. But the church accepts this kind of thing. Successful churches tell us that if we care about outreach, we must bait and switch all day long, offer a soft-core gospel on the front end, hook them, and then give them the hard-core stuff. I don't think this is faithful to how Jesus modeled discipleship. We really try not to bait and switch people. When people want to know about following Jesus, we put the cards on the table. "This is what the commitment is. It is hard. It is a narrow path. It leads to death and even to hating brothers and sisters." We lead with that stuff. That way, in five weeks or so, when they hear more of the real stuff, we don't need to worry that they will leave. Yes, in the short run it is more difficult. But I don't think we are going to know the results for years to come. In ten years, I would rather see a deep level of discipleship for a few believers than a surface level for a huge number.

For Palmer, the costly message of the kingdom has replaced a seeker-sensitive approach to following Jesus.

---

6. An unethical business practice in which customers are lured into a store to buy a low-priced item but are quickly redirected to a higher-priced item because the first item was purposefully understocked.

Just as with the disciples, the call to mission forms the very core of emerging church identity and is not reserved for those of elite Christian status. As Andrew Jones (Boaz, U.K.) states:

> Our mission is what gives us purpose, which is what attracts others to us. If we are not bringing justice and transformation to the world, we should ask if we have a right to exist. We share our mission and social agenda with seekers first, since it is often the first thing they want to know about us and may determine if they will invest their lives with us or not. In the traditional church, such an honest explanation of mission was reserved for the mature in Christ and was discussed subsequent to personal spirituality and what the church offered. Now we are up front with it. Our mission defines us more than our worship.

Anna Dodridge (Bournemouth, U.K.) expresses a similar style of ministry. "Our commitment is to be a missionary at all times. Everything we do in our lifestyle, in what we say, in how we treat people, that's all our witness. It's all mission. This may seem pretty basic and obvious, but so many people just don't get it. We are definitely all missionaries and evangelists. There are some who are more gifted for this stuff or have more of a focus on it, and they are the people who encourage and lead us in this area, but we're all involved." For emerging churches, to be a follower of Jesus is to live as a missionary.

Si Johnston (headspace, London) sees mission as forming their identity as a community. "We are concerned with mission on a local level. For example, we know all our local pubs, shopkeepers, and estates. I am unofficially a pub chaplain. We expect members of our community to volunteer time to help run our health center for the homeless and the community coffee shop. We are also developing a national movement to tackle international people trafficking. For us, mission is existence!" For a community like headspace, mission is at the core of its identity.

The kingdom represents a new way of life interrupting the old. It is not simply information about God, spiritual reality, or the future. More than words, the entire way that Jesus and the disciples lived reflected the kingdom. Describing the spiritual climate in San Francisco, Mark Scandrette (ReIMAGINE!) explains, "Most harbor hostility to the Christian faith. We want to help people consider Jesus as an option through the beauty of how we live our lives. Living in the way of Jesus is not a belief system but a reality. We believe in an 'inhabited apologetic,' and through our lives 'we bear witness to the reality of God.'"

Scandrette recognizes that the kingdom is not simply about words. "Following the mission of Jesus entails putting my whole family in the middle of the chaos in order to see what it means to see the kingdom of God in operation. We seek to discover and demonstrate a different life in the midst of the turmoil." For Scandrette, there are no mission projects or outreaches. Their daily lives point to the reality of the kingdom. Through their activities in the community, members preach good news.

If the kingdom represents an entirely new way of life, then there is no start or stop to the gospel presentation. Si Johnston (headspace, London) points out:

> Church.Co.uk is a center heading to being 24-7. It's fast becoming an urban sanctuary where people can come and experience what it's like to be in an atmosphere saturated with hope and love. We care for everyone from homeless people to young professionals to local youths. Many are committed to seeing the place become the hub of community life for the Waterloo area of London, but in turn, as a team, we are committed to helping those in our community be dispensers of hope and good news in their respective spheres of existence (based on Eph. 4). So I guess you could say Church.Co.uk is a place that includes meetings and encourages people to a way of life drawn directly from the story of Jesus.

Jesus' community embodied the kingdom. He challenged and still challenges his followers, including those new to the faith, to live distinctively as those who have been freed from exile. Emerging churches take up this challenge, creating 24-7 missional communities that seek to express the kingdom in all they do.

The Gospel of the Kingdom Transcends All Church Forms

Emerging churches create missional communities that follow the pattern set by Jesus. According to N. T. Wright,[7] the prevailing understanding for Christians in the New Testament was that in the same way Jesus was to the Jews, they were to be to the Gentiles (a light to the nations). Jesus exemplified the *missio Dei* in all its richness, serving and forgiving in his first-century Palestinian context. The Holy Spirit continues the work of Jesus, seeking to implement the kingdom of God on earth. The Holy Spirit motivates people to live like Jesus, to *lean into* the kingdom, to serve, and to forgive. Just as Jesus was, Christians are to

7. Wright, *Jesus and the Victory of God*, 660.

be in their cultures everywhere and at every time. The Holy Spirit will lead those who are willing to live in the kingdom and to participate in God's mission through the proclamation of the gospel until the return of Christ.

Dieter Zander (Quest, Novato, CA) realized that missional communities differ greatly from current forms of church planting. He no longer believes that the Boomer-derived, Gen-X megachurch is the way to engage in kingdom-focused mission (as he attempted in his first church plant, NewSong, in Pomona, California, beginning in 1986), nor is church-within-a-church (his second ministry effort, Axis, at Willow Creek, 1994), nor are house churches (smaller communities that he experimented with after Willow Creek in San Francisco in 1999). He came to the conclusion, "I needed a fast from the system. It is not about church form but about the kingdom. The kingdom transcends all forms." The answer does not reside in church structure but in the way of life modeled by Jesus and what that life looks like in our context today.

Mark Palmer (Landing Place, Columbus, OH) shifted from traditional church planting to initiating missional communities as well. "It is not that we don't do church planting any more. It is just that we begin with Jesus and the kingdom." Palmer reported that he was in fact starting his fourth church next week. "I always start a new group with a partner, and we always begin with the Sermon on the Mount, focusing on the Beatitudes. I make historical, theological, and inflammatory comments. I instigate and guide. Whenever we start a community, I do this. My job as pastor is to keep the community in the story." Keeping the community focused on the kingdom becomes the highest priority for this new work.

New kingdom communities take on the form of their context. Jason Evans of Matthew's House (Vista, CA) expresses his kingdom-centered thinking in the following terms. "We are not planting a church; instead, we want to embody the kingdom. Consequently, how much planning can we do beforehand? It is a case of the chicken and the egg. Which came first? That's our dilemma." They appreciate that the kingdom's appearance depends on the culture, for the gospel is always a response to a given context. As a response, it cannot be planned extensively beforehand. It cannot be a fixed structure. Planning for kingdom-type communities is much more tentative than it is for typical church planting. One needs to hold on to forms much more loosely.

While Rob Graham (Levi's Table, St. Louis) prepared to plant a seeker church, he read the Gospels with fresh eyes. Convicted by the claims of the kingdom, he interviewed five "successful" church planters on ways to proceed. He asked them pointed questions about the kingdom. "Is it true that your goal is not the kingdom of God but to pay your own salary, and is your vision undermined by your desire to have your salary paid?" Each of the five said yes, and some were moved to tears. Graham realized that he wanted to plant a church in an entirely different way. Graham describes this as his first church-planting "death." "At that point, I gave up my lifetime desire to be supported by full-time ministry." From then on, all church questions had to pass through kingdom criteria to be adopted.

Jesus was not a church planter. He created communities that embodied the Torah, that reflected the kingdom of God in their entire way of life. He asked his followers to do the same. Emerging churches seek first the kingdom. They do not seek to start churches per se but to foster communities that embody the kingdom. Whether a community explicitly becomes a church is not the immediate goal. The priority is that the kingdom is expressed. Inherent to kingdom activities is that the community will reflect the local context, and therefore forms vary greatly.

Challenges for the Emerging Church

Jesus created an alternative social order, one built on servanthood and forgiveness, through the activities he performed as a leader of a counter-temple movement.[8] Paul continued this model as well. "If we stated the agenda of Paul's mission in modern terms, it seems clear that he was building an international, anti-imperial, alternative society embodied in local communities."[9] In the same way that Jesus' forgiveness of sins directly challenged the power of the temple authorities, Paul's declaration "Jesus is Lord" was inherently political. Calling Jesus "Lord" was also stating that Caesar was not. It dethroned the emperor. Following the pattern of Jesus, Paul fostered local communities that embodied an alternative way of life, one built on serving and forgiving. These communities were a result of the proclamation of the gospel and functioned as both a sign and a foretaste of the in-breaking kingdom.

What a challenge to perform mission according to the pattern of Jesus! To live consistently with the life of Jesus, emerging churches need

8. N. T. Wright, *The Challenge of Jesus: Rediscovering Who Jesus Was and Is* (Downers Grove, IL: InterVarsity, 1999), 139.

9. Richard A. Horsley, "The New World Order: The Historical Context of New Testament History and Literature," in *The New Testament: Introducing the Way of Discipleship*, ed. Wes Howard-Brook and Sharon H. Ringe (Maryknoll, NY: Orbis, 2002), 13.

to proclaim that a time of exile has ended, that God has returned, and that forgiveness is available to all. They need to create and foster an international, postcolonial, and anti-empire movement. They need to build communities that have no enemies but Satan in which nationalist tendencies are abandoned and they serve as brothers and sisters. All the while, they need to forgive one another and point through their lives to the kingdom of God. The challenge to follow Jesus, for those in the U.K. and the U.S. today, proves a difficult task indeed but one that emerging churches have taken up as their challenge.

Although seeking to do mission in the pattern of Jesus is difficult, any other model proves even more problematic. As Andrew Kirk states, "Though the problems of discovering and reapplying mission in the way of Jesus may be complicated, the Christian community needs a standard by which to measure its own performance—a standard which is able to call into question its own policies, programs, and practices. Without this, mission simply becomes an arbitrary response to whatever a particular culture or moment of history throws up."[10] However difficult and complex, there is no better model for missionary activity than the way of Jesus, and it is in the life of Jesus, the gospel, and the kingdom that emerging churches receive their blueprint for mission.

The idea of a kingdom focus instead of a church focus is a huge paradigm shift, one that does not come easy. But emerging church leaders are getting the message across. Joel McClure reports of the progress they are making at Water's Edge (Hudsonville, MI). "Out on the back deck one night we were meeting, and we compared missional communities to the static perspectives of church we had all learned. People were getting it! They began to describe the differences between a kingdom perspective and a church perspective on reality. It is a slow process, but the transformation is happening—little bit by little bit." At this point in their church life, they have talked about it so much that Jesus and the kingdom are simply part of their DNA. Mark Palmer of Landing Place (Columbus, OH) echoes McClure. "Our church takes Jesus and the kingdom very seriously—and people are getting it. When someone speaks up at church and shows that they get it and understand our kingdom focus, it is a moment that gives me energy for another week or two!"

Because a kingdom perspective is so contrary to the current understandings of church, one can feel like Sisyphus pushing his rock uphill, only to see it crash back down again. Joe Boyd, founder of Apex (Las

---

10. Andrew Kirk, *What Is Mission? Theological Explorations* (Minneapolis: Fortress, 2000), 39.

Vegas), vents his frustrations. "I hate 'pop Christianity.' I tell people who Jesus is, who the Father is, and I talk about the kingdom. But then they go to the local Christian bookstore and read heretical things about Jesus and get all messed up!"

Following the way of Jesus in creating kingdom communities is difficult, to say the least. Emerging churches are inspired by the stories of the New Testament and humbled by their own experiences. However, once infected by the gospel, what choice do they have but to follow? All other options pale in comparison. An understanding of the kingdom challenges all other previous understandings and practices.

At times, the discussion of kingdom in emerging churches is frustratingly fuzzy because they are working out the very latest understandings of gospel and culture from the likes of N. T. Wright, Lesslie Newbigin, Dallas Willard, and others. They cannot look to their new paradigm/purpose-driven/seeker parents for help here, as these movements did not focus on the kingdom (with the possible exception of the Vineyard, but even there it was primarily a prayer focus). These older movements created churches with virtually the same structure that Protestant churches have had since the sixteenth century. Emerging churches are truly pioneering, and thus a little messiness is to be expected.

Conclusion

The kingdom, or the reign of God, is about our life here and now, and it is concerned not just with individual needs and aspirations but also with the well-being and mission of the community of Christ's representatives. It is directed beyond the present membership of the body of believers to encompass the world that Jesus came to save from the consequences of its rebellion by turning it in a radically different direction. The gospel of emerging churches is not confined to personal salvation. It is social transformation arising from the presence and permeation of the reign of Christ. The gospel of the kingdom is prominent throughout the four Gospels. Emerging churches are no longer satisfied with a reductionistic, individualized, and privatized message.

As an aside, today's reader must appreciate that Jesus' original Jewish first-century audiences understood the words "kingdom of God." The early church practiced the dynamics of the kingdom of God, but they did not always use the same terms, as those words would have been foreign to their hearers in a Greco-Roman context. The early Christians participated in the activities of the kingdom, redeeming through acts of service and forgiveness, but their message was communicated in ways indigenous to local cultures. Emerging churches use the term *kingdom of God,* and that is why we use it in our work. However, our hope is that a postmodern wordsmith will contextualize the word for our present time.

In summary, when a crisis of confidence hit the church, emerging churches retrieved the life of Jesus as a reference point. In Jesus, they discovered a long-forgotten gospel, the idea that we have an invitation to participate with God in the redemption of the world. Emerging churches accepted this offer, and they joined the *missio Dei,* God's outward movement to humanity. Jesus announced the kingdom of God, and this is the message emerging churches seek to proclaim in their newly formed missional communities.

4

Transforming Secular Space

There is nothing so secular that it cannot be sacred, and that is one of
the deepest messages of the Incarnation.

Madeleine L'Engle, *Walking on Water*

Even times of coffee turned into worship and to a centering on Christ.

Dwight Friesen, Quest, Seattle

By now it should be clear that in discussing the emerging church we are
not simply talking about a different style of church adapted to a particular
age range. Rather, we are talking about a radically different ecclesiology that reflects the church's call to mission in a post-Christendom and
postmodern context. This raises a range of theological and philosophical
issues. In particular, a major shift is taking place as the self-confident
construct of modernity crumbles. Secularization, far from undermining
religion with its denial of the transcendent and its insistence on verification through the senses and the application of cold logic, has created a
spiritual vacuum and a deep desire for integration. Hence, the title of
this chapter highlights the end of modernity's sacred/secular divide.

What happens when the kingdom enters cultures? Do kingdom
communities respect the arbitrary divisions societies create between
the public and the private, the sacred and the secular, or are they no
respecter of the existing powers? This chapter reveals how kingdom

65

communities, practicing the life of Jesus, interact with modern and postmodern cultures in Western society.

Tearing Down the Sacred/Secular Divide

Sacralization, the process of making all of life sacred, represents the interaction of kingdom and culture. Emerging churches tear down the church practices that foster a secular mind-set, namely, that there are secular spaces, times, or activities. To emerging churches, all of life must be made sacred. "There is an inherent rejection at Grace of dualism," says Jonny Baker (Grace, London).

Sacralization in emerging churches is about one thing: the destruction of the sacred/secular split of modernity. The modern period was characterized by the birth of the idea of secular space, that is, the idea of a realm without God. Before this time, in every culture, all arenas of life were spiritual; it was impossible to label some practices "religious" and others not. Spirituality as a separate domain was unknown. With the birth of modernity in the West, the tie between religion and the rest of life was broken. Beginning with William of Ockham and John Duns Scotus in the fourteenth century and accelerating with René Descartes in the seventeenth, the modern period created a secular space and relegated spiritual things to the church.[1] After Descartes, the spiritual place ceased to be the church and was relegated to the heart.

The marginalization of religious practice continued until the 1960s when many of the Western presuppositions about reality began to be deconstructed within the culture. Questions about Western superiority and "progress" began to be raised. A desire for a spirituality that embraced all of life began to be resurrected. Call it whatever you will, modernity was about the birth of secular space. The postmodern (or non-modern) is about the sacredness of all of life. For emerging churches, it means to give all of life over to God in worship, to recognize the work of God in formerly unspiritual things or activities. Emerging churches mark this shift to a "whole life" spirituality.

A consequence of the creation of a secular realm was modernity's penchant to break everything up into little parts for classification, organization, and systematization. Thus, in the modern period, many du-

---

1. We rely on John Milbank, *Theology and Social Theory: Beyond Secular Reason* (Oxford: Blackwell, 1993); and Zygmunt Bauman and Keith Tester, *Conversations with Zygmunt Bauman* (Cambridge, U.K.: Polity Press, 2001) throughout the book as we write on modernity.

alisms were introduced to church life that had not been problematic before: the natural versus the supernatural; public facts versus private values; the body versus the mind and spirit; faith versus reason; power versus love; and the list goes on. These capitulations to the dualisms of modernity affected every level of the church, including worship, Bible study, power structures, and mission. Postmodern culture questions the legitimacy of these dualisms. Correspondingly, every one of these modern divisions is greatly opposed by emerging churches.

The Holistic Approach of Emerging Churches

The new paradigm, purpose-driven, seeker, and Gen-X churches are not postmodern in this sense. These movements venerate the large gathering and the heart as primary spiritual domains. They do not challenge the many dualisms of modernity but rather continue the divisions between natural and supernatural, individual and community, mind and body, public and private, belief and action, and they leave controlling power structures in place. In these movements, religion and spiritual practices are activities one does apart from the culture, and spirituality is still very much at the margins. In contrast, the clarion call of the emerging church is Psalm 24:1: "The earth is the LORD's, and everything in it" (NIV).[2] For emerging churches, there are no longer any bad places, bad people, or bad times. All can be made holy. All can be given to God in worship. All modern dualisms can be overcome.

Emerging churches embody the desire to remove secular space. For these communitites, there are no nonspiritual domains of reality. This upsurge in spirituality reflects the demise of the secular as society moves beyond rationalistic modernism. "Secular space is as a bubble in the surrounding water. It is a place where God has been excluded. I don't believe in 'secular.' It shouldn't exist," says Steve Collins of Grace (London). Ben Edson (Sanctus1, Manchester, U.K.) also rejects the notion of a divide between secular and sacred. "We try to create bridges that span the secular/sacred divide because we don't make that distinction. We use secular music in worship as well as film and literature. I hope they are points of connection between people's everyday lives and their

---

2. The Hebrew adds emphasis to the fact that the whole of creation belongs to God by right of his creating and sustaining power by placing "the LORD" at the head of the sentence. The following verses elaborate by relating creation to the entire physical universe and its peoples. In the Christian church, this psalm is traditionally sung on ascension day, expressing its christological fulfillment.

faith." Emerging churches recognize the sacredness of all of life and seek to dismantle everything secular.

From Systematic to Nonlinear

Earlier surely!

The creation of a secular realm during the period of modernity led people in the West to seek control over their world. When they perceived that *they* were in control and not God, they organized and systematized all reality. This organizing principle affected church practice as well, as the modern church became highly ordered. Because of the newly literate nature of churchgoers in the sixteenth and seventeenth centuries, churches began to be structured like texts. Each part of the service progressed in logical fashion until the service was complete. As Marshall McLuhan wrote, "The medium is the message,"[3] and modern structures spoke loudly and clearly: Linearity, order, and systemization were the means through which one properly worshiped God.

Emerging churches remove linear expressions of the faith. Postmodernity teaches that linearity is but one of many narratives that could be told about a given event. In fact, postmoderns prefer that more than one narrative be told, recognizing that one systematic telling is selective and open to distortion. It is not that postmodern people do not want truth per se, but whose truth? Often the one proposing, or more often imposing, "truth" is a person in power. Why trust that person? Instead, a better way to truth, in their view, is to hear the many stories and to discern accordingly, within the context of community.

"Truths" also have bodies. Truth is not simply a set of abstract ideas; it walks and talks. We hear the truth as we hear about what God is doing concretely in people's lives. Postmodern people understand reality in multiple ways. There is more than one way to do things, more than one thing going on at a time, and more than one message coming across. It is in the confluence of these activities that "truth" is discovered. Building on that idea, narrative is key. Who wants to listen to abstract, context-less propositions when one can hear or watch a story unfold?

How is nonlinearity manifested in a worship event? In a service, there may be music or a video playing in the background, artwork to observe, or active participation in an activity even while the "teaching" is going on. The multiple events themselves may function as the teaching or as

3. Marshall McLuhan, *Understanding Media: The Extensions of Man* (New York: McGraw Hill, 1964), 7.

the experience of Scripture. Sometimes these many activities are internally consistent, sometimes not. The overall message may be where two or more distinct activities intersect or diverge.

In Todd Hunter's community (Christ Community of Faith, Yorba Linda, CA), a church meeting consists of an open mic where anyone can share at any time. The service does not come to a final resolution, nor is there any expectation that it should. Life goes on! According to their reasoning, why put an artificial narrative of closure on an experience that ought to have no end. Grace, an alternative service in London, likewise does not progress step by step in a linear fashion.

In Scripture reading, differing modern and postmodern scriptural interpretations offer a sharp contrast. Under modernity, evangelicals defended the authority of the Bible primarily by arguing for its inner consistency and for the fact that Jesus upheld the inspiration of the Hebrew Scriptures. The Bible was considered a book authored by God that gave answers to life's problems. The various books, incidents, and propositional statements provided the pieces of a jigsaw that if fitted together correctly would present a complete picture. The problem was that there seemed to be pieces missing and pieces that did not fit, no matter how hard one tried.

The Bible was a book to be defended against all detractors. The combatants came out of their respective corners for an intellectual boxing match, each opponent seeking to score points against the other. After each round, they returned to the protection of their respective corners for encouragement, advice, and refreshment. Under postmodernity, however, the boxing "ring" became a circle with no secure corners in which to retire.

Emerging churches became increasingly dissatisfied with using the Bible in a modern way. Brad Cecil of Axxess (Arlington, TX) confesses, "It has been a long journey for everyone. It is hard to repent from foundationalism.[4] Once enlightened, you can never go back, because certainty is such a warm blanket in which to wrap yourself." Nonfoundationalists such as Cecil are not implying that they have accepted a rationalistic-liberal approach to Scripture (which is also a modern construction). They are looking to the

---

4. Nancey Murphy, *Anglo-American Postmodernity* (Boulder: Westview Press, 1997), 9: "Foundationalism is a theory about knowledge. More specifically, it is a theory about how claims to know can be justified. When we seek to justify a belief, we do so by relating it to (basing it on, deriving it from) other beliefs. If these other beliefs are called into question, then they, too, must be justified. Foundationalists insist that this chain of justifications must stop somewhere; it must not be circular, nor must it constitute an infinite regress. Thus, the regress must end in a 'foundation' of beliefs that cannot themselves be called into question."

Bible afresh without the presuppositions and restricted vision of modernity. For them, the Bible presents a fascinating collection of stories that together make up a big Story that stretches from before creation to beyond the end of time. Pete Rollins (ikon, Belfast, U.K.) reflects his concern with modern ways of reading Scripture. "I was worried about the evangelical churches' way of reading the Bible as a singular book with one voice rather than as a book with many voices and many ways of interpreting."

God communicates with humanity, not primarily through the form of propositions but through a story illustrated by parables, riddles, sayings, and folk songs. It is a story that is still unfolding and in which we have a part at this point in time. The Bible is an invitation to share in the excitement, commitment, and risk of a journey of a lifetime rather than a book providing answers and a safe place. It is not a jigsaw but a painting that has exquisite detail and rich colors in some areas yet is sketchy in others. It is a finished product in the sense that we are not going to get any more, and we have to live with what we've got. But it will be complete in our eyes only when we are in the presence of the Lord at the fulfillment of human history. We are not at liberty to treat it as a paint-by-numbers canvas or to paint over what has been given either because we do not like it or because we insist on details being included out of our own imaginings or under the claim of new revelations.

From Elitist Cultural Disconnect to Engagement with Visual Culture

The Reformation was born in a literary age, and it is difficult to imagine its occurrence without the prior existence of the printing press. The Protestant church itself was a contextualization into print culture, a new form of church created for those who built their worlds around the printed page. In one way, it was the newly literate class waging war on the illiterate, as images were often the only way for the illiterate to understand the gospel. Thus, stained glass, symbols, and the teaching of story came under deep suspicion. With a focus on the logically prepared preached Word, worship became abstract, and the listeners now needed to imagine what they previously had seen with their eyes. Even the worship music was strongly text based, as the words, not the entire experience, carried the meaning. As Martin Luther said, "The ears are the only organ for the Christian." Everything became highly structured, abstract, printed. The print era mirrors the modern era, and one can argue which came first.

With the invention of the photograph in the mid-nineteenth century, the seeds of the print era's demise were planted. Since that time, the visual and aural aspects of culture, including radio, TV, motion pictures, and the computer, have had a more significant place. These forms of media were warmly received, much to the dismay of elite literary culture. The modern church, born in a literary age, has had trouble making a shift from a print to an image-based culture.

Protestant church forms were created by a literary age that no longer exists. It is hard to imagine what their particular traditions would look like without a literary, modern emphasis. The Protestant church has sided with elite print culture historically, and now there exists a great disconnect between those in the culture who venerate print culture and everyone else. "The elitism that is so prevalent in the church has created a chasm between the church and popular culture," says Ian Mobsby (Moot, London).

It is not simply an issue of preferring one culture or one style over another; the problems lie much deeper. As Mobsby says, "The gap between traditional church and contemporary culture reveals the sin of the church in failing to be incarnational and requires repentance and innovation that the emerging church seeks to live and create." Emerging churches seek to incarnate, embody, and express the gospel beyond print culture, beyond the linear approach of modernity. For example, in emerging church services, they play "secular" music but alter the meaning (not necessarily the words) of those songs. Thus, church resembles the rest of their lives.

Instead of profaning the church, secular music becomes holy, and therefore the rest of their lives becomes holy as well. For alternative worshipers (those connected to the alternative worship movement in the U.K.), music is Christian when they glorify God with it, *not* because of the lyrics or because a Christian wrote it or played it. All things can be made holy as they are given to God, whether "secular" or not. Postmodern people construct their world in nontextual and nonlinear ways, and the gospel must be embodied and therefore communicated in that same manner to be faithful in mission. In postmodern cultures of the twenty-first century, a linear or text-based ecclesiology perpetuates secularity in the church and denies the church's call to live incarnationally.

Creating a Life-Embracing Spirituality

During the period of modernity, the church accepted its diminished role at the margins. The church embraced the idea that its proper role was as spiritual chaplain to society. The church no longer addressed all of reality, just the cordoned off realm of the "spiritual." Near the end of modernity—after the 1960s—these constructions of sacred/secular were deconstructed, and new spiritualities emerged on the scene. Fearing that they might lose their corner on the spiritual market, much of the church fought these new developments. The church decried the new spiritualities that sought a holistic approach to life. Many of these new forms of faith, however, sought to remedy the spiritual lack that the church had long accepted.

The end result of this increasing isolation is that a spiritual culture now surrounds a secular church. At the sunset of modernity, the church refuses to create a holistic spirituality for its people and fights to stay at the margins of society as a spiritual chaplain. Consequently, those spiritually insightful mystics who recognize the depravity of modernity must look to other faiths to address their longings. As many church people fight to keep the dying church modern, emerging churches abandon the modern while bringing new life to the church.

Emerging churches refuse to accept the modern church's truncated form of the sacred. Instead, they create a spirituality for all of life. Such alternative spiritual practices, however, bring fear to the church's modern sensibilities. Alternative worship is similar to New Age practices in its use of ritual, ecology, creation, imagination, and the kinesthetic, admits Paul Roberts (Resonance, Bristol, U.K.).[5] "However, these are *cultural* similarities, not doctrinal ones. Alternative worship is working from a particular understanding of the world that is shaped by the belief that God has acted uniquely in Jesus Christ."[6] Roberts writes of a whole-life spirituality that has its roots in belief in Jesus Christ, a spirituality that gives no credence to the idea of a realm without God.

Embracing Both Transcendence and Immanence

Secular modernity pushed religious practice to two extremes. Whereas in premodernity God was both transcendent[7] and immanent,[8] in modernity, God could be *either* transcendent *or* immanent but not both. In this regard, both conservatives and liberals are equally modern: Conservatives stress the transcendence of God, and liberals stress God's immanence. In modern conservative churches, it follows that God is experienced

5. Paul Roberts, *Alternative Worship in the Church of England* (Cambridge, U.K.: Grove Books, 1999), 20.

6. Ibid.

7. Transcendent: God is beyond human experience and understanding, transcending the physical universe.

8. Immanent: God actively participates in creation.

outside material reality. Paul Roberts (Resonance, Bristol, U.K.) offers an example. "In charismatic worship, God is located 'outside' the physical domain. This is why charismatic worship is so focused on ecstatic experience. By contrast, alternative worship relocates God back within the physical domain, so to experience God means to encounter him in and through the created things around—symbolically, iconically, sacramentally."[9]

Simon Hall of Revive (Leeds, U.K.) shares his experience in looking to overcome the modern aspects of charismatic worship. "I think one of the biggest tensions within Revive is trying to prevent the charismatic flight from reality in worship. I remember working in an inner-city church in my early twenties, trying to get people to sing songs about their lives, and their attitude was, 'We came here to get away from our lives!' I'm trying to change that, because the consequence is that faith and real life become totally separated." Indeed, worship that focuses exclusively on celebration and transcendence can end up ignoring the unresolved questions and conflict people live with and driving them further into denial. But at the same time, recognizing God only in created things is to ignore God's otherness, his transcendence, aspects of God's character seen in Scripture. Emerging churches refuse the false choice of secular modernity, voting with neither the conservatives nor the liberals. They recognize God's deep work in material reality while at the same time embracing the invisible reality of God.

Often what becomes church in the new paradigm construct is an ugly, empty, square warehouse with bright carpet, uncomfortable seats, and a stage for performers. New paradigm churches (such as the Vineyard and Calvary Chapel) move away from "the earth is the Lord's," believing that material reality does not need to reflect spiritual reality, thereby, in essence, giving physical space over to secularization. For emerging churches, this "Boomer" hostility toward the beautiful reinforces the sacred/secular split of modernity in that it venerates the written word, logic, and linearity and gives all other reality over to the "world." In contrast, emerging churches ask, can we not know God more fully through what we see around us in the worship space, just as we see glimpses of God in the goodness and beauty in daily life?

Emerging churches use paintings, slides, drawings, and candles as visual expressions. In addition, they might show videos or television clips. On occasion, an art installation or exhibit functions as the entire

9. Roberts, *Alternative Worship in the Church of England*, 18.

"service." They might display icons that resonate with both ancient and popular cultures. Historically, although less so in Protestant circles, the arts played a large role in expressing the holy, bringing the spiritual and the physical together. By immersing themselves in all forms of media, emerging churches retrieve God's immanence while maintaining a commitment to God's transcendence, thereby creating a rich and beautiful worship environment. As Andy Thornton (Late Late Service, Glasgow, U.K.) says, "There is no point in doing this if you don't think God will kiss you on the cheek in the process."

ReIMAGINE! (San Francisco) illustrates the pursuit of transcendence and immanence in the following way. Imagine that a person parachuted and is now floating down to a city. As this person comes closer to the earth, he or she sees different things at different levels. At fifteen thousand feet, this person might see the city as a beautiful green. At five thousand feet, he or she might see it as green pixels, like a Seurat painting. As this person gets even closer, he or she might notice that the green dots are people. Everywhere these kingdom people go, they leave a little green smudge. Each kingdom person is an "incubator" of green and advocates greenness in the city.

Green is not a primary color—blue and yellow are. Yellow is the vertical axis, the spiritual axis, the pursuit of God. The higher it goes, the more faint it becomes. This is the sole pursuit of the Creator, of transcendence. Blue is the pursuit of creation, social justice, the good life, doing good to others. It becomes darker and darker as one moves away from the center. This is the pursuit of the immanence of God. Yellow people view God only as transcendent. Often, they are evangelicals and conservatives. With their focus on transcendence, they care about God but not about what God loves. Blue people love what God loves—they love the earth, humanity, the environment, and the sensuality of being human. They are liberals. With their focus on immanence, they don't love God and they deny Jesus, but they long for the kingdom.

At ReIMAGINE! the focus is green. Jesus is the ultimate green, for Creator and creation meet in Christ. People are fallen and are either blue or yellow. ReIMAGINE!'s task is to help yellow people add blue to their palette (becoming tied to creation) and to help blue people add yellow (becoming tied to the Creator). For Mark Scandrette and his community of artists, "This is the DNA of kingdom life." This is a brilliant picture of modernity's penchant to force people to focus on transcendence or immanence, but never both. It is also a wonderful illustration of how the kingdom (green) interacts with the twin poles of modernity (yellow and blue).

Incarnational Engagement with the Wider Culture

Emerging churches do not occupy a reactive and defensive stance in regard to the wider culture but rather seek to engage it as insiders. As Andy Thornton (Late Late Service, Glasgow, U.K.) points out, "It is not only missional questions that drive the impetus for creating new forms of church. What plays a major role in new forms of church is simply the desire for lifelong Christians to make sense of their two worlds: their church and their culture. The people who care most about the cultural disconnect within the church are the kids of the people in church. Look at the leaders of the alternative worship scene. Almost all are kids of influential Christian people. These kids want to stop being cultural outsiders. They look to bring their two worlds together. They seek authenticity, and, in so doing, they need to end the dissonance." Emerging churches want to stay true to both their faith *and* their culture.

Ending the fragmentation and offering integrity to the lifelong Christian is only part of a deeper issue at work here. We are commanded by Christ as his followers to live incarnationally, to overcome boundaries, to express the God-life, and to recognize where God is at work in every realm. Jonny Baker of Grace (London) has thought extensively about incarnational mission. "God is encountered in the stuff of everyday life, not outside it. So worship makes two moves: It brings the real world into church, and it enables God to be encountered back in the real world. This is a direct challenge to an experience of the church as a world apart, unrelated to the rest of life." Visions (York, U.K.) worked at clubs on Friday nights, providing visuals for local promoters, and conducted worship on Sunday nights. From an integrity standpoint, they would not do anything at the club on Friday that they would not do in church on Sunday. Their life in the world had to be consistent with their faith commitment. Correspondingly, they would not do anything on Sunday that they would not do at the club on Friday. Their faith had to be expressed in ways that were native to the culture around them. Living in culture as a local and yet pointing to the One beyond the local help keep emerging churches' worlds intact.

Worship Arising out of Local Cultural Contexts

When worship and witness are in sync, a 24-7 spiritual life is created for participants that overcomes the "secular" aspects of life with reminders of God. Sue Wallace (Visions, York, U.K.) explains, "The reason we embrace culture in worship is not only to make the place feel like home to those coming into it from the outside world but also to make us take our worship from our church space into our world. When you are in a shop or a pub, and you hear a track that has been used in church, it forges connections and makes you think about God." When people bring their culture to God in worship, then that experience extends to their daily lives when they are away from the community. These "secular" worship expressions become reminders and clues of God everywhere.

Incarnational worship implies bringing all that people have and are, from their world, to God. But opening up the worship experience to include all gifts, experiences, and idiosyncrasies creates a certain vulnerability, about which Steve Collins (Grace, London) writes with refreshing candor.

> Grace was started by someone who felt that the ordinary kind of service certainly didn't express his way of life! And it has all the good and bad aspects of that foundational concern (i.e., it deals with things and connects with life in ways that conventional churches don't). But it also showcases our aesthetic snobbery, revealed in our love of gadgets and fashion. Church as self-portrait, if you like. At least, by being unwittingly inclusive in this way, it keeps us confronting those things. When church is just about "churchy" things, it's easier to pretend we're being holy enough by going to church and don't have to do anything else. I think the attitude that church activities are enough to make me good and discharge my debt to God is a characteristic of civic religion. It's paying our dues to God in the same way that we pay to Caesar (i.e., to keep him off our backs while we have our own fun somewhere else). Coming to faith in a society that has pretty much lost its civic religion means we had to make starker, all-or-nothing choices.

Offerings of worship that arise out of the collective responses of the worshiping community, with each person contributing out of his or her personality, gifting, and experience, is self-revealing. It brings to the surface underlying issues that need to be addressed as they relate to the individual concerned or are typical of the group. In the case of Grace (London), Steve Collins identifies their predilection to gadgetry and aesthetic snobbery. Some offerings prove to be obstacles rather than channels to worship. In contrast, passive worship leaves these issues undetected. Collins brilliantly describes what happens when people do not bring their world to God: They can deceive themselves into thinking they are doing spiritual things while they are leaving their secular lives untouched. By bringing it all, people see themselves for who they are and create possibilities of redemption in all areas of life.

Distinguishing between Worship That Is Integrally Connected and That Which Is Merely Trendy

The focus of attention in the worship wars that have waged in so many churches has been between traditional and contemporary styles. Emerging churches believe this is a nonissue, for, in their view, both traditional and contemporary forms of church are equally secular and modern. Each type of church is marginal to the culture at large and addresses only spiritual things. Thus, emerging churches refuse the modern temptation to create a trendy, youth, young adult, or Gen-X service, for although it promises to be postmodern, this is a ruse. Such services inevitably leave all of modernity in place.

Recognizing that people bring their world to God, emerging churches are strongly tied to local culture. These churches do not use cultural expressions because they are trendy but because they are rooted in people's lives, and this is the only way to be honest before God. Kester Brewin (Vaux, London) describes how their goal is simply to live the faith in a way that is true to their context right now.

> I guess there have always been struggles between those in charge of the traditions and teachings and those who seek to raid the temple vaults and put them back in the public domain. Those Christians who fought for ignoring Jewish food laws, for the Bible to be translated into English, and for contemporary music to be used in worship are all in the line of Christ, sweeping the obstacles out of the way of those who try to come to worship as normal people. Without wanting to be over-grand about it, that is really what Vaux is about. We want to speak about God in the vernacular. It just happens that our local dialect is urban and design savvy.

Vaux looks to communicate the gospel in language that both they and their hearers understand in the context of a world they both share. They create worship for themselves with all their local particularities, thereby making sacred the many activities of their lives. Vaux creates small, highly creative, indigenous worship events that give honor to God using the language of their urban and design-savvy world.

Worship That Expresses a Body/Mind Holism

The sacred/secular split of modernity separated the body from the mind. The mind/spirit/heart was sacred, and the body, as part of material reality, was secular. The church followed suit. For example, modern worship focuses on the mind. To understand the foundational truths of Scripture and right doctrine is the highest priority. The body is a necessary evil but certainly not to be valued as highly as one's thoughts. The focus on mind was the modern church's strategy to be relevant to a Cartesian society. However, after three hundred years of a cognitive-based Christianity, we have entered a new era in which such a reductionistic focus on mind has been discredited by the culture at large. In the postmodern era, there is an embrace of both body and mind. Body and soul are no longer separate but are seen as parts of the whole human system.

Emerging churches bring the body back into the worship event. Whereas the Reformation removed many rituals from the worship service, postmodern worship restores these activities. The Reformation focused on the spoken Word, while postmodern worship embraces the experienced Word. Thus, emerging church worshipers may respond with the sign of the cross, more often associated with Catholic worship, and openly receive the deep mystical aspects of communion, candles, and incense. They may retrieve ancient rituals and create new ones involving the body; they may dance in different venues. Emerging churches create their own music, as at Solomon's Porch in Minneapolis, where they also practice yoga, massage, and physical prayer. They believe that what is good for the physical body is good for the spiritual body and vice versa. In both their worship and their community life, emerging churches look to overcome the modern dualisms in regard to body and soul.

Finding God's Fingerprints within Popular Culture

Ian Mobsby (Moot, London) believes Christians must identify and redefine the signs and symbols in pop culture that point to God, thereby reclaiming these aspects of culture for God. For Mobsby, people can identify God's grace only if they are first immersed in a particular culture. People must be insiders to know how God is communicating to a particular culture at a particular time. Jonny Baker (Grace, London) contrasts an incarnational way of engagement with "'escapology theology' (like that espoused in the Left Behind series of novels by Tim LaHaye and Jerry

Jenkins) that sees a future in heaven after the earth is destroyed." Instead, Baker advocates that Christians need to invest themselves in the current culture, not live on hold until time runs out. For both Mobsby and Baker, Christians must dwell in culture *now* and point to God *from within*, not from without. Only in this way can culture be redeemed and secularization overcome.

Because Christians share cultures with those around them, worship should not be foreign to their friends. Unfortunately, churches that are indigenous to postmodern culture are quite rare. Paul Roberts (Resonance, Bristol, U.K.) states, "The problem is that most organized forms of evangelism fail to pass through the cultural net, so many alternative worshipers give up on the idea of intentional mission, whether they would admit it or not. This is bad. The groups then end up being therapeutic and grow by transfer, but in my opinion, they are not exploiting their full potential in evangelism."

A common desire among all emerging churches is to create a venue where Christians can bring their friends. Truly living within a culture and creating indigenous forms of worship help make this possible. Many churchgoers would be embarrassed if their friends and neighbors were to attend church with them, but Ben Edson (Sanctus1, Manchester, U.K.) presents a different scenario. "Our people have confidence in the product. Although this is a marketing term, it is really quite important. When people bring their friends to Sanctus1, they know that they will be fully welcomed and have a good evening. People have confidence and therefore are happy to bring friends along. Unfortunately, this confidence does not exist within a lot of churches."

Evangelism as a Way of Life, Not an Event

Evangelism that overcomes the sacred/secular split of modernity must be a natural part of one's everyday life. For example, in the U.K., serving in this way is intentional, as in clubs. Anna Dodridge (Bournemouth, U.K.) writes about evangelism in the following terms.

> I guess it is quite central to what we are about really. The idea that the church as an institution was not doing anything for the world and that none of us would want to involve our friends and family in such a mess of an establishment was a big motivator for getting the community functioning. It really is something that people, non-Christian and Christian alike, can be involved with and a part of. I guess we all have areas where evangelism is focused. For some of us it's mainly the

clubs. Others are into the housing estates where they live or places where they socialize.

Postmodern evangelism may also involve living everyday life with friends who happen to live within postmodern culture. "As well as the more overt missions in our lives, there is also the everyday meeting people, hanging out with people, that is important. I guess as a community we have recognized, through discussion and prayer, that lifestyle evangelism is very important. It's what Jesus was about. We are aware of the fact that every attitude we have and every move we make affects the people around us, whether or not they are Christians, so we are careful to look out for one another, to be accountable, to question any suspect behavior" (Anna Dodridge, Bournemouth, U.K.).

Postmodern evangelism is really about living like Jesus in postmodern cultures through one's relationships. Dodridge states:

> Part of discipling each other is to get to know each other very well and to know areas of struggle that will in turn affect evangelism. There's the everyday lifestyle evangelism that touches everyone we come into contact with (and is clearly the hardest thing), but then we each have our little projects, where we do things specifically to bring about relationships. For example, our work in the clubs provided opportunities for us to meet lots of local DJs and promoters. We met a few clubbers too. So arising from that club night, we now have a bunch of new friends whom we see out and about and hang out with. They know we are Christians, and they see how we live. For us, that is evangelism.

Emerging leaders represent a spectrum of thought on the topic of evangelizing, but no matter whether they are to the right or to the left, they all regard evangelism in terms of an open-ended conversation and an embodied way of life as distinct from a result-geared confrontation. This stance reflects their own negative experiences and also a keen sensitivity toward the kind of people among whom they minister. Johnny Sertin (Bartonka, Bournemouth, U.K.) agrees.[10] "You say the gospel by living it. Changing worship might be interesting, but the focus must be the incarnation. I won't live or die for a worship meeting, but I would give my life for living incarnationally, and ultimately Christianity is about what you would live and die for."

10. Johnny Sertin was an early founder of Bliss (mid 1990s) and the nightclub Bartonka (late 1990s), both located in Bournemouth.

Rock Bands and Club Music

In emerging churches, especially in the U.K., there is a movement away from the rock band form of church where performers lead worship from onstage. Rock 'n' roll worship, pioneered by the Vineyard and other movements, invites listeners to look onstage for direction. Much of the focus is on the people up front, even if the hearers are encouraged to focus on God.

Although songs are still sung in many emerging churches, they are not always the primary way these churches experience worship. Instead, music serves as a support for other activities such as prayer, silence, and liturgy. In club-culture worship, music surrounds the worshipers, who may not even see the DJ. One does not focus on a stage up front; in fact, there may not even be a stage. Steve Collins (Grace, London) compares the immanent style of club-culture worship to a New Testament, post-temple sort of worship, one that emphasizes the immanent sort of worship Jesus spoke about to the woman at the well. In club music, one feels immersed in God's presence.

The roots of club culture's influence on churches go back to the U.K. in the 1980s. Collins tells his story. "I was a clubber in the mid-1980s and saw the beginning of rave culture in 1988. I felt God on the dance floor, not in church, and at the end of the 'service' I felt clean." His fellow clubbers pursued God's presence and found it in the club. For Collins, a question gripped him. "Why is the church not plugged into this subculture?" Ian Mobsby (Moot, London) explains the initial birth pangs of alternative worship.

> Alternative worship was initially a contextual reaction to the rave culture. It presented a way of being church that was born out of the community vibe of clubs and raves. This, for me, was mostly "Gospel Garage": Suddenly, I was worshiping God in a very unchurched place. This was a paradigm shift, which I think many others experienced. So a new way of being and doing church was born in alternative worship. Alternative was a cultural movement in the late 1980s that was for some very liberating until it led to drugs. So alternative worship grew contextually out of that.

Again, this reflects making holy what was once secular.

It is primarily in the U.K. that we see new forms of church indigenous to club culture. Beginning with Nine O'clock Service (Sheffield, U.K.) and continuing to this day, the alternative worship movement in the U.K. has the longest history of club forms of church. In 1995, Kenny

Mitchell, a DJ missionary from Brooklyn, introduced club worship to Pete Greig and Warehouse, creating what would be one of the first club venues for the descendents of the house church movement.[11] The Cultural Shift network, of which Warehouse is a part, has since then focused on planting club-culture churches throughout the U.K. (NGM in Bristol has a significant role in this, and Rubik's Cube in Bristol is their primary venue.) The movement looks to create up to twenty-six club-culture communities in the next year. In addition, Cameron Dante, a former BBC Radio One DJ and former member of Tribe (Manchester, U.K.) has had ambitious plans for club-culture communities throughout the U.K.

The First Emerging Church

We finish this discussion on emerging churches and their transformation of secular space with a case study of a community in the north of England: the Nine O'clock Service (NOS). What gave rise to NOS? Paul Roberts (Resonance, Bristol, U.K.) explains:

> There was definitely an emergent set of cultural forms in the late 1980s in the U.K., arising from a growing self-realization that postmodernity was something real and new, and also through things like the "second summer of love," which took place in 1988 and put the whole independent (now illegal) rave scene on the map. This transformed the music that was being produced by the most innovative young people of the time and also in turn video and art. Clubs started using multimedia, so it was inevitable that we [the church] would start to as well.

The birth of a postmodern worshiping community began in Sheffield, U.K., in the fall of 1985, when John Wimber, leader of the Vineyard movement, held a series of renewal and healing meetings at the invitation of St. Thomas Crooke's Anglican Church. Young people were called out and anointed under the leading of the Holy Spirit. Toward the end of 1985, Robert Warren invited the newly formed Nairn Street Community (a community bound by a common purse and mission) to perform church services at 9:00 p.m. on Sunday nights (hence the name Nine O'clock Service) on a one-year trial basis. Their mission was to reach those the church could not, the eighteen- to thirty-year-olds. They combined

---

11. But Warehouse was not alone. Bliss in Bournemouth, under the leadership of Johnny Sertin and others, was throwing club culture parties at that time.

the feel of a nightclub with the charismatic theology they had learned from Wimber. They conducted worship and teaching and then invited the Holy Spirit to fall. However, the Sheffield team's style of music was more harshly urban than the suburban soft rock typical of the Vineyard at that time. The NOS folks said to Wimber, "That music of yours is 1960s Righteous Brothers. Our God is stronger than that!" As Andy Thornton (Late Late Service, Glasgow, U.K.) explains, "NOS was much bolder. It cut through. It worked for people, particularly those who felt emasculated by the softness of charismatic evangelicalism."

Over the next few years, NOS pioneered an entirely new way of worship within the Anglican Church. To be clear, NOS's innovation was locally derived and not sourced in the Vineyard. "What the Wimber mission did was help them realize that they could continue to work in an existing church setting *and* be authentic to the culture in which they were working and living" (Paul Roberts, Resonance, Bristol, U.K.). NOS leaders created expressions of eucharistic worship using forms indigenous to club culture. By the end of 1986, NOS numbered 150 people. The growth came from both the unchurched and evangelicals disillusioned with the form of the institutional church. In 1987–88, NOS created two venues, a eucharistic service and a teaching service. The eucharistic service utilized symbol and expressed the bread and the wine using multimedia. Much of this service stressed God as "other," emphasizing the mystery of God. The teaching service utilized dance culture. During the teaching, film loops further expressed what the speaker was saying. These film loops displayed culture, nature, and other visuals. Over time, NOS integrated the very best high-tech sound and video technology into the service. In 1987, NOS was considered to be a success and was continued indefinitely.

NOS had "sweepers," the name they gave to those in the community who reached out to clubbers, inviting them to attend—and come they did. NOS sought to have the clubbers always outnumber the church people. Any clubber was welcome; however, non-clubbers were visited by a pastor who determined if they were right for NOS. The pastor explained the high cost of joining in terms of a commitment to community, simplicity, and financial giving. In addition, each member needed to listen to dance music, go clubbing, and read club-culture magazines. A NOS stylist helped them buy clothes and adopt hairstyles that were indigenous to club culture.

By the late 1980s, there were four hundred members of NOS. As time went on, NOS left its charismatic roots and adopted a creation-centered theology. At the 1992 Greenbelt Festival, members of NOS performed "Passion in Global Chaos," which "scandalously" featured bikini-clad dancers.[12] In 1993, they created the Planetary Mass, a service that seventy people worked to create each week.

But NOS contained a fatal flaw from its very inception. Utilizing an aberrant form of a charismatic leadership structure, in NOS, the top leader could not be questioned. The controlling nature of the leader crushed the identities of all those in leadership, who became severely traumatized. From his position of authority, the leader made inappropriate advances among the females of the leadership team as well. In 1995, the behind-the-scenes story of NOS came to the forefront, and the group disbanded in the midst of a scandal that gained national media attention. Most members of NOS never returned to church.

Despite its tragic end, the NOS phenomenon made a profound impact on many who experienced its highly creative worship. Simon Hall of Revive (Leeds, U.K.) explains his first encounter with NOS: "Just down the road some guys about five years older than me were coming out of the goth[13] scene and experimenting with the dance music coming over from New York and Chicago (we're talking 1986 now). They were doing something radical, creating worship with this awesome music, and visuals, and in the dark. Man, it was overpowering. It was called the Nine O'clock Service, and it all went haywire, but it changed my life forever." Hall also experienced NOS at the Greenbelt Festival in 1988.

I was a fairly regular twenty-year-old Christian, continuing to live in a dualistic world of Graham Kendrick's music and a group named the Cure, somehow managing to balance my life outside the church (the darkly beautiful world of goth and Indie)[14] with the very different environment within the sacred walls. The walls fell down that summer, and I knew there was no way back for me: no way that I could ever again eagerly expect the latest Vineyard songbook, no way that I could live the enforced

12. "In fairness to NOS—the wearing of bikinis was and is normative at any summer clubbing event in Europe. Heat is a big issue when dancing to hi-BPM music, especially when taking Ecstasy, which can cause overheating and dehydration if not counterbalanced by imbibing water (not alcohol) and chilling out. So in wearing bikinis, the NOS girls were just doing what anyone in clubs did anyway. The shock engendered in some of the Greenbelt attenders just indicates how far the church was from club culture and the willingness of NOS to identify authentically with it" (Paul Roberts, Resonance, Bristol, U.K.).

13. Goth is a musical subculture that began in the 1980s. It evolved out of the punk music scene of the 1970s and stressed melancholy and darkness and was characterized by the wearing of black clothes.

14. Indie is an early form of alternative music that was recorded by non-mainstream record labels during the 1980s.

lie that my church was relevant. I was ruined. Many people my age and older saw in NOS a hope for a different kind of church.[15]

For Mal Calladine (Tribal Generation, Sheffield, U.K.), the experience was equally significant. "I would come back from the services in tears—they were so powerful. I saw guys come to faith at NOS. The power of God was certainly there." Paul Roberts (Resonance, Bristol, U.K.) says, "I visited NOS in 1991, and it knocked me out." Ian Mobsby (Moot, London) describes his experience. "In the middle of the rave scene in the north of England in the early 1990s, I experienced Visions in York and the Nine O'clock Service in Sheffield, where my cultural world and religious world hit head-on. It changed my outlook, and traditional church never appealed the same way again." For Barry Taylor (Sanctuary, Santa Monica, CA):

> NOS was like a breath of fresh air. I hadn't seen or experienced anything like it at the time. It was visually stimulating. The energy of the space—the idea permeating the air that there could be a collaborative expression of worship—was heady stuff given the time period. It was a challenge in that it was definitely pushing some theological horizons. For the most part, I found it immensely liberating because it allowed me the personal space to begin my own process of reflection and recontextualization.

According to Paul Wilson, "NOS was the most exciting club in the U.K., for Christians *or* non-Christians. The Holy Spirit was there. It was amazing dance culture, it was creation spirituality, and it was a gritty urban expression of church." Paul Roberts (Resonance, Bristol, U.K.) says, "NOS impacted the perceptions of those of us who were in our twenties and thirties then, because we realized that even the most cutting-edge charismatic and evangelical forms of church were on a different cultural planet to where the wider, younger end of the culture was going." Andy Thornton (Late Late Service, Glasgow, U.K.) agrees. "People often reach a breaking point with evangelicalism in their late twenties as they see that the world is overwhelming, that the way they were taught and the way the world actually works no longer fit. You either subjugate yourself or get out of it. NOS gave them some certainty while not leaving them in cultural backwaters."

Even though they never visited, some felt encouraged simply by the existence of NOS. Steve Collins of Grace (London) says, "I knew about

---

15. Web article written by Simon Hall, Revive, Leeds, U.K. Link no longer active.

the Nine O'clock Service. It was a sign of hope to me, that some Christians somewhere were indeed engaging with club culture (which had quickly become the dominant culture of people under forty in the U.K.) and the secular world of the 1990s. I didn't know of anywhere else." Dave Tomlinson (Holy Joes, London) says, "We knew of NOS in those days and greatly admired what they were doing, though none of us had ever been there. But they were an inspiration." Andrew Jones, then in California, says, "I had heard about it when I was doing rave worship in California and was inspired by the fact that the Brits were actually doing it."

Looking back at NOS years later, Andy Thornton says the following: "NOS was incredibly innovative. They had a confident faith. Twenty-four of them shared a common purse, and they had many creative people who were uncompromising in their integration of urban music and art." Paul Roberts (Resonance, Bristol, U.K.) offers his assessment. "I think the contribution of NOS was enormous, brilliant, seminal, God given. Shame it all went so badly wrong. If they had been non-cultic and more open to cooperation with others, alternative worship would be a serious missional force to be reckoned with in the church today." Thornton adds, "In alternative worship, a core question is what to do with art and faith. In every alternative worship group, you will have frustrated evangelists and completely internalized artists—a great incoherence. One side measures the meeting by lives transformed, the others if their art was expressed. NOS found a home for these two types."

After the formation of NOS, other alternative worship[16] groups started popping up around the U.K. Sue Wallace, a pioneer with Visions (York, U.K.), says, "NOS was a catalyst (either directly or indirectly) for people to see what was possible for multimedia worship. Seeing the Nine O'clock Service at Greenbelt in 1988 was an inspiring and life-changing moment. Our ideas of what worship should look, sound, and feel like were turned on their heads by seeing this amazing loud, multimedia service that at the same time was deeply worshipful. I remember thinking, 'Wow! That was really interesting, but I could never do it in a million years.'" In 1989, Wallace began to explore alternative forms of worship, and what was to be Visions was born in 1991.

Andy Thornton's band played at Greenbelt, and he remembers seeing NOS play in 1988. He thought their show was quite interesting, but he

16. The label "alternative worship" was possibly given to the budding movement in 1991 at Greenbelt. Contextual forms of the mass were seen as early as Jim Friedrich's work in 1969. "'Circus Mass' is a good example of an early alternative worship experience that was responding to the West Coast (California) art scene" (Andrew Jones, Boaz, U.K.).

didn't think anything more of it. In 1991, Thornton was asked to lead worship for a Scottish youth night in Glasgow, U.K. "I remembered back to NOS at Greenbelt, and with my contacts from many artistic fields, I brought things together. We had visuals, images, and there was no front. Some liked it, and some got confused." Soon thereafter, Thornton began the Late Late Service in Glasgow.

Paul Roberts (Resonance, Bristol, U.K.) describes how NOS inspired him to begin a service. "I always felt the idea of NOS was highly exportable, and I knew I'd need to build a community to do anything like that. This came together in the summer of 1993, when I spent a sabbatical reading postmodern texts and visiting other nascent alternative worship communities around the U.K. and meeting up with Mark Pierson, then at Cityside Baptist in Auckland, New Zealand. This in turn led to people putting me in touch with people who had recently moved to Bristol. I persuaded our church to let us run services there in the autumn of 1993, and Third Sunday Service (now Resonance) got going in January 1994."

The innovation of the alternative worship community influenced not only the church community but the wider culture as well. "In the early 1990s, the clubs in parts of northern England were looking to alternative worship groups like Visions and NOS for their video resources. It was said that NOS's mass was the inspiration for Enigma's debut album, although I've never been able to verify it. The album certainly sounds uncannily like the NOS mass. Both used dance music and Gregorian chant" (Paul Roberts). Andy Thornton echoes Roberts. "U2's Zoo TV was said to be inspired by NOS. It is important to realize that NOS was much more influential than just church. Their multi-screen, postmodern use of imagery was a cultural trend at that time within the pop-culture scene."

Although the Nine O'clock Service ended badly in 1995, it has much to teach about the emerging church. Its primary contribution was its ability to overcome the sacred/secular division of modernity, as identified in this chapter. Moreover, it created a highly participatory and creative spirituality for its community. NOS serves as a powerful example of an embodied gospel in postmodern culture.

Conclusion

Modernity pushed the church to the margins of society and gave it the task of religious provider. The church returned the "favor" by allowing the rest of society to be beyond its domain, inhabiting the realm of the secular. As modernity's rule began to crumble, the modern church shared its fate. A desire for a holistic spirituality filled the culture, but the church found itself ill prepared for the task. Holistic spiritualities formed to address all of life, and the church found itself defending its modern ethos.

Emerging churches face a formidable task as they endeavor to distinguish between the parts of church life that are rooted in modern culture, to be discarded, and the parts that are gospel and need to be maintained. If the emerging church errs in regard to culture, the church dies, but if it gets the gospel wrong, it loses its identity. Emerging churches have at their disposal three primary tools to dismantle and re-create church: the gospel, sacralization, and the life of the community. Having already explored the gospel in the previous chapter, in this chapter we explored how emerging churches seek to end secularity by overcoming linearity, print culture, systemization, and the dualisms of invisible/visible and body/mind and by creating a whole-life spirituality in all realms of society. The next chapter explores the kind of community required to engage culture in the ways described here.

5

Living as Community

In our current cultural crisis, the most powerful demonstration of the
reality of the gospel is a community embodying the way, the truth, and
the life of Jesus. Healthy community is the life of Jesus living in us and
through us. For community to last, our love for one another must be
surpassed only by our love for Jesus. If the relationships are grounded
on anything other than Jesus, the community will fall—and the sooner
the better!

Jonathan Campbell, Seattle

On one occasion, after spending hours with her at the Living Room, the
church's café, a guest asked Karen Ward (Church of the Apostles, Seattle),
"When is your church service?"
"You just had it," replied Ward.

The ecclesiology of emerging churches flows out of their understanding of the gospel, proclaimed and lived by Jesus, and the mission he
entrusted to his followers. If the church is to be the body of Christ on
earth, what key characteristics does the church need to function in such
a capacity? In other words, what kind of community life must exist
so that the church has the ability to practice the way of Jesus in every
sphere of society?

This chapter explores how emerging churches must create a space
for the kingdom to come, that being a member of the church means
first and foremost identification with Christ and his community of

followers. It also examines the practice of peoplehood. The church is primarily a *people,* not simply a *place* to meet. It is a movement and not an institution. Drawing on the understanding that secular space no longer exists, church is a seven-day-a-week identification, not a once-a-week, ninety-minute respite from the real world. The church lives as a committed community *in* this world, which desperately needs redemption.

The relationship between the church and the kingdom is a complex one. The two cannot be exhaustively defined, and there is a significant overlap. The reign of God existed before the coming of the church, and it will replace the church at the consummation of all things, when Christ will reign supreme and unchallenged. The church, for its part, is a servant and a sign of the coming kingdom, which was inaugurated with the coming of Christ and was established, in its provisional form, with his ascension into heaven and the imparting of his Spirit. The church, as a servant of the kingdom, constantly points beyond itself to the Lord who is its head and who requires unreserved and comprehensive submission.

The dialectical tension between the church and the kingdom cannot be resolved. The church exists between the time of the inauguration and the consummation of the reign of God on earth. Therefore, it is always the "pilgrim" or the "becoming" church. Furthermore, it is made up of forgiven sinners, not perfected saints, who are at various stages of a life journey of discipleship. Yet the dialectical tension has value in that it safeguards the church from becoming self-focused, institutionally self-sufficient, and intellectually complacent. The strains and stresses brought about by the dialectical tension provide a forcible reminder that Christians are called to live by faith, love, and hope until they stand transformed by the presence of Christ at his glorious return.

Emerging churches draw their inspiration and model from the example of Jesus. They recognize that they have moved from the physical proximity of Jesus to his presence in the midst of their community by his Holy Spirit. The risen Christ now works by his Spirit, who operates through the community as well as beyond it, in the furtherance of his purposes in the wider world. As Si Johnston of headspace (London) writes, "Authentic community is not a utopian vision. Instead, we believe that it is centered around principles drawn from the story of Jesus. Our values aim to reflect his story and transparency, his love and life, his need for recreation, his connections and solidarity with people in life's predicaments, and his reflection and dialogue, all of which should continue to mark our ethos and community practice."

Those who pursue the kingdom as their first priority find that a community forms that is made up of people on the same journey. But it is not just any kind of community. Such people become a community with Jesus as their king, an alternative community that is unlike all others. The kingdom gives rise to the community and not vice versa. The church is first the product of mission before it is an agent of mission. The church consists of those people who have been called *out* and called *together* in order to be sent into the world to witness to the kingdom. "For me, the intention to follow Jesus' call to be one of his disciples determines whether a group of people is trying to do church or something else," says Paul Roberts (Resonance, Bristol, U.K.).

First and foremost is the kingdom, and the church follows. Consequently, to ask church questions without reference to the kingdom is fruitless. Emerging churches represent this viewpoint of kingdom before church. They are built on the premise that the mission God has entrusted to his church is concerned with actualizing the kingdom by being available to God and responsive to the leading of the Holy Spirit. The focus of emerging churches on the "gospel of the kingdom" as distinct from a "gospel of salvation" has produced a new ecclesiology. More accurately, it has signaled a return to an ancient ecclesiology in which mission is integral to church.

Preparing the Way for the Kingdom

Believers must give up old loyalties in order to create a space for the kingdom to come. Nationalism, individualism, and consumerism are a few of the ideologies that must be reappropriated or completely abandoned in light of the coming reign of God. In addition, some of the most cherished church forms may be more a hindrance than a help in regard to creating space for God. When such forms are removed, often what is left are simply tight-knit communities that hunger for the coming of God's reign.

By identifying with Jesus, believers undergo a profound change of allegiance. They die to self and recognize that their primary identity is as adopted daughters and sons in the family of God and that the local expression of that family is the church, understood as a community of Christ followers seeking to live out their new identity in all the circumstances of their daily lives.

According to N. T. Wright,[1] Jesus stated that all loyalties had to acquiesce to loyalty to the new kingdom. All forms of power had to be relinquished. Satan, not Rome, was their enemy now, thus ending all forms of nationalism and violence. If one wanted to pursue the kingdom of God, old, former loyalties had to give way to new kingdom-oriented ones. We see this changed set of allegiances most clearly in the community Jesus gathered to himself.

Any attempt to join people in a community presents a challenge for individuals who have been nurtured in the culture of modernity, in which independence, individual rights, and privileges are the norm. Such people are often disturbingly silent when it comes to their corporate responsibilities. Because of the pervasive nature of culture, people are largely unaware of the extent to which they have become individualized and privatized.

Looking back to the outset of modernity, after Duns Scotus, humans were on their own, and they needed to protect what was theirs.[2] Personal property rights ensued and created the modern individual. A new understanding arose that gave every person unlimited sovereignty over his or her individual person. Philosophically, all people could be sure of was their internal being. Because material and immaterial reality were no longer connected, people could no longer be sure of their observations. All connections with others became "extra" and discretionary rather than understood as essential to being human. Even religion became a universal condition that one could objectify and describe, and therefore, people could make an individual decision as to whether to accept or disregard it. Individualism, currently at its zenith, had its birth at the very outset of modernity.

At this time in late modernity, communal bonding occurs when individuals consume goods alongside one another. It is at the shopping mall where this connecting occurs, as shoppers buy similar products and share "fellowship." Many American churches function similarly. The shopping mall ideology of the seeker church caters to the spiritual search of the American consumer. These churches justify the removal of all religious symbols and anything else that does not conform to consumer culture.[3]

1. N. T. Wright, *Jesus and the Victory of God*, vol. 2 of Christian Origins and the Question of God (Minneapolis: Fortress, 1996).

2. As we write on modernity, we are indebted to John Milbank, *Theology and Social Theory: Beyond Secular Reason* (Oxford: Blackwell, 1993); and Zygmunt Bauman and Keith Tester, *Conversations with Zygmunt Bauman* (Cambridge, U.K.: Polity Press, 2001).

3. Kimon Sargeant, *Seeker Churches: Promoting Traditional Religion in a Nontraditional Way* (New Brunswick: Rutgers University Press, 2000).

Often in new paradigm churches, the only community expression in worship is the casual glance at other people who are enjoying their own personal worship. In this way, it is glibly assumed that community is formed in the process of mutual recognition. However, the biblical understanding of community signifies so much more and far exceeds this individualized expression of worship.

As already mentioned, a church-within-a-church does not challenge the autonomy of the individual either. Spencer Burke (Newport Beach, CA) discusses the problematic nature of a church-within-a-church, the most common expression among the seeker/Gen-X style of church.

> Early pioneers were initially optimistic that this form of church would work out. However, these younger leaders desired to move away from the seeker model, which does not challenge individual sovereignty. These younger leaders were quite limited in that they did not have the freedom to change their theology, or the way they do budgets, or how they baptize. The difference between seeker and Gen-X communities always reared its head eventually. Often the church plant would start with a half-million-dollar budget and a big Sunday morning event. The ultimate goal was to be big in celebration, always built around the preacher/teacher, buildings, and staff. Actually, it was the same old system. If the younger leader wanted to start a network of house churches for the sake of community or for the kingdom, he would lose his job.

Burke concluded, "The church-within-a-church always collapses upon itself at some point."

Emerging churches challenge the priority of the individual assumed in seeker, new paradigm, and even traditional Protestant churches. This challenge is seen most clearly in postmodern worship, especially in club music found primarily in the U.K. It is not simply a new type of music. The event experienced at the club necessarily involves community expression and the active participation of all. By contrast, in soft rock or hard rock worship events, individuals usually ignore other church members as each person focuses on God and the band members. In club-culture worship, participants do not ignore their friends but become fellow travelers in a "very near" experience of God. They experience God in association with their friends and also go through the experience together. It is a shared event that binds people closer together. The Cultural Shift network utilizes club culture as its primary worship form, and it is also used in alternative worship and various independent mission movements such as Tribe in Manchester, U.K. To be clear, we are not saying that club culture is the only way to worship in postmodern culture. The ways are endless, and these varied expressions are explored in chapters on participation, creativity, and spirituality.

Why is it that so many churches do not go deeper, allowing the kingdom to change church practices into more substantial forms of community? The simple reason is that it is easier to alter surface forms than it is to tear down church practices to make room for the kingdom. Spencer Burke (Newport Beach, CA) notes that most churches, even if they promote themselves as seeker, purpose-driven, Gen-X, or post-modern, deconstruct maybe only 10 percent of the church while leaving the other 90 percent intact.

> These churches might change their style, but they don't alter who gets paid, who tells the community what to do, or the weekly nature of church (i.e., meeting at a particular place at a particular time each week). They do not change who is able to preside at the Lord's Supper, and they do not change the marks of success, usually translated into money and numbers of people. To allow the kingdom to deconstruct these issues is to touch the 90 percent, and that is taboo for most churches.

If a church chooses to position the kingdom before the church, then the other 90 percent comes into question, and an entirely different church emerges. The need for such a radical dismantling of the church is understandable given the nature of the kingdom. When Jesus levels everything, then everything is up for grabs. This is a far more painfully demanding process than the minute adjustments of church services.

The focus of emerging churches is on incarnating the gospel, not numerical or economic success. They believe the gospel of the kingdom levels all other expectations of what success means. Ultimately, Mark Scandrette (ReIMAGINE! San Francisco) does not care if he is success-ful. "I am on a journey to find where heaven and earth come together in order to really experience the gospel. The goal of this is to see the gospel expressed, not necessarily in any terms of budget or number goals."

Because of the ongoing, nonstop nature of the faith, participation in a tight-knit, perhaps smaller, community is essential. It is the only way to ensure that each person can participate in life-transforming activities. The focus is not a service but a way of life together. The cost is high to live as a community of the kingdom, and to do so, these communities completely redefine their understanding of success.

Emerging churches create a space for the kingdom to come in their midst. They prepare themselves by abandoning other allegiances, such as individualism and aspects of consumerism. They choose to dig deeper, letting go of their ideas regarding church as they display a willingness to give up cherished church forms if they hinder the kingdom. They create venues to share their stories and struggles with one another.

How Kingdom Practices Deconstruct Church Practices

The shift to a kingdom emphasis from a church emphasis does not simply mean a new style of doing things or the addition of new programs. It entails a radical restructuring, redirecting, and reenergizing of the church. At Three Nails (Pittsburgh), they use the life of Jesus as a model to deconstruct church forms. Holly Rankin Zaher explains, "We refer to Luke/Acts to see who we are as a Jesus movement, utilizing that account of the life of Jesus and of the church he founded to both deconstruct and reconstruct church practice. For the whole first year, I said, 'I'm a pastor of deconstruction' because we had to rethink everything we did."

Emerging churches may not appear as legitimate forms of church to those who are not wrestling with ideas of church practice. "The people who come and stay at Water's Edge (Hudsonville, MI) know that something is wrong with church as we know it. If newcomers haven't had that realization, they come and say, 'This isn't church' and leave" (Joel McClure). "Part of our view is that there needs to be a place where this wrestling can take place."

Church is a place where those on the journey can meet up with one another. For Water's Edge, the church is not a safe haven for people who have "arrived" but a meeting point for those on the journey of faith. Kester Brewin of Vaux (London) writes the following:

> I guess our ecclesiology has been evolving since before we even started Vaux. We work things out through praxis. Our theology is not static—a stone tablet that informs what we do. Rather, what we do informs our theology through a process of exploration. This has been particularly true of our views on church, in that we didn't start with some grand idea about how to set up a new style of church, all planned out and documented on paper first. Quite the opposite. In a sense, even that mode of beginning has come to mean a lot to us in our idea of what church is: It is simply a meeting point for those who are journeying.

Mark Scandrette (ReIMAGINE! San Francisco) identifies a pattern showing how emerging church leaders evolve. First, a desire forms in leaders to create something new, something to which they could bring their friends. Their first inclination is to perpetuate the institutional model, that is, a Gen-X or young adult service, which is simply a modified seeker service. These models constitute a minor change to the existing megachurch model. After a time, leaders become disillusioned with the entire megachurch model and the kind of Christianity it represents. They then move to a house church model in which leaders are not paid and there is no official institution to support. At some point, however, they realize that the church simply moved location, from the church building to the house, and that the fundamental structure of church did not change. Such leaders develop a growing conviction that the real issue is not where a church meets, the style of the service, or even the structure but that the kingdom of God is embodied in the life of the community. They move to establish their practices around Jesus and the kingdom, and the church "service" decreases in importance.

Emerging churches utilize the kingdom as a tool to deconstruct all aspects of life, including virtually all church practices. They understand that the kingdom gives rise to the church, not the other way around. Forms and structures of church are variable in emerging churches, especially in comparison to new paradigm, purpose-driven, and seeker churches, which keep most of the traditional structures intact. These older movements maintain an emphasis on paid senior pastors, the Sunday service as what constitutes church, outreach that focuses on lapsed suburban professionals, and the idea that Christians come to church, primarily understood as the church building. Utilizing the kingdom of God paradigm as a tool of deconstruction, emerging churches dismantle many forms of church that, although viable at one time, increasingly represent a bygone era.

Redefining the Meaning of Church

Emerging churches raise basic questions about the nature of church. Is it the place where weekly worship services are conducted, or is it a network of relationships? Emerging churches utilize the gospel both to dismantle and to rebuild church forms, marking a significant shift of emphasis from church to kingdom.

The practice of inclusion creates a new kind of family. "Who is my mother, and who are my brothers?" Jesus asked his followers (Matt. 12:48 NIV). Jesus turned the family structure on its head. Yes, the followers of Jesus lived as family, but this new family was not connected by blood relations. Those who pursued the kingdom served as brother and sister to one another. Again, it was alternative, as this family had no father other than God in heaven. The followers of Jesus belonged to this family, which took precedence over all other associations and allegiances.

Creating a vital community is a challenge in our current cultural context. People are both hungry for relationships and yet at the same time ill prepared for the costs involved. In a culture in which casual relationships or contractual relationships are the norm, it is difficult to build relationships on deep foundations that can survive disagreements and disappointments. People are more prone to walk away when the going becomes difficult than to work through a crisis to the point where a new depth of understanding is reached.

A Family, Not an Institution

Emerging churches pursue the "new family" practices as modeled by Jesus and his followers, and their embodied way of life operates similarly to the life of an extended family. What characteristics of family in our culture might shed light on emerging church practices? Families consist of relationships that are not based on choice. Individuals typically do not choose their families and are connected to them whether they like it or not. One does not choose *when* to be a family member. People are part of a family when they sleep, when they are at school, or when they are with friends. In addition, people do not even need to like their families. They are with them when the feelings are there or not. Whether a family meets one's needs is rarely considered.

If a church begins to look like a family, then all its institutional practices will undergo change. Church as family is primarily about relationships. It is not about meetings, events, or structures. Such rubric questions do not make sense when discussing relational issues. The alternative family structure of emerging churches seeks a sort of family commitment. People are part of a kingdom community even if they don't get their needs met and often whether they feel like it or not. "I believe the commitment is relational more than institutional. Emerging people commit to one another and to God, and that commitment is deep and lasting. We are stuck together as family, even if we don't like one another" (Andrew Jones, Boaz, U.K.).

For many churches, the structure itself prevents family-type connections. An institutional way of being church must give way to relational ways of being. Joe Boyd describes what happened at Apex (Las Vegas):

"We wanted the church to become a family, God's family. We needed to structure church as a family, not a rock show, or a business, or a convention, or a university. We could not think of how to do that with four hundred people! We wanted God to be the father and Jesus to be the leader. We wanted the big meeting to be something *less than* church for these people." Boyd deconstructed a "successful" form of church in order to create a space for family-type relationships to develop.

A church is a family not just in terms of communal identity but also in terms of the support it provides among its members. In the early days of Landing Place (Columbus, OH), Mark Palmer's wife, Jennifer, was diagnosed with cancer. "This was earth shattering. Jennifer's story and the way she bore her sickness through its various stages enabled the community to form in a special way and continue to exist and thrive. Furthermore, the way the community lived through this ordeal brought a lot of people into the community. It was an amazing commentary on God and the story he is writing. Through all of this, Landing Place acted as my family."

Emerging churches have strong family ties that remain firm in the face of adversity and in spite of differences. Steve Collins (Grace, London) describes his experience of community: "One of the beneficial things I learned from my first church was that Christians need community, especially in a society like my own, which is indifferent or passively hostile to Christianity. I was taught that you won't find the perfect church but that you need to be in community with other Christians, however unlike you they may be. So find the church you feel God is calling you to and stay there until you are called onward. That's what I've always done."

Just as with any family, the challenges can be significant. Anna Dodridge (Bournemouth, U.K.) says:

> The problem with all this is that it is so incredibly hard. Because we are in part relying on people, it's easy for things to collapse. It can make a big difference in a small church when one or two people aren't "feeling it." I would say we are having a bit of a season of that right now. People have begun to lose focus. There are a few people who have drifted a long way off, and it is tough because, although we are committed in relationship to one another, I can't push people or instruct them in too forceful a way. It's good because, at whatever place people are in faith, we still maintain those relationships. People still show love and service. It's not like leaving a congregation and taking a few months away with people trying to sort out your backsliding and then giving up on you.

There is still that link as a community, and people remain committed. That's so important.

Just as with families, Dodridge's community rises and falls depending on the quality of relationships.

These examples are in sharp contrast to the consumer form of church, in which people shop to get their spiritual needs met. Brad Cecil (Axxess, Arlington, TX) makes the distinction between a *consumer* church and a *communal* church.

> We are not interested in short-term relationships or meeting a person's needs or functioning as a spiritual vendor for people. Rather, we want to be a community of people committed to sharing life together. We don't desire growth for growth's sake but rather a community that grows slowly through natural introductions. We don't measure our success by numeric growth. We have decided to measure by other means, such as, How long do relationships last? Are members of the community at peace with one another? Are relationships reconciled?

As Cecil points out, when people change the success rubric from numbers to levels of connectedness, then much of the church's activities get called into question.

A People Rather than a Place, a Community Rather than a Meeting

The desire for church to be a meeting at a particular place and time is hard to shake admits Alan Creech (Vine and Branches, Lexington). "The systemic need to have a building for legitimacy is still ingrained in people. We feel illegitimate because we don't have a building. The desire to call a place church hinders all expression of the body." According to Creech, "These are theological problems that stem from deeper roots. It is all a matter of spiritual formation. Buildings and professionalism create a deformed spiritual formation. The church as located somewhere, in a certain place, in order to connect with God, is not consistent with the New Testament. The 'church in a place' contains and confines spirituality too much. It doesn't allow me to pray without ceasing."

The term *church* (Greek, *ekklesia*) is more a verb than a noun. It refers to the calling out of a people. In its broader use in the Roman city, it referred to a town meeting in a public place. The modern church has identified too closely with the centralized temple worship of the Jerusalem church rather than with the household basis of the Pauline model of church. The household was not simply a domestic unit in the first century. It was the basic socioeconomic unit in a preindustrial society in which so much of life depended on patronage. The household included, in addition to the extended family, slaves, the clientele who regularly traded with the family, and friends of the family. In light of this background, a first-century Christian would have been puzzled by the question, "Where do you go to church?" for church was a network of people to which one belonged. It was not a once- or twice-a-week association but rather a community of continuous interaction that included a range of activities related to every aspect of life. The community supplied a circle of people who provided both identity and security.

For Three Nails (Pittsburgh), community took precedence over ordered or stylish worship. "Our worship gatherings are messy," Holly Rankin Zaher confesses. "Our focus is on connecting with one another." Three Nails puts a higher priority on community formation than the church service. "We have such a pool of talent in our church that we could have a totally kickin' worship gathering, if that is where we wanted to place our energy. However, we made an intentional decision *not* to make that happen." The Three Nails community wants their energy to go into the relationships within the church, not the gatherings.

Kenny Mitchell, DJ and leader of Tribe (New York), also understands church as a communal way of life, not a service per se. Tribe describes itself as a community that looks out for one another. They feel they don't have a context for going to church because they are "being church." Church for them is their "living space" as a community. Tribe sees church as relating to a wider network of relationships. In their own terms, they "push relationship more than the cell group." Yet they commit to friends through the cell structure to maintain contact. For Tribe, a minimal church structure helps with the relational goals of the community.

Anna Dodridge (Bournemouth, U.K.) points out the differences between a meeting focus and a relational focus.

> I suppose most Christians to some extent have this kind of community with at least some of the people with whom they attend congregational meetings. However, their focus is still on the gathering, whereas our focus is on the relationships. We spent a lot of time in the beginning talking about what we think being the church is about, what form it should take, where the structures are and aren't proving helpful. Through that discussion process, the people who were interested emerged, and we were able to identify the common need and desire for serious relationships, for loving one another, for being committed to one another rather than being task focused.

The relationship questions needed to be answered before official meeting questions could be discussed.

When church is equated with a meeting that meets in a building at a particular time, it implicitly leads to a split between church life and the rest of life, thereby creating a sacred/secular divide. Christians can be led into thinking that the church meeting is the primary spiritual activity of their lives, thus creating a secular sphere. Alan Creech (Vine and Branches, Lexington) believes that the idea that people are spiritually formed in a meeting is seriously mistaken. "The notion of how we are spiritually formed—that we have to have some big speaker to make us better Christians, or a big church, or feel something big going on so we can feel something *is* going on—is mistaken. Our spiritual formation is gauged by feelings and spectacular events. This is very dangerous, and it is rampant. We need to return to slow, journey-like growth."

Community is a long-term process and does not happen overnight. Si Johnston (headspace, London) maintains:

> We are most definitely not just a set of meetings. Sure they happen, but they're just a part of the spectrum. Meetings have a place, but they are *not* church. We literally have nothing in terms of financial or material resources. We have realized that it's possible to build a community without the flash and savvy gadgetry you'd associate with a bigger inner-city church. Despite the fact that Steve Jobs or Bill Gates wasn't around at the time, it wasn't the lack of Keynote or PowerPoint or technology that caused Gandhi to reject Christianity. It was the lack of love and community. At the moment, we're carrying out a community audit so that we can take what little we do have and try to meet local needs with it as efficiently and professionally as possible. It's a process, but then so was evolution.

Changing the perspective of an entire community presents challenges. At an informal gathering of Water's Edge (Hudsonville, MI), one woman started chanting, "We hate church!" in response to a focus on the language of "missional community." However, Joel McClure and Randy Buist corrected her, saying, "We *are* the church. It is the 'church merely as meeting' idea that is so wrong." Mark Palmer (Landing Place, Columbus, OH) shares how difficult it is to convince people that church is a way of life and not a meeting. "Maybe 70 percent of Landing Place gets it—that church is a way of life and not a meeting. However, I tend to focus on the 30 percent, whom I describe as the 'why can't we sing more, teach more, I'm going to miss church this Thursday' sort of people."

Karen Ward (Church of the Apostles, Seattle) describes her relational understanding of church. "Church is not about a building or strategies or programs. Church is relationship in, with, and under God as Father, Son, and Spirit. To be church is to participate in the Trinity/divine life of God. Because God is the source of all relationality, to focus the church on relationships is to be Christian at the core." For emerging church leaders, to be a faithful Christian without a community is a logical impossibility.

Emerging churches confront deeply entrenched notions that church signifies a performance-based gathering. They believe church is not about a meeting at all. It is about a community. Yes, there are meetings, but they do not define church. The meetings are scheduled to support the life of the community or to flow out of the community, but they do not create the community. Church is not an occasion or a periodic event. "One of the things we emphasize is that church is not an event but a group of people," Joel McClure (Water's Edge, Hudsonville, MI) says. Water's Edge recently printed T-shirts that on the front say, "Don't *Go* to Church," and on the back say, "*Be* the Church."

Because emerging churches function as a community, the church service itself, if the community has one, may just be a small window into their entire life together. Andrew Jones (Boaz, U.K.) explains what church signifies for emerging church leaders.

> You cannot understand how the emerging church worships simply by looking at what happens in a worship service. Take a look at our weddings, our funerals, our meals, our birthday parties, our street parties, our festivals, our pilgrimages. Look at how we seek to infuse our ordinary rituals as well as how we display our worship on a stage so traditional church people can enter in. The latter is necessary (we do it at large conferences), but it is not the most accurate reflection of who we are or what we normally do.

The Sunday worship service was the most obvious entry point into the traditional church and perhaps the most straightforward way of ascribing its identity. But the emerging church is a different animal. Many of the groups that started recently are meetingless in this sense. They have moved away from a central gathering. They are relational, organic, and flowing. However, because they have no regularly scheduled meetings, they meet more often than churches that are formally organized.

Anna Dodridge (Bournemouth, U.K.) says, "We don't really *do* formal meetings. We encourage one another to go to things such as the

Bournemouth prayer meetings with other churches, so I guess that's where any formal meeting comes in. People tend to go to what suits them. We have get-togethers, such as weekends away, barbeques, and meals together. We arrange evenings to touch base as a group and to see which direction we're going in."

"We now have many small relational communities that network together to form Apex," Joe Boyd reports. "Church for me consists of my twelve friends with whom I spend most of my time. Many of our relational communities engage in everyday life together. We operate as an organic extended family. We share what we have. Currently, we have twenty-five house groups. Only fourteen can be found on the Web; the other eleven are hidden because they have no official meeting. They simply function as communities. They meet often but at no particular time. They are not organized but rather completely decentralized."

There is also a strong aversion to regimentation, even at the small group level. Church might happen in twos and threes. Dwight Friesen of Quest (Seattle) declares, "We deconstructed small groups. Who does 'this or that' felt artificial to orchestrate. Now, we hook up with a friend or two intentionally for conversations. We covenant to co-spiritually direct each other for a season." They seek "organic connecting." Church happens whenever two or three come together. The church is not a particular time or place but the connections that happen when followers of Christ come together. Kester Brewin of Vaux (London) concurs. "When Christ said 'wherever two or three gather,' we believe that he meant that church was happening at those moments. It's not a place to visit but a dynamic that occurs when people who are journeying come together. As we've explored more deeply, we've come to see that the genesis of the early church holds a pattern for church now."

Mark Scandrette (ReIMAGINE! San Francisco) feels that to call his "urban swarm" a church is to formalize their function and deaden the experience. "There is so much baggage from the idea of church, so I hesitate to call it that." There is no official gathering, but the community gets together quite often as people participate in kingdom life together. "It didn't make sense to be intentional about spiritual things anymore. For some reason, we just needed to be real and be friends and to let something develop naturally. We share values, not just beliefs. We wanted integrity about how we are living." There is a strong antipathy toward a program approach to ministry. Instead, their activities arise spontaneously out of their values and lifestyle.

"We have a swirl of life together, but we have no name for this. We are 'enduring urban tribes.' It is a multi-portal view of Christian community. It is not about an external structure but about people seeking the kingdom." Scandrette's community has no official name, and no one is officially in or out.

Some see the church as a rhythm rather than a routine. Spencer Burke (Newport Beach, CA) questions why Christians set aside a particular day for church. "Instead, why don't we ask what we are doing for church this week. How about church as rhythm, not as schedule? What is a natural rhythm for church?"

Landing Place's (Columbus, OH) network of three organic churches may get together for a potluck dinner or a night of liturgy, but "we don't ever meet in a church as a church," reports Mark Palmer. "We are a decentralized movement of churches. We are not house churches in the formal sense (i.e., we do not adopt the house church strategy of worship in houses, reaching certain people, and multiplying)."

These moves toward meetingless church illustrate some of the radical questioning regarding the nature of church. They illustrate what church may look like as a 24-7 way of life. They also raise the issue of what to do with growth. How can emerging churches continue to emerge without destroying their DNA in the process? Jonny Baker of Grace (London) says, "People are very committed to Grace and being a part of it. We go to extraordinary lengths to create amazing worship at times. The size is small enough that it works in this loose way. If it gets a lot bigger, it may have to function differently." Joel McClure (Water's Edge, Hudsonville, MI) looks to the future of their groups with some disquiet. "If we grow, we are not sure what we will do: get bigger or create smaller units." But McClure points out that "small is not the answer, and big is not the answer. It is about faithfulness."

Paul Roberts (Resonance, Bristol, U.K.), long a participant in organic forms of community, cautions that church cannot be confused with simply hanging out with friends. "I think it's easy to equate church with enjoying friendship. Friendship is good and God-given, and healthy church requires it, but it is a bit more than this." Roberts warns that "if the definition of church is opened up without boundaries or structure, then it is just a warm, fuzzy, transient-shared experience and risks doing very little in causal connection to Jesus of Nazareth." For these organic communities to serve as church, they must remain committed and focused on Jesus and the kingdom.

A Place of Mutual Accountability

For some emerging churches, church is equated with a set of commitments. Simon Hall (Revive, Leeds, U.K.) explains, "We're moving toward membership of Revive having nothing to do with attending a particular meeting. Instead, it's about being accountable (through a small group, prayer triplet, soul friend, spiritual director, etc.) to five basic values of discipleship. There is no law (you shall pray for this length of time, four times a day), but there is a sense of movement (this is my next step in following Jesus). I thought many would be against something that sounds judgmental and exclusive to liberal ears, but pretty much everyone is up for it."

Anna Dodridge's community (Bournemouth, U.K.) stresses commitment as well. "We see church as the people and the relationships we have with one another. So we identify with being committed to one another as church, but that extends to being committed to all the church in Bournemouth, whatever meetings and buildings people attend. I guess that stretches out to being part of the church of the nation and the world in the long run. It's about being church everyday, growing our relationships, supporting one another, helping one another learn, sharing with one another, and being accountable." For Dodridge, commitment and accountability—not attendance at a particular meeting—mark one's membership in the community.

Commitment that is deep and long lasting is a strongly held value in emerging churches. "We make decisions through consultation with one another. Our commitment outlasts any relationship to institutions, but since there is so much mobility in our world, only a commitment that is relational and nongeographical will last for a significant period of time. I expect to have many of the same relational commitments to the same people in thirty years' time, regardless of where we live or what institution we may be linked with during that time. And I would expect those in my church to hold to the same relational commitment. We will live together forever. This is the kingdom—and it starts now" (Andrew Jones, Boaz, U.K.).

Time alone will tell whether such high aspirations can be maintained over the course of years. But the eternal dimension Jones emphasizes must not be overlooked. Quality of life together here on earth points to the richness of relationships that can be fully realized only when the kingdom and the church coalesce with the return of Christ, but Christians must endeavor to embody that vision now.

Relationships That Give Rise to a Gathering

Given that emerging churches see themselves as committed relationships and not church services per se, what role does an official gathering play? Is a weekly church meeting even necessary? After dismantling their existing ideas of church, Joel McClure and Randy Buist (Water's Edge, Hudsonville, MI) initially came to the conclusion that meetings were inherently a bad idea. However, in the past two years, they have changed their minds and have come to realize that meetings can be a good thing, given their proper place. Kevin Rains (Vineyard Central, Cincinnati) also has had a change of heart. "We've been down the road of deconstructing the idea that church is *just* a meeting, but now we stop short of saying that church has nothing to do with gathering. We have found that it's too simplistic and ultimately unhelpful for people's spiritual formation to say that church has nothing to do with gathering." Even though church cannot be reduced to a meeting, meetings can still be useful.

What then is the proper role of the gathering? Todd Hunter (Christ Community of Faith, Yorba Linda, CA) states that meetings must be redeemed, not eliminated. "We can't throw out meetings, but we must give them a new purpose and ask what they accomplish." Indeed, when meetings are purposeless, they can become a waste of time. Roger Ellis of Revelation Church (Chichester, U.K.) explains, "If you don't value meetings, they immediately become boring." Ellis has discovered that it takes some planning to create a gathering that is meaningful. "We want creativity, artistic expression, and to hear from one another." A meeting is only as good as the purpose behind it. A meeting should be a place where the kingdom is expressed.

Gatherings may also have a positive role if they facilitate a deeper sense of community for their members. Steve Collins (Grace, London) says, "I use the word *church* in two senses: (1) Christians in community, which focuses on people and how they relate, and (2) forms of faith expression, which is about what Christians do. I think particular kinds of faith expression, meeting, building, etc., are there to serve the relational needs of the community."

For Collins, meetings are valuable if they serve the community. On the flip side, the depth of relationships determines the quality of the church gathering.

The church service flows from the community. We couldn't produce the service if we weren't good friends, and the business of producing the service is the core around which the friendships grow. So we're a community in a loose way, but we do see a lot of one another, and we socialize as friends too. I suspect that saying "we're just friends" sounds too weak for many Christians. But friendship is amazingly strong glue, and all the heavier forms of commitment fall apart without it. As friends, we get a lot more done, because we like one another and don't want to let one another down.

For Grace, church services flow from the friendships of the community, and these services in turn deepen those same friendships.

A Movement on a Mission

Traditional churches exhort their members to be consistent and articulate witnesses in their workplaces, communities, and other social networks, but they have no support structure to facilitate such outreach. Emerging churches place an emphasis on witness within the broader community by ensuring that their structure is missional in nature. Such churches contain communities of service and witness, and a decentralized approach makes these churches accessible and appropriate to each context. Furthermore, the relationships that exist between the Christians and their wider circles of friends are both natural and maintain a low threshold, eliminating barriers of exclusion and alienation.

Emerging churches share a common mission in the world. Kevin Rains (Vineyard Central, Cincinnati) says, "Church is a weekly gathering, a monthly gathering, *and* a people committed to one another. For us, the primary gathering point is either a weekly meeting in a home with between five and twenty-five friends or the daily rub of living together in a household community. But *primarily,* church is the people of God on mission together." For Rains, church is a set of strong relationships supported by gathering together. All the while, the people in these relationships recognize that they exist for those outside their community.

Chris Matthews of Red Café (Swansea, U.K.) explains that the church gathering serves as a support for people's lives in the community. "We are very much a community seeking to remove the distinction between church and nonchurch activities. Rather than sucking things into serving the church, our focus is to be out and about being church." He recalls, "I know that I would find it hard to revert back to being a part of a meeting-based church that existed to serve the vision of a leader or a group of leaders. Yes, it's helpful to consider styles of worship, approaches to teaching, discipleship, and prayer, but far more important is *doing* what we think church is all about."

Perhaps surprisingly, the communities that emerging churches share with people outside their faith communities are as strong as those within. "We belong to each other, but our primary connection is to the world. We belong to others in the church but *without* intimate connecting," says Rachelle Mee-Chapman (Thursday PM, Seattle). Members of Thursday PM commit to living the kingdom together as church. "However, we do not feel that we need to be best friends, divulge everything, and spend all our time together. Our primary relationships are with those outside the community." Mee-Chapman continues, "For me, my primary relationships consist of the Fremont Arts Council and my children's school." Joe Boyd (Apex, Las Vegas) agrees. "My pagan friends are church for me as well. While with them, I spend time with Jesus because he is with me. My community with these Las Vegas actors is just as strong as my Christian community, and I am slowly introducing Jesus to them."

Emerging churches carry this kingdom-like community into their other spheres of life. Ben Edson (Sanctus1, Manchester, U.K.) states:

> Faith within Sanctus1 is all about lifestyle. I guess I hope that our meeting together helps facilitate people to live within that lifestyle. There are also a number of people who are involved in campaigning on issues in regard to social justice, and issues such as fair trade are really quite important to people within Sanctus1. I guess it's about holistic faith and the fact that although Sanctus1 is a church, it is above all a set of relationships—relationships with one another, relationships with God, and relationships with the world. As soon as we start thinking Sanctus1 is just about meetings, then it suffers. It stands for a lifestyle choice.

Sanctus1 is not a community just for the sake of community. It is an open community with a purpose: to establish a group of Christ followers who will act as change agents in the world. "Inviting people into the kingdom means inviting them to where you are that night. Evangelism is bringing your friend to IHOP [International House of Pancakes, a chain of restaurants], because that is where your friends are. In this way, people become immersed in the community" (Joe Boyd, Apex, Las Vegas).

Evangelism is not seen as a program but as a communal living out of the gospel in everyday routines. For Brad Cecil of Axxess (Arlington, TX), "Evangelism is a way of life. By this I mean we are a community and introduce people into our community all the time. We don't really feel as though the gospel can be packaged into a proposition that is dispensed in slick programs or presentations. So evangelism happens naturally as we introduce people into the community." Revelation Church (Chichester, U.K.) encourages a range of activity groups ranging from the arts to Frisbees. They include both Christians and non-Christians in the same groups. This avoidance of differentiation is another common characteristic of emerging churches. They do not want to create "us" and "them" distinctions, which they feel would be both discriminatory and destructive of group participation.

Emerging churches meet as a community to support their lives outside the community. For those outside, it is often the distinctive life of the community in their midst that communicates the gospel. Doug Pagitt (Solomon's Porch, Minneapolis) says it well: "Hang around us for a while, and we will recognize the God-life in the world together. We will discern what harmonious living in God looks like. It is an invitation to live in the kingdom of God. This invitation is not the sole property of Christians. Jesus calls us to live in particular ways, in his ways." Karen Ward (Church of the Apostles, Seattle) echoes Pagitt. "Everything we do has an outward leaning trajectory. We take our name seriously (Apostles means those who are sent out). Nonchurched people can pick up the gospel from us as we form relationships, as the gospel is a holy virus that is spread from person to person (the most effective means of transmitting anything). We are the carriers of Christ. In our very bodies, we are carrying out the life, death, and resurrection of Christ both in and for our world."

Emerging Churches Consist of Decentralized Communities

Because of the highly relational, continual, and missional aspects of community, emerging churches tend to be either small groups or networks of small groups. Their ways of life together are as varied as the people who make up the communities. The groups take a variety of forms and may meet in response to a range of objectives expressing both presence and connectedness.

Small Groups Are the Essential Meeting of Church

For many emerging churches, small groups often meet as full communities and consist of between eight and fifteen people. The basic structure of emerging churches must remain small because of the high commitment to relationships. According to Dwight Friesen (Quest, Seattle), "Relationship is our organizing principle. In our informal research, we learned that twenty-five to forty was the upper limit for relational connectedness. Any bigger than that, and the group needs to organize functionally. Consequently, we committed to never growing beyond forty, and so we never built the infrastructure to enable us to go beyond that. We believed that our community would self-regulate. We have a radical commitment to being small."

Emerging churches have no desire to grow big. Their missional commitment is expressed in their desire to reproduce when they begin to stretch relational aspects too far. Rachelle Mee-Chapman (Thursday PM, Seattle) says, "We do not want to grow in numbers. We do not want full-time staff or a building." However, she reports that often other church leaders do not consider what she is doing church. Todd Hunter (former national director, Association of Vineyard Churches) says, "The way many young church planters conceive of being church does not fit the criteria for being an official Vineyard church. It was widely assumed that you are not a real Vineyard if you can't support a pastor financially and have at least four home groups. However, the young people I've mentored do not want a church over a hundred. Unlike their Boomer predecessors, their issue is not how to keep growing." Speaking out of his experience with the Late Late Service in Glasgow, U.K., Andy Thornton says that "while each community has a different way of doing leadership, forty people is the biggest a group can get and still feel democratic."

Those at Quest (Seattle) do not want their group to grow any bigger than it currently is. In fact, they would like it to decrease in size a bit. They now have twenty regulars, but Dwight Friesen believes fifteen would be ideal. Some in the community live together. They read one another's blogs or instant message one another every day on their cell phones. Their community has approximately ten people who are married and ten who are single, with very few kids. While similar to house churches, they dislike the label. "We are not house church in the 'react against institution' mentality of the late 1960s and early 1970s. But we are house church in the sense that we encourage that kind of connecting" (Dwight Friesen, Quest, Seattle).

Challenges Facing Small Communities

Small communities face a unique set of challenges. Three years after Eternity (Bracknell, U.K.) started, their gathering became quite popular.

People brought their youth groups over, and it began to number three hundred, with visitors making up 70 percent of the total attendance. Those within Eternity became frustrated. "We had to hire a school hall to accommodate everyone. This began to destroy the work of community that God was doing, so we changed the format, venue, and style of the service to serve best those members of Eternity" (Mark Meardon). Large crowds were destroying the form of community to which they felt called.

A community needs to remain a certain size in order to ensure the participation of all. Andy Thornton (Late Late Service, Glasgow, U.K.) says, "Alternative worship is highly participative, and that is why they never get bigger than twenty-five people. If you want group participation, there is a ceiling or limit." Yet at the same time, such groups can become monochrome and insular. There are both benefits and drawbacks when groups are composed of the same interests and lifestyle. On the positive side, they can relate more readily to a wider circle of people like themselves. On the negative side, they can become self-centered and exclusionary.

Whenever the issue of small groups is raised, the debate rages as to whether they represent "birds of a feather flocking together" or whether diversity brings greater creativity and personal growth. Jason Evans (Matthew's House, Vista, CA) prefers diverse house groups rather than grouping people according to their generation or interests. He believes the segmenting of the church is the biggest thing wrong with church as a whole.

The Relationship between Small Groups and Their Wider Community

The small group structure of emerging churches, coupled with their decentralized, networking structure, may lead to increasing fragmentation. The question is then, What is the relationship between emerging churches and their wider community?

At Revelation Church (Chichester, U.K.), the commitment to remain small through a network of diverse cells is part of their DNA. As a church with twenty-five cells, the challenge is how to remain one church with one vision. "We don't simply want house church through lots of small groups. The church is called the community of the kingdom, and there is both unity and diversity" (Roger Ellis). They need a clear vision and mutual commitment to a way of life together.

Dan Kimball (Graceland and Vintage Faith Church, Santa Cruz, CA, and author of *The Emerging Church*) made the shift from viewing the large weekend service as the primary way to define church to developing a network of house churches (home communities). The home communities meet midweek, and then on Sundays, they all meet together in a large worship gathering. "When I was leading Graceland, we communicated that small groups were the extra, and now, for Vintage Faith, we are communicating that the big meeting is the extra. This is not easy, as most people have been taught to view things the opposite way."

When emerging churches meet in a large congregational setting, they widen their community ties and build on the intimacy developed in their small groups. These networks of small groups may gather together on a monthly basis. However, the large group meeting is of secondary importance. Apex (Las Vegas) had weekly large group meetings. However, they became sparsely attended as the home groups increased in importance.

Kevin Rains (Cincinnati) explains how home churches become connected to Vineyard Central.

> Generally, people join home churches, and home churches join Vineyard Central. Each home church decides what the criteria for membership or covenanting together looks like. For some of the intentional household communities, this takes the form of vows. The baseline minimum, of course, is commitment to the person of God revealed in Jesus, which is different from belief in a set of propositions. However, we do say the Nicene Creed at our larger gatherings, as we believe that it, along with several other creeds, summarizes our core beliefs. The churches that relate to Vineyard Central are expected to send delegates (leaders or representatives) to a monthly leadership community meeting, which involves a potluck meal, storytelling from the various groups/ministries, sharing direction/vision, worship in song, and prayer for one another's groups and needs. They are also expected to give financially in some way to the wider network of churches, meet regularly with an elder, and have a one- or two-page written plan for making more and better disciples in their group/ministry. That plan gets shared with the entire leadership community for accountability.

Large groups are similar to the small groups in that the meetings of large groups are based on the extended relationships of the participants. Mark Palmer (Landing Place, Columbus, OH) explains how their network functions. "We're really committed to proximity. The majority live within walking distance of one another." Many live in communal housing arrangements. "Amy,[4] my son, and I live in community, and many in the

---

4. In the fall of 2004, Mark Palmer married Amy, a woman who had been a part of their community for two years.

three churches live in community together. The three churches interact in informal ways; we get together for parties, social action, meals, and art. We are a network of churches consisting of three different groups that meet separately. We are each a church consisting of ten or twelve persons. Our groups do not meet for regular monthly times but whenever we feel like it. It feels pretty right for us." For Water's Edge (Hudsonville, MI), the large meeting is the occasion when the extended community gets together as a whole. It is highly relational and interactive. Most demonstrate their commitment to the larger community by showing up and being together.

Unlike the stereotypical house church, emerging churches do not exist in isolation but establish networks for mutual support and encouragement. Church is expressed through the small, primary, face-to-face group and also in the groups meeting together as the church in the city or region. Each person involved sees the other communities as church because he or she has a stake in those communities through the many cross-connections expressed through relationships and affinities.

From Solid Church to Liquid Church

Karen Ward (Church of the Apostles, Seattle) cites Pete Ward's book *Liquid Church* as giving substance to the idea that the kingdom precedes forms of church. "The liquid church is the kingdom of God," she has concluded, coupled with the conviction that "structures are created as they are required by the gospel."

What does a liquid church look like? Pete Rollins (ikon, Belfast, U.K.) explains, "We are often presented with a Tesco (the U.K.'s leading supermarket chain) model; in other words, all your goods under one roof. People at ikon resonate more with a matrix style of community in which the community is made up of various elements. For example, someone may go to a local church on a Sunday, work with Concern on a Tuesday evening, meet and pray with people on a Friday afternoon, and attend ikon on a Sunday evening. Much of what we offer in this matrix is a sense of minimal community (community that is not focused on concrete belief systems but is more a shared feeling or milieu)."

Liquid churches offer church "slices" instead of one primary meeting. In addressing the issue of the centrality of the meeting for the building of community, Spencer Burke (Newport Beach, CA) is of the opinion that "all the church doesn't necessarily need to be together for each meeting." Some might meet in one area and others in another. Burke's community does not do much in the way of Bible study at the meeting. "I'm not convinced a church can do an effective Bible study because of the size." He believes that for the community to engage Scripture seriously it must be organized into groups in which all can participate.

It is difficult to get a sense of how large a community is within a liquid church. According to Anna Dodridge (Bournemouth, U.K.), "It's hard to number the community, because when we gather as a kind of larger group, it's not always the people who are fully involved. Quite a few are people who are interested or want to be a part of what we are up to but have regular congregational church homes and are kind of on the sidelines of what we do. I guess when you count everyone at a wider gathering, there would be about thirty people. But the people who have stepped out of their former congregations and are totally involved with us number about fifteen."

Consistent with the liquid church idea, Dodridge's entire community rarely gets together. "We tend to gather rarely as a whole. Weekends away and special together days are the only times we specifically gather as a whole, although we do tend to all be at the prayer room from time to time. So when we get together, everyone who comes along, including both the core and the fringes, all are a part of what we do. But in terms of everyday community, there are only a few who are really pushing things and moving things and devoting time to this."

Liquid churches are networked communities. Ian Mobsby (Moot, London) says, "Fluid or liquid forms of church reflect networks of people. As cultural expressions are now fluid and networked, place or geography are far less important these days. However, Moot has 90 percent network membership, and a significant 10 percent local membership. Our culture in London is fragmented and multilayered, so it would be impossible for one church to reflect its locality without it looking like a warehouse."

Kester Brewin of Vaux (London) expresses his convictions in eucharistic terms.

> We see the act of the Eucharist as a powerful symbol of what we believe about Christ and the body of Christ. In the breaking of the loaf of bread, what was singular, physical, and fixed in one place is split up, transformed, and taken out into the cities in which we live. Church for us then is perhaps simply a network of the infected. Each time two nodes in this network communicate, church is happening, the body is evolving, and Christ is being formed. So is there any commitment to one another? Of course. Otherwise the network would collapse. Is there a stress on living

like Christ? Of course. It's only when Christlike activity occurs between nodes that synapses are strengthened and the body emerges.

Conclusion

Emerging churches believe that the church should shape its corporate life in accordance with the practices of the kingdom of God that Jesus inaugurated in his ministry. Their understanding of the Christian life is strongly Christocentric, drawing much inspiration from the Gospels. Emerging churches create a space for the kingdom to enter their midst. They commit to the community that follows this King and let their other loyalties take a backseat. An unchastened consumerism and anonymity are not options within their ranks. They display a willingness to abandon old church forms as they dramatically restructure their communities. They abhor the idea of church as a meeting, a place, a routine. Clearly, for these communities, church is a people, a community, a rhythm, a way of life, a way of connectedness with other Christ followers in the world. These communities are small, missional, and offer space for each individual to participate. Emerging churches form tight communities. It is through living as a community that emerging churches practice the way of Jesus in all realms of culture.

6

Welcoming the Stranger

I'm more convinced than ever that we don't have a clue about Christianity. I'm not an orthodox Christian anymore; I'm not a Protestant. The kinds of questions we are asking are very different from the questions asked at other times. Is Christianity necessary? Whose religion is it anyway? What does it mean for us to incarnate Christ, to live redemptively in a materialistic world?

Dwight Friesen, Quest, Seattle

The last chapter outlined how emerging churches form community. This chapter is the first of two chapters on hospitality within that same community. This chapter covers welcoming the outsider, the practice of including those who are different. The next chapter covers the generosity extended to that same outsider.

The Inclusive Practices of Jesus

As already mentioned, emerging churches are deeply influenced by teachings on the kingdom, and at the heart of the kingdom practice of Jesus is the practice of inclusion.[1]

1. The following insights are based on N. T. Wright, *Jesus and the Victory of God*, vol. 2 of *Christian Origins and the Question of God* (Minneapolis: Fortress, 1996).

In ancient Israel, the categories clean and unclean maintained identity and established boundaries, and contact with outcasts, sinners, or lepers made one unclean. In conjunction with the holiness codes and food laws, the priest declared who was in and who was out. The sinners, the outcasts, the oppressed, the poor, and the hungry were despised and were definitely out.

Jesus promised a new day, that the time of exile was over. Jesus initiated a counter-temple movement that rendered religious observation redundant. Although the early believers in Jerusalem observed the hours of prayer, no longer was there a need to go to the temple to become clean or holy. Forgiveness and acceptance were offered *on-site* in Jesus' alternative community. Jesus' community shared the benefits of the kingdom with those who were excluded. The end of exile meant that the kingdom was for all who would come. Jesus fed the hungry, included the outcast, announced forgiveness to the sinner, healed the leper, declared the unclean "clean," and gave good news to the poor. While remaining in the culture in virtually all ways, he broke every regulation that presented an obstacle to the kingdom.

Modernity and Exclusion

As already mentioned, modern people chased God out of a particular realm and labeled that realm "secular." Because of their fear of being alone in the universe, moderns felt they needed to control every aspect of reality. In their relentless pursuit of order, Western cultures sought to assimilate people by making everyone the same. Inherent to the logic of modernity was a resolve to remove the ambivalent remainder, to remove all that did not fit. Those who refused to fall into the ordered plan of modernity were removed. Thus, nonconformists of any kind found themselves isolated and without social value.

In modernity, the outcasts paid the highest price. In Germany during the 1930s and 1940s, the Jews did not fit the modern category of Christian or pagan, so it was determined that they needed to be eliminated.[2] The pursuit of order, welded by the myth of the Aryan master race, created tragedy. Without the technical and scientific communities, the Holocaust could not have occurred. For Bauman, the Holocaust did not occur because it was so irrational but because it was a rationally planned modern experiment in social engineering.

2. Zygmunt Bauman, *Modernity and Ambivalence* (Ithaca, NY: Cornell University Press, 1991).

Postmodernity represents, on the other hand, a time when plurality is accepted and order and control are relinquished. Within culture today, both modernity and postmodernity exist side by side. Risking oversimplification, modernity is evidenced in those areas in culture and society where control, homogeneity, and universals reign, whereas the areas that express freedom, difference, and plurality are postmodern.

Jesus faced the exclusion of first-century Palestine and confronted it with an inclusive community. The exclusivity of modernity, with its pursuit of the same and the exclusion of the other, needs to be similarly challenged. Any social entity within modernity that desires to model the kingdom must confront the ordering and controlling aspects of our current context.

Practices of Inclusion

As an expression of their great love for Christ, emerging churches, as a matter of lifestyle, include the outsider, even those who are different, knowing that the "other" both clarifies and defines the boundaries of their faith.

Moving the Eucharist from an Occasional Observance to the Central Act of Worship

A truly missional church integrates worship with welcome. This does not mean that such churches merely welcome people over the threshold of the church. Rather, they demonstrate welcome by identifying with people of all walks of life in their contexts. The door is open not only to invite people in but also to send members out into the wider world as servants of Christ and agents of his reign. Worship and welcome find expression in witness, both verbal and acts of kindness and sacrificial service, and in the pursuit of peace and justice. In the ancient eucharistic liturgies, the final word was the sending forth of the participants as Christ's representatives to a needy world.

Sharing a meal with others is a welcoming act of hospitality. Many emerging churches place a great emphasis on the Eucharist as a central act of worship. Others celebrate the Lord's Supper in the context of an actual meal, which was the practice of the early church. The ethos of the service is one of hospitality, and all are invited to the table. At times, the eucharistic celebration takes place in a home or café setting. This enables a group to demonstrate hospitality in a culturally appropriate manner.

When Landing Place (Columbus, OH) starts a new church or a new gathering, there is only one nonnegotiable for the new community. At each meeting, they must share a meal together, because they believe that the shared meal is central to becoming the people of God together. Mark Palmer explains, "Communion for us is our sharing the bread and cup in the middle of the meal. Everyone is equal when we gather. In Scripture, we notice that Jesus does cool stuff in the midst of meals. Maybe, if we share a meal, Jesus will do cool stuff in our midst as well. Somehow through shared meals, open to everyone, the kingdom is extended and the gospel is proclaimed." Joe Boyd of Apex (Las Vegas) expresses the same point: "Eating is very important for meetings. It is mysterious what happens through the meal." The early church's prayer "Maranatha," which is Aramaic for "O Lord, come!" or "The Lord has come!" reveals both the expectation and the actualization of the ascended Lord's presence.

Changing Hospitality from a Christian Extra to a Central Practice

Hospitality is at the core of all they do at Solomon's Porch (Minneapolis). Doug Pagitt declares, "Hospitality has the ability to show up in many other practices. We do it in every setting, and it is dominant in every place it can function." Karen Ward (Church of the Apostles, Seattle) expresses their ministry of hospitality in terms of "a monastic ethos." "Those people who come in the door are Christ. It is a variation of the monastic guesthouse—inspiring us to treat and to regard people who come to our door as angels who visit us every day."

At Quest (Seattle), members take hospitality seriously and train for it. Each person in the church is taught how to be hospitable and how to host a gathering at his or her home. Members are shown how to make a home warm and inviting. Such skills are not always intuitive.

Hospitality is a way of life at Three Nails (Pittsburgh). Holly Rankin Zaher declares:

> Our ethos is Jesus focused. We provide space for people to belong before they come to believe. We build real relationships with people, regardless of the end result. We want to be able to share life with people, whether or not they choose to follow Jesus. We have three houses of people who live on the south side. They invite people in. They are amazed at the variety of people who have said yes to Christ. People become interested in God because of how we live together.

Turning a Welcome Space into a Safe Place

Emerging churches, if they are to be faithful to the way of Jesus, must welcome the outsider. Ministries of inclusion welcome anyone God brings to them and create a safe place in which people can dwell. Solomon's Porch (Minneapolis), which moved out of the suburbs and into an urban environment, felt they needed a building from day one. Doug Pagitt explains, "We wanted a place where we could invite and welcome others. We wanted to make our surroundings better. It made sense to have a space. If we truly were to be creative, we needed a space to do it."

Hospitality includes creating a safe space for all to worship. "There are some labels we would wish to attach. The most important is we provide a 'safe space.' The worship space has to be safe for the vulnerable and not a place where people are ostracized for their gender, race, doubts, disabilities, depression, or orientation" (Sue Wallace, Visions, York, U.K.).

Hospitality extends into the world and creates a safe zone in which people can dwell. Through buying an old café in the heart of the town, Linden Church demonstrated hospitality in the center of Welsh youth culture. "We built Red Café because we needed to create space for young people," says Chris Matthews of Linden Church (Swansea, U.K.). "We created a service, Extreme, at the café for the new Christians. The traditional church didn't feel right for them. It would have required too much of a cultural change for the young Christians. A church ought to look like a pub, bright and inviting. My desire is that a church would be a pub, 24-7."

Dave Sutton (New Duffryn Community Church, Newport, U.K.) explains his church's ministry commitment as welcoming whoever comes their way. He says, "We have picked up broken people along the way. We have an inclusive feel to everything we do. We attract those who can't handle normal church." New Duffryn looks upon Christianity as a journey. "We have seventy people in the community, but only a small number is involved in the base groups. Hopefully, all of them will eventually become a part of a group. We also offer lots of therapeutic counseling. We have a holistic way of working with people."

The notion of a safe place is highly significant for people who have stepped out of abusive relationships or have encountered hostile or exploitative work environments. In our society, people need sanctuaries and sacred places where healing and reconnecting can take place. This is especially important for congregations consisting of many displaced young people or singles in search of trustworthy relationships.

Welcoming Those Who Are Different

Ministries of inclusion include those who are different. Anna Dodridge (Bournemouth, U.K.) comments that when a church refrains from church marketing, it might get the "wrong" people, which makes church life more difficult.

> In the congregational setup, people choose their church based on its style, theology, and so on. But because we are so limited in numbers, it doesn't really work that way. It's also hard because we all have different ideas about what we want and what we believe Scripture says and so on. We all agree on the fact that church should be viewed and done differently, but beyond that there are not so many areas of common thought. Among our number are evangelicals, postevangelicals, Pentecostals, liberals, etc. I think it works well because the mixture keeps us balanced and challenged, but it can cause some problems sometimes when people think they know *the* right way to do things and others don't agree.

Emerging churches resemble the kingdom when they contain many differing perspectives yet remain committed in relationship.

As Joe Boyd (Apex, Las Vegas) experienced in the Las Vegas show community, other people can help us discover who we are. "I've finally found a people like me. I never knew I was an actor until I met them. They were me, and I've been sheltered from them my whole life." To the extent that people isolate themselves from other people and out of insecurity refuse to lower their guard, they face an identity crisis. People discover who they are not by navel gazing or through a counseling program but in authentic relationships with other people. Community is an essential ingredient of identity.

Emerging churches do not need to motivate their members to reach out to those who have different beliefs. That is where they live. Debbie Blue (House of Mercy, St. Paul) reports, "We don't have any formal ways of interacting with other faiths, though we have a community that is, I think, constantly interacting. We don't really need to lead our community there. For the most part, they are already there."

Although they are inclusive with all who come, emerging churches are exclusive in their devotion to Christ. "A group of people who are merely reading Jesus together as one among a range of possible sources of inspiration for a shared life journey (or a slice of it) are different from a group of people trying to follow him as the Lord of their journey" (Paul Roberts, Resonance, Bristol, U.K.). Simon Hall also emphasizes the Christ-centeredness of his community (Revive, Leeds, U.K.). "We are very Christocentric, which means that while we recognize God's presence in other religions and in people of no faith, we still see Jesus as the most perfect revelation of God and therefore the surest route to God."

At the same time, however, emerging churches do not believe that their wholehearted embrace of Christ excludes them from including all who draw near. Debbie Blue (House of Mercy, St. Paul) says:

> We preach that God acted uniquely in Jesus to redeem the world and that we have been redeemed by the blood of Jesus. We acknowledge that trying to figure out what that means, especially in relation to our activity in the world, is a little bit of a wild ride. We are definitely not out on the streets trying to get people to accept Jesus into their hearts so that they can be saved from hell. We are hoping and praying that we will be able to live and act in the world in a way that witnesses to God's mercy in the world and by so doing point to Jesus.

Moving from Perceived Arrogance to Transparent Humility

Emerging churches approach discussions with others in humility. "We are very aware that we have a faith construct that works for our community," declares Brad Cecil of Axxess (Arlington, TX). "That means we have a community of strongly held historic Christian beliefs, but we are always aware that we could be wrong. We are not foundational empiricists who feel that we have reduced our faith to the point of irreducible certainty. So we engage in a very broad spectrum of discussions for such a small group, yet without fear. We engage. We do not do any intentional outreach to engage other religions. We are just a community, and because we are a community, we are diverse."

Emerging churches engage in dialogue with others, fully aware that the church has often erred when it has made claims about God. Jonny Baker (Grace, London) says:

> We have developed instincts around hospitality, welcome, and grace so that we try to offer unconditional acceptance to anyone. It is from this foundation that we can have an open conversation about our faith that is real to us. But I think we look for that to be a dialogue rather than us telling people what to think. We once did a service called "we're right, follow us" that explored the discomfort we all feel with that old-school, arrogant approach to evangelism. I know it's very postmodern, but while we are confident in our faith, we want to make humble claims for it,

recognizing that people have claimed various things in the name of God and have been a long way from the kingdom.

Standing up for the truth or fighting the culture wars has no appeal to emerging church leaders. Debbie Blue of House of Mercy (St. Paul) says:

> We are not very oriented toward apologetics. Russell Rathbun [her co-pastor] just told me that a woman called him yesterday to tell him about a march in Washington to defend marriage. She was willing to help us organize our church to go. Russell said he didn't think we would be interested in that. She said, "Don't you want to stand up for God? Defend God?" He said, "No." She hung up abruptly. I think we're highly aware of our need for God to speak to us and disorient us from our ways, confound us, smash our idols (all the images of God we create and believe in), and we don't feel very suited to the task of defending God. We are comfortable with having a lot of unanswered questions. We think maybe that's what it's like being in relationship with a living Being. We think it's more honest than providing a lot of answers, abstract notions of truth.

Emerging church leaders are under no compulsion to stand up and fight for truth.

Those outside the faith are more interested in the ethics of Christians than their doctrines. "One person in Revive went to an Alpha course and was helped by it, but most people are somewhat cynical about the 'there *must* be an answer or else God is not God' philosophy behind some apologetics," says Simon Hall (Leeds, U.K.). "We are working more on an expression of faith that we can believe in without having to screw ourselves up. People seem to be more interested in our values and lifestyle than in whether we have a coherent doctrine of the Trinity." Emerging churches do not deny the truth of Christ when they approach others, but they also are aware that they see through a glass darkly (1 Cor. 13:12).

Moving from Verbal Apologetics to Embodied Apologetics

Traditional apologetics offer a reductionistic approach to God, ignoring Christians' spiritual and communal way of living in favor of a cognitive approach to truth. Pete Rollins of ikon (Belfast, U.K.) explains, "In contrast to orthodoxy (right belief) and orthopraxis (right practice), we advocate believing rightly and practicing rightly. In other words, one should speak and act in a manner that respects others and transforms their existence. In this way, we have a moral agenda, but it is a minimal one that focuses more on the how of belief and practice than the what." Andrew Jones (Boaz, U.K.) is of the same opinion. "In a world that is increasingly spiritual and less secular, our apologetics has more to do with helping people discover the truth that is near them. Our biggest critics and persecutors tend to be the Pharisees and religious rulers. But that was the case for Jesus also." Apologetics should increasingly take the role of spiritual direction rather than confrontation.

A community committed to the gospel of the reign of God provides the most convincing apologetic of the gospel. Brad Cecil of Axxess (Arlington, TX) explains, "We are not evidentiary apologists and don't feel we can reduce the Christian faith to an irreducible point of certainty and build up from there. To borrow a phrase, 'community is our apologetic.' The only answer to others we have is our community. We say all the time that if you want to understand the community join us." One cannot understand the truths of Christianity as an outside observer. One needs first to experience the embodied truth of the community.

Perhaps emerging churches' reaction against apologetics is based on the premise that it is of necessity based on the rationalistic assumptions typical of modernity. But this is not always the case. Apologetics can mean simply being prepared to give a reason for the hope that is within with meekness and humility. It can demonstrate that people have thought through the assumptions behind their beliefs and have honestly faced the challenges to belief. It can be more concerned with establishing plausibility than with proof. Jones (Boaz, U.K.) continues, "We will always be giving an answer to those who ask. And we will always be seeking to live in such a way that makes people ask. And we will always be exporting our living environment to be closer to those people God puts on our hearts. But what's different? I would say that power and prayer are heightened, as is a sensitivity to God's timing and people's process. And experience precedes explanation rather than following it. Please don't let anyone say that it replaces it, because both explanation and experience will always be present." One must demonstrate the faith with both actions and words.

Si Johnston (headspace, London) says, "With recent epistemological shifts and cultural change, we find it easier to look for patterns, to use Graham Cray's terminology (Anglican bishop of Maidstone, Kent). These indicate where the Holy Spirit could be at work in the lives of people and interpreting that for them. Generally, this happens relationally over pizza in our homes, the local pub, or wherever. Apologetics for us (as I expect for many cultural creatives) has moved from atomized abstract presuppositions to narrative-based apologetics of building plausibility structures using narrative and in particular the biblical narrative." Such an approach does not mean that intellectual barriers to belief are discounted but that they are not assumed at the outset of a conversation. Furthermore, there is an acknowledgment that one can present strong arguments for the plausibility of one's beliefs yet make no impression on the other person. Such a view also acknowledges that when apologetics is about winning an argument, people may be antagonized.

Emerging churches are typically unimpressed by forms of apologetics that presume to have definitive answers to every barrier to belief. In other words, they reject the confidence of the modernist mind-set, believing it is based on shallow, reductionistic thinking. However, there is an acknowledgment that a certain type of apologetics is acceptable, given all the caveats listed above. "Our policy as far as I see it is that we are friendly with other faith/religious traditions. We are more about dialogue and discussion with them than about obliterating them with heavy-handed apologetics," explains Si Johnston. "But discussion involves listening, and listening should precipitate change. We would all probably want to affirm themes and aspects of other world religions but claim that they find their fulfillment and end in the story of Jesus. We don't do Josh McDowell–style apologetics because it has little mileage in our culture. Yet we find that it is impossible to do any kind of mission without apologetics of some kind."

Moving from Having an Agenda to Letting the Holy Spirit Carry the Agenda

Emerging churches dislike categorization that separates insiders from outsiders. Rachelle Mee-Chapman (Thursday PM, Seattle) speaks of her problems with the traditional understanding and practice of evangelism. "Much of my church is into incarnational living, but they are concerned about seeing people as objects and marketing God. Can I have an agenda with someone and still be genuine? Can I be truly loving when I want to convert someone? Can we love people and let the Holy Spirit do the converting?"

Emerging churches avoid a contrived proclamation of good news, one that does not flow naturally out of one's life. Ben Edson (Sanctus1, Manchester, U.K.) says, "I am licensed as an evangelist within the

Anglican Church, but I find that people's understanding of evangelism is very narrow. People still see evangelism as manipulative and abusive; therefore, I rarely use the language of evangelism. However, evangelism is fundamentally important. There are a couple of principles that I have noticed over the few years I've been here. The first is that evangelism must be organic and honest. It is organic in the sense that the best evangelism happens naturally. If we try to force it, then our approach becomes contrived. People will see through that and become more disaffected."

Edson recounts the following incident. An outside speaker "came to Sanctus1 and was talking about evangelism. At the end we had a prayer time, which he led. In this prayer time, he invited us to think of one or two friends we could target to bring to Sanctus1. At this point, there was uproar. People's friends were their friends; they were not targets. They would feel dishonest in their friendships if they were aiming to get them into Sanctus1. Of course, Sanctus1 people speak with their friends about their personal faith and the faith community to which they belong, but they are doing that organically rather than in a contrived way."

Steve Collins (Grace, London) is also quite critical of prevailing evangelical practices. "'Coming alongside' means faking who you are in order to trap others. Instead, we ought to look at the communities of which we are already a part. We come from these very subcultures." He affirms, "I intensely desire everyone to know God and to be saved. However, the methods need to be different." Such concerns are deeply embedded in a culture that places a high value on authentic relationships as a statement against the forces of manipulation so prevalent within Western culture. In relating to postmoderns, Christians must have no hidden agenda, and all that they contribute to a relationship must be for the benefit of the other person rather than to enhance their own position.

Some leaders feel that friendship evangelism denies the very gospel they seek to communicate. Chris Matthews (Linden Church, Swansea, U.K.) is concerned that friendship evangelism results in attention being focused on the potentially responsive to the exclusion of those who are indifferent or hostile to such approaches. He expresses this concern with candor. "The concept of friendship evangelism has always been something we have struggled with, as this is hardly unconditional love! We feel the call to serve the community and to be a presence for good, and our prayer is that along the way we will see people find faith."

Changing from Salespersons to Servants

Christians must simply *be* the good news and not have an ulterior motive. Dieter Zander (Quest, Novato, CA) illustrates this point from personal experience. A strange couple lived down the street. He typified them with the comment, "I bet they sell Amway!"[3] Indeed, at one point, they came over and sought to sell him Amway products. He replied with a firm no, and he hasn't had any further contact with them in four and a half years. God nudged him through that contact. How he felt about that couple is how most non-Christians feel about Christians. Zander faced the challenge, "How can we be friends with people so that they don't feel this way about us?" His new agenda is to do good, to bless others as the Abrahamic covenant commands. He wants to be good news to people consistently without another agenda.

Dave Sutton (New Duffryn Community Church, Newport, U.K.) is critical of Christians who make a gospel presentation, seek a response, and then leave that person to go to the next one. "It can't be about how many you converted this week or bound by the latest evangelistic five-step strategy. We are not interested in becoming a megachurch. We are interested in getting as close as we can to following Jesus." Jesus did not push for a decision in order to promote a hidden agenda. He expressed the welcome of the kingdom and embodied the end of exile and the forgiveness of sins. Christians should strive for nothing less in their communities.

In contrast to a salesperson, a servant does not present a product but gives himself or herself. From a biblical perspective, service does not entail demeaning servitude. Rather, it is a term of honor, applied to Jesus, who saw himself as the fulfillment of Old Testament prophecy. The twelve disciples were prepared for leadership characterized by servanthood, and the apostle Paul frequently referred to himself as a servant in his letters to the churches of the New Testament world. Emerging church leaders, in their disdain for titles, status, and aspirations for a professional career path, are eager to model their leadership style on the humble servant.

Moving from Changing Beliefs to Changing Lives

Emerging churches focus on changed lives rather than changed beliefs. People do not want to be converted, but experiencing the life of the king-

---

3. Amway (now a part of Alticor) is a popular multilevel marketing company prominent in the United States.

dom may be welcomed by many. The focus is to create cultures of the kingdom and to allow God to do the work. For Steve Collins of Grace (London), "Church is a minority pursuit, and churches that make a fuss about what they're doing are suspected, quite rightly, of trying to make converts, and nobody wants to be converted. Our non-Christian friends, who know what we're up to, are interested, but they won't come. It feels a little too risky, like we might trap them in some way." Brad Cecil of Axxess (Arlington, TX) concurs. "Axxess is missional but *not* in the sense that we are trying to save all the individuals we are engaged with in the culture so that the kingdom will advance and Christ can work. Instead, we are trying to make our community a place where you can feel the kingdom of God, and we don't think we need to save everyone for this to happen."

"Evangelism is the invitation to the conversion process for someone. It is inviting someone to change their life." Doug Pagitt (Solomon's Porch, Minneapolis) goes on to address two fundamental questions: What is the gospel? and How does one convert? Pagitt believes that the old view perpetuated the idea that changed ideas (conversion) lead to changed behavior. Pagitt believes, however, that a changed life (conversion) leads to changed beliefs. "We are much more involved in inviting them to live differently than to believe differently."

Moving from Speaking about Grace to Grace Speaking through Lives

For emerging churches, evangelism takes the form of presence rather than proclamation. Sean Stillman of Zac's Place (Swansea, U.K.) has a good relationship with local Muslims. It is low key, relational, and nonconfrontational. He recognizes that he is on a "learning curve" in relating to this community as he seeks to "earn the right to speak." He is comfortable being friends with people who have different worldviews. He is prepared to engage with them for the long haul, "and maybe over five or ten years the situation might change, as the grace of Christ speaks through my life."

For some in emerging churches, whether one is in or out is not the concern. Spencer Burke (Newport Beach, CA) maintains, "God encourages us never to separate the wheat from the tares. But we do. Every time we do that we hurt the work of God. We need to soften the ground, plant seeds. Let's quit making it tough to get to the inner circle. Maybe some have wandered away because of our attitude." Sue Wallace (Visions, York, U.K.) is also concerned not to build barriers that preclude the possibility of an ongoing conversation. "We don't like rigid barriers between the ins and the outs. We will welcome everyone equally. We believe faith is a pilgrimage that we are all on. Within the group, we may disagree on matters such as conversion experiences, but we are pretty orthodox in the central matters of faith, salvation, and the unique character of Jesus."

Some groups express their relationship with other faiths by serving them. Humble service expresses generosity toward others, which is the root meaning of grace. The artists of Thursday PM are redoing a day care center for the interfaith hospitality network. Mosque, synagogue, and others are working on this as well. Their attitude of service reflects a true openness regarding other religions. Rachelle Mee-Chapman explains, "We try to make as much space for people as possible. We breathe on what God is doing in people's lives, see if we can fan the flame. We are not concerned with differences but whether we can dance in the overlap. Maybe the rest of who God is will be worked out through relationship."

Moving from Privatized Faith to Public Faith

Emerging churches typically emphasize ministry in the community and the workplace rather than ministry largely restricted to church members. They recognize that Christians, especially in urban settings, are living in a multi-faith society. Consequently, there has to be mutual understanding and respect as people live and work together. Rachelle Mee-Chapman (Thursday PM, Seattle) explains her determination "to create a rhythm of living that allows our faith to have feet and relevance."

Christians need to live their lives publicly so those from outside the church can be attracted to the faith. For many, such as Simon Hall (Revive, Leeds, U.K.), the word *evangelism* has a bad odor. "Our evangelism is pretty poor. The word itself barely gets mentioned. Everyone who has become a Christian through Revive has done so through friendships. The people in Revive are very cynical about any evangelistic techniques. My own vision is simply to put the people of God out there in the marketplace and hope that we live a life that attracts people to God. That is the hardest option of all, because it's 24-7 evangelism." Chris Matthews of Red Café (Swansea, U.K.) echoes Hall's sentiments: "Throw us into the midst of culture, and see what happens!"

Evangelism involves sharing the deep experiences of life with those outside the faith. Pip Piper of maji (Birmingham, U.K.) states:

My view on interfaith stuff is simply that Christianity has to stand up in the wider marketplace, and that means more gatherings and events that bring together those faiths. We share a lot together, and art and film can help that link and help people explore and express their distinct faith journeys without having to feel under attack or undermined in any way. Each is stronger for the encounter. Evangelism or mission for me is no longer about persuading people to believe what I believe, no matter how edgy or creative I get. It is more about shared experiences and encounters. It is about walking the journey of life and faith together, each distinct to his or her own tradition and culture but with the possibility of encountering God and truth from one another.

Rachelle Mee-Chapman (Thursday PM, Seattle) agrees. "Regarding interaction with those outside, it is primarily presence and participation. It consists of spending time with friends."

Nanette Sawyer of Wicker Park Grace (Chicago) started meeting with the residents of Wicker Park, listening to the spiritual journey stories of the locals. Her goal was to get to know them, to care for young adults. She wants Christians to find a way to welcome them as the church. She desires to do "evangelism without imperialism; to go into a community and be with them; to become them, knowing their stories, letting them know me, and letting myself be changed by them. We meet at a tea house for spirituality discussions."

Some members of emerging churches spend time in the public arena in intentional acts to connect with others. Kevin Rains (Vineyard Central, Cincinnati) leads a gathering called Jesus @ the Pub, which meets for discussion of a gospel passage most Thursday nights. Out of the ten people who attend, seven do not regularly go to church. The church also hosts neighborhood parties. Rains says, "We're serious about being intentional in our efforts and not just calling whatever happens evangelism."

Moving from Evangelizing to Being Evangelized

Christians cannot truly evangelize unless they are prepared to be evangelized in the process. In sharing the good news, people are enriched by the spiritual insights, honest questions, and depth of devotion demonstrated by those of other faiths. Including others involves listening to them and, in so doing, learning from them. Much of what exists in other faiths may not necessarily be hostile to the kingdom. Christians can learn much from other walks of life.

Pete Rollins of ikon (Belfast, U.K.) reports, "We have been actively engaged with other faiths through the evangelism project. Evangelism has an important role but is seen as a two-way process designed to open others and ourselves to God." Their evangelism project is the reverse of most forms of evangelism. They visit people of other faiths and spiritualities and allow themselves to be evangelized in order to learn more about other walks of life. "We deemphasize the idea that Christians have God and all others don't by attempting to engage in open two-way conversations. This does not mean we have lapsed into relativism, as we still believe in the uniqueness of our own tradition, but we believe that it teaches us to be open to all. We are also genuinely open to being wrong about parts and perhaps all our beliefs—while at the same time being fully committed to them."

Listening to other faiths expresses an openness to the possibility that something might be learned from them. Emerging churches believe there is much to gain from other cultures. Dieter Zander (Quest, Novato, CA) expresses his viewpoint. "God brought me to San Francisco because I needed to learn the ways God's Spirit moves apart from Christians. God has used other religions and other persuasions to draw me to him. God works in these religions in mysterious ways." Dwight Friesen (Quest, Seattle) echoes Zander. "One week, we pulled quotes from Christian, Hindu, and Muslim mystics, and we engaged in conversation. What does it mean to be a spiritual person from that tradition? We learned that the teachings are similar on a mystical level. How these traditions approach mystery is very similar. It shocked some of us."

Spencer Burke's community (Newport Beach, CA) visits different Christian traditions every few weeks. "We're in *and* out, so we honor everyone. Yes, we lead from a particular story. I think the difference is that even though we are looking at church, we hold true to the Christian tradition. However, the Christian tradition could hold to an inclusive model, not an exclusive one. We have a community hermeneutic. We read other sacred writings, then get back to Scripture and decide together how to interpret what we have read from the literature that other religions hold to be sacred."

Burke's community is prepared to learn from faith traditions outside the Christian fold. There is a Buddhist family in their church. As a community, the church visited a Buddhist temple. They participated in a guided meditation with this family. Burke celebrates the many ways God is revealed. He recognizes that the Spirit has been with these people all along. The community celebrates other traditions. They reach out to other traditions, and they see them as beloved children of God.

With a focus on kingdom rather than on church, people find that their relationship with other faiths changes. "As someone who was a

Buddhist for twenty years, I have a deep respect for other people's faiths," says Dave Sutton (New Duffryn Community Church, Newport, U.K.). "My understanding is that if the kingdom is what God is about, then God might be involved in other faiths. . . . We very much see our work in relation to the unique person and work of Christ. If other religions are involved in that work, that is fine."

Because emerging churches believe the presence of the reign of God is beyond the church, they are accepting of other faith communities. Ben Edson (Sanctus1, Manchester, U.K.) reports, "We had a guy from the Manchester Buddhist center come to Sanctus1 a couple weeks ago and talk about Buddhist approaches to prayer. We didn't talk about the differences between our faiths. We didn't try to convert him. He was welcomed and fully included and was really pleased to have been invited. We gave him a positive experience of a Christian community, which is in itself an important act of mission." The underlying values that determine their relationships with sincere adherents of other faiths are respect, humility, and inclusivity. Emerging churches are prepared to engage in an open interchange and to leave the outcome in God's hands. The underlying principle is inclusivity. Therefore, all are welcome, and this is reflected in people's everyday lives as well.

Those with an interest in ministering cross-culturally, be it in club culture or with other faiths, need to learn the art of critical contextualization. Otherwise, their witness will be compromised, and they will simply mirror the mood and mantras of contemporary culture rather than the light of the gospel. The light of the gospel will affirm elements of culture, fulfill aspirations that cannot be realized by any other means, as well as pass judgments on aspects that are narcissistic, addictive, and destructive. In the process, Christian witnesses will find themselves challenged. They will see ways in which they have skewed and narrowed their understanding as a result of their own cultural blinders. Those who witness in cross-cultural situations will find themselves changed in the process.

Conclusion

Modernity teaches its inhabitants to exclude and to conform. Members of emerging churches, however, display the hospitality of Jesus and include and welcome others into their midst who are different from them. Emerging churches hold to Christian orthodoxy, affirming the uniqueness of Christ. This understanding, however, rather than being a reason to exclude, empowers them to include those of other faiths, cultures, and traditions. Because of their confidence in Jesus, members of emerging churches venture out and truly listen to those of other faiths and even seek to be evangelized by them. They no longer feel that they need to argue for the faith. Instead, they believe their lives speak much louder than their words. They do not believe in evangelistic strategies, other than the pursuit to be like Jesus in his interactions with others. They do not target people or have an agenda but rather seek to love all those whom God brings to them. They do not hope for a belief change for their conversation partners as much as a life change. Because of their high level of engagement with other cultures, the sacred/secular split is overcome as they practice the kingdom in their midst, in community.

7

Serving with Generosity

On one occasion, our community was getting kicked out of a park because of our interaction with the homeless. "You can't feed the homeless here; you need a permit," the policeman said. I replied, "We are not feeding the homeless. We are having a picnic. We're eating *with* them."

Spencer Burke, Newport Beach, CA

I no longer believe in evangelism. To be postevangelism is to live our lives in Christ without a strategy but with the compassion and the servant posture of Jesus Christ. We do not do evangelism or have a mission. The Holy Spirit is the evangelist, and the mission belongs to God. What we do is simply live our lives publicly as a community in the way of Jesus Christ, and when people inquire as to why we live this way, we share with them an account of the hope within us. We are to love one another, and that creates its own attraction. Taking care of the sick and the needy creates all the evangelism we need.

Karen Ward, Church of the Apostles, Seattle

In their many activities, emerging churches strive for the kingdom, and the very essence of the kingdom is generosity. The last chapter showed that emerging churches welcome the stranger. This chapter represents the other side of that same coin of hospitality: serving the stranger. Hospitality is manifested in emerging churches as members seek to serve those both inside and outside their communities in all spheres of life.

Emerging churches find the culture in which they live to be a challenge, as a marketing orientation permeates all spheres of society. Self-interested exchange, which is pervasive in modernity, is the opposite of the free gift of the gospel. Emerging churches stand out significantly as they reject the economic rules prevalent in culture and practice hospitality by serving with generosity.

Kingdom-Inspired Generosity

Emerging churches root their practices of hospitality in their under-standing of Jesus and the kingdom. Through a distinctive way of living, Jesus and his community served to fulfill the Torah. As those who had been freed from exile, they sought to love and not to hate, gaining the reputation of those who loved one another. They lived lives of justice and held one another accountable not to prefer one over another. Liv-ing in such a way followed the example of Jesus. Through serving and forgiving, Jesus revealed the way of life God has always desired for the people of God. Jesus inspired his followers to live under the rule and the reign of God, thereby becoming a light to the nations and participating in the *missio Dei*.

At the core of the gospel is God's generosity embodied in the concept of grace. Jesus served in this way, and those communities who decide to follow him must do likewise. God continues to pour out his love and mercy in the world, and the church is entrusted with the opportunity to join God in this work. As emerging churches seek to do so, they confront the practices of consumer churches.

The Consumer Culture of Exchange

In our late modern or early postmodern time, the economic sphere permeates all other spheres to the extent that virtually all parts of so-ciety are touched by economic concerns. Most Western cultures today are permeated by marketing and the media, none perhaps more than the United States. The advertising and marketing industry has a sig-nificant influence at all levels of society. Marketers create tastes, wants, and understandings in order to stimulate sales. Ultimately, marketers significantly influence how people live.[1]

1. M. Alvesson and H. Willmott, *Making Sense of Management: A Critical Introduction* (London: Sage, 1996), 105.

Advertising and marketing, which are so seductive and pervasive in culture, have a profound impact on spirituality and the pursuit of God. Today, typically, individuals come to spirituality as shoppers. They *consume* spiritual experiences.[2] They pursue the next experience that promises to take them to a higher spiritual plane and yield greater growth. On the producer side, merchandisers of consumer spirituality sell sensations to those desiring higher peak experiences.[3] Given the reality that we live in an economically permeated culture in which individuals act as spiritual shoppers and spiritual vendors offer higher and higher peak experiences, what effect does this have on the church?

Churches that adopt a marketing approach treat their visitors as customers, numbers, and potential converts instead of simply as people. A culture of self-interested exchange permeates the life of consumer-oriented churches, where the "customer's" financial support is solicited in exchange for spiritual services rendered. Those on staff in marketing-oriented churches see themselves as customer service workers. The staff is motivated to ensure the satisfaction of customers by anticipating and meeting their various needs. Even though staff members who treat church as a customer service center often have good intentions, seeing themselves as good stewards of the faith, their work fails to achieve their goals. The underlying assumption is that customers are never satisfied and are liable to take their business elsewhere. Satisfaction is an elusive target, constantly moving and taking on new forms.

Much of marketing practice borders on manipulation by creating needs.[4] Until one sees or experiences a product, one often does not "need" it. The creation and the presentation of a product create the need. When churches decide to make entertainment their main focus, they create a continued expectation and desire for more. Marketing is not neutral; it fosters human desire as much as it satiates it.[5]

Marketing makes a science out of the relationship between producers and consumers. The pastor or church staff must relate to a church visitor in a prescribed way so that the person is moved to the next step in the marketing strategy. In the process of identifying and meeting needs,

2. Alan Aldridge points out that there are two ways to view consumption. Consumption is often characterized negatively as hedonism or narcissism, or positively as choice and autonomy (Alan Aldridge, *Religion in the Contemporary World: A Sociological Introduction* [Cambridge, U.K.: Polity Press, 2000], 186–90).

3. Zygmunt Bauman, *Globalization: The Human Consequences* (Cambridge, U.K.: Polity Press, 1998), 80.

4. Alvesson and Willmott, *Making Sense of Management*, 95.

5. Ibid., 20.

what the organizers and promoters perceive to be visitors' needs often become the visitors' desires. Thus, the church itself creates an artificial need and then sets out to fulfill that created need.

Marketing churches may say they are only meeting the felt needs of individuals. But like all marketing organizations, they have a strong say in what those felt needs are. They create desires as much as they fulfill them. In that respect, they cease to be a neutral provider and instead are using their power to control individuals. Their consumers are wired to seek the fulfillment of their needs. They adopt cultural narratives that say that every person lacks something, is impoverished, and needs a particular product to be satisfied.

Churchgoers associate the consumer church's products with "need satisfaction." There are areas of an individual's life that are ambiguous and insecure, to which the church seeks to respond by creating and of-fering products that will address those gaps. Consumer churches present a relationship with Jesus as the answer to widespread feelings of angst. Thus, Jesus is turned into a product that satisfies needs. The problem is that Jesus won't satisfy individual needs, for the gospel is primarily about God's agenda, not ours. For true satisfaction to take place, needs must be reformed and transformed to correspond with the gospel.

When Jesus is presented as a product and ceases to satisfy, as all prod-ucts cease to satisfy at some point, one must then move on to another spiritual expression. By marketing Jesus, therefore, the consumer church actually makes the pain worse, for now even God, from a visitor's per-ception, cannot help. Instead of challenging the logic of the economic system, which the kingdom does wonderfully, the consumer church blesses the economic rules and creates transitory surface-level Christians in the process.

The Kingdom Comes as a Gift

Emerging churches do not allow anonymous consumers to continue consuming. Rather, in short order, they become active participants. Gen-X churches, which copied a seeker model, allow individuals to consume and to leave anonymously. Emerging churches signify a determined stand against the consumer, one-hour, drive-through sort of spirituality.

A letter written by Si Johnston to the headspace (London) community reveals this prevailing anti-consumer emphasis. "Along with the rest of the leadership team, I am concerned that headspace does not fall into the trap of being solely a service to be consumed. Instead, it should be a collaborative and generative community, together discovering new art, new dreams, new direction, new thinking, and new action. We need to open up the conversation and enable collective ownership."

Brad Cecil (Axxess, Arlington, TX) takes up the same theme:

> It is our conviction that one of the reasons Christianity is so consumeristic is that we have prioritized the individual and have commodified God. The church must share some responsibility for this monster we have created. We have made Jesus out to be the ultimate consumer commodity. He is packaged in a convenient needs-driven format of the one-hour God experience that happens every Sunday morning. We are trying to flip this and prioritize the community and work to make the culture a place in which the King reigns. Social service and activism are how we do this.

This critique of a consumerist society reveals the extent to which the church itself has become subverted by the wider culture. The church, as a sign of the kingdom of God, must demonstrate an alternative society. Consumerism both pacifies and disempowers people and robs them of their individuality and creative potential. Consumerism destroys community by discouraging active participation.

Unbridled consumerism also leads to greed, acquisitiveness, and wastefulness as people become dissatisfied and bored with their possessions and strive for the latest and the biggest (or the smallest, in the case of gadgets). Emerging churches believe that people need to be delivered from their covetousness and selfishness so that they can be liberated for a life of service and generosity.

Consumer churches promote self-interested exchange and thus violate an inherent part of the gospel, that of the gift. They want satisfied customers who will return the next week. This distorts relationships among church members, who expect certain things from others depending on whether they play the role of consumer or producer. Emerging churches insist on a radical shift of emphasis by first forming a community that can be both faithful and generous. Once such a community has been established, then and only then can it focus on addressing needs based on the priorities of the gospel of the kingdom and not self-centered agendas.

We must accept that we live in a consumer culture and are consumers. We cannot leave our culture. For that reason, communal life will contain aspects of consumer culture. Yet people do not need to accept the logic of the economic system when it differs from the gospel. People must think through what they adopt and what they refuse. As Jonny

Baker (Grace, London) wisely says, "We do a lot of reflection on what it means to follow Christ in a consumer culture, which includes both engaging and resisting it."

The Generous Acts of Hospitality

Hospitality, as taught by Jesus, means reaching out to one's neighbors, first to meet their immediate needs and then to address their deeper, long-term needs. It recognizes that people may have needs of which they are unaware or to which they are not prepared to admit. It entails establishing a relationship of trust in which people are not exploited in their vulnerability or treated as objects. At the same time, the practice of hospitality is not based on triumphalism or a false self-confidence that one has the answers and the resources to fix any personal or societal problem. This was the mistake of humanistic liberalism. True hospitality represents an offer to others of all that has been received from God. People who offer hospitality realize that they too are continuing to learn how to go to God in faith, humility, and contrition and to receive his blessings.

A ministry of hospitality assumes greater importance in an individualistic and inwardly focused society that excludes the vulnerable and the lonely. The early church recognized the importance of hospitality in its social context, in which many were widowed, orphaned, excluded, or ostracized. Hospitality restored human dignity to the slave in a society in which as much as 80 percent of the population was indentured laborers.

From Disembodied to Embodied Spirituality

In the past, a strong commitment to social action all too often degenerated into a human activism in which those involved believed they were building the kingdom. This overlooks the fact that it is God's kingdom. It is something that only God can bring into being. As Jesus reminds us, the kingdom comes unexpectedly as a gift and a surprise. The popular phrase "building the kingdom" does not occur in the New Testament and is alien to its understanding of the nature and the dynamic of the kingdom.

Kingdom activity must never be divorced from its roots and nourishment in the gospel. It takes place only through the operation of the Spirit of God through, although at times in spite of, God's people. Recognizing this important understanding, Landing Place (Columbus, OH) endeavors to link social action with an equally intentional spirituality. Mark Palmer states, "One cool thing we have done is to create the Urban Center for Spiritual Formation. There we try to marry spiritual disciplines to social action. We experiment to do these two together. We have a desire to do spiritual practices and turn them into social action."

The typical emerging church approach to spirituality represents a reaction against an escapist form of revivalism in which groups of earnest Christians look back to a significant move of the Spirit with the heart cry, "Do it again, Lord." Rather, revival emerges out of the mission of the church.

The leaders of Red Café and the church plant Extreme in Swansea were of the opinion that "the closest thing to revival was Soul Survivor 2000, when all those young people went to Manchester and served in the inner city" (Peter Mannion). This event attracted over six thousand young people to an economically depressed area of Manchester with Europe's highest crime rate. The young people camped out in an inner-city park, learned about urban challenges, and served the community for a week by painting over graffiti, picking up trash, and working in the gardens of the elderly. In this high crime area, the police inspector told the young people at the end of their stay that there had been no reported crimes that week. Their involvement was in conjunction with a long-term commitment to the area on behalf of teams of young Christians who had moved into the area and taken jobs locally. This outreach is known as the Eden Project, and it currently involves more than ten teams with thirty people in each team. They invite their neighbors into their homes, which have become centers of hospitality. Crime has been significantly reduced since 2000, and the teams have earned the respect and the support of the city council, schools, and police.

Si Johnston of headspace (London) sees his job in the following terms. "My job is to see that people understand the breadth of the kingdom and live accordingly. The DNA of our spirituality is that intimacy with God comes only through involvement in society. In other words, they fund one another. Intimacy with one another without involvement in the wider community is shallow and narcissistic, and involvement without intimacy is backbreaking and short-lived. We therefore encourage a spirituality that is by nature activist and missional. This seeps into every aspect of our community life."

Kenny Mitchell of Tribe (New York) expresses his deep social commitment in the following terms. "We talk about Jesus quite a lot. Unless the widow is being taken care of, we are not following Christ. The basic ingredients of gospel are not fused in our life if we are not purposefully aware of what is going on in our neighborhood. We believe that Christ is all about single moms and drunks. Therefore, as a church, we must be socially and politically aware. To be authentically spiritual, we have to be engaged in what Jesus talked about."

From Social Programs to a Socially Engaged Way of Life

Emerging churches move away from social programs and move in the direction of hospitable living. At Quest (Seattle), social programs are generally discouraged. Dwight Friesen insists, "We discourage programs in our faith community. Almost everyone is involved in social service as a career. On the fifth Sundays, we do a social project: picking up trash off the beach, painting a playground, working at a food shelter. Much of our giving goes to members going through crisis moments. We live generously, giving with a kingdom perspective in which individuals support others. We give of our time."

Sanctuary (Santa Monica, CA), led by Barry Taylor, also serves the poor and has worked with Habitat for Humanity. However, they avoid formal programming. Instead, in the context of their lives, they take care of the marginalized. "Many were serving God in the culture before coming to church. They already understood that Jesus hung out with the marginalized. They didn't need to be taught that. It is only when they come into the church that they unlearn generosity," Taylor wryly comments. Rather than extracting people from the world, the church should empower members to engage more effectively in the ministry and mission that God has already entrusted to them in the world. Members should serve the world through their vocations rather than through church-administered programs.

Si Johnston of headspace (London) also dislikes social programs. He says:

> We don't see it as social service. This term smacks of right-wing inflammatory labels hurled at the earlier liberals within Christendom. Social service can be construed (certainly in the U.K.) as devoid of spirituality. Instead, we encourage and teach a "joined-up" spirituality, which sees evangelism and social service/action/justice in a synthesis. Loving God and loving your neighbor are two sides of the one coin. The Enlightenment has forced a wedge in here that seems to erode the composite nature of shalom. I use the term *social engagement* as a composite for evangelism and social action. We understand shalom/re-creation/salvation as being

the bringing about of well-being to every level of people's existence in the here and now.

For some communities, serving becomes habitual—it is just what they do. Revive (Leeds, U.K.) provides a telling example. Simon Hall states:

Community ministry is very important in Revive, because we live in an inner-city community and we are Christians. Our gospel would be toothless and hypocritical if we were not serving our local community. But I don't think anyone thinks like that. They just do it. We have a team of people cleaning the local park and streets, some guys do prison visiting, others work with drug addicts and prostitutes. We have a number of youth workers doing sex education in schools, and we put on two big parties a year for the local community: a party in the park in the summer and an open air carol concert at Christmas.

Anna Dodridge's community (Bournemouth, U.K.) ministers to the marginalized in the community.

People have their own areas of interest. Some of us are involved with Amnesty International. There are some people in our church community who are very involved with international students. Some of the students among us provide services for other students. Some of us are involved with the homeless. We live in a vicarage, and so we get a lot of homeless people calling on us, and we invite them in for cups of tea and time for a chat. It is an area of awareness that has emerged during our times of discussion, in which we have learned that social service is a central part of who Jesus was and therefore who we should be. One of our plans is to open some kind of night stop-in place that offers space, shelter, and tea for clubbers and anyone else wandering around in the wee hours of the morning.

Tribe (Hollywood) works with foster kids who are children of parents with AIDS. Some members went to Kosovo and made a film about the situation there. On the local front, they gather food to take to downtown Los Angeles. "Most service is pretty organic, in the form of individual initiatives rather than planned programs," reports Rebecca Ver Straten McSparran. This bottom-up involvement is typical of their approach to ministry, in contrast to a programmatic, top-down approach, which requires the selling of an idea and appeals for volunteers to commit to support the initiative.

Emerging churches still participate in one-time initiatives, but that is not their mainstay. For Tribe (New York), asking for volunteers to support a project on a one-time basis "still seems gimmicky," according to Kenny Mitchell. "We really want to deal more with a lifestyle of serving. We are concerned with where people in our community shop. After the devastating September 11 attack, we gave money to people in the Middle East, to Palestinian kids, to refugee kids. We gave our church tithe to them without creating any official programs. We simply wanted to support the people so that they could do what was appropriate in their context."

This viewpoint expresses the concern that a programmatic approach can lead to a commodification of the gospel. Furthermore, such programs can lead to the majority of the congregation opting out of personal responsibilities by using the church as a proxy. Emerging churches seek to replace a programmatic approach with an organic response. Authentic love expects nothing in return. Unconditional love does not lay down conditions and does not discriminate. It eschews "acts of love" that carry a hidden motive and are in reality self-serving. It rejects opportunism and gimmickry. An act of love cannot be turned into a photo-op or a publicity promotion.

Members of emerging churches practice hospitality through sharing meals and opening up their homes and hands to those outside. They offer food and a safe place to others. They see this as a spiritual practice, not social service. They look to serve others as part of a holistic way of life.

Communicating the Good News

A great deal of rethinking is taking place in regard to the task of evangelization. Younger leaders ponder why the good news is so often projected as bad news. This arises from the sin-focused presentation of the message and the fact that many who seek to evangelize lack credibility and demonstrate inconsistency. The good news presents the opportunity to participate with God in the redemption of the world, and emerging churches communicate the good news through service.

Demonstrating a Life of Service in Which All Are Invited to Share

Emerging churches participate in life with the outside community. Mark Scandrette (ReIMAGINE! San Francisco) organizes initiatives to serve the homeless but adds, "The ideal is a lifestyle of service. I already live in an inner-city neighborhood. It doesn't have to be a program." The insider's perspective leads to a far more radical approach than that offered by those who come from outside.

"One great thing about this community-type church," says Anna Dodridge (Bournemouth, U.K.), "is that we can involve non-Christians in our community. They can hang out with us, eat with us, and get served by us. That to me is evangelism as it should be. People can belong to the community and really get an idea about our day-to-day lifestyle. This approach puts a lot of pressure on us and how we behave and our attitudes, but isn't that what picking up the cross and following Jesus is about?"

Dodridge's comment reveals a move away from an exclusively verbal and often confrontational style of evangelization. Emerging churches are wary of engaging in acts of kindness simply as a means of gaining an entrance to present the gospel message. They do not see their service as a means to a disguised end but rather as an expression of the love of Christ. They engage in relationships with those they are helping, and in so doing, issues of faith invariably arise. The sensitive and compassionate way in which the service is offered gives rise to questions and the opportunity to bear witness to the reconciling work of Christ on the cross.

Becoming Good News People before Proclaiming the Good News Message

Landing Place (Columbus, OH) places an emphasis on living the good news before speaking about the good news. Mark Palmer expresses his deeply held conviction that "we are really committed to being people of God by being a loving community. To the extent that we are doing that, people will be drawn to that expression of love and will be reached." He adds, "We steer clear of negative aspects of evangelism." They see this in terms of a prepackaged, judgmental, we-have-it-all-together approach of aggressively confronting individuals in a way that lacks respect and sensitivity. Levi's Table in St. Louis shares this aversion to a strategic approach. For them, in seeking to share effectively the good news of God's love expressed in Christ, the fundamental question is how to form people in the kingdom. In seeking to answer this question, they have felt it necessary to "jettison all methodology" (Rob Graham).

Emerging churches do not so much target people as love them. Joe Boyd's (Apex, Las Vegas) comment about his own journey, from that of a successful large-church pastor to his present mission involvement with actors in Las Vegas, is both sensitive and revealing.

You have to love them first. You can't serve people whom you can't love. I'm so emotionally involved with them. I'm in love with them, and it has been only eight months. I pray for them because I love them. That for me is huge! It is something I saw in Mother Teresa. I love them and then serve them, not because it is one of the five purposes of our church either. I tried serving people, mostly Christians, all my life. God did not give me a heart for others before. Maybe I have a heart for them because of my own failure as I reflect on my recent history. How many churches go from six hundred to thirty in one year? I couldn't figure it out. What did I do to run all those people off? Maybe I love these show business actors because I walked into it having failed in my first career. I came into their lives broken and out of my brokenness spent time with them. It was mysterious.

Sometimes the most effective ministry is a consequence of painful experiences that give depth of understanding and empathy that would not have been possible otherwise.

Moving from a Spiritualized Gospel to an Embodied Gospel

For emerging churches, the kingdom is not as much a spiritual kingdom as an alternative kingdom. Si Johnston of headspace (London) explains how they see people in relation to God's kingdom.

We see the kingdom as having a political agenda. Put simply, politics equates to the affairs of the people. Jesus was a politician before he was a preacher or a philosopher. The word *gospel* was a familiar construct in the ancient Near East and could mean things like "a new deal" when a new emperor came to power. Jesus' new deal seems to us to be very concerned with the here and now and is therefore very social in its nature. This is great, because the single mother walking around a nearby supermarket who's got three kids to feed and an estranged husband doesn't care as much about her spiritual state as whether she has gone 50p over her government allowance of £54, which will cause great embarrassment at the checkout. How is the church helping to bring dignity and security as well as spiritual healing to her life? Working closely with government, we are privileged to see that they actually admit there are deep-rooted problems that superficial social policy won't address. So in many ways, this is a moment of opportunity for the church (emerging or otherwise) to step up and show that it cares and delivers based on a faith that works.

Moving from London to Arlington, Texas, the message is the same. Brad Cecil of Axxess explains his vision in the following terms.

We have the feeling that God wants us to create a culture that is kingdom-like so that in that culture the poor, the widows, and the orphaned are cared for, the hungry are fed, the children are safe, and the community lives in peace. This will come about not necessarily so that the King returns but that the King reigns—in other words, so God can work freely. We have said that we don't measure our success by how many people attend our staged events but by how God-like the culture is. Are the poor fed? Is the crime rate down? Are the widows cared for? Does the hospital have enough volunteers? Does the community have public transportation? Is art supported? Is beauty valued? Are people educated?

The kingdom is a specific response to a specific context. Brad Cecil (Axxess, Arlington, TX) explains, "The community decides what our cultural condition is and works to transform these areas. For example, we are working to bring public transportation to Arlington, as we are the largest U.S. city without public transportation. We feel that it would be kingdom-like to allow people who live in this community to spend money on other things besides multiple vehicles. This is one way by which we want people to feel the presence of God in our community."

Dave Sutton (New Duffryn Community Church, Newport, U.K.), serving as leader of a base community in the poorest part of Wales, says, "This is not a new method but a new way of thinking." He frankly admits, "What we are doing won't work from an evangelical point of view. It's about God's children who are in desperate need. My job is to show love and compassion to them, and hopefully they will start a faith journey. How long I work with them is immaterial."

Moving from Proclaiming a Message to Demonstrating Personal Concern

Becoming good news to another person includes much more than conveying a message. Evangelization in the changing Western context is as much demonstration as it is proclamation. In the words of Dieter Zander (Quest, Novato, CA), "Evangelism is 'good newsing' people. If Christians in the U.S. would be quiet for a year and only do good works, that would be evangelism. Our actions are way behind our words. There are a thousand ways a day one can good news another." As he engages with the people of the San Francisco Bay area, he is motivated by a deep and sustained longing. "Let me take advantage of every opportunity to good news someone today. If I take every opportunity to do that, then that is a good day. I need to leave the results to God and spread seed everywhere." In San Francisco, "the 'harvesting mentality' does not work. The soil is dead. It needs soil rejuvenation. One day, maybe my kids or grandkids will harvest. Right now, in our context, we just need to replenish the soil." That is especially true in a post-Christendom context that is becoming increasingly neo-pagan.

God planted Joe Boyd (Apex, Las Vegas) in a community of actors who are not Christians. He was inspired by Mother Teresa's model of ministry, applying it to his very different context. "I take Mother Teresa's perspective and apply it to the field of acting. I am not trying to convert anyone. My entire life I have tried to convert people and failed at it. I love actors, and now I'm their community shepherd. I was a terrible shepherd at church. I was more of a motivational speaker. But now I'm a pastor to drug addicts, to gay couples breaking up, and it is the most rewarding profession I have ever had. I am more sure now that I am doing ministry than I ever was before."

Working among the clubbing culture in Bournemouth (U.K.), Anna Dodridge says, "We are a pretty left-wing socialist bunch, so social action is very important. It may be one of those common points that draws us together. A lot of what we do with the clubbers is social service, like pastoral work with people, putting in time to help them out practically. I guess they aren't particularly the poor and needy in financial terms, but they are needy emotionally and spiritually, meaning *they need us.*"

If the poor aren't in one's sphere of influence, one needs to pursue them. In this way, Rob Graham's (Levi's Table, St. Louis) perspective on evangelism has changed. "The poor and marginalized are critical to who we are. If you don't know and aren't known by poor people, you have a crisis at the center of your Christianity. Knowing and being known by the poor are essential." Mission includes being interested in all who are overlooked. At Water's Edge (Hudsonville, MI), they work in a downtown soup kitchen once a month. They don't serve the food, but they talk with the people. NGM in Bristol (U.K.) reports that in their church-planting efforts, community projects are highly important. Members intentionally work with the socially excluded. NGM has a heart for the poor, and social justice is a key value. They work alongside people rather than for them, giving them life skills and arts training.

"You need a core group of very committed people around you who are willing, if necessary, to move into the area and help in the mission," reports Si Johnston of headspace (London). Several members of Vineyard Central in Cincinnati have relocated to a poorer neighborhood and have bought homes there. It is the same neighborhood where the church has property and offices.

If God is with the poor, then Christians should give high priority to giving to the poor. For emerging churches, the concept of hospitality is integral to their work among the poor. They do not offer help from a distance, which emphasizes the distance between those serving and those being served. They work in and among, not from the other side of a divide. They minister out of a relationship, for compassion signifies feeling *with*, not simply *for*, another person.

Moving from a Dualistic to a Holistic Gospel

Social service is integral to the church's understanding of discipleship. Members of emerging churches do not separate the Great Commission (to make disciples of all peoples) from the Great Commandment (to love one's neighbor as oneself). They do not engage in debates over which mandate has priority. Rather, they see them as different sides of the same coin. The church consists of a community of Jesus followers committed to live out a distinctive kingdom lifestyle, proclaiming it by deed and word. Simon Hall of Revive (Leeds, U.K.) reports that "friends who have visited Church of the Saviour in Washington, D.C., tend to return like people who've been to the seventh heaven. They have weaknesses, but what these people have in common is a holistic view of the gospel, while also sharing a very serious commitment to discipleship."

Alternative worship services address issues such as poverty, sexuality, racism, and the environment. In some services, justice and environmental issues are integral. In the Cultural Shift movement, spearheaded in the U.K. by Revelation Church (Chichester), NGM (Bristol), and Sublime (Southampton), there is a renewed emphasis on all aspects of life. Revelation Church (Chichester) has a sign language program, "overcomers" for addicts, and visitation for the lonely. They cater to disabilities; donate food; offer a referral system; provide food for the homeless; help children; and offer parenting skills, "green" environmental audits for homes, and a domestic violence forum. In addition, they advocate justice for the poor, primarily through fair trade. They have a passion to see the kingdom of God proclaimed and worked out. Revelation Church also has Peaceworks and Christian Research, Education, Development (CRED), which advocates for justice worldwide. Tribal Generation (Sheffield, U.K.) advocates for justice issues through Jubilee Plus, Tear Fund, Drop the Debt, Adbusters, Campaign against the Arms Trade, and hungerweb. Tribal Generation deemphasizes the church service and reemphasizes service in the world.

"We are increasingly engaged in our communities. The church has a bad press, and by doing good, I believe we can see a shift take place in people's minds," says Billy Kennedy of Sublime (Southampton, U.K.). Red Café (Swansea, U.K.) performed such extensive social service that government programs gave them substantial aid. Chris Matthews admits:

> Some are very suspicious of our motives, but I always try to be up front about faith being the engine that drives the project and the motivation to be involved in the community, without forcing our views on others. This is sometimes an issue with funders, but invariably once we've talked it through, it isn't a problem. Our experience has been that as the project has developed we've been much more active in the mainstream, particularly in the voluntary sector, education, and social services. We've gained a huge amount of credibility in all sectors and now work in partnership with all of them. We have discovered that working together has helped dispel some of the myths.

Emerging churches participate in the larger community while at the same time offering a unique contribution expressed through allegiance to Christ, obedience to the gospel, and the life-transforming experience of the Holy Spirit. Dave Sutton's (New Duffryn Community Church, Newport, U.K.) radical stance is of heightened significance in the U.K., which is a post-Christendom context. "The church has no voice. I work with the most vulnerable people and families. As I work with them, the people begin to think the church is relevant. And what if that begins to happen on a larger scale? The message of the church, the gospel, can then be heard. It is very much about working slowly, doing achievable activities, supporting what is going on. And that is what is attractive—when we see the needs of the community met."

In both the U.K. and the U.S., there is a growing realization of the strength and effectiveness of faith-based initiatives that are supported by volunteers and enjoy the goodwill of the communities they serve. They have earned increasing government support precisely because they have had the greatest impact and are the most cost effective.

Moving from Tithing for the Church to Tithing by the Church

Emerging churches tithe to the needy with whom they have a prior relationship; they do not believe in anonymous giving. Joel McClure (Water's Edge, Hudsonville, MI) teaches that tithing in the Old Testament went to something that burned (sacrificial offering), provided for the poor and the widows, or went to throwing parties. He is cautious about using the language of tithing when talking about giving money. "The temple was built on heavy taxation and forced labor. It was a holy flat tax. If you are going to use the language of tithe, then apply it to what the tithe referred to in the Old Testament. Money should go for people who can't provide for themselves or for throwing parties. Malachi 3:10 is about not bringing in the whole tithe (i.e., stealing from those who can't provide for themselves). Instead of placing the emphasis on the tithe, we teach being generous. Where we see a need, we give to that, for people who are truly in need."

There are about twenty adults and ten children at Levi's Table (St. Louis). No one gets paid, and everyone tithes. The bulk of the money goes to a local food pantry. When the local food pantry came to them with the sad news that their truck had broken down and they needed eleven thousand dollars to fix it, the community did not hesitate. Rob Graham responded, "Done. What else do you need? An extra two thousand dollars for anything?" Even a church of twenty adults can do significant things when the money does not support salaries and buildings.

Moving from Serving in the Church to Serving Christ in Vocations

James Child-Evans (Bliss, Bournemouth, U.K.) advocates that the church ought to be a network of Christians who serve the world through their vocations. In so doing, he deemphasizes the church service as the primary expression of church. Spencer Burke (Newport Beach, CA) concurs, pointing out that for the poor in many places Sunday is a day of work. For that reason, churches often do not have poor people in them. Therefore, Christians must go to them.

Vaux (London) established an unbroken link between worship and vocation. Kester Brewin states, "Our worship is simply an attempt to offer the gifts we've been given, the same gifts that we are hopefully using in our workplaces. Someone once asked why Vaux didn't run a soup kitchen. It's a non-question for us. We have senior civil servants, teachers, social workers, and urban planners who are part of the 'network of the infected' and are involved in the nitty-gritty issues of urban life every day. To open a soup kitchen may sound worthy, but it does little for our view of the worth our work has throughout the week."

For Johnny Sertin (Bartonka, Bournemouth, U.K.), "There are both gathered and scattered views of church. I advocate scattered. Scattered is the only truly incarnational option." Scattered Christians "go into a particular sphere as empowered people living their lives in society. The church serves to refresh them, but their focus is what goes on in society. They run their own businesses, and they participate in the art world. As anonymous people, their vision is to transform society."

Mark Scandrette of ReIMAGINE! (San Francisco) notes that teachers, lawyers, and others are all under God's reign. Scandrette does not want to pull people away from their life but to push them farther into it. Doug Pagitt of Solomon's Porch (Minneapolis) asks his church members if they, through their work, are participating with what God is doing in the world. "Our job as leaders is to show how the kingdom of God is within people. God recognizes what we don't recognize. The good news of God is that God is near. We can step into the kingdom and live it!"

Conclusion

It would be a serious mistake to interpret the foregoing conversations as simply a return to the liberal, social gospel of the 1920s. Emerging churches are committed to Jesus and to making him known. They are not guilty of a conspiracy of silence by failing to name the name of Christ in their ministry of presence. But their evangelizing does not consist of a strategy in which their social involvement becomes the bait on which new converts are hooked. They participate in relationships with those they serve, and they do not treat them as objects. Because of this shared relationship, conversations invariably turn to God. They serve with generosity, expecting nothing in return. A good deed inspires reciprocity on the part of the recipient. However, such reciprocity is not directed toward the person who initiated the kindly act but toward a third party, preferably someone outside the faith community. Repaying the other person would be self-serving, not self-giving. Generosity is never calculating. It is extravagant.

Authentic kingdom living provides both the credibility and the opportunity to point inquirers to Christ. Having been recipients of God's grace, mediated through the group, some people will want to belong and participate and, in so doing, will come to believe.

Members of emerging churches are committed to nonmembers. They see the church as a place offering hospitality to all, in concrete ways, and they do not reject those who are deemed undesirable. Their emphasis is on ministry in the surrounding community and to worldwide needs rather than ministry that is primarily focused on church members. They are able to place such a strong emphasis on serving others because they are not preoccupied with running programs, enlisting volunteers for the departments and programs of the church, and raising support for salaries and building maintenance.

Emerging churches also have a strong desire to distance themselves from the prevailing models of evangelism, which they regard as intrusive and manipulative. They seek to work alongside from a position of respect and concern for the whole person. Evangelization is not a hit-and-run activity but one that entails a long-term commitment. They stop to consider what constitutes good news from God to a person in his or her total life situation.

Emerging churches overcome the cultural pull of self-interested exchange and offer the gospel, the good news of God, freely. Often this gospel is experienced as service by a Christian. It also includes a relationship with redemptive agents as they seek to live like Jesus in every sphere of society. Members of emerging churches believe that by their very lives they embody the good news.

8

Participating as Producers

Sitting in pews; standing up; sitting down; the same format each week. It just wasn't working for us. As artists, writers, creative people, the single, fixed configuration of soft-rock worship and three-point linear preaching was a body not only we felt uncomfortable in but was dying around us. We were frustrated. We sat each week surrounded by some of the brightest talents in film, TV, theater, art, social work, and politics who were made to watch in virtual silence because they didn't play guitar and didn't preach. These were the only two gifts that were acceptable as worship. It just seemed such a waste. We just thought it was outrageous that we had all these gifts that were being used in the corporate world, in the market economy, and were being snubbed for poorly done soft-rock and two-bit oratory in church. We saw that if worship was about gift, then what we brought to worship had to be integral to us, something meaningful from who we were.

Kester Brewin, Vaux, London

The gospel makes possible full participation with God in the redemption of the world. In regard to Christian worship, full participation means bringing all that we have to God. We bring our world, our context, our material reality to God as an offering. In other words, worship is not an escape from life or a masquerade; it does not represent a dividing of the secular and the sacred, leading to a bifurcated existence. The combination of sacred and secular is the only way we can ensure that the gospel is incarnational. The insights offered by emerging churches into a participatory, indigenous worship challenge the rigidly maintained sacred/secular division of modernity.

As noted throughout, the kingdom is of top priority to emerging churches. One important aspect of the kingdom is that all sit at the Lord's Table, both outcast and insider, from all parts of society, as they share in God's generosity to them. There are not two classes of people who come to the Table. There is just one class consisting of a new type of people. All divisions are overcome in the new social order. These people recognize that they are not seated because they have earned their place or by the luck of the draw but by God's grace. Once seated at the table over which the Lord presides, the participants together represent the reality of the universal priesthood, a kingdom of priests, in which all have equal say.

How the Church Has Changed

To appreciate the extent to which the church has been corrupted and compromised by the culture of modernity, it is helpful to contrast the church in its earliest decades with the church we have come to know in our lifetime. It is all too easy to consider the church we have experienced as normative, when in reality its present form would be hardly recognizable to Christians of New Testament times. This is not to say that the church should not be reconfigured in response to changing circumstances. Emerging church thinkers are not arguing that the early church represented an ideal or pristine form of church. It was as full of problems as churches are today, as is attested to in the letters of the New Testament, many of which were written in response to local challenges. Rather, emerging churches are drawing attention to the dysfunction of churches shaped by modernity and are drawing fresh inspiration from the early church in terms of becoming a missional presence in the contemporary context.

The Participatory Church of the New Testament

In the early church, the "rule of Paul"[1] prevailed. That rule provided space for everyone to have a voice at a meeting. Priests did not run the gathering. Instead, God's will was made known through being atten-

---

1. John Howard Yoder, *Body Politics: Five Practices of the Christian Community* (Scottdale, PA: Herald Press, 1992).

tive to and participating in a discussion that submitted to God's voice. In writing to the church in Corinth, Paul offers his position on worship. "Well, my brothers and sisters, let's summarize what I am saying. When you meet, one will sing, another will teach, another will tell some special revelation God has given, one will speak in an unknown language, while another will interpret what is said. But everything that is done must be useful to all and build them up in the Lord" (1 Cor. 14:26 NLT). Seeing the kingdom at work through egalitarian ways of being was not simply a theory for the early church—it was an observable social reality. However, it was not without its challenges, some of which Paul addresses in his letters and which we will consider later in this chapter.

The Consumerist Church of Modernity

The chapter on hospitality discussed self-interested exchange as one aspect of consumerism in our culture. This chapter focuses on another aspect of consumer spirituality, that of the spectator or the passive recipient. In late modernity, capitalism combined with spirituality, thereby filling religious expression with materialistic desire.[2] Rather than focusing on God, spiritual consumers turned attention on themselves as they sought spiritual goods to help them construct a life with minimal commitment or belief requirements.[3] The consumerist and privatized spirituality of modernity is all too evident in the American church, as exemplified by the seeker movement, which caters to the consumeristic demands of the spiritual seeker by removing all traditional practice, avoiding the classic spiritual disciplines, and providing tools so individuals can construct a portable faith.

A consumeristic faith assumes a "faith to go," as one's faith is not tied to a particular religious institution. Spiritual consumers are free to shop around in their search to improve upon or supplement what they already have. As Wade Clark Roof writes concerning the faith journey of the Baby Boom generation, "With *believing* disjointed from *belonging*, it amounts to a 'portable' faith."[4] With a mobile faith, one unceasingly searches for new and innovative spiritual experiences. A declining loyalty

2. Linda Woodhead and Paul Heelas, eds., *Religion in Modern Times: An Interpretive Anthology* (Oxford, U.K.: Blackwell, 2000), 345.
3. Ibid., 470–71.
4. Wade Clark Roof, *A Generation of Seekers: The Spiritual Journeys of the Baby Boom Generation* (San Francisco: HarperCollins, 1994), 200.

to inherited religious traditions means that people have no compunctions about abandoning the faith of their forebears in their ongoing personal spiritual quest.

When church is understood primarily as a place rather than as a people, the physical church property becomes a place where people receive spiritual products. The service is built around the consumption of these experiences. The marketing church structures itself in such a way that visitors expect to be served. It creates consumers out of visitors. Over time, members come to believe that church represents programs and services done to them rather than participants who are all invited and expected to contribute.

To be attractive to consumers, seeker churches offer music that is either light rock or soft jazz, use videos and PowerPoint, employ drama if there is sufficient talent within the congregation, and dress informally. Messages explore and apply biblical teaching to the circumstances of life, family, character, finances, and so on. Seeker churches attract people by promising "relevant application" through addressing felt needs[5] and offering a plethora of choices.

There is nothing inherently misplaced in any of these elements, for worship ought to arise out of the culture of its inhabitants. Indeed, emerging churches are equally creative, but in their case, the congregations are *contributors to* rather than *recipients of* worship.

Worship Services in Emerging Churches

It is relatively easy to critique existing models of church when we see them as the products of modernity. It is a far more difficult task to redirect or replace them with a more contextual alternative.

For the church to be a place where people feel at liberty to share their journeys and to offer up their lives, a gathering must have no sense of being dominated from the front. Instead, each person must be given space to share in a setting in which he or she feels at home. For example, Church of the Apostles (Seattle) created a café called Living Room and opened it to the public. The café is now at the center of their community. Emerging churches strive to create an environment in which the freedom to participate flows freely.

5. Kimon Sargeant, *Seeker Churches: Promoting Traditional Religion in a Nontraditional Way* (New Brunswick: Rutgers University Press, 2000), 72, 114.

Moving the Community from Consumers to Producers

Emerging churches are determined to move from a consumer to a producer form of church. According to Mark Palmer of Landing Place (Columbus, OH), "There is still the expectation that I do the stuff and they consume it. But we are moving away from that. I want it to be about being sent, about being priests. At our house groups, I function as a facilitative leader, and I speak little. When groups start, I speak more, but as we move on, I speak less and less." Todd Hunter concurs as he discusses Christ Community of Faith (Yorba Linda, CA). "At our services, we did not want to give our visitors anything to consume." The only way they received the benefit of the service was through participation, not through detached observation.

This is a hard concept to get across even to members of a new church. Those individuals who are transferring from other churches tend to bring their traditional expectations with them. Even people who were not previously churched may come with a consumer orientation because of the models of church they have observed as outsiders or seen on television programs aired by local churches.

Although it can be quite difficult, Mark Palmer of Landing Place (Columbus, OH) seeks to maintain full participation in their gatherings. He issues the following challenge. "We have a commitment to Paul's letter to the Corinthians only to the extent that we gather to the ideals behind it. Paul makes it clear that every single person has a gift (1 Cor. 12:7, 11; see also Rom. 12:5–8; Eph. 4:7; 1 Pet. 4:10). Unless every person makes an effort to use his or her gift, the community is not healthy. We make every effort so that there is space to use those gifts. We ask the Holy Spirit to give us the gifts we need for this place."

Full participation is an alternative to consumer church, where the attenders are simply the recipients of a program or service. As Jonny Baker of Grace (London) describes, "I think participation and involvement are key. In a consumer culture, it's all too easy for worship to be something else we consume. So for us, we consciously want to get people involved in worship creation rather than in worship consumption. We also feel that being involved and taking part is a better way to learn anyway. It also enables more gifts of the community to be used. And it's more fun, with a much greater chance of surprise!"

One cannot truly worship from a detached standpoint. Certainly, an inspiring worship team and preacher can lead the assembled company into the presence of God. But Baker warns that worship cannot remain vicarious. Christians need to be enfolded into the worship experience through the gifting of those who lead, but each person has gifts to offer both to extend and to enrich that worship experience. Furthermore, worship is not confined to the event when the entire community is gathered. It continues throughout the week as the members of the community meet in smaller groups and are dispersed in their family, work, and neighborhood contexts. Christians are worshipers not one day in seven but seven days a week.

The challenge this transition presents is in moving people from their former experience of imported worship expressions, which demanded little of them, to one in which they are relating their own culture and experiences to their worship expressions. This is much more demanding, for it requires people to integrate the whole of life with their faith commitment. In other words, they must remove the wall separating the sacred from the secular.

By turning from consumers into producers, worshipers feel a sense of ownership, and in the process of being actively involved, they are more likely to be significantly affected by the worship experience. People are more engaged when they are part of the drama rather than members of the audience. As observers, they may feel the emotional impact, but the impression soon passes as it is replaced by stronger stimuli. This alternative model has to be taught, experimented with, and demonstrated, but it is an understanding of church that arises directly out of the New Testament.

Taking Personal Responsibility for a Worship Service

Kester Brewin (Vaux, London) is candid about what he wants to see: "Those of us who are looking and hoping for the church to respond to the challenges of this new century are not longing for the day when St. Paul's Cathedral goes multimedia. Rather, we are looking for the time when people begin to take responsibility for presenting worship to God which has integrity for who they are, involves their own struggles and gifts, and shows some personal investment in communion with their creator."[6]

For worship to be authentic, it must be indigenous rather than imported. People must be able to express themselves in a natural way, not in a way that is foreign or forced. Just as DJs are highly creative in the

---

6. Kester Brewin, "What Makes It Alt," http://www.vaux.net/greyspace/PolWMIA.htm (accessed June 3, 2005). For more, see Kester Brewin, *The Complex Christ* (London: SPCK, 2004).

way they mix and match in order to create something new, so these churches delve into ancient traditions and refashion them so that they are made not only accessible but also attractive and contemporary.

"Being rooted in your culture does not mean playing banging house music over sermons, or using multimedia presentations, it simply means getting people who spend 95 percent of their time 'out there' in the big nasty world to create their worship using the very same tools that they use the rest of the time."[7] Kester Brewin (Vaux, London) offers the following advice on how to get started using participatory worship. "So if you want to begin in alternative worship it is very simple. Just be yourself before God and encourage others to do the same. Begin to express yourselves using tools that you understand. You may understand graphic design; you may understand Bulgarian nose flutes; the media is irrelevant. What is important is that you, like Abel, brother of Cain, whose sacrifice was accepted by God, present as worship something that has integrity and importance for you."[8]

Originally, the challenge for alternative worship was to express the faith using only the materials from contemporary culture. After over a decade of such activity, Steve Collins (Grace, London) took a step back and reflected.[9] He notes that alternative worship succeeded. It was much more than simply style, however; it was a new method to create worship. What is that method? Simply put, "People make worship for themselves in forms that fully reflect the people they are and the culture they live in." As Collins writes, "Perhaps the crucial legacy of the method is that it makes church that belongs to the people who made it, rather than church designed for someone else, some third party we think it'd be good to reach. The alternative worship approach to mission is, if our church doesn't work for *us*, how will it work for anyone else? If it doesn't represent *us* to God, won't it ring hollow to visitors? It imposes the humility of starting mission with our own people rather than trying to be people we're not."[10] Alternative worshipers do it for themselves and not to market to someone else.

Emerging churches create an environment as a context for the worshiper, but they don't script it. As Collins continues, "This hands-on approach to church is hard work. The reward for all the effort is

7. Brewin, "What Makes It Alt."

8. Ibid.

9. Steve Collins, "Bring Back the Pews (Not)," http://www.smallritual.org/section7/sfcolumn sept01.html (accessed June 3, 2005).

10. Steve Collins, "A Method Called Alternative Worship," www.smallritual.org/section6/aw method.html (accessed June 3, 2005).

church that is a natural part of your life. It's your own worship, you and your friends made it as a gift to God and one another. It's what you wanted to say to God, not what someone thought you should hear. Church can be what it was meant to be—the direct expression of Christians' lives with God and one another, in the world not out of it."[11]

Incorporating Flexibility

For meetings to be highly participatory, they need to be small, usually under thirty people. Such meetings are highly dependent on the gifts of those who attend. The meeting *is* the people who attend. Joe Boyd of Apex (Las Vegas) describes how their house gatherings are flexible. The home group may decide just to take care of the kids for eighteen months. Or the women may do a study. If they want to have an in-depth Bible study for all the adults, they would need to have someone watch the kids, so they mostly do things with one gender at a time. "Just because you opened your Bible and bowed your head doesn't mean you had church," declares Boyd. He doesn't want to be too hard on those who, because of their life stage, simply watch their kids and don't do too many intense spiritual activities. The type of meeting held depends on the kind of people present, the needs they bring, and the initiatives taken by various group members to meet those needs.

If the church really is a body, then each additional member ought to influence the body as a whole. Solomon's Porch (Minneapolis) wants to make sure that the presence of each new person contributes to change in the church. It is a dynamic they want to maintain. Anyone can come and change the overall code. It is that flexible—and that vulnerable. Karen Ward of Church of the Apostles (Seattle) says, "We want Linux, not Windows. With Linux, everyone is a coder [i.e., computer programmer writing code]. The code determines how the system works, and for Linux, there is great freedom to determine how the system works because each person can code or customize the system. With Windows, there is a fixed structure [i.e., much of the structure is already set by someone else, and one simply needs to work within that structure]. If new people come, the code changes. Each person is involved in shaping what goes on from the very first moment he or she walks in." She invites people

11. Ibid.

to give their testimony. Each can take on a leader role immediately. The code is always changing. However, the source code, the language itself, is proprietary. It is given by God.

James Childs-Evans (Bliss, Bournemouth, U.K.) cautions that groups should not strive to be something they are not. They must begin by asking what God has uniquely endowed this particular group to be and to do. "Groups can only be what their members are. We can't copy what others are doing. We first need to identify the resources of our group. Who are we, and what can we give to God?" Their ministry will arise out of their gifting and calling.

Providing an Opportunity for Each Person to Contribute His or Her Story

Emerging churches create a space so everyone can share his or her story. Rob Graham of Levi's Table is concerned that churches only give lip service to the priesthood of all believers. To combat that, each participant at the Sunday morning meeting prepares a one-page paper. The members hear what everyone has to say as they eat breakfast together. For example, one Sunday a person wrote on prayer and encouraged members to try a spiritual practice that week and to share about it the next week.

In Dave Sutton's community (New Duffryn Community Church, Newport, U.K.), members meet in small groups to share their stories. "We relate our faith to real life issues. We go from the situation and look to Scripture to solve the nitty-gritty problems with everyday life. We share stories, and we give each person the opportunity to examine those stories. For instance, in considering the story of Jesus stilling the storm, we ask, What kinds of storms do we have?"

Members of Quest (Seattle) meet in homes twice a month. On one of those occasions, they share their journeys with one another. Their story night is called "Seeing one another. Seeing the Christ in one another." They give one another a point of connection, a glimpse of their life. They have a time of silence afterward and respond in worship after that. Besides the story nights, everyone is invited to participate at every meeting. Dwight Friesen states, "Everyone can share, and most times everyone does."

New Duffryn Community Church in Newport (U.K.) features full participation within a traditional church structure. Dave Sutton explains, "We discuss things and seek to include everyone, within the limitations of the Anglican Church structure. In everything we do, we try to include people. Everybody has a voice. We value everybody, even if they are not articulate. We force people into speaking, and we are constantly amazed."

For a season at Sanctuary (Santa Monica, CA), the church meeting took the format of an open mic. The Sunday gathering became a spiritual club night in a dance club. It was an attempt to have a discussion about God in an entirely different context, an exploration of religion and spirituality outside the comfort zone of the church being in charge. Thus, the leaders had no control over the outcome. In addition to an open mic, there was a prayer room, a conversation room, and an art room. The events were heavily participatory, providing multiple ways for the congregation to worship.

A metaphor for a participatory kind of service is karaoke. Karen Ward of Church of the Apostles (Seattle) says, "Karaoke is the model of alternative worship we have adopted. One woman was awful and sounded like a gerbil! Everyone cheered her on. 'You go girl,' they shouted. These are gospel values, singing their hearts out to God. They give their best. This is much better than auditioning a worship team. I would much rather have the gerbil-voiced woman! I have one woman who plays accordion out of tune. She is awful, and yet we love listening to her."

The individual stories of each member and the collective story of the faith community are seen in the context of God's story as it unfolds throughout Scripture. Theology becomes a dynamic, unfolding reflection on God's dealings with people in the changing circumstances of life.

Fostering Full Participation

Emerging churches see the leading of worship not as a priestly role but as a role assumed by everyone present. Individuals exercise control and provide the principal input. "Our worship style is similar to alternative worship in the U.K. and differs from the rock-band orientation of American worship," Karen Ward (Church of the Apostles, Seattle) explains. "For the most part, we have no up-front leader, no stage, no presiding priest, no big pastor." According to Ward, "The Gen-X church is no different from what preceded it. Simply stated, the band replaced the pastor. It is still personality centered. In contrast, Church of the Apostles is multigenerational and highly participatory. On one Sunday, we finger painted. We made a cloth altar, and everyone put their painted hand on the cloth. This is like 'godly play,' like Montessori[12] church."

Taking her cues from alternative worship, Ward leads worship as a curator in a museum in contrast to a moderator of an assembly. She facilitates but does not draw attention to herself. In emerging churches, no one person necessarily presides over worship. In fact, sometimes the technology presides over the worship experience.

Encouraging Interactivity and Dialogue

In modern churches, the senior pastor does the teaching. Some emerging church leaders, however, challenge the traditional concept of the pastor as the primary or, in many cases, exclusive preacher and teacher. Their leaders are no longer the ones who speak up front at the corporate gathering. Rob Graham of Levi's Table (St. Louis) concurs. "I had to give up the idea that I get up and download all the information to everyone else. Yes, I have spiritual authority, but it is manifested differently."

Typically, Doug Pagitt's (Solomon's Porch, Minneapolis) sermon is a running commentary with a discussion. The themes to be addressed are not decided by the preacher in isolation but with the participation of the entire group. At a midweek Bible study, members determine what Scripture passages will be discussed on Sunday. They discuss what the community needs to hear. This dialogue is Pagitt's preparation for Sunday. In essence, the community leads the pastor so that the pastor can lead the community.[13]

Some leave the teaching time out of the service altogether. "My blog is my pulpit. I rarely will preach in a church. It is on the blog where theological issues are discussed" (Rachelle Mee-Chapman, Thursday PM, Seattle). This provides the forum for an ongoing dialogue of how to live out one's commitment to Christ in the midst of the perplexities and challenges that face believers on a daily basis. The electronic media takes the conversation out of an ecclesiastical setting and provides opportunities for people to be honest and for everyone to participate. It also promotes a sense of immediacy.

12. Montessori is an educational approach that allows students to be self-directed. The teacher creates a context and sets out the tools for creativity rather than functioning as the source of information.

13. Doug Pagitt, *Reimagining Spiritual Formation: A Week in the Life of an Experimental Church* (Grand Rapids: Zondervan, 2004), 85–99.

Involving Planning by the Community

The worship planning team is not necessarily the leadership team. An unusual part of Three Nails, an Anglican church-planting initiative in Pittsburgh, is that the priest is not involved in the design of the monthly worship gathering. The only limitation placed on the planning team, reports Holly Rankin-Zaher, is that Holy Communion must be from the Book of Common Prayer.

In emerging churches, everyone is invited to help plan the worship event. Jonny Baker (Grace, London) says, "Anyone can come to our planning meetings." According to Ben Edson, the same is true for Sanctus1 in Manchester (U.K.). "The planning group sets the program and makes decisions regarding the future of Sanctus, and this is open to all." At Water's Edge (Hudsonville, MI), the leaders do not plan the meetings. "Other groups plan the meetings. Leadership is fluid. It is not the same leaders who lead the different events," explains Joel McClure. According to Steve Collins (Grace, London), "Alternative worship is more about radical power structures than radical presentation styles. Groups work as teams of equals, whether or not there are ordained persons involved. There are no fixed hierarchies or predetermined roles; no one is pastor for this and that. The team isn't an elite group, delivering expertise to the congregation, but a representative group, creating something on behalf of the congregation. Consequently, boundaries between team and the congregation are fluid and hard to spot."[14]

Andy Thornton, formerly of the Late Late Service (Glasgow, U.K.), points out the pros and cons associated with open planning for worship services.

> The downside of participation is that some have no tolerance for the discussion. Others are gifted at it. Perhaps the worship leaders are those with the patience. The upside of a small group doing it on behalf of the whole is that the small group can help the large group get on with it. The positive side of a large group being involved is that there are more stories and more varied processes of growing in faith. Consequently, people are all the richer for hearing from a variety of people, each describing his or her own faith journey.

For Thornton, worship planning receives the participants' contributions as gifts. "Alternative worship always receives what people have as their

14. Collins, "Method Called Alternative Worship."

gift from God to the community. All are invited to share their faith experiences and stories."

Including All Ages in Worship Gatherings

Andrew Jones (Boaz, U.K.) says:

Worship in the emerging church is usually on the defensive from the traditional church. But there is much in the emerging church that should challenge the traditional church. I have seen the best examples of integration with the elderly and the very young in our own alternative worship experiences. One event in Texas had a retired professor projecting his own slides and my seven-year-old hosting the dance space. A ninety-one-year-old man came back two years later for the next event and participated in the drum circle.

For some churches, encouraging young people to participate creatively in their own worship services is a high priority. At the youth congregation Warehouse (Revelation Church, Chichester, U.K.), Dan Slatter preaches maybe monthly, and the youth pick up the remainder. His ideal scenario is to work himself out of a job. Slatter is adamant that Warehouse is not a youth group but a true congregation. He makes the following distinction. "Youth groups in churches are babysitting groups. We are not called to be a youth group. We are called to be disciples, to build the church—which in our context is a youth congregation—to see the lost come to Jesus, and not because Mommy and Daddy are in church." These churches have a high level of participation by the youth. The older leaders function as facilitators.

Hosting a Corporate Gathering

Brad Cecil of Axxess (Arlington, TX) describes the growing pains of full participation in a corporate gathering. "We thought a dialogical approach would be necessary, so we had a large discussion format every Sunday evening. But as we grew, the discussion became a frustration, as an increasing number of people couldn't participate. We abandoned the discussion format." Joel McClure describes similar growing pains. "When Water's Edge (Hudsonville, MI) first started meeting, each person would share, and this would take about an hour and a half. After that we would go to prayer. As it grew, this became untenable." To address this challenge, Axxess adopted a more decentralized approach, creating smaller gatherings (house churches).

Axxess also went to a more symbolic, experiential, free style of worship for its large group gathering. Such celebrative worship events are not focused on celebrities on a stage but on worship leaders as servants around the communion table. "We have transitioned away from discussion in our larger gathering, though it is appropriate to comment or to ask a question. In fact, many feel comfortable taking the initiative. It happens frequently." Cecil's and McClure's frustrations reflect not only the issue of including more and more people but also changes in the dynamic of the congregation as it moves beyond the face-to-face community to one of greater diversity and less intimate relationships.

Mark Meardon reports that the cell groups each take turns leading the large group gatherings at Eternity (Bracknell, U.K.). Dan Kimball of Vintage Faith Church (Santa Cruz, CA) also describes that each home community rotates to take responsibility for the main service. Quest in Seattle adopts the same approach (Dwight Friesen). Axxess endeavors to express its fundamental value within the context of the larger gathering while at the same time accepting the inevitable limitation in the number of people who are able to participate. They have moved from full participation to identification with representative individuals from the congregation. Neither type of large group acts as a substitute for full participative worship. In each of these congregations, the smaller meeting is highly touted as essential.

Bringing Openness and Vulnerability

When all are allowed to participate in a meeting, the community is placed in a vulnerable situation. Karen Ward (Church of the Apostles, Seattle) talks about the susceptibility that participative churches experience simply because of their open structure. "There is always the threat of a virus in the form of a crazy person. However, this is okay, because the rest of the coders aren't crazy, and they can figure out a way to disable the virus, take down the page, communicate that the community's values are different from those of the one who was just sharing. They take the person aside and deal with him peaceably, and they model the change they seek." Ward is sober about the risks they take. "The possibility of death does exist. It is part of living together. We risk death to the system, which could be destroyed by the virus. It is always a possibility. There are crazy people in every family, just as there are diverse people in communities. However, we can absorb these problems."

Kester Brewin (Vaux, London) shares how they deal with those who are a troubling force to the open community. "A good example of each person having a voice is provided on the website slashdot.org. Here, anyone is free to post, but you can choose to view the site at various levels, from just seeing posts from people who have shown they consistently write interesting stuff to seeing all the junk that anyone posts. Dirt is not excluded but managed. Vaux has done a lot of thinking about dirt that represents the ugliness in people's lives that comes to the surface."

Offering a Range of Gifts in the Service of Others

Some emerging churches have come to the realization that the expression of the gifts of the Spirit is not restricted to the worship event or confined to the ministry needs of the members. Dieter Zander explains how his own thinking has changed. At NewSong (Pomona, CA), where he served from 1986 to 1994, he desired that everyone use his or her spiritual gifts at church. "We wanted everyone involved in some way with no such thing as nonparticipation." Everyone was responsible to serve at NewSong. Now, instead of participation at the church service, the kind of participation Zander seeks is outward, away from the church service. How can I "good news" my neighbors and my coworkers? is the question that always comes to the fore. Members, in the exercise of their gifts in their life settings, become good news as they function in the way in which the ascended Christ has equipped them in accordance with his purposes.

Zander says, "I think we are moving rather quickly away from teaching people how to serve in the church to serving like Jesus apart from the church. Through our teaching on gifts, we were training them to be loyal church members, not missionaries. We have now come to realize we need to train people as missionaries to serve outside the church service. Currently, we are scaling down the large groups so people can meet their neighbors. The small group serves to help each person 'lean out' weekly." Zander speaks of an incarnational approach to ministry that is increasingly typical of the missional approach of emerging churches. Full participation is not just for the church service. It is for the church's service to the world.

Embracing Both the Transcendence and the Immanence of God

In worship, emerging churches embrace both the transcendence and the immanence of God. An undue emphasis on the former makes God remote and disconnected, whereas an exclusive focus on the immanence of God can lead to an inward preoccupation or an attitude of presumptive intimacy. In some circles, God has been reduced to a special "buddy" who provides comfort and support but seldom challenges. It is in the dynamic tension between the immanence and the transcendence of God that people encounter the holy, the *mysterium tremendum* that both attracts and causes people to withdraw in awe-inspired, reverential fear.

Among emerging churches, there is a growing reaction against stage-managed and celebrity dominated worship events. They feel that upfront, stage-managed worship emphasizes the transcendence of God by removing his presence from the main body of the worshipers. It also places the human performers between the worshipers and God. The performers become a distraction, making God remote as they become the focus of attention.

In seeking an alternative, contemporary worship model appropriate to urban cultures, some have opted for the DJ model, which in their minds provides a better approach than the worship band. The DJ engages the audience, inviting people to express themselves. The music surrounds the listeners. They may not even see the DJ. They do not focus on transcendence up front but the immanence that surrounds them on the dance floor. A band, however, creates a spectator environment. This insight is especially significant for Grace (London) and those working within the club culture that is so widespread among eighteen- to thirty-five-year-olds in Europe.

Unrelieved noise and an upbeat atmosphere characterize both Boomer and Gen-X seeker services. Silence and inactivity at the front would represent a loss of control. By contrast, emerging churches value changes in pace, pauses, and periods of silence. They provide a "breathing space" in which worshipers can be sensitive and responsive to the leading of the Holy Spirit. It is in times of silence that healing takes place and lives are redirected.

Challenges to Full Participation

In their attempts to redefine and reconstruct church as a fully participative community that points to the kingdom of God, emerging church leaders make no claim to have all the answers. Most admit that they are on a steep learning curve. They acknowledge their areas of confusion and the mistakes they have made along the way. They identify a number of areas in which they continue to struggle to find answers and to make adjustments. New movements often begin with high ideals, but with the passage of time, they have to face new challenges lest their ideals become compromised.

It is one thing to state the ideal of full participation; it is another to actualize that ideal. It is affected by the mobility of members and the reticence of some people to get involved due to their existing commitments. Single parents face a particular challenge, especially if they are divorced or separated and have custody of their children on a periodic basis. Furthermore, leaders can exclude people from participation because of the limitations of their vision or their concern that their own leadership positions could be challenged.

Creative energy is required to maintain an interactive model of worship. The strain is partly relieved by the fact that emerging churches are not aiming for professionalism but are emphasizing a natural expression that flows from the gifting of members.

Movements that start out as radical expressions of church immersed in popular culture can, over the course of time, begin to create their own subculture. As emerging churches become increasingly insular and detached, they may become nostalgic. Consequently, the future of emerging churches will be determined by their readiness to recognize the challenges of active participation and indigenous creative worship and their determination and creativity in responding to them.

Groups face the prospect of becoming increasingly insular in order to maintain the small size necessary to preserve relational bonds. If they are committed to remaining small, they must at the same time be committed to establishing new groups. Only by birthing new groups that carry their spiritual DNA will they be able to remain missional.

Many people need encouragement to overcome their reluctance to speak in public. Emerging churches require small venues to create a level of affirmation for such people. There is nothing new in an emphasis on participative worship. It has been the position upheld by the Quakers (Society of Friends) and the Plymouth Brethren. In their meetings, any individual moved by the Spirit is free to speak. However, with the passage of time and the emergence of certain individuals who have biblical knowledge and discernment or, in some cases, who like to hear the sound of their own voices, the same individuals speak at each meeting.

This predictable routine can be avoided when everyone is involved in the planning of the worship experience.

Conclusion

Emerging churches have a strong desire to provide a genuine community expression of worship that reflects the level of understanding and the richness of experience of the members. This worship form is not constructed elsewhere and imposed upon the community. Instead, it arises out of a response to the grace of God at work in individual lives, their corporate experience, and the signs that God is actualizing his kingdom both among themselves and in the communities they are called to serve.

Irrespective of the style of worship, from written ancient liturgy to spontaneous contemporary forms, the worshipers engage with energy and intensity. Their worship is highly intentional rather than casual and distracted. There is a Godward focus as members recognize that God is both audience and participant. Unlike congregations that are shaped by modernity, congregations of emerging churches are not an audience watching the people at the front as the principal performers. Rather, the entire congregation is actively and creatively engaged in offering worship.

Emerging churches demonstrate a high level of participation at their worship gatherings as well as in discussion of issues and decision making in relation to every aspect of the community's life and witness. The extent of the participation of each person in worship is not confined to predetermined congregational responses. Rather, participation includes the full range of activities that make up a worship event. Participation is not orchestrated but consists of both prepared and spontaneous contributions. The community has a space for everyone to share his or her story, gift, and offering. Emerging churches seek to put the doctrine of the priesthood of all believers into practice.

Consumerism teaches people to be passive spectators, objects, receivers. Emerging churches, in their efforts to resemble the kingdom, create a space for all members to act as producers in their gatherings. As each person brings his or her world to worship, the sacred/secular split is overcome. By being so open to all, emerging churches make themselves vulnerable, but these participant communities consider it a risk worth taking.

9

Creating as Created Beings

God created us to be creative, to be partners with him in making something beautiful, which in turn inspires others to turn toward God in wonder and awe. It constantly amazes me that when Christians work together as a team, what they create together is often way more than the sum of their parts, as God's Spirit, too, joins in and turns something mundane into something prophetic. There are times when we are at a loss for words. Either the existing words are not sufficient, or they have been overused to the point of cliche. It is here that the arts step in, offering us a thousand words per creative act. But we know that it does not have to be perfect. That would crush us with perfectionism. It just has to be true, an honest expression of our love for our Creator. As Mother Teresa said, "Make something beautiful for God."

Sue Wallace, Visions, York, U.K.

It's important to note that I was the "normal" person here, doing what normal young Londoners were doing, listening to that music, wearing those clothes, going to those clubs. This wasn't some grubby freak underground but the creative edge of mainstream culture. But where were the Christians?

Steve Collins, Grace, London

With the inauguration of the kingdom of God, Jesus initiated the new into the old and invited his followers to join him in redemptive activity. Part of that redemptive activity involves participating with the Creator

in seeing entire realms of reality come to life. When Christians participate in this way, they share in the creativity of the Creator. Emerging
churches participate with the Creator, utilizing all of creation, sacred
and secular, as their canvas.

Creativity forms in the context of the emerging church's emphasis
on the gospel and the end of secular space. Members participate with
God in the redemption of the world. Such participation, as noted in the
last chapter, means playing an active role in that redemption and not
watching as spectators. One way they play a redemptive role is through
creating beauty from what was considered ugly, thereby making sacred
what was once profane.

Creativity and aesthetics witness to the dynamic and the beauty of
the kingdom of God. When God originally created the universe, he
looked at what he had made and declared it good. Re-creation within
the reign of Christ seeks to respect and restore the goodness and the
beauty of God's creation.

This chapter is intimately tied to the previous one. Creativity without
full participation has minimal value for the worshiping community.
Creativity by a few instead of the many, although it may inspire, does
little for the priesthood of all believers and the development of gifts
across the body of Christ.

McDonaldization and the Church

Modern culture presents challenges to the dynamics of creativity.
Creativity could not be more different from the McDonaldized context
that characterizes so much of modernity.[1] McDonaldization is the process
by which the principles of the fast-food industry influence other realms
of society. Those principles are efficiency, calculability, predictability,
and control. George Ritzer asserts that McDonaldization is the most
powerful social process in the world and that no culture will remain
untouched by its influence.

Even if one doubts Ritzer's McDonaldization metanarrative, there is
little debate that McDonaldization greatly affects contemporary culture.
Outside the economic realm, it does not take much imagination to see
McDonaldization in health care, education, and even in the church. Mc-
Donaldization is evident in American appropriations of church growth

---

1. George Ritzer, *The McDonaldization of Society: An Investigation into the Changing Character of
Contemporary Social Life* (Thousand Oaks, CA: Pine Forge Press, 1996), 121–42.

principles. It is also apparent in the seeker and purpose-driven types of churches, although many older churches have caught the bug as well. Some churches have literally sent their staffs to McDonald's University for training. Jonny Baker (Grace, London) says, "A lot of independent churches over here made 'modernizing' moves and ended up with plastic coffee cups and school halls and fluorescent lights, which seemed like a big mistake! In contrast, the aesthetic of alternative worship is much more about reengaging with tradition and ritual as well as with contemporary culture. So reframing sacred spaces kind of fits."

The transformation of secular space communicates that the earth is the Lord's and that material reality, the part we see, holds out the possibility of redemption. Much evangelical practice has held in high esteem the invisible reality, the life of the mind and the heart, while giving visible reality over to the world, to non-Christians, and to the devil. However, if all physical reality is to be redeemed, then Christians must use their hands, eyes, and feet in an ongoing and comprehensive involvement with the whole of life. Christians must touch things, create things, and beautify things. Emerging churches are attempting to participate with a creative God and to make the physical expression and the spiritual experience one.

A Theology of Creativity

Worship expressed both verbally and through a full range of artistic expression is a uniquely human activity on earth. Witness and mission are the outflow of that worship commitment. Consequently, it is given the highest priority.

The urge to be creative is not ego driven but rather arises out of a theology of personhood and community identity. Its starting point is the affirmation that we are made in the image of God and that God is by nature creative. The opening words of Genesis declare, "In the beginning God created . . ." Humans' subsequent alienation from God through willful disobedience did not destroy this creative potential. Rather, it led to its misdirection and misplaced motivation. Yet the image of God in humankind was not totally destroyed. The beauty and genius that remain are evidence of God's common grace and of the hope that finds its fulfillment in Christ. The urge to create is an indication of the spiritual longing that still resides in the human spirit.

Jonny Baker (Grace, London) highlights the central importance of creativity. "It's a core value for me and Grace. I would say that being made in the image of God, among other things, is about creativity. I also think that in a consumer culture we need to help people move from consuming worship to producing it." "The creativity of God is linked to the realization of the kingdom of God in our midst," says Doug Pagitt of Solomon's Porch (Minneapolis). "The phrase 'the kingdom of God as the creativity of God' I made up as a way of explaining how God and humanity interact." The entire story of redemption as it unfolds to the present time represents God's ongoing creativity. It is a story that Christians eventually find themselves having a part in, no matter how small.

Every Member Is a Created Being and Is Therefore a Creative Being

Where do the roots of creativity lie? For Si Johnston of headspace (London), it goes back to creation. "All of us have some amount of creativity because we were created. And what we create can have traceable roots back to the original. Thinking innovatively about worship means that we're constantly trying to stand outside the box that the media and advertising continually try to put us in and to express something of the redeemed within us. This means that we aren't about excellence but about supporting one another in our gifts of worship regardless."

Worship services that reduce people to passivity or to routinized responses fail to recognize the true nature and calling of the individual. The performance of the few becomes a restricted recognition and utilization of gifts and reduces the bulk of the congregation to the status of nonpersons. In Spirit-filled worship, people celebrate the diversity of God's gifts, gratefully acknowledge the gifts he has given to others, and discover their own gifts that can be offered on the altar as a gift to God and used in the body of Christ to enrich worship.

Creativity Is Participating in God

Paul Roberts of Resonance (Bristol, U.K.) translates the creative urges of the congregation into worship by interrelating their gifts into a corporate worship offering. In so doing, their potential creativity is actualized in its highest expression. "We use creativity in worship. Being creative and working with others is one of the greatest of human privileges. The problem with most forms of Christian worship is that they demand very little from most of the congregation. At worst, it can seem like watching TV and just singing along with the songs." In traditional worship forms, the congregation is often reduced to passivity or, at best, to orchestrated responses. Worship that results in suppression is a contradiction in terms.

Individual and corporate creativity expressed in worship becomes participation in a God who is both creative and the source of creativity in humankind, created in his own image. For Karen Ward of the Church of the Apostles (Seattle), art invites people into a godly encounter. "Creativity is an expression of being in God. Art is our participation in God. Fancy art has no more value than other kinds of expression. There is a full range of quality." Artistic expression is not restricted to an elite group but is something in which everyone is invited to participate, whatever his or her level of ability.

Creativity Is in Itself Worship

The creation of art directed toward God is in itself worship. Part of the ethos of alternative worship is that constructing worship is part of the worship event itself. Times of creativity are worship. "Alternative worship for us," explains Dave Tomlinson, "sprang out of our giving room for artists to express their art as worship."

Alternative worshipers hold the strong conviction that planning, brainstorming, and trying out ideas are in themselves worship, not simply the preparation for the worship gathering. "Creativity is very important to what we do. It is an expression of our devotion to God," says Sue Wallace of Visions (York, U.K.). In worship, people offer back to God the richest expression of his presence among them, motivated by their gratitude for his grace. Creativity arises out of giftedness at conception and at regeneration, and it is evidence of the continuing work of God's Spirit in people's lives. Recognizing that all are gifted by the Spirit, each person needs to be encouraged to offer back to God his or her gifts as an offering in worship.

Gift Offering Is an Expression of Worship

Worship is offering a gift. Kester Brewin (Vaux, London) provides a thoughtful reflection on this topic.

We create because we are created. The act of creation is fundamental to being fully human. We create to keep the gift moving. If the gift stops or is turned for profit, it dies. In short, the act of giving created gifts is central to our worship. We bring something of who we are, something that has taken our time, not just our money, something that uses the gifts we have been given, and offer that in worship. Not songs we don't really like. Not money into the collection plate. Not just oratory and guitar playing. We welcome the expression of any gift: dance, writing, film, graphics, installations, meditations, etc.

In short, we feel that the wider church has lost something. Its gift practice is too often distorted. By restricting the types of gifts that are really appreciated, mostly to preaching and a narrow musicianship, and by giving space only to those gifts, churches are denying people the opportunity to worship in a way that truly comes from them. Though we don't always realize it, as created people, everyone has a basic desire to be creative in some way, and if the church will not accept their gifts, they will take them elsewhere. Mostly, they will go into the marketplace to exchange their gifts for cash. And most people know that this can be ultimately unsatisfying.

Creativity gives worshipers the opportunity to embrace aspects of God's character they normally would not acknowledge. This comes about as they see the diversity of his creativity through their gifting and the influence of those gifts in daily life. Brewin (Vaux, London) gives a final charge.

All churches, wherever they are and whatever tradition, need to become places in their communities where people can exchange gifts—not just spiritual gifts but any gifts: providing toddler groups, creating places to hang art, opening cafés for passersby, providing peaceful refuges from noisy streets, running seminars, making available financial advice, and providing practice rooms for young bands. In the exchange of gifts, relationships are always catalyzed, always strengthened. Then and only then can the talk turn to the one who gave everything for us.

As has been frequently noted, there is no comprehensive list of gifts in Scripture, and many gifts are simply mentioned without any definition or description. The gifts listed are simply offered as examples of the many ways in which the ascended Lord continues to operate through his Spirit to accomplish his mission on earth. Furthermore, the context in which gifts are expressed is not restricted to ministering to the needs of church members. Gifts should be used as an expression of God's concern for the needs of the world.

Preserving Tradition through Constant Change

Placing a strong emphasis on creative worship raises the question, What is the relationship, if any, between contemporary expressions of worship and the worship of the church as it has been expressed across the centuries and within many cultural settings? Is this rich tradition simply ignored, or is it mined?

Tradition is honored and celebrated not in attempting to reproduce the past in a very different present but in seeking to re-create the traditions, reinterpreting them so that they make the same impact today as when they were originally created. In seeking to be loyal to a form, people may thereby be guilty of destroying its intent.

If worship or church life is to remain indigenous, and if space is to be given to people to bring everything they have to God, then worship must constantly change, for culture is dynamic. Unfortunately, most churches are set up to function as static systems. The key is to ensure that structures do not prevent dynamism and connectivity.

Expressing God's Creativity

Creativity within the context of the emerging church is not simply an expression of the human spirit or a demonstration of personal ego. Rather, it provides evidence of the fact that we are made in the image of God. Creativity represents the outpouring of the gifts of God in all their amazing diversity and generosity. For creativity to be truly worshipful, it must point beyond the persona and the giftedness of the individual or the team of artists to the one who has enabled them to exercise their creativity. This means that the artists bring their skills under the reign of Christ and use their gifts to bring glory to God rather than to serve themselves or to attract the adulation of an audience.

Cultivating a Climate of Creativity

Emerging churches are characterized by creativity. Christ Community of Faith (Yorba Linda, CA) experimented with Quaker spirituality. Todd Hunter reports, "It had a Gen-X feel to it. Everyone shared a piece of art, poetry. All participated. Most were unsure of church." Chris Matthews (Red Café, Swansea, U.K.) says, "Creativity was definitely encouraged. It is part of our DNA now."

Holly Rankin Zaher of Three Nails, an Episcopal church plant in Pittsburgh, describes the tension between full creative participation and the professional performance of a few. "We are still trying to figure out how this works out. We are not wanting to be cheesy, and we have amazing musicians." She describes one highlight. "We had a church service called 'Redemption' in which some artists took garbage and made it beautiful. It was an installation piece. It was powerful. With art stations, we seek to create ways to be corporate and individual at the same time." Sometimes the church uses art installations and then ties them together with the Eucharist.

The encouragement of artistic expression entails experimentation and being prepared to take risks. Barry Taylor of Sanctuary (Santa Monica, CA) works with a community that is embedded in the arts and entertainment community and reflects this openness. "We were uncertain if it was even church when we were meeting weekly on Sundays. We were willing not to set anything in concrete. Instead, we explored what others were doing, and we read fairly broadly. Our church was always an experiment. Church was sometimes a conversation and sometimes liturgical. We changed everything at one time or another."

Creativity is not restricted to large communities with a range of gifted artists. Rachelle Mee-Chapman describes Thursday PM (Seattle) in the following terms. "We are a neo-monastic house church. We have art in our house meetings and create big events with lots of art. For Lent, our artists created a piece of art for each week. I picked out meditative parts for those art pieces, printed them, put them on the altar, and we had *lectio divina*. We learned about God from them." Another time, they created a labyrinth, a pathway laid out on the ground along which people walk in meditation. "I tell my crew they need to sink into the story, find their place in the story."

Roger Ellis of Revelation Church (Chichester, U.K.) admits that creative people are often disorganized and idiosyncratic. Consequently, they need an accountability structure in which to operate as a community. "Artists often can't initiate and are massively disorganized. They need a stage manager to coordinate and provide the environment, to listen to what is going on and integrate creativity. Leaders are there to hear and understand and create an environment. Good leaders serve as hosts in order to create an environment of high morale and trust where people can do their stuff."

Debbie Blue of House of Mercy (St. Paul) believes that a creative environment must permeate the entire church. However, this does not mean that leadership is not required. "I sometimes think we are more like artists than ministers of the institution. That means there is quite a bit of institutional chaos and a lot of creativity. I think it is what has made House of Mercy thrive. It also means we tend toward disorganization. The congregation is made up of a lot of artists, and it is no wonder. There are enough organized types, though, that we can pull together and muddle through whatever we need to."

Bringing What One Already Has

Dwight Friesen of Quest (Seattle) says, "People bring instruments and share songs, and I might bring a guided centering prayer as part of a worship experience, or we might sing at communion." People also bring icons, crosses, candles, statues, crowns of thorns, and artwork to their gatherings.

Sometimes the focus on creative gift giving is a matter of economics. Andrew Jones (Boaz, U.K.) says, "There is a lot of emergent thinking these days about gift giving, alternative economies, generosity, simplicity, frugalness. And, of course, most emerging churches don't have any money or a budget, so what they create will be simpler and less dependent on material forms than the more established churches that have a bank account to match their opportunities." Simon Hall of Revive (Leeds, U.K.) says, "Creativity has been a huge part of our practice and theology. I have a highly developed theology of worship that values the homemade gift more highly than the shop-bought gift."

For Mark Palmer of Landing Place (Columbus, OH) art is simply a part of what they do when they get together. "During the meetings, the arts are manifested somehow: through music, written meditations, poetry, liturgy, and stories from the early church. There is the opportunity for everyone to share. It is an open forum." In other words, their artistic expression is homegrown rather than reliant on outside sources.

Prioritizing Authenticity over Relevancy

Often, congregations and groups that are preoccupied with being relevant lose their authenticity in the attempt. When they try to be someone else, all they succeed in doing is providing a pale imitation. Those they are attempting to relate to see them as phony, no matter how well intentioned their efforts. In both worship and witness, it is essential to be oneself. Andy Thornton (Late Late Service, Glasgow,

U.K.) states, "Most people who actually experience something of God don't care how cutting edge it is. I'm aware that if I were to make worship with the belief that I am culturally in tune, I am deluded. When I listen to my music, my melodies are not contemporary. In general, that is where people come from. Most creativity is a bit of a mishmash. If you aim at being cutting edge and miss, it is five times worse than saying something authentic but a bit out of date."

Jonny Baker (Grace, London) says:

> Creativity is more authentic than seeking to target or be relevant. Alternative worship was often put into the youth box and didn't like it at all. It was at pains to point out that it wasn't a youth thing. I think youth stuff makes youth a target market to attract. The kinds of people coming to alternative worship hate being a target market via advertising, so they don't want to be involved in a church that is doing the same thing. I guess it's about a notion of authenticity. It feels more authentic to produce worship that we can relate to and other people will hopefully get than to say we are making worship to target someone else.

As the worshiping community is given permission to express itself, it gains in authenticity. It declares to all those with whom it comes in contact, "This is who we are. We are just like you, and you can be a part of us."

Involving Lighthearted Playfulness

Creative inspiration is not always intense. It can also be playful, as in the experience of Karen Ward of the Church of the Apostles (Seattle). "Visuals are a way to reimagine the kingdom. We play in the kingdom through ritual. Through exploring the parables of the kingdom, we worship, we play, we rehearse. We playfully act out the kingdom of God, play at the things of the gospel. Just as kids play dress up in grown-up clothes, in worship we purposefully play at acting out the kingdom in a small, broken way. We are participating in God."

It is important to capture this attitude of lightheartedness as a corrective to either the emotional intensity that leads to exhaustion or the somber dullness that prevails as a pall over worship. An emphasis on playfulness provides a safeguard against artists taking themselves too seriously and against downplaying the contributions of others. The playful approach also dispels intimidation and inhibition caused by a concern that one's contribution will not be up to the same standard as that of others, especially when the church contains highly talented art professionals.

Making Worship Sustainable

Sustainability is a struggle for a number of groups. Joel McClure reports that for a while at Water's Edge (Hudsonville, MI), they were creating worship installations (24-7 prayer rooms, stations of the cross, etc.), but it became too much work on a weekly basis. Now they do it on a monthly basis or when the artistic need arises. As Jason Evans describes, Matthew's House (Vista, CA) works similarly. Their creative activities lie primarily outside the home group at the monthly gathering. At their large monthly meeting, they set up art installations and a communion station. Most groups that put together these creative events do so monthly or quarterly. A weekly event is untenable. "Sustainable worship is a high value for us. We want most of our energy to be focused on the outside community, not on the service," declares Mal Calladine (Tribal Generation, Sheffield, U.K.).

Involving Rituals

Rituals, whether routinized expressions (consisting of familiar responses such as gestures or set prayers) or creative expressions, are meaningful and encourage participation when they provide an opportunity for the entire worshiping community to play an active role. Participating in rituals is like learning to dance. At first you may feel self-conscious while you are learning the steps. But you soon forget yourself when you find yourself dancing with freedom and hopefully with grace. Rituals facilitate and encourage participation of the congregation. They serve not only to facilitate a coordinated congregational response but also to enhance the collective impact. An absence of such ritual reduces a congregation to consumerism and passivity.

Sue Wallace of Visions (York, U.K.) says, "Image and action can reach people in a way that words alone cannot." Although intimidating at first, the obstacles to creative worship can be overcome. Wallace continues, "Multimedia isn't all that hard after all, when you have a chance to play and experiment with it in a safe environment." Dave Sutton of New Duffryn Community Church (Newport, U.K.) agrees. "We dabble in alternative worship and house music. We use liturgy quite a lot with rituals associated with symbols, pictures, banners, incense, candles."

"Very early on we realized that ritual was important," declares Andy Thornton (Late Late Service, Glasgow, U.K.).

> We put our worship together with ritual arts and a strong narrative. We wanted those who came to experience freedom within the rituals. In our services, we might sing together, introduce a theme, make some sort of a response with stations, light candles, and offer unspoken responses. At the end of the day, you didn't just listen. You were asked to move physically within the worship space. Consequently, you put your mark in the sand and declared, "This is where I stand." They didn't always articulate it, but generally people wouldn't leave without moving. They could make decisions without feeling that they were being watched.

Paul Roberts (Resonance, Bristol, U.K.) expresses the vision he and others had for a church to which attendees felt they could bring their spiritually minded friends who had never darkened the doorway of a church. "Part of the original vision of most groups begins with a sense that they could never in a zillion years bring a non-Christian friend to worship at the church they used to attend." Pete Rollins (ikon, Belfast, U.K.) describes their worship experience in a similar way: "Lots of people who attend and participate are artists and musicians. The words, rituals, use of painting and music are all created in-house rather than imported. Use of all the senses is vital."

Communicating Spirituality Publicly

Creativity, when pursued as an ultimate value, can result in groups that are simply expressing themselves in a self-focused manner. It is art for the sake of art. As a counter to this tendency, worship should be not only offered to God and shared among the members of the faith community but also offered to the world. Witness takes the form of overheard praise. Pip Piper describes his participation in maji (Birmingham, U.K.), which took the form of a monthly spiritual evening held at a local night spot that incorporated music, DJs, visuals, and art installations. "The key for me was that it was open to all and held in a venue constantly open to the wider public. It was an opportunity to express creatively something of Christian spirituality in a public arena and not just a public venue we had rented and then closed off for our own purposes."

Anna Dodridge (Bournemouth, U.K.), a member of an arts-centered Christian community, says, "For my core community group, creativity is very, very important. Most of us are connected in some way with creative stuff through music. We also have some artists, photographers, designers, and so on. I suppose it's another common point of interest we have. It is seen as very important that we use our creativity to honor God and to draw people to be interested in who we are and what we do. It's a brilliant way to meet people and something we can hopefully become influential in. If we can influence people, we can turn them on to God."

Ian Mobsby of Moot (London, U.K.) clarifies how Christians redefine the symbols of consumer culture and redirect these signs in worship to God. In this way, the church engages in the deepest parts of the culture, in a sense making their spirituality "public" while remaining consistent with the biblical tradition.

> Creativity is key to Spirit-led worship, and passionate living as a Christian in our postmodern world is important. It is not about selling out to our materialistic culture or the unquestioning embrace of materialism as a way of life. It is the counter-sanctification of redefining signs and symbols in our culture that point to God. God speaks into culture, and it is for us to follow where the wind blows. Yes, it is about not living a life of idolatry, such as thoughtlessly conforming to a totally consumerist way of being community and church. But we are a church that lives and operates within a consumer culture. The difference between living *in* but not being *of* consumer culture is key. The Puritans who withdrew from culture as an act of holiness did not recognize that the cost of this isolation was not to follow or to trust Christ in the culture. It is no coincidence that in a recent poll of evangelical Christians 90 percent feared contemporary culture. This is withdrawal, and the emerging church, as a much-needed corrective, is reengaging with our current culture seeking to follow what God is already doing.

Anna Dodridge (Bournemouth, U.K.) says:

> Some of us are part of this group called Nth Degree. The group is meant to be a community place for local Christians involved mostly in music but in other areas of creative arts too. It means that we all know one another and can work together, support one another, use one another's talents, like web design, film graphics, videos, recording, and so on. There is a big element of the Bournemouth music scene that is Christian. It seems to be an area God is really working in. It means we are meeting people, lots of people, sharing creativity that is God given, and knowing influential people and being influential ourselves. It's really very good stuff.

Worship "for us" and "by us" is not necessarily inward looking. Sue Wallace of Visions (York, U.K.) says, "I would be worried if there was no sense of vicarious worship (i.e., worship for 'them,' 'them' being the world outside, embracing the city and the people we meet day to day). We want our worship to inspire us to live our lives in such a way as to make a better world."

Taking Seriously the Context in Which People Live

Most churches rely on resources drawn from outside. In the case of traditional denominations, the resources come in the form of orders of worship and hymn collections. For independent and seeker churches, they consist of songs made available under performance licenses. Emerging churches are more concerned with developing indigenous forms of worship that take context seriously. Si Johnston of headspace (London) says, "We are trying to help people see that worship and mission need not be thought of in the traditional way. Thinking innovatively about mission means that we're constantly taking into account the ever changing contours of urban living. London living, as in Los Angeles, is constantly accelerating in nearly every way. Culture is driven from here, and so to be redemptive and not merely reactive in our mission, we've constantly got to be thinking creatively about this." Creativity allows for positive engagement with culture.

Mark Scandrette of ReIMAGINE! (San Francisco) creates environments, "green spaces," for Christians and local artists. Scandrette supports art installations, parties, experimental projects, and events. At an arts warehouse, the group hosts art-making weekends and studio nights. One night featured intercession and sculpture. On another occasion, members wrote graffiti prayers and ate meals with heroin addicts under the freeway. Through all these events, Scandrette's community seeks the kingdom of God in their context.

Andy Thornton reports that in the early days of the Late Late Service (Glasgow, U.K.), they had no interest in talking to other creative groups in the alternative worship movement. He respected the Nine O'clock Service in Sheffield, but he did not want to copy it. "We felt we should look like the externalization of our internal journeys and express our own spirituality. We didn't talk to anyone then. Each alternative worship group then was doggedly determined to keep its independence. In doing our own creative act, the Spirit became most manifest. It would have been less authentic if we had done what others did. It would have been less evangelistic as well." In other words, they believed their expression of church had to be fully indigenous to be authentic. They did not want to be labeled.

Barry Taylor of Sanctuary (Santa Monica, CA) says, "Our worship was naturally creative. We gathered together to talk about spirituality and made contextual music focused on the reality of our own experiences regarding the God we served." They write many of their songs and compose poems to describe their own spiritual journeys and to raise the questions and issues with which they struggle in the course of that journey. Their worship arises from the here and now as opposed to borrowing from elsewhere and another time.

Tribe (New York) throws parties at which Kenny Mitchell is the DJ, and the resulting atmosphere creates an access point with those outside their community. NGM (Bristol, U.K.) has a special ministry in training DJs for the club culture. Phil Ball reports, "Regarding visuals, NGM's DJs do stuff in clubs. In addition, they paint, have meditation, dance. A lot of our activities are in schools, at events, and at rock nights between 10:00 and 12:00 p.m. on Friday nights."

Creating Using Adaptation

Andrew Jones (Boaz, U.K.) provides some helpful insights regarding the subject of creativity, distinguishing creative adaptation from creation *de novo* (developing an original concept or image).

It should be said that, in first place, we are really talking about co-creativity over consumerism. We want to be involved creatively in the processes rather than become consumers of someone else's creative efforts. Second, creativity should not always be the process of creating new things. We are living in a post-novelty world. Things are not more valuable if they are newly created. Creativity in the sense of inventing new forms (how traditional church views it) can be a negative thing. There is a surplus of invention and resources. No one, for example, wants another web browser, and no one wants another computer system to add to PC, Mac, and Linux. Much better to have improvement and competence within existing standards. Much better to retrieve old and ancient practices than to invent new ones. The past is better than the future. The future is not a big deal—it will happen and is happening now. But the past is a precious resource that must be protected and rediscovered. This should be the focus of our creativity: making the old live again today in the forms we already have. If we need to make a new form, so be it, but new for newness sake is just more confusion and more work for everyone.

Using Technology

In some communities, media becomes the host, the lead person in the service. Andy Thornton of the Late Late Service (Glasgow, U.K.) highlights the significance of technology. "Media enabled one to get away from the cult of personality. We would put four or five images near one another, and they would speak to us with a certain resonance. With a narrative theme, worship could become a powerful environment. This would be over and against the one person who encourages us to worship from up front." However, he recognizes that technology must play a supporting role. "The technology stops, one person reads, acts. It's about our humanity. There are items that are especially important, like someone who would bare their soul."

Thornton also recognizes that there is a downside to technology. "People want to use technology to the extent of hiding behind the technology. The worst side of alternative worship is guys staying up late creating video loops while relationships with people who need them suffer. They don't get involved in helping people but in creating technology only."

Using Popular Culture

Andy Thornton (Late Late Service, Glasgow, U.K.) describes the tension between artists and evangelists that may apply to any emerging community.

> For many, art is its own justification, and this is one end of the spectrum—art doesn't need to fulfill a social function to have value. On the other end of the spectrum is the desire to achieve transformation within those who receive your outputs—changing lives. Artists don't ask the question, Did that work? It is the same difference between high art and commercial art. For the high artists, it is enough that the art was expressed, whereas for commercial art, the ends achieved are what matter. My take is that worship is a public event and that other people have to *get* what you are trying to say. People have a communal experience from what the artist brought. We are servants of a communal experience, and unless the congregation recognizes what you are doing, you are really not serving them.

Andrew Jones (Boaz, U.K.) explains that the use of popular culture involves prophetic critique as well as embrace.

There is a use of the culture's tools, as there should be. Jesus probably used a chisel. But there is a rejection and a prophetic reversal of the culture's tendency to embrace materialism. Emerging church people are leading the way in this. I can tell you of emerging church leaders who refuse to buy products if they suspect child labor, and of emerging church services that would not allow clothing with brand names into their holy place. In this area, emergents have gone farther than their parents in addressing the rampant consumerism and materialism that plagued the traditional churches.

Using Giftedness

Full participation, explored in the previous chapter, fosters creativity. When each person is empowered to express and develop his or her gifts, increasing diversity can be expressed, resulting in both creativity and ownership. By contrast, in a controlling environment that demands conformity and reduces people's responses to predetermined channels and patterns, creativity is frustrated. Despite a flood of literature on spiritual gifts and every-member ministry, the great majority of church members still have not been enabled to discover their spiritual gifts and the areas of ministry for which God has already equipped and called them. Emerging churches, with their goal of full participation and their appreciation of the distinctive contribution of each person, address this challenge.

Creative potential will be realized only to the extent that the leadership has a wide and comprehensive view of gifting and is able to develop individuals by providing opportunities for them to give expression to their God-given talents in a community that provides both affirmation and honest assessment. Emerging churches make space for creativity in their services. They encourage each person to bring what he or she has from culture into the worship space. Worship thus has integrity and reflects members' context.

Conclusion

Jesus ushered in the kingdom of God and invited his followers to join him in redeeming the world. Part of this redemption is participating in God's works of beauty, making all things holy. By creating as God's creation, we give back worship to God as a gift. Emerging churches make space for imagination to thrive. Worship is so important that everyone must bring all that they have, and that includes materials from their own worlds. Full of joy, these worship gatherings reflect the love the creation feels toward its Creator.

It is important to maintain the link between creativity and participation, otherwise creativity will become elitist and disempowering of those not considered creative by those who have talent and have been given the opportunity to hone their skills. Such a view is rooted in the theological conviction that every person is creative in one way or another for the simple reason that every person is the outcome of a Creator God, in whose image all have been made.

Creative acts of worship in which all participate are offered to the wider community as evidence of what God can do with seemingly ordinary material. Worship is part of the witness of the faith community to the wider community that God restores alienated humanity and in the process bestows beauty and creative energy. In a church service, boredom occurs through routinization and disempowerment. As part of a creative community, people are reenergized by the presence of the Spirit within and among them.

10

Leading as a Body

I would not make a good CEO, and I realized it would cost me too much to try to be that. It seemed like the most alive and best things about me would not thrive in the role of pastor. I also found out that I loved to write sermons and that I could preach, that people were really compelled by my sermons and my classes and my prayers and how I talked about God and the Bible. It just didn't seem like the church was the place to do that. To be a pastor, you had to be more CEO-ish and less an artist and interpreter of the faith.

Debbie Blue, House of Mercy, St. Paul

The preceding chapters examined the nature of the good news of the reign of God as demonstrated and proclaimed in the Gospels. They then related this message to the end of the sacred/secular divide, arguing for a holistic spirituality. They showed that the kingdom must be embodied in reproducible communities that are both a foretaste and a servant of the reign of God on earth. These communities need to engage in generosity within a pluralist society. Full participation and creativity are required for a community that takes the new life of the kingdom seriously. The task of leadership is to create or to help foster the above characteristics—not a small endeavor at all. It is evident that each of these practices requires discerning, multitasking leadership.

The Kingdom and Leadership

Participating in God's good news has a direct bearing on issues of leadership. Modernity has had its effect on leadership as well, with its various expressions of control in bureaucratic or McDonaldized forms. Emerging churches, in their attempts to resemble the kingdom, avoid all types of control in their leadership formation. Leadership has shifted to a more facilitative role as emerging churches have experimented with the idea of leaderless groups. The leader's role in such groups is to create a space for activities to occur.

Jesus, the Kingdom, and Modernity

In the new covenant, there are no patriarchs in the kingdom, for that place is reserved for God alone. Jesus is the head of any community under God. Leaders in local churches provide leadership and facilitate the wide range of ministries exercised through the membership of the body. The very nature of the kingdom of God leads to a reexamination of all views of power, as all previous power structures are made relative.

During modernity, the idea that Christians "participate with God" was lost.[1] Participation was replaced by a willful God who commands all reality through his awesome power. The modern God no longer had humans' ultimate good in mind. Rather, this God simply wanted complete obedience.[2] By reducing God to power, modernity removed the sense that a good and beautiful God participates with humans. Modern people fled from this God of unbridled power. They sought to create "safe zones" (the secular realm) so that God would not interfere with them.

Modern churches resemble this modern God. Their leadership is based on power, control, and submission to authority. For the church to resemble the kingdom of God, current notions of church power must be drastically altered. The church needs to operate as a consensual process in which all have a say in influencing outcomes. The church should resemble God's beauty as it displays a peaceable community through the nonhierarchy of the priesthood of all believ-

1. John Milbank, Catherine Pickstock, and Graham Ward, "Introduction: Suspending the Material: The Turn of Radical Orthodoxy" in *Radical Orthodoxy: A New Theology*, ed. John Milbank, Catherine Pickstock, and Graham Ward (London: Routledge, 1999), 1–20.

2. William Cavanaugh, "The City: Beyond Secular Parodies," in *Radical Orthodoxy: A New Theology*, ed. John Milbank, Catherine Pickstock, and Graham Ward (London: Routledge, 1999), 186.

ers. Individuals should be transformed as they become members of the body of Christ.

Leaders face the great challenges of pursuing the kingdom and motivating others to do the same, yet without using the primary tool of modernity: control. As Paul Roberts (Resonance, Bristol, U.K.) says, "For me the snag with controlling leadership is that it amounts to a denial of Paul's theology of the Spirit working in all members of the body." The only tools allowed in the kingdom are noncoercive (those that work within consensual processes of peace). Thus, the only legitimate mode of kingdom leadership is persuasion. However, control is very deceptive. Even using the language of "team," "customer," "empowerment," or "servant leadership" may simply hide the many areas of control within an organization. "Pastors must go beyond the rhetoric of the universal priesthood. 'Every member is a minister.' *You* can preach it a few times a year from the pulpit. But it is *you* who is still in the pulpit, and *you* are still seeing people from *your* office, as they make appointments with *your* secretary." In Alan Creech's view, "There are deep systemic problems with the whole deal" (Vine and Branches, Lexington).

When organizations find themselves in the midst of discontinuous change, occurring both within the institution and throughout the broader culture, leadership becomes a crucial issue. It goes without saying that leadership is always an issue in the life of any institution, but during unpredictable times, established leaders need to be prepared to jettison established patterns of operating that are no longer applicable in the new reality. They also need to learn new insights and skills to meet fresh challenges.

The church is no exception in this regard. It too must retrain existing leaders, especially when they represent a culture out of step with the changes taking place. The church must set a high priority to build new leaders who will function as different kinds of leaders. Emerging church leaders are already pointing the way. Yet at the same time, new leaders need adequate recognition, accountability structures, and appropriate training so that they will work with the kingdom and not against it. In other words, are they able to lead communities by consensus, persuasion, and without hierarchy?

While some point to the practices of the early church as a model for the priesthood of all, Ian Mobsby (Moot, London) puts forth his own ideas regarding the theological roots of participation.

It starts with an understanding of the Trinity as a community of mutually inclusive and serving components of God. There is no hierarchy. We are attempting to model this trinitarian understanding by having an active community approach that empowers all to have a voice, to help make decisions, and also a fluid community that people are free to leave or join. Services happen and are run by different people every time. I, as an Anglican deacon, have a role to advise decisions and to raise theological and other considerations. But it is the group that makes decisions.

Although Mobsby roots normative forms of leadership in the Trinity as opposed to the kingdom or the priesthood of all believers, the prescription is the same: give everyone a voice. In a nonhierarchical community, all members help make decisions and take turns leading, actions that serve as a counter to the control and oppressive tendencies of modernity.

For emerging churches, the key challenge is to dismantle all systems of control and to reconstruct a corporate culture according to the patterns of the kingdom. Leaders in emerging churches ask how they are to express the life of Jesus in this culture at this time. These are not questions of church structure per se. Much more fundamentally, they are kingdom questions. Structural questions of church can be considered only after the kingdom has proper priority. How much emerging churches utilize the kingdom as a leveling force determines the ultimate shape of their communities.

From Stifling Control to Creative Freedom

Emerging church leaders are opposed to any hierarchical understanding of leadership out of the conviction that it inevitably stifles people and creativity. Sue Wallace (Visions, York, U.K.) describes how Visions has changed in its understanding of leadership.

In the early days, we were quite hierarchical. We copied the way Nine O'clock Service (Sheffield, U.K.) publicly organized its leadership. So we had people in charge of various groups, such as music or slides, but these people in turn were accountable to the group leaders. We soon changed this, as we sensed that it was not a healthy way to run this sort of thing. We discovered it stifles creativity and crushes people. Other alternative service groups around the country who had a much more communal leadership structure, which felt freer and healthier, also inspired us. So in a sense, our structure was in reaction against NOS, which was structured like a bad example of a house church, complete with heavy shepherding.

But also our experimentation with different models of leadership was part of our journey to create a better way of being church.

Emerging churches form networks, not hierarchies. Joe Boyd maintains that Apex (Las Vegas) is nonhierarchical in that any house church can break with the Apex network at any time. The congregational network to which Tribe (Hollywood) belongs encourages its member congregations to each create its own covenant. The network strongly advocates for the priesthood of all believers. The network also affirms the global church, indigenous churches worldwide. The network is nonhierarchical, and through this network, churches are connected with local bodies elsewhere in the world.

From the Vision of the Leader to the Vision of All

Emerging church leaders regard the way vision casting is performed as a manifestation of modern systems of control. Brad Cecil (Axxess, Arlington, TX) says:

> I should say we do not desire the mission/vision process that is currently in play in corporate America and megachurches, as community cannot be defined by mission but rather by relationship. We *are* because of relationship. So we measure our success by our ability to maintain relationships rather than an arbitrary mission determined by a handful of leaders and driven down through the organization. While we tend to respond negatively to the Jim Collins (direction of the bus) [an example from *Good to Great*][3] style of focus, we do understand that mission and vision are in play. People have hopes and dreams. So we encourage the process of articulating the hopes and dreams of people to see what is common, and then leadership determines what resources should be committed. In a real sense, we are creating mission and vision all the time.

Emerging church leaders see the way vision statements are put together as ultimately mechanistic and reductionistic. Doug Pagitt of Solomon's Porch (Minneapolis) explains:

> The reason we don't have a mission statement is that it would be too long. It would change as new people come each week. Mission and vision statements are wrong when one person says this is why the community

---

3. Jim Collins, *Good to Great: Why Some Companies Make the Leap . . . and Others Don't* (San Francisco: HarperCollins, 2001).

exists and this is what we're doing. I ask these people why they are so reductionistic. Why can you only do this one thing? Most vision statements are nice thoughts, but they don't really cast any sort of vision. I just think these statements are so mechanistic. They have a fundamental misunderstanding of humanity. We're not called to any one thing. One person can't plan for everyone else.

Emerging church leaders do not disagree with vision statements, provided that the kingdom is not violated in the process, everyone is invited to share in the creation of the statement, and the Holy Spirit is in charge. Jason Evans (Matthew's House, Vista, CA) has no problem articulating a mission or vision statement, putting together what the Holy Spirit is saying to the community. Evans is not opposed to vision statements provided that each person can participate in its generation. To Alan Creech (Vine and Branches, Lexington), the value of vision/mission statements "depends on how much weight you put on these things. A bunch of what I wrote in 2000 still stands, but it has evolved. It is the Holy Spirit who is moving, and I don't know everything, and we move on and continue to listen as we go."

From Powerful Group Leaders to Leaderless Groups

Many emerging churches have experimented with the idea of leaderless groups. The Late Late Service (Glasgow, U.K.) was the first emerging church to structure itself as a leaderless group (1991). "The leaderless idea came in part from Glasgow's Late Late Service, which was fiercely democratic, reflecting the Scottish Presbyterian model, and partly arose from the postmodern culture of the people who set it up" (Paul Roberts, Resonance, Bristol, U.K.).

Some see the roots of leaderless groups going farther back. Andrew Jones (Boaz, U.K.) says, "I am sure there are many parallels with biblical and ancient forms of worship, which were more interactive and participatory than Reformation models. But for a more immediate link, I believe a lot of the thinking came from the 1960s counterculture, which is where almost all elements of emerging church can find some roots."[4] Perhaps another source of the leaderless idea was simply the postmodern critique of modern forms of control. Steve Collins (Grace, London) reasons that

4. For the purposes of this study, however, the Jesus People movements, although strong in community and social service, did not overcome the sacred/secular split. Therefore, they do not fit the criteria for emerging churches.

perhaps it was rooted in "postmodern philosophy and its deconstruction of power structures. Any reimagining of church in postmodernity was going to have to take that on board."

Other roots of the leaderless group in emerging churches stemmed from past experiences with controlling leaders. For Jonny Baker (Grace, London), "It is partly in response to very heavily led evangelical and charismatic leadership that people definitely don't want to repeat." Steve Collins (Grace, London) adds, "People who wanted to do church experiments quickly ran up against the existing power structures of the church. Maybe the powers that be wouldn't give permission, or they'd take it away once you'd started, or they wouldn't get what you were about. So the whole area of power immediately became problematic. It was something you needed to take a stand on or rethink, and the people who pushed through these envelopes to do something had been radicalized by their experiences and weren't going to behave the same way toward others."

Even if a leader is culturally savvy, emerging churches are wary of the powerful charismatic leader, and understandably so. Ian Mobsby (Moot, London) explains, "When the Anglican Church of England ordained the leader of the Nine O'clock Service, they modeled leadership on the same style as many evangelical forms as power leadership from the front. This eventually brought about its downfall. Their power-based leadership style led to a cult and to a moral scandal. This tragic downfall of a group that began with so much promise provided a lesson for all churches." It underlined the need for accountability. Emerging churches are wary of anything that resembles the unchecked power of the charismatic leader, which is not surprising given that many of the present leaders came out of charismatic churches that ran into the ground in the late 1980s.

The roots of the leaderless group could be as simple as the desire to be treated as a peer and with respect. In the words of Jonny Baker (Grace, London), "People are adults and want to be consensual about how they operate." For example, the Late Late Service (Glasgow, U.K.) was highly intellectual, with five Ph.D.s in the group. Shared leadership was the only decision-making approach that would be tolerated, according to founder Andy Thornton. "Shared leadership kept most people happy."

Whatever the roots of the leaderless group, be it Scottish Presbyterianism, the 1960s, postmodern deconstruction, a reaction to controlling charismatic leaders, or the desire for respect, some within emerging churches believe the leaderless option may be going too far. According to Kester Brewin (Vaux, London), "Some people are massively anti-leadership, which I think is more a reaction to poor experiences to the extent that the baby goes out with the bath water."

Paul Roberts of Resonance (Bristol, U.K.) reflects on the lessons he has learned in leaderless groups. "I am older now and am convinced that it does not work to strive for a leaderless group. If we had a clearer understanding of leadership, I think Resonance would see much more happening now, as I would have been able to build up leadership and pass it on prior to my change of job. To a degree, our idea of leadership didn't work. It didn't properly evolve, and in the end, it was a lack of consistent group support for the de facto leaders and their disenchantment that resulted in the services closing down."

Andy Thornton (Late Late Service, Glasgow, U.K.) is equally self-critical of the leaderless model. "If I were to start another group, I would definitely use a different model of leadership. Power in egalitarian groups such as ours manifests in who gets to say what, what is read, what is printed as the final statement of worship that night. The group had seven songwriters who challenged one another with the question, 'Who gave you the right to say what is a good lyric?' We had unspoken leadership, but this was not healthy."

Todd Hunter, formerly of Christ Community of Faith (Yorba Linda, CA), likes participation by all, but he does not like the idea of leaderless groups. He recognizes that participation by all does not necessarily imply that there are no recognized leaders. He asks, "Is it possible to give the gospel more than lip service yet not end up in a leaderless place? Once you put the church in its proper place, then leadership can be there." He asks an important question: If the kingdom is at work, if the community gets behind it and supports it, can the community then have leaders?

Leaderless groups do not advocate no leaders but simply that leadership be fluid, that all have a voice, that there be no named or appointed leader, and that leadership be flexible so that the right people lead the right things. In leaderless groups, there are those who function as leaders, depending on the task at hand. "I don't like the word *leaderless,* since all things are led, in some way. Every organization or movement is led. But like a flock of birds, that leadership is dynamic rather than static, and it is continually transferred to the right person at the right place at the right time" (Andrew Jones, Boaz, U.K.). So-called leaderless groups seek first to get the kingdom right and then talk about leadership.

From Leadership Based on Willingness to Leadership Based on Gifting

Some form of leadership is not only advisable but also inevitable. Whenever a group of people meets together for any length of time, someone will emerge as a leader. One individual may automatically take the lead, or the leadership may change according to the particular situation. The same individual may not constitute an appropriate or effective leader in every circumstance. That is the big difference in emerging churches.

A generally held opinion among those involved in emerging churches is that leadership is based on gifting. What no longer exists is one leader for all things. Kester Brewin (Vaux, London) says:

> I believe in leadership. People need direction. But we need to find models of it that have nothing to do with power. One of the most helpful things we've ever done at Vaux was to identify what roles people naturally take in a group situation. Some are really good at sparking off ideas; others are good at bringing them to completion, while others network. What is key is that to have a successful team you need all these gifts to be functioning. There are those who typically say very little in the heat of a discussion about an idea for a service but at the end of the evening are able to draw the whole thing together and rationalize what may have been a hectic brainstorm. We always make a point of referring to them, and it's amazing how well they distil stuff.

Leadership based on gifting requires people to give place to others. This means they acknowledge their own limitations as well as the gifting and the leadership authority and potential of others. One person leads one thing, and another leads another thing. Doug Pagitt of Solomon's Porch (Minneapolis) states, "Someone is always in charge, but it is not always the same people. Just because you lead something doesn't mean you lead everything. It's like chores. I do that right now. It is task oriented, not position oriented." Rob Graham of Levi's Table (St. Louis) says, "Leadership depends on what is going on and what we are trying to accomplish at a particular time." When gifts are respected and affirmed, leaders can take turns. Dave Sutton of New Duffryn Community Church (Newport, U.K.) is committed to setting a personal example. "I actively encourage people to get involved. We take turns leading."

Once gifts are discovered, the individuals with those gifts can be expected to lead in certain areas. Anna Dodridge of Bournemouth (U.K.) says:

Part of our commitment to one another is to invest in exploring one another's gifting and areas of strength and to help people develop their God-given abilities. After identifying areas of strength, we can then look to people to lead in those areas. For example, a couple of people in our community have been identified as particularly prophetic, so we invest in helping them develop that gift. They in turn help to lead prophetically and to encourage us in prophecy. The same goes with teachers, apostles, evangelists, pastors, and so on. Natural leaders emerge in the sense that people are naturally strong in certain areas.

Natural leaders emerge in the areas of gifting when given permission to do so.

A single leader produces a truncated form of Christianity, one that does not offer the richness of all gifts shared. Doug Pagitt (Solomon's Porch, Minneapolis) sees that shared and multi-gifted leadership is essential for the church to realize its true nature as the body of Christ. "I realized, as a professional pastor, I couldn't get to the kind of Christianity I wanted to live on my own. I needed other people around me to help me do that." Having many gifted leaders equates to a rich and vital community.

From Leadership Based on Position to Leadership Based on Passion

In emerging churches, those most passionate end up being the leaders. It is leadership by displaying enthusiastic and committed interest. Anna Dodridge (Bournemouth, U.K.) makes the following distinction: "I guess there is a difference between the core and the fringes. There are people who are very committed to the cause. They are committed to the idea of community church and also to the people involved. I guess these people are the main motivators, the ones who keep things happening. Their initiative and power to motivate make them mostly in charge of decisions because they are the ones implementing things as well as the ones that the decisions affect the most." She admits that it is a struggle to get a high level of commitment from everyone. "There are also people who are interested in the idea of community church and so come along to some of the more 'gathered' things we do, but they are mostly still part of passive and disconnected congregations and are not fully sold on the community church. There are people who are connected with us simply by being around and by being in relationship with us."

The hardest workers and those most active are the leaders. As Paul Roberts (Resonance, Bristol, U.K.) states, "Leadership at Resonance worked on the basis of a 'get-off-your-ass-ocracy' (i.e., those who were prepared to do stuff got the most say in how things happened)." Anna Dodridge (Bournemouth, U.K.) agrees.

> I guess leadership is linked with activeness. The people who emerge as obvious leaders are those individuals who most demonstrate passion for seeing the community develop and are really pushing for that. There are a few people who meet up to chat about the community and to pray for us and tend to coordinate the various things that are happening. Two of them have had leadership roles in congregational churches in the past. I suppose many of us are more concerned with our relationships in the community and aren't that bothered about the form the community takes. Others are really passionate about community itself as a form of church and want others to catch hold of that. The latter tend to take more of a leadership role in terms of shaping and developing the community.

From Authority Based on Position to Influence Based on Track Record

Leaders who have a good history with a group are those who wield the most influence. Although at Vaux leaders bear no official title, those who serve well are received as leaders by the group. As Kester Brewin of Vaux (London) describes:

> I guess you've probably bought something from Amazon z-shops or E-bay at some point. My developing view on leadership is that the systems on those sites that allow feedback ratings to emerge have something important to tell us. We can choose to buy from whom we like, but we are more likely to buy from those who have an established track record of trust and good service. In the same way, while Vaux has no specified leadership, it does have an unspoken trust/merit system where more weight is bound to be given to the ideas of those in the group who have shown consistent commitment and have a track record of good output. We've come to see this as essential to stop what is effectively an open community of artists being diverted off course by any old person who turns up and has a view.

Steve Collins (Grace, London) echoes Brewin. "A bunch of friends doesn't mean no leaders, just no formalized positions but rather leaders who deserve to be so considered. Their status is given by the group rather than taken by the person or imposed by an institution."

Those who have something significant to say are the ones others listen to. But as open as this model is, it can still disguise subtle forms of exclusion. Jonny Baker (Grace, London) says, "We have discussed on several occasions that while we have an open process there are people who hold a lot of personal power (i.e., they get listened to, have sway). This is often a difficult thing to see and name, but it is a danger. We have wondered at times whether we are in danger of having hidden decision-making processes because of this. But my hunch is that as long as we keep the discussion about that going, it's okay."

"There are always power issues in worship," concedes Sue Wallace of Visions (York, U.K.). "After the public downfall of the Nine O'clock Service in Sheffield [1995] and the leadership team's abuse of power came to light, we reacted against this. We brought in a group dynamics counselor to work with us to make sure that even in our communal decision making we were not silencing the quiet people or manipulating anyone in any way. We were wary of making any leadership decisions for a while for fear of being manipulative. Over time these fears passed, and now we have a fairly healthy method of running Visions."

From Closed Leadership to Open Leadership

Joel McClure of Water's Edge (Hudsonville, MI) says, "Anyone who showed up in response to a general invitation could lead. Anyone who wanted to be part of the leadership could come. The meeting was open. Six decided to commit to that, four men and two women. We aren't against structure, but we are for healthy structures." Doug Pagitt of Solomon's Porch (Minneapolis) echoes McClure. Leadership is open to anyone at Solomon's Porch. It is the same at Sanctuary (now called New Ground) in Santa Monica, California. Anyone who shows up can be a part of things. They feel the risks entailed in having too many voices are far less than the risk of being exclusive, reports Barry Taylor.

For Pip Piper and maji in Birmingham, U.K., leadership is open to both first-timers and the most experienced. "The leadership is organic and open. Everyone, whether they have been around and in relationship with people like myself for years or they have been here only twice, has equal access and voice to help shape the next gathering or to offer assistance and participation."

For Tribe (Hollywood), the idea of a segregated leadership meeting was anathema, says Rebecca Ver Straten McSparran. "There will always be people who have different jobs, but to have a tier of people who meet privately as a special group of leaders is not what we want. Anyone is invited to leaders meetings. There are no secrets. No group is meeting in isolation planning for everyone else."

For Rachelle Mee-Chapman of Thursday PM (Seattle), leadership is modeled on Dorothy of *The Wizard of Oz*.[5] "Everyone who wants to come along can come along. Eschatology is Oz, the kingdom. I only know how to tell them to get back to the yellow brick road. I am rethinking what it means to be a leader. Leadership is totally open. There may be some who come who are better leaders. My job is simply to make sure they are on the yellow brick road."

From Leaders Setting the Agenda to Congregational Agenda Setting

In many emerging churches, leadership is implicit rather than explicit. In other words, leaders emerge naturally through the recognition and affirmation of the community. It may be the case that nobody bears an official title. In the Late Late Service (Glasgow, U.K.), no one was assigned to do anything; all were volunteers. All owned the community. It was egalitarian, although as Andy Thornton points out, "Natural leaders emerged." Each year, five were elected as the steering group. However, the most experienced leaders were often looked to regardless of their elected status. As Mark Scandrette of ReIMAGINE! (San Francisco) says, "Leadership is implied, and no one calls it Mark's group." There is often a deep concern with giving one person a title. Alan Creech of Vine and Branches (Lexington) describes his situation in the following terms: "Yes, there are elders and leaders, but what do we mean by titles? Does that title mean I am the dude through whom everything happens?"

In emerging churches, the authority to speak is rooted in the congregation. Peter Rollins describes how ikon (Belfast, U.K.) is looking to do some very different things, but they do it together. "The leadership model is quite directional in the sense that we have a strong sense of attempting to chart a different path. But there is a high level of participation, and the directorial type of leadership arises from democratic, organic flows of communication and reflects the desires of the people. If there is conflict, we will not push ahead in an area. In this way, the 'voice from the front' is the voice of the congregation echoed back."

5. Brian D. McLaren, "Dorothy on Leadership, or How a Movie from Our Childhood Can Help Us Understand the Changing Nature of Leadership in the Postmodern Transition," *Rev. Magazine* (November/December 2000), www.emergentvillage.com/downloads/resources/McLaren/Dorothy onLeadership.pdf (accessed June 2, 2005).

Emerging church leaders do not set an agenda but rather facilitate a process by which the community sets the agenda. Karen Ward, Church of the Apostles (Seattle), says that she would use material only if someone from her community were excited about it. As a pastor, Ward does not initiate new programs. It must come from the community. "We're organic in that way," she insists.

When leadership is understood as servanthood, the power remains with the people. As Sue Wallace says, "As a Visions (York, U.K.) employee, I do make decisions at times. Sometimes, someone has to! But I defer to the group wherever possible. Sometimes I have to jump first and ask later, but in reference to what I previously know the group's will to be. For me, the difference is that I am the servant of the group, not its ruler. So it is more a question of where the power rests. The power rests with them, not with me."

From Exclusive Decision Making to Inclusive Consensus Building

When leadership is exercised by a community as a whole, and when leadership functions change according to the situation, how are decisions made and adhered to?

The process of consensus decision making can be quite difficult. Jonny Baker of Grace (London) shares his experiences. "I actually found the leaderless thing quite a challenge at first. I had come from leading a Youth for Christ team where we were much more directive, albeit as a team. But it was a good discipline for me personally to submit ideas to the group knowing that no one's viewpoint carried more weight than another's, and if the group didn't like them, then it was tough. But it was definitely a group-owned decision-making process. I think it is an important value."

Consensus decision making involves differing levels of agreement. Simon Hall describes the way Revive (Leeds, U.K.) makes decisions.

> The leadership team has a monthly day of prayer and fasting. We meet in the evening, with anyone from the church welcome to join us. Being a Baptist church, we have church members' meetings and have so far made all our decisions by consensus. We try to distinguish between "I think this is a bad idea, but you're my community, and if you want to do it, I'll still back you," and "I really believe God is against this." If we get any of the latter (and we have occasionally), we don't make a decision. I realize this can put a lot of pressure on the dissenters, but we try to take them seriously. We try to get agendas out as early as possible and

ask people to pray over them. We also have days away/retreats when the church needs time to think about things seriously.

Emerging church leadership is bestowed by the community rather than claimed by an individual. It arises out of an intrinsic authority that the community recognizes and acknowledges rather than out of a formal position or title. It is invested from below rather than imposed from above. Because leaders are affirmed by the congregation, decision making is necessarily consensus based. A consensus determines which way a church goes. The leaders simply create the context for this to occur.

Team Leadership

Emerging churches share the conviction that leadership must not be invested in one person. Spencer Burke (Newport Beach, CA) expresses this in a radical form when he claims, "I'm still a sheep, not a shepherd. We might have older and younger sheep, but we're still sheep. I am a fellow traveler." If there is a specified leadership team, the leaders make their decisions in community. Debbie Blue of House of Mercy (St. Paul) states, "Since there are four of us (Russell Rathbun, Mark Stenberg, me, and Chris Larson) as leaders, there are really four different styles of leadership. We've often joked that it's a benevolent multiheaded dictatorship, and there's probably a shred of truth in that. As a staff we work out a lot together, make decisions, figure out what seems a good direction to go or event to have, and then we present it to the board. They trust us and are inspired by our vision."

Ben Edson of Sanctus1 (Manchester, U.K.) reports:

We're exploring the whole leadership thing at the moment and expanding it out. Basically, I am the leader because I am a full-time, paid Anglican minister and my job was to set up and run Sanctus1. However, leadership within Sanctus1 is a bit more shared. There is a woman who is part of the leadership team with me and also another woman who has taken on a pastoral role. We are currently in the process of delegating some responsibility for pastoral care within Sanctus1 to two core people. This will enable a greater level of pastoral care for the members of Sanctus1 and develop particular gifts. We are also establishing a group that will develop the wider mission of Sanctus1, again encouraging and developing gifts.

Team leadership facilitates leadership initiatives and helps all members identify and exercise their various gifts. A leadership team that operates as an elitist group and marginalizes and disempowers the membership is a debilitating factor.

Transitioning from Open Leadership to a Community of Leaders

Many groups that begin with the ideal of open leadership come to recognize that some individuals are the problem solvers, vision casters, and initiative takers. Brad Cecil of Axxess (Arlington, TX) describes the process by which they went from open leadership to a leadership community. "The larger community had open leadership. We allowed anyone who desired the opportunity to participate in the decisions of the greater community. As we have grown, we have transitioned from a leadership community consisting of those who responded to that open invitation into a representative leadership team. This is a representative style of polity that has voices from each of the communities instead of anyone who wants to come."

Evolving to Representational Leadership

As churches grow, it becomes increasingly difficult for everyone to be involved in the decision-making process. Some churches then move to a combination of consensus and delegated decision making. In some cases, churches transition completely from participatory to representative leadership. To avoid this, some churches spin off new smaller congregations. However, when churches decide that it makes more sense to continue to grow, then the leaders must be proactive to ensure that they do not become increasingly distanced from the congregation. When that happens, people can become disempowered, disgruntled, or passive.

Sue Wallace of Visions (York, U.K.) reports:

Leadership is not always consensus based. Our group consists of a number of fairly easygoing people who are willing to go ahead with a majority sometimes. However, day-to-day service-running decisions are more based on a delegative structure. Paul's body analogy is the best one here really. On any one Sunday, someone will be delegated to run slides, someone to do video, someone to DJ, someone to be responsible for whatever form of teaching happens, etc. They will effectively be in charge of that item that night. The next week it will be someone else. It's not really that different from the structure Paul mentions in 1 Corinthians, when everyone comes to the meeting with something. The service theme is taken from the lectionary. The general feel and angle of the service are planned by the whole group in a·fairly informal way (usually over food), and the details are left to the people in charge that night. I organize the rotation as to who is doing what and when, but according to people's own wishes. In that sense, leadership merely becomes organization.

In the same way, Ben Edson (Sanctus1, Manchester, U.K.) combines both shared and delegated forms of leadership in an effort to remain truly representational in a situation of numerical growth and population mobility. "I try to share the leadership, but I find that if Sanctus1 needs to be driven, it is helpful to have the authority to do that." When leadership becomes decentralized to the point that it permeates the entire group, it can paralyze the group rather than empower each member. Ian Mobsby (Moot, London) shares his experience. "The Epicentre Network ended because the group was not sustainable. People disagreed about everything to the point that there were two different groups—one very cynical, which felt very disabling, and the other wanting to move on, which was the beginning of Moot. When a church gets like that, it needs to end."

Representational leaders need to ensure that there is an extensive communication network and that subgroups representing various areas of ministry are reporting decisions to the community. At Tribe (Hollywood), the smaller leadership group reports its decisions to the larger community. It is this openness that resonates with members. "How we bring our discussions back to the community is key. Making decisions together is part of what everyone likes about Tribe. We bring our discussions back to the larger community, always aware of how subtly we can become secretive and exclusive" (Rebecca Ver Straten McSparran).

What Leaders Do

Leadership represents a wide range of functions. Each leader, in addition to functioning as a generalist, brings specific skills to bear that are in line with his or her gifting, technical training, and experience.

From Mediators of God to Facilitators of Ministry

Emerging churches work more like an extended family or a movement than an organization. They are not seeking to create organizations but organic movements. Unfortunately, this is a different sort of challenge than is put forward in many leadership books. Most leadership training reinforces the clergy/laity division. "The problem with the theology of most leadership material is that it causes people to believe that they don't have access to God except through their leader. They can't help others because they aren't ministers. They feel less-than the ones in charge, those who stand at the front" (Alan Creech, Vine and Branches, Lexington). Creech believes this teaching is dangerous to the body. Jason Evans of Matthew's House (Vista, CA) comments, "According to the old way, the leaders were still regarded as mediators. Instead, we want the people to follow the Holy Spirit, *not* us." When someone asks Karen Ward (Church of the Apostles, Seattle) who the leader is, she responds, "We hope the Holy Spirit. We want to allow the Holy Spirit to lead." Unfortunately, much leadership material does not help leaders overcome modernity—how to step back, refuse forms of control, give space for the Holy Spirit to work, and create contexts for the priesthood of all believers to be expressed.

Leaders who see themselves as mediators instead of facilitators usually operate as people who control rather than people who make connections. Controllers operate on a principle of divide and conquer, whereas facilitators bring people together who can become creative through collaboration. Andrew Jones (Boaz, U.K.) reflects:

> I think the type of leadership found in alternative worship is similar to how leadership is exercised in other disciplines: art projects, collaborating on group projects, creating new organizations, leading in a chaotic environment. Emergent theory in computer systems and biological organisms is showing us why Solomon told us to observe the ant (Prov. 6:6) and its ability to build community without a single big leader calling the shots on every decision. The business world is now quoting Scripture to help itself give leadership to its projects. Maybe it's time for the church to put down the management books and pick up the Bible to see what all the fuss is about.

Emerging church leaders function as facilitators by overcoming the sacred/secular divide and enabling people to recognize their skills and experience as gifts from God to be used for the furtherance of his kingdom in every domain of life. By inculcating this realization, leaders can facilitate a much fuller participation as more and more people recognize the significance of what they have to offer.

Steve Collins (Grace, London) adds, "Leadership becomes facilitation—creating and protecting something that treats other people as creative equals. You don't know who is going to be God's leader for the next situation. It might be anybody. It might not be you. So this lack of structure isn't just a game; it's an open door for the Spirit." Chris Matthews (Red Café, Swansea, U.K.) makes this same point. "Leadership is facilitative rather than directive. Many people have participated in leadership, sometimes for a specific period. We have lots of people around who have been involved in leadership in the past and are still part and parcel of the church even though they aren't leading now."

Si Johnston (headspace, London) states:

> Facilitative leadership allows for community-led leadership. My intuition is telling me that church should be wholly communitarian in its setup, but it also needs leadership. So how can it be communitarian yet also have leadership? While I detest the CEO approach to church leadership and would much rather have the more passive approach, people, even sophisticated London Gen-Xers with their alleged hermeneutic of suspicion toward authority, desire leadership. I want them to view my leadership as more of a facilitative kind, which advises and keeps things orthodox. I sense that it's largely nondirective and much more supportive, which is a conscious effort because I'm an entrepreneur and have the ability to run over people to get things to where I think they should be.

From Using a Centralized, High-Control Approach to Using a Relational, Decentralized Approach

A controlling style of leadership is more masculine, and male domination within the church has firmly entrenched this particular style. Rebecca Ver Straten McSparran of Tribe (Hollywood) represents a different approach. It is clear that she is the pastor, but not in a traditional sense, because she does not control things. She created a different model of pastoring. "I have a female way of doing things."

However, a high-control versus a relational style must not be regarded as a gender issue. Mike Breen, who has moved on from being rector of St. Thomas's Church, Crookes, Sheffield, to lead the Order of Mission launched by the church, describes his leadership style as "zero control, high accountability, and low maintenance." Under his leadership, the church has grown to be the largest of any denomination in the north of the U.K. But the model is a decentralized missional expression of church in contrast to the centralized megachurch.

In the U.K., the most vital movements are those in which no control is exerted over the various subgroups within a larger church community.

High accountability without control is amply illustrated by Mike Breen's relationship with Mal Calladine. The decentralized manner in which Tribal Generation is run is impressive. Many leaders are empowered, energized, fully engaged, and supportive of one another. Roger Sutton's (Altrincham Baptist Church, Manchester, U.K.) hand-off approach toward Cameron Dante, who works as a DJ in the clubs of Manchester, while holding himself accountable to the board of deacons of the church, is noteworthy as well. Sutton models the high-accountability, zero-control model. Steve Collins of Grace (London) adds, "I get cynical about events that claim to be alternative worship that leave the power structures untouched. The change in power structures creates the innovation and ensures its authenticity."

Decentralization empowers, whereas centralization disempowers. Leaders who use a decentralized approach delegate responsibilities along a chain of command. "We've pretty much stopped organizing things centrally because nobody enjoys doing them," comments Simon Hall of Revive (Leeds, U.K.). "The main downside of this is that it's very hard to do anything that requires 'a long obedience in the same direction' (to quote the title of a book by Eugene Peterson), because there is little structure to keep things going if someone loses heart."

From Creating Tasks to Creating Space

Leaders must create a space for others to do the work. If they do not, they will end up carrying the entire responsibility for the tasks of the congregation. According to Si Johnston (headspace, London):

> We, as a leadership, have emphasized maximum participation but found that week after week the leadership team had to accept full responsibility for services. We were talking about participation but not facilitating it structurally. This was consumer church with an alternative worship gloss. Now, after a year, we've cancelled one of the fortnightly leadership meetings and have decided to have a community-planning meeting where we plan services and talk "church and mission." The core community, which numbers about thirty to forty, turns up for this when we plan and pray together.

Gift-based ministry does not flourish in a controlling environment. This is evidenced when controlling pastors preach sermons and lead seminars on spiritual gifts, but all their teaching fails to translate into getting more people involved in a wider variety of ministries. Creating awareness without creating space simply leads to mounting frustration followed by apathy.

Among the leadership team, space needs to be created for individual leaders to explore fresh avenues of thinking and to start new initiatives. Mark Scandrette (ReIMAGINE! San Francisco) wants to be an explorer leader. He asks, "Who wants to go with me? I want to dabble in many things. I am very interested in how cultural forms express the kingdom of God. I want to explore the message through the arts. I want to create a spoken-word piece of humanity and divinity together." Mark's comments reveal his role as a thought leader, connecting the dots to come up with new concepts.

From Equipping Members to Equipping Missionaries

Leaders must embrace more than simply giving space and opportunity to others. They must at the same time help people increase their competency level as missionaries. According to Simon Hall (Revive, Leeds, U.K.), leaders are to equip "the saints for ministry." And this ministry is in the world. "I happen to think that ministry doesn't refer to doing stuff in church meetings." To equip others, their gifts must be identified and affirmed. Members also need the space and the opportunity to develop their gifts through the hard knocks of experience.

Such participation includes every age group within the faith community, especially the youth. Phil Ball of NGM (Bristol, U.K.) says, "First, the leaders lead cells, and then the youth lead cells for their friends. If youth want to create something, the leaders facilitate it, knowing that they learn through doing, through being trusted. The leaders, working in teams, help them. They seek to be leaders who work themselves out of a job." For NGM, identifying and equipping new leaders is a high priority. As Chris Matthews of Linden Church (Swansea, U.K.) explains, "We currently have a large team of NGM volunteers: singers, musicians, DJs, youth workers, etc., who are involved in supporting the work here in Swansea as well as in other locations in Wales."

From CEO to Spiritual Director

Leaders stand at the side and ensure that groups are healthy. Ian Mobsby (Moot, London) sees his role in the following terms. "My role is to help keep the community healthy, to be a pastor for prayer and pastoral needs, to be a mediator when things go wrong, and to be custodian to a vision to keep the group journeying together. This form of leadership operates as facilitator, advisor, empowerer, envisioner, and permission giver. This helps others to lead sessions and the group. I think it works well at the moment."

Rebecca Ver Straten McSparran (Tribe, Hollywood) is heavily involved in spiritual direction and mentoring. Alan Creech of Vine and Branches (Lexington) maintains the same ministry priority. "My view of pastor/overseer has changed radically from a person in charge, one who had to exercise hierarchical control or risk chaos, to pastor as spiritual director, as a person who sits back and watches the community as a member of it. I look and see how things are going. I listen to God about the community. I am much more familial and more relational. Pastor is not a title, does not receive a paycheck, and has no positional authority. I have functional authority as I operate in charismatic giftedness at a certain maturity level." Simon Hall (Revive, Leeds, U.K.) adds, "I am trying to follow people through the process of growing up and helping people at different stages of faith listen to and appreciate one another."

Dwight Friesen of Quest (Seattle) says, "The church might employ someone in the future, but probably not to do the things that everyone should be doing. We are moving toward leadership being a bit more about *paraclesis,* that sense of coming alongside as an advocate, friend, encourager, and defender. So the whole team is going to be trained as spiritual directors." Alan Creech (Vine and Branches, Lexington) says, "I'm the pastor, the leader, the overseer, but it doesn't mean I can do anything I want. I have vision input, but the group changes what I put out there. It evolves with everyone's input. No one asks my permission to do things. I am the spiritual director of the community." Creech continues, "I used to tell people what to do, trying to solve their problems. I don't do that now. I refuse to solve their problems. I don't have to have an answer to their problems. I want to fix someone, come up with a great answer, be the wise guy, but instead I need to listen."

Mark Palmer (Landing Place, Columbus, OH) shares the same opinion. "I'm less about making things happen and more about just being available, to be a guide. Although I am only thirty, I am the spiritual father to this community. I pour myself into their lives. I want them to be so much farther ahead than when I was twenty-four. The best thing I can do is be available to them." But the task is by no means easy. "Dismantling bruised egos is a tough job in order to help them come to a healthy place of faith and life," says Si Johnston of headspace (London).

Spiritual direction comes even before membership. Quest (Seattle) does not "possess" its members. In fact, Dwight Friesen encourages people to move on when need be. He asks, "How do we decrease so God can increase? What are your dreams, and how do we help you get there? We are highly educated and motivated people in Christ and his cause. We have some really good people, and it is a shame to keep them in one spot." Friesen wants to help them find their next step of ministry.

From Mobilizer to Participant

Mobilizers are concerned to get people involved to cover a multitude of tasks. They should first ask themselves whether *they* should be the ones to get involved. By taking the initiative, they may become an inspiration to others who will want to get involved rather than feeling obligated to do so.

Leadership emerges as people are led by the example of servant leadership. Levi's Table (St. Louis) enlisted the help of Church of the Saviour (Washington, DC) to train them in servant leadership on a monthly basis. Rob Graham recounts the following story, which illustrates some of his change in thinking. As the dates for the Servant Leadership School approached, Graham was frustrated that no one in the community had volunteered to watch the kids. His wife asked, "What is the name of the school?" Graham says, "Bam! That hit me. I volunteered to watch the kids during the leadership school. The words came alive for me and for the group. 'The greatest among *you* will be the servant.' If we want spiritual power, we must be the servants of all. It is then that we gain the authority to speak."

From a Staff Approach to a Volunteer Approach

Andrew Jones (Boaz, U.K.) offers a pragmatic reason why so many emerging churches do not have formal positions and a paid leadership. "A lot of emerging churches don't have professional leadership. It would be easy to say this is a biblical response—that the New Testament church had a plurality of elders, not a single pastor. But the fact may be more pragmatic and economic. With the current movement of thousands and thousands of emerging churches globally, within a short period of time, there are neither the resources nor the strategic desire to place a paid professional at the head of each emerging church."

Most emerging churches are small, and many do not enjoy the sponsorship of a denomination or parent church. Therefore, financial concerns are a big issue. In the case of Grace (London), Jonny Baker explains, "Grace is very small. The people involved are professional and incredibly busy. We struggle to all get together to plan anything. It's that life stage for us all. There is no one employed to work on behalf of Grace as a pastor/facilitator/administrator/priest, so it's a volunteer thing."

Some leaders, such as Simon Hall (Revive, Leeds, U.K.), see paid leadership as disempowering of or taking initiative from other leaders.

> Where we're headed at the moment is that I think I need to step down from paid employment by the church. Humanly speaking, I started this thing, and I am still running it. That leaves little room for others to innovate or even take major responsibility. We recently had a church weekend away, and it was only after someone had said something to me that I realized that over the weekend I had defaulted into lone-ranger, do-it-all mode. The reason was a combination of knowing that this was the path of least resistance and no longer having faith that people wanted to participate. I think there might be quite a few people who agree with me that I'm the best at doing everything (for the record, that's irony and a confession rolled into one), so I need to get out of the spotlight to help people do it themselves.

Alan Creech (Vine and Branches, Lexington) sees a paid professional ministry class as extremely crippling and feels that there is a revolution currently under way to challenge that long-held concept.

Conclusion

Leading in such a way that points to the presence of the kingdom—through servanthood and consensus expressed in collaboration—requires leaders to recognize that God's kingdom always precedes them. They must lead as servants, facilitators, and consensus builders. Living in such a peaceable, consensus-building way is itself a prophetic witness to the rest of society, which is so often destructively competitive and polarized. It demonstrates God's order, which contrasts sharply with modern methods of control.

Within the church, many leaders represent a hierarchical and controlling understanding of leadership. This has resulted in a growing restlessness among many younger leaders who represent a culture of networking, permission giving, and empowerment. Many discussions of leadership disregard the life of Jesus, as if leadership involved a set of neutral principles to be applied in any context. The kingdom disrupts these power structures. In the kingdom, the servants rule, not the powerful elite. The ones who have no voice are given a voice. So a new set of questions emerges: What kind of structure is required for a community that pursues the kingdom? What kind of structure does not violate the very nature of the kingdom?

To Dieter Zander (Quest, Novato, CA), the primary qualification for leadership is that one is actively learning how to live in the kingdom of God as an apprentice of Jesus. What is needed is an alternative form of leadership that embodies the servant model demonstrated and espoused by Jesus himself and that he expected from his followers. This style of leadership operates for the benefit of all so that each person can realize his or her full potential. It is not a style that disempowers and inhibits. Such leadership must always benefit those who are led rather than enhance the power and prestige of a few. Such leadership functions as a team. It is constantly forming additional teams, each contributing to the overall vision of the community. Leaders who follow the kingdom lead not by controlling but by connecting. They bring people together to generate synergy through the combining of visions, gifts, and experiences for the diversifying of the church's mission and its continuing outreach in society.

Emerging churches have been greatly influenced by the kingdom, and this includes their ideas regarding leadership. They look to avoid modern forms of control at all costs. The key idea is that leaders emerge based on the activity at hand and are not the sole leaders of a group. All are welcome to the leadership table. Consensus decision making is the norm. If a leadership team is chosen, these leaders operate as spiritual directors, mentors, and facilitators.

11

Merging Ancient and Contemporary Spiritualities

We needed a way of life, a way to pattern our lives on Jesus. Historical practices are ways to do this. They make sense of the world and provide a framework for our lives.

Jason Evans, Matthew's House, Vista, CA

It's funny how we talk of "bringing things to God"—like he wasn't there all the time. What we're really doing is bringing our attention to bear on the relationship between things and God that already exists and maybe making a few conscious adjustments to our own place in that relationship.

Steve Collins, Grace, London

It was easier to define the spiritual when the sacred/secular split was intact and the kingdom was not a central pursuit. Then the spiritual was all the things one did at church or in one's heart or in holy places. It is harder to define the spiritual now that communities are overcoming the sacred/secular split and are pointing to the kingdom in all spheres of reality. Because spirituality connects to all of life, both life as an individual and life in the faith community, is there a danger it will lose its significance? If welcoming the stranger and feeding the poor are spiritual activities, then what about prayer? Is it spiritual or more spiritual or even necessary?

When Jesus taught his disciples to pray, he taught them to ask for the kingdom to come and for his will to be done as it was in heaven. The new way of life that Jesus inaugurated, the incoming reign of God in which the outsider was included, the poor were shown generosity, and enemies were loved, was to continue to be their focus in prayer. Taking our cue from Jesus and the disciples, we see that prayer is one aspect of spirituality, just as caring for others is. It is not the sole act or a superior act of spirituality, but it is a necessary act all the same.

The pervasive practice of spirituality in Western culture marks the beginning of postmodernity, for as mentioned, modernity created secular space. Modernity separated spheres of reality into neat boxes. The so-called fact realms of the economic and the political were separate from the so-called value spheres of art, music, and religion. The recognition that this division was artificial demonstrates the pervasive influence of postmodernity, and the interest in spirituality is a significant manifestation of this shift. We live in an era in which interest in religion is hitting new lows while interest in spirituality has never been higher.[1] Unlike in the period of Christendom, lower church attendance does not equate to lower interest in spirituality.

Adherents of postmodern religions (actually all religions that are not modern) tend to practice a holistic way of life. They observe that all of reality is sacred and that all dualisms are simply metanarratives proffered by those in power. Postmodern culture pushes for boundaries to be overcome. For the most part, however, the overcoming of the split between the sacred and the profane is foreign to mainstream church practice, as shown in chapter 4.

Spirituality is something of a buzzword throughout the Western world. In part, it represents a reaction to the soul-starved secularization that has permeated culture. It represents a longing to experience both the transcendent and the immanent in all realms and to give a sense of intrinsic worth and cosmic significance to the individual. It also serves to integrate body and soul, the internal and the external world. In a society characterized by fast-paced living, increasing uncertainty, growing demands in the workplace, and family pressures, spirituality is valued as providing coping mechanisms.

Within emerging churches, there is also a strong emphasis on spirituality. Among many postmodern evangelicals, it is especially attractive as a counter to the hyperactivism that has characterized particular traditions.

1. David Lyon, *Jesus in Disneyland: Religion in Postmodern Times* (Oxford, U.K.: Polity/Blackwell, 2000), 84–85.

Hyperactivism arose as churches emphasized performance and achievement while undervaluing contemplation and physical relaxation. Hyperactivity ignores the need for a healthy, balanced rhythm. Spirituality is also a reaction to the adrenaline addiction created by some high-energy, high-volume, contemporary worship styles. Such postmodern people are searching for a quiet place with subdued lighting to provide respite from the din of high-power amplifiers and the glare of strobe lights. They are seeking to express a form of spirituality that differs from the individualistic therapeutic models, which often reflect a retreat from the world rather than provide resources to engage the world. They are retrieving practices that sacralize all space, representing a hearkening back to premodern times, when all of life was holy. There is nothing magical about ancient practices. They are not valuable because they are ancient. Rather, they serve as resources from a time when the church did not practice the Western heresy of secularism. Today, they can be modified in ways that seem culturally appropriate.

Spiritual Roots

More than one source has influenced the contemporary emerging church movement. Tracing its roots will help us understand its various emphases and styles of spirituality.

Emerging from Third Wave Charismatics

The visits of John Wimber to the U.K. beginning in the early 1980s had a profound and lasting impact on many evangelical churches, especially within the Anglican Church. Churches hosted seminars that were attended by many Anglican clergy and lay leaders. The movement associated with Wimber and the Vineyard became known as the Third Wave,[2] a term coined by C. Peter Wagner to describe a Holy Spirit emphasis that differed from classical Pentecostalism and the charismatic movement. The style of the Third Wave was quieter and was influenced by the Quaker tradition of Wimber as well as his soft-rock musical preference. The Third Wave distanced itself from the other two traditions in not stressing tongue speaking as the sign accompanying baptism in the Holy Spirit. Especially appealing was Wimber's habit of

2. C. Peter Wagner, *Changing Church* (Ventura, CA: Regal, 2004), 43.

inviting the presence of the Spirit rather than *commanding* a particular manifestation.

In the U.K., virtually all the leaders of emerging churches were rooted in the charismatic movement (some Third Wave, some not) in the 1980s and early 1990s. In the U.S., this is not as evident, although two of the most influential leaders in emerging church networks, Todd Hunter and Brian McLaren, have strong Third Wave charismatic roots. For the most part, however, neither the U.K. nor the U.S. leaders brought a charismatic style of worship into emerging churches.

Connecting with Ancient Spirituality

Emerging churches reach into the past for many of their spiritual practices. But they do not simply reach back for anything ancient. Instead, they select highly participative practices that integrate body and spirit. Certain ancient spiritual practices find their origins in the early church fathers and medieval saints. Jonny Baker of Grace (London) says, "We link to the broad range of Christian spiritual traditions and have often had others from other traditions come and lead us in Ignatian prayer, Jesus prayer, and the use of icons. A lot of these practices are on the more contemplative side of faith."

More in evidence in the U.K. than in the U.S. is the embrace of Celtic spirituality. Andy Thornton says, "The Late Late Service drew its inspiration from the Iona Community. From Iona, there was a range of orthodoxies and much more liberty. It was a form of institutional faith quite different from the Church of England or the Church of Scotland." "The Iona Community in Scotland has helped groups to understand new ways of working with liturgy and ritual," reports Sue Wallace of Visions (York, U.K.). Roger Ellis, founder of Revelation Church (Chichester, U.K.), affirms, "Celtic spirituality is part of the DNA of our church. Celtic spirituality gives us a good reflection of the big picture. It is full of desire, passion, creation, mission, and speaks to the poor of heart." Ellis admits that "traditional Celtic worship sometimes feels like music for manic depressives. Yet there is much to explore of the wild, celebratory, and creative that could also be called Celtic."

The Celtic revival finds echoes in Wales, which shares cultural roots with Scotland. Dave Sutton of New Duffryn Community Church (Newport, U.K.), reports, "We rely on Celtic spirituality via the Iona Community. Through their teaching, we are geared up to include people." The Iona Community emphasized a spirituality that not only embraced the whole of life but was also inclusive of all people within the broader community. In other words, their spirituality was outwardly directed and not simply inner focused.

Whereas Christians can learn valuable lessons from the spiritual practices of a more leisurely and community focused age, they must not idealize or romanticize those practices, many of which were influenced by pre-Christian superstitions. Also, extreme aesthetic practices and bodily self-abuse can contribute to hallucinatory states of mind, which must be distinguished from authentic spiritual experience. Kester Brewin of Vaux (London) says, "We wouldn't say we were heavily into Celtic or stuff like that. I think people in Vaux are a bit dubious about going too far down those roads, as it can often seem like people are buying into something just to feel justified and ancient. However, we do feel part of a tradition and don't really think we are somehow being totally original. We are doing what people throughout the ages have always done, but in our own time and place."

Andrew Jones (Boaz, U.K.) is anxious to broaden the conversation among emerging churches:

> I would say that monastic Christianity over the past fifteen hundred years is giving us more resources than the more centralized, formal, Constantinian churches. There is also much in the Old Testament feasts, parties, and pilgrimages that resonates with contemporary practices of emerging church. The ways of Celtic Christians have been especially meaningful to me recently, especially as we create a monastery in the Orkney Islands. But our monastery will not be a retro, return-to-a-dead Celtic ritualism. Rather, it will, like its predecessors, function as a cultural portal, pilgrimage center, new-media resource base, micro-business enterprise, and a place of spiritual strength for the dispersed community.

Creating a Post-charismatic Spirituality

Rachelle Mee-Chapman of Thursday PM (Seattle), a congregation within the Seattle Vineyard, contrasts the emerging church with the modern church, specifically referring to her experience with the Vineyard. "We are so different from the traditional church. Modern churches, such as the Vineyard, focus on the building and the paid pastoral staff, and if there is any money left over, evangelism and mission. In addition, they must look very evangelistic in all they do. On the other hand, Thursday PM spends money on art parties, on paying rent for someone who needs it. We stay organic in all ways possible. My main goal of the Thursday PM meeting is to create a weekly Sabbath, to hear from God. For us, what counts as spirituality is to offer a listening space to others—to be present to people. Also, living with authenticity is a big spiritual thing."

Mee-Chapman continues, "In emerging churches, all things are worship: everyday conversations or watching kids skateboard and seeing their devotion to practice, passion, and skills." When asked if emerging churches can be charismatic, Mee-Chapman replied, "Yes, but we're more contemplative now with less about prayer and intercession. We are more eclectic, having added some actual traditional practices, and we are more 'everyday life,' more subtle. A big part of our spirituality is everyday living."

Constructing an Eclectic Spirituality

The emphasis on spirituality that is so prominent within emerging churches is a blending of traditions in the contemporary context. The leaders are determined to resist an elitist spirituality that alienates the majority with its high demands and esoteric language. Paul Roberts, vicar and leader of Resonance (Bristol, U.K.), reflects this broad perspective. "We have been very eclectic. That's been the name of the game from the beginning. Sometimes we use the stuff we have made up ourselves and sometimes stuff from books (e.g., Henri Nouwen), stuff from classic writers on spirituality (Teresa of Avila, Julian of Norwich, Ignatius Loyola), and stuff from the culture (for example, we used Douglas Coupland's *Girlfriend in a Coma* quite a bit when it was first out).[3] Often it's been in the juxtaposition of texts old and new that the most stimulating stuff has come out, as that is an exercise in spiritual hermeneutics."

Drawing from a variety of traditions to produce a newly created mix is the liturgical equivalent of DJs working with a mix of songs to produce fresh expressions and moods. The eclectic approach of the emerging church is also in sync with the wider culture's approach to spirituality, which has become divorced from institutional religion and the control of dogma. Yet emerging churches provide correctives to popular spirituality in that they are rooted in the practices of Jesus in both the Hebrew and the Christian Scripture. They are also rooted in the ancient practices of the Christian tradition and are

3. Douglas Coupland, *Girlfriend in a Coma* (Toronto: HarperCollins, 1998).

strongly corporate in their expression. The latter point is especially significant in a Western cultural context of extreme individualism and subjectivity.

Corporate Spirituality

Spiritual exercises are not exclusively privatized and internalized. They relate to the life of the corporate community of faithful people and provide the values, spiritual stamina, and sense of calling for their mission in the world. They provide the discipline of learning to listen corporately to God for a clear sense of his leading. This corporate emphasis is especially important in response to the excessive individuality that has influenced churches in the West and has undermined their community life. It also provides a challenge to self-reliance and the belief that humans can bring about the kingdom of God through their own activities. Christians need a renewed realization that God's mission can be engaged only as they are open to the leading of the Holy Spirit and recognize the need for his presence in their lives.

Overcoming Hyperactivity

As noted, hyperactivity is a feature of traditional evangelicalism and charismatic churches. Their high-energy worship leads to increased expectations and hype generated by adrenaline addiction. Rebecca Ver Straten McSparran of Tribe (Hollywood) recognizes the need to relate to her cultural setting. "I don't want a hyperactive church. I want reflection and silence, where art is central." She wants the church to be more sensitive, discerning, and open to the inspiration of the Spirit in recognition of the gifts that have been given to each individual through both genetic coding and the work of regeneration. The cultivation of the arts requires space, imagination, encouragement, and the opportunity to grow through participation in community. Artistic expression that is both rich and deep in its insights requires time, stillness, and unhurried reflection in order to flower.

Spirituality must be integrated with the rhythm of life, according to Dwight Friesen (Quest, Seattle). "We're just a bunch of friends doing the best we can. It's a journey, and sometimes our corporate spirituality just falls flat. But we made it flat, so that is okay. It is part of the process, just as the rests, like the notes, are part of the music." In other words, creativity cannot be programmed; it takes its own time and carves its own path.

Embracing Liturgy

Some structure and rich content are needed to sustain a community over the long haul. When these are absent, a Christian community is at the mercy of the spiritual ebb and flow and creative output of the current leadership. Among emerging churches, liturgies are welcomed, provided that they are made culturally accessible with adequate explanation and relational authenticity. In emerging churches, liturgy is not a straitjacket that inhibits and controls but a rich resource that nourishes and stimulates.

For those who have emphasized performance and contemporary expressions of worship, liturgy has negative connotations. It conjures up images of irrelevance and mindless repetition. However, there is an increasing desire to reconnect with ancient liturgies that inspired past generations and sustained the church across the centuries. Sue Wallace of Visions (York, U.K.) says, "*Liturgy* and *ritual* do not have to be dirty words. They can be rediscovered, and if they are relevant and meaningful, they can be amazingly powerful." For Ian Mobsby of Moot (London), "Liturgies from all around the world, ancient and new and in particular those around the Eucharist, are key."

Si Johnston identifies the sources that headspace (London) draws from. "We use various resources for spiritual formation and worship. I've just finished *The Prymer*[4] and so used some of that in our liturgy. We occasionally build various creeds into our liturgy as well. Since I provide spiritual direction or mentoring for some of those within headspace, I recommend various resources depending on who they are. Some are using prayers and meditations from the Northumbria Community,[5] some the Anglican Book of Common Prayer."

House of Mercy (St. Paul), rooted in the Baptist tradition, nonetheless embraces many ancient traditions. Debbie Blue reports, "We pray a lot in the service. We do a confession, the Eucharist, and have incense every Sunday. We've appointed a thurifer (the person who swings the incense pot). It was a real position in the historic church on par with the exorcist. We have a really beautiful candle stand for people to use

---

4. Robert E. Webber, *The Prymer: The Prayer Book of the Medieval Era Adapted for Contemporary Use* (Orleans, MA: Paraclete, 2000).
5. See www.northumbriacommunity.org.

to light candles in prayer after communion. On another occasion, a lot of people participated in making those candles at a do-it-yourself workshop."

Vine and Branches (Lexington) also stresses liturgical practice. Alan Creech grew in the conviction that liturgical practices could be spiritually healthy. Members participate in communion each week, and at their meetings on Tuesdays, they pray an abbreviated office. They use silence and antiphons. They intersperse their evening service with *lectio divina,* chanting, a discussion of what they have read, and the reading of Scripture (not necessarily teaching). "The liturgical thing is erupting everywhere. It is not necessarily house church, but it is not incompatible with it either. It can be both free form, organic, and liturgical." Matthew's House (Vista, CA) began using liturgy in 2001. Jason Evans says, "We read the Book of Common Prayer together at our meetings, and we read the Psalms out of Eugene Peterson's paraphrase *The Message.*"

Rebecca Ver Straten McSparran describes a typical service at Tribe (Hollywood), a community started in her downtown Hollywood home several years ago.

> As we get started, we always sit in a circle. Our typical service is very liturgical. I love the liturgy in Isaiah 6. The drums start, and we call everyone together. We sing one song, and we light the Christ candle as a poem is read. We do congregational drumming, or Taizé, or guitar, but usually drumming. Someone prays. I might lead a prayer of confession, or others might take turns. It might be an artistic/community prayer. Often we break into groups for prayer. We lift our hands over our heads. We listen and pray, and we imagine that Jesus comes. Sometimes the sermon is art, and sometimes I don't speak. But when I do, I start with a reading from the Word, and I read Scripture through *lectio divina.* My preaching is fairly dialogical, and I engage where people are at. We have a time of meditation that lasts about twenty minutes, with classical or ambient music to help in the process. The room is dark, relying on candlelight for the entire service. We gather everyone for communion, the words of institution. We use wine, pass the cup around, and say the Lord's Prayer together. After a benediction, we bring food in, and everyone eats together. We start the gathering around 6:00 p.m., and the service lasts two and a half hours. Dinner starts at 8:30 or 9:00. As the night moves on, the service emerges, and I simply listen to the move of the Holy Spirit. My preparation for the evening was simply jotting down some notes.

Thursday PM (Seattle), a typical home group, has soup, bread, wine, an Irish blessing, and a communion prayer. Rachelle Mee-Chapman never preaches, except through her blog. The members all teach and learn from one another. They plan to spend the summer doing an Ignatian examen.

Sanctus1 (Manchester, U.K.) practices communion and prayer techniques such as the Jesus prayer and body prayers (prayer through gestures rather than through words). Ben Edson says, "We have communion twice a month, as I believe that within communion there is a point of connection to the past and also a hope for the future." Ian Mobsby of Moot (London) declares, "We use a lot of old Celtic Christian material, including labyrinths, as a postmodern reinterpretation of premodern Christian forms of worship." At the House of Mercy (St. Paul), Debbie Blue reports, "We have a stations of the cross service on Good Friday. We invite various artists to create one of the stations. Last year the artists created all fourteen stations on fourteen- by sixteen-foot canvases, and then we displayed all fourteen interpretations together. We use the traditional Catholic liturgy to walk the stations." At Water's Edge (Hudsonville, MI), members participate in *lectio divina,* which was foreign to the group initially. They have times of silence, and they meditate with PowerPoint images.

Another ancient liturgical service that has seen a resurgence in popularity is the service of compline, in which the community commits itself to the Lord's safekeeping for the coming night. Debbie Blue (House of Mercy, St. Paul) says, "We had a compline service every Wednesday for a while that included silent prayer, meditation, and the Eucharist. We plan to resurrect that for Lent each year."

For some, an appreciation of the ancient liturgies of the church extends to a realization of the significance of the Christian calendar and the seasons of the year that cover the various aspects of the ministry of Christ: preparing for his coming (Advent); the Christmas season; the penitential season of Lent; Holy Week, climaxing in the celebration of the resurrection on Easter Sunday. The ascension of Christ is associated with the giving of his Spirit and the commission of the church to take the good news to all peoples. Matthew's House (Vista, CA) follows the Christian calendar, and some have adopted the Jewish calendar as well.

The discovery of liturgy and the ancient prayers of the church reflects a desire to be rooted during a time of profound cultural upheaval. It also illustrates the desire to express devotion in a variety of forms. Words are used not just to express a logical sequence of ideas but to create moods. Repetition is important, and sometimes it is accompanied by music that relaxes the mind so that people can listen to the words with renewed sensitivity and openness. The liturgical tradition is also associated with a valuing of artistic expression. In reaction to the hard-edged rationalism that characterized modernity, emerging churches appreciate mystery and recognize that in dealing with issues beyond their comprehension they must be comfortable with ambiguity. An emphasis on the Lord's Table rather than the pulpit is central, emphasizing hospitality and inclusion.

Retrieving a Monastic Spirituality

Emerging churches have shown a renewed interest in monastic spirituality, in which community is fostered through the practice of daily spiritual disciplines and mutual accountability. In reviving the concept of the Celtic mission community, emerging churches demonstrate their commitment to living corporate life as a welcoming presence by which the wider community can see and experience the transforming power of the gospel. Members of Vine and Branches in Lexington pray the hours. Mark Scandrette of ReIMAGINE! (San Francisco) reports, "We entertain an idea of monasticism that stresses engagement and not only contemplation. We present a holistic and integrated picture of the gospel and not a reductionistic gospel." Phil Ball relates that members of NGM (Bristol, U.K.) participate in meditation and different seasons of prayer. "We are a new monasticism. It is the nature of who we are. We have a sense of call to mission, one another, relationship, God, and community."

One of the most integrated approaches is that of the Order of Mission in Sheffield, U.K. The order provides training in Christian discipleship based on a series of diagrams called LifeShapes.[6] Those who join the order take vows of simplicity, purity of life, and mutual accountability. Their mission is to send out teams to establish communities of fellowship and witness. Members observe the hours of prayer but in a postmodern way. Most members of the order have jobs and so are unable to meet together throughout the day. Instead, they receive their intercessions through text messaging on their cell phones.

The Order of Mission, arising out of St. Thomas' Anglican Church in Sheffield, represents an impressive contemporary mission inspired by the Celtic model. Whereas the first Celtic pilgrims were effective in the evangelization of northern Europe, their hope is that their new

---

6. You can read more about this in Mike Breen and Walt Kallestad, *The Passionate Church* (Colorado Springs: Cook, 2005).

movement will make a significant contribution to the reevangelization of Europe.

Twenty-four-seven prayer rooms started in Chichester, U.K., in the fall of 1999 as part of the Revelation/Warehouse community. Now these prayer rooms are in many countries all over the world and within local churches of many traditions that are committed to intercession for personal and corporate spiritual renewal. These prayer rooms reflect the creativity of youth culture with a range of approaches to God and to the ministry of intercession. In a prayer room, people take part in experiential and meditative activities such as the examen (thinking back through things with God, noticing). They also feel the "thorns" of a cut soda can, wash their hands as a symbolic act of cleansing from sin, write a prayer response to a psalm and post it on a bulletin board, and pray the liturgical prayer book. They also pray nonverbally with music, dance, poetry, and painting.[7] Members of Vineyard Central (Cincinnati) pray "the psalms like a bunch of monks, without the robes."[8] They find that praying the hours offers them a contrast to individualism and narcissism.

Roger Ellis, at Revelation Church (Chichester, U.K.), sees Celtic monasteries as models of mission. "They had a simplicity of lifestyle, and they served their community through literacy education, growing food, creating schools, and mission training. Likewise, we want our prophets and our intercessors to be partners in social justice." The monastic model is attractive because of its holistic understanding of spirituality, its emphasis on community support and accountability, and its commitment to mission beyond the brotherhood. Emerging churches are re-creating this model to fit changing times. Like the ancient orders, they see life as a pilgrimage and that in the course of their daily walk they will encounter the presence of God and receive his guidance and grace.

Restoring the Centrality of the Eucharist

In emerging churches, the symbolic aspects of worship are central. As a result, there is an appreciation of the Eucharist as the central act of worship. Brad Cecil (Axxess, Arlington, TX) states:

7. See http://www.24-7prayer.com (accessed June 2, 2005). Prayer rooms have given rise to a form of church built around the prayer room idea: the boiler room. Boiler rooms are a neo-monastic form of church that highlights community, hospitality, justice for the poor, prayer, and the arts. At this point in time, boiler rooms are limited to the U.K., but they are likely to spread along the same lines as the 24-7 prayer movement.
8. See http://www.vineyardcentral.com/hours.

We started moving to a more participatory and symbolic worship expression after about two years of slowly seeing people bring ideas. For example, we configure our Eucharist to be the center of the auditorium and the focal point, and we are seated around it with the band located in the back and dimly lit. We open our service by proclaiming that Christ as symbolized by the Eucharist is the reason we gather, and we invite people to partake when they are ready. They can partake any time during the service. Most people move to the center, kneel on the prayer rugs, and spend some time before the elements. The band plays for about forty minutes, but there is no talking between songs, and art is displayed as well. We have about twenty minutes of the spoken word, which we view as art as well. It takes some getting used to in Texas, as most are used to a distinct focal point, well-defined structure, and group activity as opposed to individual activity. The biggest adjustment is to the preaching, as it is not the reason we gather. Since we view preaching as an art form rather than the transformative transfer of correct information, most people really like it. It is usually creative, short, and inspiring but very different from what they are used to.

The central place given to the altar or communion table has strong symbolic significance. The community is gathered for a meal. It is an offer of hospitality. This is in marked contrast to the focus placed on a pulpit located on a stage. It is a move from the celebrity to the celebrant, from someone who is speaking at you to one who is eating with you and who welcomes you to the feast on behalf of Christ.

Integrating Tradition and Contemporary Culture

Sue Wallace (Visions, York, U.K.) comments, "Because we believe what we say and sing, liturgical reform is important. We need the flexibility to be able to express what we really want to express while being real and true to the angst of our society and the pain of the world. This will change on a week to week basis. But there are also some things that will not change, the framework of orthodox belief in a saving God, for example. Plus, with communion, we do not have to reinvent the wheel."

Alternative worship remains indigenous. It always reflects the lived environment of the worshipers. It may at times look consumer oriented, but that is because people are consumers bringing their everyday lives to God. People cannot stand outside culture. They stand squarely within its bounds. "It's pointless denying our consumerism, for God knows what we possess. Some of it is good and may be useful for furthering our relationship with God" (Steve Collins, Grace, London).

Personal Spirituality

Individuals in emerging churches participate in a spirituality that integrates the corporate and the personal. Andy Thornton (Late Late Service, Glasgow, U.K.) expresses it this way: "The church service is not about the artistic. It is about how the service fits into your own life narrative, which then gets expressed back into the communal setting."

Emerging churches encourage their members in the practice of the spiritual disciplines. Jason Evans (Matthew's House, Vista, CA) says, "Individually, each adopts what practices they want and asks for help. Some do the Book of Common Prayer, some the divine hours, and some the Eastern Orthodox prayer book. We find that even outsiders participate with us in these." At Landing Place (Columbus, OH), members practice Celtic spirituality. Mark Palmer says:

> Probably 75 percent of our community is using the Northumbria Celtic Daily Prayer Book, but not necessarily together. It is not encouraged in any sort of coordinated way, but people have taken the project on individually. Some groups meet morning and evening to do the prayer. At my house, people pray between 8:30 and 8:40 a.m. each day. I haven't pushed it. Praying the same prayer book adds a cohesiveness and a rhythm to the community. Somehow in the midst of that God moves the community in the same direction.

Participating in a Holistic and Mystical Spirituality

Spirituality is not confined to meditation and contemplation. It also involves artistic expression. With Mark Scandrette of ReIMAGINE! (San Francisco), artists work through books on the connections between art and spirituality. They adopt common practices, journal three pages a day, and create a piece of art once a week. They are accountable to one another. Scandrette encourages a holistic pursuit of God, including exercising, eating right, praying, and studying Scripture.

Andy Thornton shares similar convictions, combining the mystical with a regard for the whole person: body, mind, and spirit. "Late Late Service attempted to create a broad, cultural, and social approach to faith very early on. We sought to create an emotional, intellectual, and mystical spirituality. We sought to awaken our mystical side, to be body oriented. Meditations helped us with this." Spencer Burke of the Ooze (Newport Beach, CA) agrees. "A move away from intellectual Christianity is essential. We must move to the mystical."

Fostering a Worshipful Way of Life

Sue Wallace (Visions, York, U.K.) expresses the integration of worship into life in personal terms.

> I think for most of us worship is a way of life. We have been heavily influenced by Celtic spirituality, which tries to turn everything into prayer. Church for us is more than the service, and I'm not sure it could exist properly for us without, at the very least, the pub. Not because of the beer, but because of the chance to sit in a relaxed way around tables and share our happiness and angst with one another. Eating together is very important for us too, and so we share meals together midweek on a two-weekly basis.

Doug Pagitt (Solomon's Porch, Minneapolis) believes that for him and his community worship is more in the streets than in the so-called worship service. "I believe in Romans 12:1 worship. Praise from the lips is not what worship is supposed to be. Rather, it consists of lives offered up to the agenda of God. That is how we worship God. It is in the stories of the people in the church where the good things are to be found."

All too often people separate their church life from the one they live throughout the rest of the week. This is most frequently because the teaching and intercession conducted in church are concerned with people's personal lives and ministry in the church with little or no connection made with the decisions members have to make in their professional lives. In contrast, one of Si Johnston's (headspace, London) most satisfying aspects of ministry is "seeing people connect their vocational lives with their spirituality and faith."

Steve Collins (Grace, London) expresses his commitment in terms of a "whole life faith." "We'd all consider anything less to be seriously defective or even not Christian. The stuff we do at Grace is the expression of that." Collins elaborates on the whole life faith idea in which one brings all that he or she is to God. "My conversion was the standard 'give your whole life to God' type. All that you are and all that you own are now God's. God will now choose the path of your life. So I always felt that it was all his anyway, and if it wasn't, I shouldn't have it!"

Receiving and Giving Spiritual Counsel

Members of Quest (Seattle) organize retreats at a local priory, where they are now regulars. Dwight Friesen reports, "The sisters coached us in how to listen to one another and to God, how to speak redemptively into others' lives, and how to equip people to be co-directors with one another. We learned how to sacramentalize all of life. We turned meals into communion. Even times of coffee turned into worship and to a centering on Christ." From the sisters, they learned that "full devotion is for everyone." Emerging church participants receive spiritual direction from their mentors as they seek to live a balanced rhythm of life in all spheres of reality, balancing prayer, community, and outreach.

Engaging the Culture with Spiritual Practices

As mentioned earlier, spirituality is growing in significance in the broader culture. Emerging churches are in tune with this trend and are seeking to respond to it, not only by affirming the value of a search for the transcendent but also by making resources available. They do this by living as "spiritual" communities within their neighborhoods and among the networks they serve. They invite others to join them, welcoming them as people with contributions to offer.

Chris Matthews of Extreme (Swansea, U.K.) expresses the conviction that "there is a hunger for spirituality in our culture, but our structures keep them away." To make themselves accessible within their context, they hold their meetings in a café in the center of town. Steve Collins of Grace (London) is also concerned to make spirituality accessible, and not just physically. Grace wants to make it manageable so people are not overwhelmed or discouraged. "People hunger for New Age spirituality, but our methods (quiet times, Bible studies) do not fit this age and culture." He asks, "Why not short moments? Why not have spirituality in small snippets?"

Although spirituality is a talking point within culture, not all spirituality is Christian in inspiration and content. It is as likely to be influenced by alternative spiritualities or by the mystic traditions within Judaism or Islam. The various New Age festivals provide venues for alternative spiritualities to display their wares and to engage in conversation with the crowds who flock there out of curiosity or spiritual need. Some Christian groups are taking advantage of this opportunity. For instance, Sanctus1 assisted in the running of a stall at the Mind/Body/Spirit Fair in Manchester, U.K. Ben Edson describes their involvement. "We spent two days at the fair and provided a sacred space for people to drop in and also to receive prayer for healing. It was an amazing weekend that enabled Sanctus1 to connect with some genuine spiritual searchers."

For Thursday PM (Seattle), their spiritual practices include missional engagement with the Fremont Arts Council through involvement with the annual solstice parade. To prepare for the solstice event, members performed an Ignatian examen of light. They asked themselves, Where have we experienced light? Rachelle Mee-Chapman says, "This year we spent four weeks building floats with the community, eating soup with them. That was church for us." Members of Thursday PM are prepared to set aside their own program to immerse themselves in the activities of the wider community. Seattle is a center of alternative spirituality and has one of the lowest church attendance rates in the U.S.

Identification with alternative spiritualities does entail some risks. But such exposure leads to a deeper appreciation of the gospel as people respond to questions and are challenged by the intensity of the spiritual search of those who do not follow Christ. "Our favorite ways of evangelism are bringing the church to the people in some way. For example, our sets of prayer installations that are regularly placed in our local Christian café. People can wander in and interact with them as they wish. On Good Friday, particularly, this has been amazingly powerful and has resulted in life-changing moments for some customers. Those people haven't joined our church, but that doesn't matter. They met God, and that is what is important" (Sue Wallace, Visions, York, U.K.).

Peter Rollins of ikon (Belfast, U.K.) provides the following account. "At ikon, I realize that people sometimes do meet God there. Just two nights ago a drunk guy at the bar participated in one of our rituals. He went into a room, put on headphones, and looked at an icon of Christ. Afterward he had to write his experience on a piece of paper. This guy went in drunk and came out sober. He said, 'Christ's eyes were sad, and they were sad for me.' He experienced God, and we did nothing but provide a space for God to give God."

For Tribe (New York), "big hugs" are meetings that are open to anyone. Kenny Mitchell says, "We do not intend the 'big hug' to turn into a seeker meeting, but that is always what happens. It might be a meditation night with focused prayer or chill-out healing vibes. Both are becoming more and more popular with those outside the community. These appeal to people who are leaving church in order to find God." Jonny Baker (Grace, London) has discovered that the ancient practice of walking the labyrinth has a broader appeal. "The labyrinth has been a great outreach thing. We recently ran it for the whole parish with lots of new visitors attending, and it has done a two-year tour around the U.K., including in schools and prisons."

The people in Tribe's (Hollywood) surrounding community are very arts oriented. They are involved in art and film and are very spiritual *and* very pagan. Rebecca Ver Straten McSparran explains, "We live and play in this community. God called us to minister to people who have a high sense of spirituality. Church is the last place they would be. We are also very involved in the Burning Man Festival."[9] She recognizes the need to relate to her cultural setting. "We are apprentices of Jesus, spiritual Christians, and our task is to find the spiritual non-Christians."

Members of emerging churches connect and communicate their faith within the spiritual language of postmodern culture. Their rhythm of life, both corporate and personal, often rooted in premodern forms, connects to a culture that has wearied of modern religion.

Conclusion

Spirituality is a major emphasis in emerging churches, more important than numbers gathered or even the celebrative nature of the worship. The real concerns are the extent to which lives are changed and gaining depth through the richness of encounters with God. Members of emerging churches recognize that there is no instant formula. Rather, spiritual disciplines have to be learned through costly exploration. They draw upon a variety of traditions and combine them in a creative mix.

The spirituality they pursue is corporate and personal. It is explored not only in the mind but also through the body. It is related to the whole of life and is not confined to a retreat or ecclesial setting. It is as much concerned with mission outreach as with personal development.

These final observations complete the circle. Emerging churches represent kingdom living, insisting that the ascended Lord reigns over the whole of life. The faith community exists here on earth as an anticipatory sign of the presence of Jesus. It is commissioned and empowered by him and in its life of obedience to his calling discovers his presence within and around in surprising and sustaining ways. It is the church on the move, the church that will always be emerging, the church in mission that discovers that the Lord is true to his word: "Surely I am with you always, to the very end of the age" (Matt. 28:20 NIV).

9. See http://www.burningman.com.

Conclusion

All emerging churches have their unique place and expression. Each has its place for as long as it's around. Which will last and which won't, time will tell. It depends on the continuing passion and motivation behind it (i.e., the people's desire to see it continue). The exciting thing for me is that each will live on in the sense that even if the structures and names and bank accounts go, the people behind it all and who have been involved will continue to seek ways to live and express their faith. My hope is that what they have created and experienced has been full of freedom and hope and hasn't sucked the marrow of life out of people and left them wondering where their faith and life went. Let's hope.

Pip Piper, maji, Birmingham, U.K.

This study sought to identify the essential practices of emerging churches in the U.K. and the U.S. As explained, after five years of research, we identified nine practices of the communities that are engaging postmodern culture. To clarify, emerging churches are not young adult services, Gen-X churches, churches-within-a-church, seeker churches, purpose-driven or new paradigm churches, fundamentalist churches, or even evangelical churches. They are a new expression of church. The three core practices are identifying with the life of Jesus, transforming secular space, and commitment to community as a way of life. These practices are expressed in or lead to the other six: welcoming the stranger, serving with generosity, participating as producers, creating as created beings, leading as a body, and taking part in spiritual activities.

The example of Jesus, as he engaged his culture with the kingdom, is exemplary for emerging churches. The gospel, as he announced it, was to participate with God in the redemption of the world. It is this gospel that emerging churches embrace.

Modern culture created a secular realm and chased all spiritual things to the margins of society, first relegating them to church and religion and then to the individual's heart. What used to be a faith for all of life came to address only a small sliver of reality. To follow the way of Jesus, emerging churches address all of reality. They travel to all spheres in society and make them holy, giving them back to God in worship. Emerging churches do not submit to the dualisms presented by modernity: sacred versus secular, body versus mind/spirit, male versus female, clergy versus laity, leader versus follower, evangelism versus social action, individual versus community, outsider versus insider, material versus immaterial, belief versus action, theology versus ethics, public versus private. Instead, they seek to overcome these divisions.

Emerging churches are communities that follow Jesus and the kingdom into the far reaches of culture. Emerging churches destroy the Christendom idea that church is a place, a meeting, or a time. Church is a way of life, a rhythm, a community, a movement. Emerging churches dismantle all ideas of church that interfere with the work of the kingdom.

Emerging churches hold to the uniqueness of Christ, yet they welcome all who come. Without insecurity, they place themselves in the midst of others, recognizing that there is much to learn from others, even those of other faiths. For churches to resemble Jesus, they must include the stranger and not recognize two types of people. Modernity is a culture of exclusion. For emerging churches to look like Jesus, they must be countercultural through inclusion.

Emerging churches are generous because they see hospitality as rooted in the kingdom. Sharing is seen as a spiritual practice, and emerging churches perform acts of sharing in all spheres of society. They offer generosity in a culture in which self-interested exchange is promoted. Emerging churches build relationships with outsiders; they do not treat them as evangelism objects (as do fundamentalists) or as social objects (as do liberals). Instead, they form relationships with them in which they share the good news at all levels.

There are no spectators in God's kingdom. God has given all members a task, a talent, a voice to share. Worship in emerging churches is by producers, not consumers. Outcasts and sinners all get to participate. Part of God's redemptive activity involves calling creation back to God's original intent. That calling back is to infuse beauty into all things. In worship, emerging churches bring the world to God.

By encouraging the creative spark that is implanted in each person by virtue of the fact that all are made in the image of God, emerging churches hope to reconnect people with their true selves. In a consumerist society that distracts and ultimately dehumanizes, the rediscovery of creativity is itself a work of God's grace that makes people authentic and invests them with an appreciation of self-worth. It liberates those who are encumbered with a poor self-image. In the act of creating, people are sensitized to the voice of God, stirring their spirits and redirecting their lives.

The task of the leader is to create an environment so that all of the above can happen. Modernity taught leaders how to control, and Christians have adopted this practice rather than challenging it. Emerging churches seek to carve a new way. How do we lead without control? How do we lead in such a way that we submit to the kingdom? How do we lead so that every voice is heard, every gift is expressed, and a consensus is reached? The only acceptable tool for the leader who forgoes control is persuasion.

If all can be made sacred, both caring for the poor and painting murals under freeway underpasses, then what is spirituality? For the Christian, spirituality involves a way of life, a lived prayer. Members of emerging churches use ancient practices to give all of their life to God in worship. Such practices move beyond individualized forms of spirituality and tie people to the historical church, past, present, and future.

For a number of reasons, this has been a difficult book to write. In the first place, we are not the authors of much of the material. We wanted emerging church leaders to be heard in their own words. Our roles have been that of interpreter and commentator. We refrained from acting as censors or critics when something was said about which we have our own opinions. We sought to include leaders who had walked away from their previous ecclesial tradition out of frustration and disillusionment as well as those who continue to work within a tradition, seeking its transformation.

Another difficulty was in trying to present a snapshot of a rapidly changing scenario. We are acutely aware that we may have missed elements and significant people and places, despite our best efforts. Furthermore, between submission of this manuscript and its eventual publication, emerging churches no doubt continued to evolve and to morph. Our effort, therefore, is time sensitive. But we trust that by focusing on the issues evident at the time of our research, we have created a record that will have value for some time to come.

In preparing this manuscript, we learned much ourselves. We have fresh hope for the church as it embarks on a new millennium. The challenges are enormous, but we are grateful for the insights and the courage of past generations of leaders. We commit ourselves afresh to support and interact with the new generation that God is raising up to take their place.

As we complete this project, we are all too aware of the diversity of the situations we have introduced as well as the wide spectrum of leadership perceptions. Many of the churches and groups visited are new, fragile, vulnerable, and in locations subject to rapid change. We hope this book will inform a generation of church leaders who may as yet be unaware of the significant developments taking place. We hope it will provide a useful resource for those training for or are already engaged in ministry to postmodern culture, to those who have walked away from the church or for whom the church is remote. However useful it proves to be to others, we testify to the extent to which our own spiritual lives have been enriched by the risk taking and outpoured love of Christ that the leaders here described have demonstrated. We thank them for their warm hospitality and for trusting us with both their vision and their vulnerability. Their love was as overwhelming as their faith was inspiring. We are sure that having read their reflections you will want to get to know their personal stories. So read on!

Leaders in Their Own Words

Here are the stories of fifty leaders, in their own words, of how they came to be where they are today. Some stories are very long, and some are very short. That is because of the length of the contribution, not our valuation of the significance of a particular story. Some entries were submitted in writing, and some are based on phone and in-person interviews.

Jonny Baker, Grace, London

I was born in a Christian home in 1965 in Cheltenham. My father was an Anglican minister. It was in the early days of charismatic renewal that my parents were filled with the Spirit. At that time, there were few resources around to help them make sense of their experience, but those were exciting days.

When I was four years old, my dad took an associate vicar's job at St. Mark's in Gillingham, Kent. This church had similarly experienced a wave of renewal. John Collins was the vicar and developed a team ministry. (He went on to be vicar of Holy Trinity Brompton in West London.) W. Graham Cray arrived as the young long-haired curate. My dad's role in the ministry was particularly to minister to people who were deeply broken for a variety of reasons: They had been in the occult, had experienced deep rejection, were schizophrenic, or whatever. Our house was invariably filled with characters whom my parents loved and who were gradually transformed.

For me, this was a great environment to grow up in. I loved God, or rather, knew I was loved by him, from an early age. I actually received the gift of tongues when I was just four years old! I never rejected God and grew up being loved. There were of course several meetings where there was an appeal to commit your life to Christ. I used to go forward at all of them until I finally realized I must be "in"!

When I was eight, we moved to a village church in Newick, Sussex, where I lived until age eighteen. We developed a youth group there that was very formative. We got excited about worship. Our youth leader would take us to open meetings at the Hyde, which was a nearby Christian community run by Colin Urquart. The worship there was like nothing we had experienced. I got a guitar for my eighteenth birthday, as I wanted to lead this kind of worship. That began a journey with worship and music. I quickly began to lead worship for the youth group and continued when I went to university. I seemed to have a gift for it.

A few things made an impact on me in my teens. A bunch of us read Nicky Cruz's *Run Baby Run*. I was also asked to help lead the eleven-to-fourteen group at the church, which made me take responsibility for my faith a lot more. Then one weekend there was a knock on the vicarage door. It was a local hippyish character who wanted to talk with the vicar. My dad was away, and we had some people staying. One of the chaps staying with us was a Christian, so he met with this hippy character. It turned out that the man had read the book *Jesus of Nazareth,* and then there had been a bird with a broken wing that he had prayed for. The bird had been healed and had flown off, so the man wanted to know about Jesus! Having spoken with him, our friend asked me if I would read the Bible with him. I was about fifteen at the time. I said yes, and we arranged to meet on Friday nights. I chose the book of Philippians because it looked short. I told a couple of friends about it, and they asked if they could join in. Before I knew it, a small group was meeting weekly to study the Bible. I was the leader. I borrowed commentaries from my dad, and we gradually made our way over the next few years through the books of the Bible. This was an amazing group.

Finally, I remember around the age of seventeen or eighteen feeling challenged to take my faith a lot more seriously, and I committed to read the Bible in a year and to pray for an hour a day. This again ended up being transformative. I still feel I have a grasp of Scripture that is undergirded by the years that followed that decision.

At eighteen, I went to university. I avoided the Christian Union at first, preferring to play on the university basketball team and to engage in a local church. During my first term, I went to a meeting nearby where Colin Urquart was a speaker. On the way I had an uncanny sense that God was going to speak to me. At the end of his talk, Colin said God had laid some things on his heart. The last one was that there were people present who knew that God was speaking to them. He was calling them to work full-time for the kingdom. (With my theology now, I realize that sounds a bit dualistic, as we should all be doing that!) I knew this was God speaking to me and calling me to ministry in some way, so I responded.

At the end of that term, I was ready to leave university and go to Bible college, but after chatting and praying with people, I felt I was to stay at university and the call would work out. After a year, I got involved in the Christian Union, leading a worship band, speaking, etc. I also remember inviting members of my math course to hear Billy Graham. A couple friends became Christians at that time.

While at university, I got involved in a church that was the most exciting community/church experience I had encountered. The vicar was influenced by the philosophy of Herman Dooyeveerd and had connections with people like Brian Walsh at the Institute for Christian Studies in Toronto. What was so liberating about this time was a theology that seemed to engage with life. It embodied a Christian worldview that was framed as creation, fall, redemption, and a vision of the future that was a renewal of creation, not an escape from it. We discussed what Christian politics, science, etc., might look like, tackled sexism, and so on. I was on the leadership team at age twenty-two and was a churchwarden. I had my eyes opened in a completely new way to how faith engaged with culture.

After university, I got married to Jenny that summer. I wondered whether I should become a vicar and went for an interview about it, but I was told to come back in a few years. I worked as a statistician, but my passion was not in it. Shortly after that, I got involved with the local Youth for Christ team as a volunteer. Gerard Kelly was directing it, and we became very good friends. My wife worked for them as a school worker, and I subsequently got involved full-time. We had a brilliant time doing evangelism over the next few years and developing a nightclub as an outreach.

Reading Pete Ward's books and articles, on relational outreach and incarnational approaches to youth ministry, shaped my thinking about youth ministry. I discovered that cross-cultural mission seemed to be where the clues were to be found for how to do ministry in our own context. Partly because of Youth for Christ and partly because of the church, we decided to write our own worship songs. This initiative was theologically motivated because there just were not songs around on the themes we were learning about.

Another factor in shaping my life was the Greenbelt Festival, which I had been to every year since the age of eleven. This was where I first encountered alternative worship along the lines of the Late Late Service. It just made sense with the cross-cultural insights and the retheologizing we were trying to do in songwriting. My life changed as a result. I realized that the kids we were working with were not making the cultural leap into church, and this encounter helped me find a missing piece. It dawned on me that church, not just evangelism, needed to be grown and reimagined in the soil of the culture of the people we were working with.

We had two children (now age twelve and fourteen). We made a decision when they were born to job share work and parenting. This was possibly the best decision of my life. I can't understand why more people don't do it! At the time, it was highly controversial, but we persuaded the management of Youth for Christ to let us do it, and they couldn't argue with the results.

During those years, I went to a couple alternative worship gatherings. I started to read a lot more books. Then we felt God call us to move to London. This was about nine years ago. It was similar work to what we had been doing, but now we were helping to plant and support new ministries rather than run one. When we moved, we found Grace, which was an alternative worship group that had almost burnt out and was taking a six-month break. We quickly joined and helped to restart it. I had been leading a worship band at various events and was finding an increasing discomfort with the performance thing and the Christian subculture. The move helped me break from it, and Grace was a new space in which to reimagine what worship might and could be like.

Grace is a loose community/network. By that I mean anyone is welcome to come to anything from services, to planning meetings, to meals in people's homes. But there is no pressure to sign up. You can be as involved or uninvolved as you like. This is actually a very Anglican approach. We describe ourselves as a congregation of St. Mary's Church in Ealing, West London. This is to help people understand the relationship with St. Mary's. We are to embody a way of life. We do not have an explicit rule of life or anything like that, but we do say that we are Christian and orthodox, seeing ourselves as part of the global body of

Christ and locally part of the Church of England. We are happy to be linked rather than independent.

I also set up a recording label in Bath with two friends, Jon Birch and Aad Vermeyden, on which we could do what we liked, having been frustrated by working with Christian record labels. Proost is the label, and it proved to be a creative outlet for the new worship we were creating. I was definitely in left field as far as Youth for Christ was concerned, but they liked that and supported it. I think they felt it gave them a different edge. I was often asked to lead events for staff.

One of our successes was creating an outreach in 2000 in St. Paul's Cathedral in London, called the Labyrinth, which has now gone global. I have since completed an M.A. and have begun to write and to try to publish some of our thoughts and discoveries for a wider audience.

Two years ago, I started working for the Church Mission Society, one of the largest Church of England mission agencies, as the youth coordinator. This seemed a surprising move to a lot of people, but I have actually always been in and around Anglican churches. And it seemed exciting to come back to missiology, as that is what had shaped my approach to ministry. It is still early, but we are changing what a mission agency looks like in a postcolonial, postmodern world, and part of that involves engaging with the challenges of mission in our own context and the emerging church movement.

Phil Ball, New Generation Ministries (NGM), Bristol, U.K.

I was born in 1971 to church planters and was raised in a Christian home in the cities of Bristol and Bath in the west of the U.K. I began ministry by working in schools, missions, and churches. In the 1980s, a band Heartbeat had a couple of Top 40 songs. As a kid, I had a dream to be a drummer with Heartbeat someday. In 1989–90, I began working with Heartbeat as a lighting technician and then filled in as drummer. My dream had come true! New Generation Ministries grew out of Heartbeat, building on the discipleship/music ministry from the band's music ministry in schools. In 1990, I started 65dba, another band established to continue Heartbeat's ministry of sharing the gospel among young people. Gradually, these ministries evolved into church plants.

In 1991, teams started working for one year in an area, seeking to create a "new wineskin" and see what developed out of the experiment. In Swindon, forty to fifty miles east of Bristol, NGM started the Gap. Four or five churches sponsored a team to work in the schools, create

244

cells, and work with kids on the street. The Gap worked with twelve- to eighteen-year-olds. There were one hundred in that group.

The predominant pattern is for local churches to sponsor and partner with a team from NGM, which seeks to plant churches. NGM has three resource centers where it trains youth: Bristol, Birmingham, and Swansea (U.K.). Currently, it is attempting to plant churches through Rubik's Cube, started by Doug Ross. Rubik's Cube is a Monday night venue at Bar Latino's in Bristol. It is an access point through which we build relationships with DJs and promoters in other clubs. A cell group, currently numbering six or seven members, meets before each club night and seeks to plant a church within the club culture. Planting churches is the primary focus. NGM seeks to plant "new wineskin" churches that grow out of the culture rather than importing models from elsewhere. We pioneered this model of working alongside a local church in planting new churches. Throughout the U.K., NGM currently has seven centers/partnerships with churches.

Debbie Blue, House of Mercy, St. Paul

I am from the Midwest, born in Cedar Falls, Iowa, in 1963, but went to graduate school in the East and had some of my most life-changing time in the West. So, I want to say I'm not thoroughly Midwestern, though I probably am. There is something about that region that influences one's being in the world. I came to the Twin Cities (Minnesota/St. Paul) because I knew a group of people here, and my husband came from the Twin Cities.

I grew up going to a General Association of Regular Baptist church (GARBC). It's pretty small, very conservative, and convinced that it's the only church that has it all quite right. Most of their cultural beliefs were not tenable for someone like me, but one good thing I took away from the church is that I learned a way of life in which God is something that I could not imagine not struggling with.

It was very cave-like. People were afraid to venture outside the small cave they lived in because it was dangerous out there. But I found the more and more I ventured out, the more beautiful and true things I found. I encountered ideas worth considering and the freedom to think. It wasn't just the GARBC that read the Bible; other people read the Bible and cared about it, and there were no questions that you couldn't ask and nothing that you needed to avoid reading or studying or liking because it would threaten your faith. And so, what if your faith was threatened? It wasn't your faith that mattered as much as God's activity in the world. There was a point for me when it began to seem like the "fundies" believed less in a living God than almost anyone. It was what *they* did and *they* believed that was a matter of life and death to them. It was almost as if God didn't exist outside their box.

My life turned during the Oregon Extension [a semester study program in southern Oregon's Cascade Mountains], when I realized God might really be alive and unthreatened by our fumbling and questioning and sometimes crazed dialogue. Actually, it might be exactly in the midst of that turmoil that good theology happens, rather than in the cave. I got excited about the Bible and theology and decided to go to seminary. I was especially interested in Karl Barth. I never wanted to be a pastor. For me it wasn't the church that seemed hopeful and alive and full of the gospel. I experienced the church more as a barrier than as something that gives truth and hope and life.

But after being at Yale University a couple years (and loving it), I realized that my love was not purely academic. It had so much to do with finding the gospel incredibly and gorgeously freeing and wanting everyone to be freed, and clearly the church was more the realm for that sort of thing than academics, so I thought I should see what it was like to be involved in church. I took an internship with the Lutheran Campus Center in Madison, Wisconsin. I worked for the Campus Center and two big Lutheran churches and decided almost for certain, after that, that I just probably couldn't work that well within the institution of the church. You had to care about things that I couldn't care about very successfully, like the parking lot and attendance patterns and church growth and what sort of impression you make on everybody. It's like my brain just doesn't function in an organized sort of institutional way.

I would not make a good CEO, and I realized it would cost me too much to try to be that. It seemed like the most alive and best things about me would not thrive in the role of pastor. I also found out that I loved to write sermons and that I could preach, that people were really compelled by my sermons and my classes and my prayers and how I talked about God and the Bible. But it just didn't seem like the church was the place to do that. To be a pastor, you had to be more CEO-ish and less an artist and interpreter of the faith.

I ended up working at the Campus Center for a couple years and loving the people I worked with. They loved me and thought there was a place for me in the church, but after I met Jim, my husband, who was a painter, it seemed much more compelling to travel around and to write, backpack, watch birds, grow a garden, and paint, so I left to do all that.

I had known Mark Stenberg (now my co-pastor) for years, and for years he had been saying he and Russell Rathbun wanted to start a church. They had both been solo pastors in the Seattle area and realized how much better it would be to do something together. They asked if I would ever want to do it with them. I said yes, because I knew Mark loved what I loved, which was the gospel. We were theological soul mates, and it seemed if we did something together it would be different and theologically thick and mostly about the good news. So when Mark and Russell ended up in the Twin Cities (because Mark's wife, who is a doctor, got a job in a clinic here and Russell's wife got accepted into graduate school here) we started House of Mercy.

I guess I don't *really* believe we had theological convictions that could not be fulfilled in any other venue, but we did have a do-it-yourself sort of spirit and wanted to do things ourselves. We wanted to work with one another, and it seemed more possible to create something alive by starting something new. We had a very evangelical approach in that we believed very much in the good news as the center, but we wanted to avoid emotional manipulation. We wanted there to be plenty of room for cynicism and a critical spirit with respect to the church and the church's methods.

We wanted a church that was lively and full of questions and very much about good theology. I guess we didn't see many churches that felt like that to us, not that there aren't some out there. Mark and Russell had both been active in the Newman Center in Berkeley, where they had a rota of preachers who preached sort of thick and intellectually rigorous sermons. Mark and I had both studied the Bible with John Linton from the Oregon Extension. He has a pretty unique approach to the text. He takes it very seriously but hardly ever reads it in the expected way. I think we had the conviction that the Bible is pretty wild and fascinating and that biblical sermons are what we need (not life-application messages). We didn't want the usual church organization, where there are lots of unproductive meetings. And we didn't want a hierarchy among the staff. We liked the idea of liturgical eclecticism and the freedom to draw from different traditions within the church, but we definitely wanted to draw from tradition. We were sure we didn't want praise music!

Joe Boyd, Apex, Las Vegas

I was born in 1973 in Kentucky. Since the age of eight, I was part of the Christian church. I later felt the church was conservative and narrow, but I didn't think that when I was young. My perspective then was "we're right and everyone else is wrong." I began to preach at the age of eleven, and at the age of fifteen I committed my life to vocational ministry. I attended Cincinnati Bible College and Seminary to prepare myself for my calling. At the age of twenty, I moved to Las Vegas to help with a church plant called Canyon Ridge. In one year, the church had grown to fifteen hundred people. I knew the pastor, with whom I got on well, and went on staff.

We began to have a church-within-a-church service, much along the lines of Axis at Willow Creek. From the start, for the sake of our autonomy, we wanted a church-within-a-church, not simply a young adult service. In 1997, we started the service, which we called Apex. We had our own elders, but these elders reported to the elders of Canyon Ridge. We struggled for the first six months and then grew from fifty to six hundred. One of our strengths was that perhaps 80 percent of the people came from outside the big church.

We were considered creative and successful. During 1999, however, the elders and I became increasingly dissatisfied because our convictions about what church was had changed dramatically. The people loved the show. We were funny and hip—we even had painters on stage—but I didn't want to provide church entertainment for the rest of my life. We saw on paper how big we were going to get, that we were destined for megachurch status, and that I was destined to be the CEO. But all I wanted to do was tell stories! If you are a good performer and a religious kid, you are encouraged to be the preacher.

I read the Gospels over and over. Nothing I was doing on Sunday was what I thought Jesus would be doing if he were here. I read other books, the most influential being Dallas Willard's *Divine Conspiracy* but also Stanley Hauerwas's *Resident Aliens,* John Yoder's *Politics of Jesus,* and the writings of Hans Küng. I grew tired of church structure.

Beginning in 2000, I preached on house churches, Jesus, and the kingdom until people became blue in the face. Eight elders sought to coordinate this kind of structural transition for six hundred people. We made many mistakes in trying to get the church to achieve this major epistemological shift in two months. We wanted the ones we had led to faith two years prior to change their entire view of church and Christianity. We discovered that few were prepared to make the shift, even those whose entire experience of faith was with Apex. The church went from six hundred to thirty in the span of one year! We sought to destroy the church as we knew it, but we didn't know what route to take for its destruction. Our big service was, for many, still the significant event of the church.

Our theology shifted from a "sin management theology" to a kingdom theology under the influence of Dallas Willard in *The Divine Conspiracy.* We came to trust that Jesus came to establish the kingdom of heaven. We believed that the parables were church-planting parables, meaning that Jesus would grow the church, not us. He would grow it the way he wanted to, and we surrendered our control of the church to him.

We became kingdom-oriented groups. The church became a family, with God its Father and Jesus its leader. Church became about our daily lives in relational community. We shared meals together, and we operated as a family. If we met someone new, we invited that person to where we would be that night (evangelism is about bringing a friend to where your other friends are hanging out).

There are twenty-five house groups at Apex now. Many of them meet together daily, sharing what they have together. Only fourteen of these groups are listed on the Internet; the other eleven have no official meeting but meet frequently—either every day or every other day. These groups are too decentralized or disorganized to be listed.

Apex is nonhierarchical. It functions as a church-planting organization, and any house church can break with Apex at any time. Our weekly all-church meeting has decreased in importance, and we are currently restructuring for a monthly celebration. We wanted to meet weekly, but people tend to come every four to six weeks, so we are thinking about a quarterly retreat instead.

Now my church is the twelve friends I spend most of my time with; they are my missional and lifelong community. My pagan friends are church for me as well—while with them, I spend time with Jesus because he is with me. My community with these Las Vegas actors is just as strong as my Christian community. I am slowly introducing Jesus to them.

Kester Brewin, Vaux, London

I was brought up in a Christian home. My father is an Anglican minister who has journeyed with the evangelical/charismatic wing of the church since the late 1970s. I was born in 1972 in a vicarage in Sheffield and lived the church life inside out. I can point to a Billy Graham rally in 1984 as a conversion, but that was really more of a moment of strengthening a faith that had always been there. I have attended church ever since but have been encouraged to stay broad, not to box faith up.

In London in the late 1990s, I found myself worshiping at a large, lively evangelical church of perhaps six hundred young adults each Sunday

night. It was there that Beki, my wife, and I met Nic and Sooz. Sooz
was the only one of us not from a vicar-kid background. At first we
were surprised at the coincidence, but we now see that the alternative
worship scene is full of us, people who were brought up "on the inside"
and do not want to throw it all away but are ready to change things and
are equipped with the know-how to attempt it.

Sitting in pews, standing up, sitting down, the same format each
week—it just wasn't working for us. As artists, writers, creative people,
we felt uncomfortable in the single, fixed configuration of soft-rock
worship and three-point linear preaching. We felt the body was dying
around us. We were frustrated. We sat each week surrounded by some
of the brightest talents in film, TV, theater, art, social work, and politics
who were made to watch in virtual silence because they did not play
guitar or preach. These were the only two gifts that were acceptable as
worship. It seemed such a waste. We thought it was outrageous that all
these gifts were being used in the corporate world, in the market economy,
but were being snubbed in the church. We saw that if worship is about
gift, then what we bring to worship has to be integral to us, something
meaningful from who we are.

Initially, and typically for our generation, we defaulted to the professionals for help. We went to Jonny Baker (Grace, London), a good
friend of ours, and asked him to start another Grace in our area. He
righteously kicked us up the backside and told us to do it ourselves. Vaux
surfaced in November 1998 after some years of labor. Four of us were
there at the beginning: me, my wife, Beki (the current festival manager
of Greenbelt Festival), Nic, and Sooz. Nic is one of the leading graphic
artists in London, and his aesthetics have driven the look and feel of
Vaux. We had a logo before we had a venue.

Vaux was initially designed as a place where people could come and
offer their gifts, whatever they were: dance, liturgy, video, monologue,
installation, meditation, graphics, sounds. We simply tried to curate this
stuff into a sort of coherent whole, to help people see that worship is
not about coming to get but coming to give. To get anything in return
is a bonus, a moment of grace.

We have a core group of twelve or so that meets weekly. As many as
eighty or as few as ten meet for services. We have a few hundred on our
mailing list, many of whom are tourists who passed through. Others are
linked to other churches in London. The age range is pretty wide. Kids
love the services because they are so visual, and many find the space and
the openness a great break from the usual fare they get in their home

churches. We have sometimes described ourselves as "worship architects," designing spaces within which people can worship as they like rather than demanding that people worship in a fixed way.

Spencer Burke, the Ooze Website

I was born in 1958 and raised in Southern California and Sacramento, the capital of California, where my dad was a legislator. My family was not a churchgoing family, but in my junior high years, we became involved in a conservative Baptist church, which was when my faith became real to me. I spent my junior and senior high years in this conservative Baptist church. After graduating from high school, I spent a year in Berkeley with the World Liberation Front, a theologically conservative, politically liberal Christian commune. After that year, I interned for a year at Arcade Baptist Church in Sacramento.

I then went to Biola University from 1979 to 1983, after which I returned to Sacramento, where I spent some time in radio. After that I enrolled at Talbot Seminary (at Biola), where I began an M.A. degree in biblical exposition. After graduation I taught courses in photography at Biola from 1984 to 1990. At that time I was also part of a Vineyard church plant in Newport Beach with Kenn Gullickson. I did an internship at South Coast Community Church, following which I had a full-time job at Covenant Presbyterian Church in Orange County, California. In 1990, I left Biola to start a youth ministry at Mariners's Church/South Coast Community Church, where I served until 1998.

I led an alternative service at Mariners's—it was about having a unique worship experience compared to the other services. I taught in story, used video, and served a full meal beforehand for six hundred people. There were a few rules I had to follow: I could play different music before and after the service but not during. I could not use candles, but I could use lots of video. We wrote our own songs, and we had a coffeehouse as well.

I went to the Young Leaders Network conference in 1996 and thought it was very generational. I couldn't do the generational thing because I knew too many people from a wide variety of ages, especially in the recovery community, who were interested in changes in worship. I saw a wide recovery of practices such as experience, arts, authenticity, honesty, healing.

I had funding to start a church-within-a-church or a church plant. Or I could stay at Mariners's. As I thought about this, I realized I needed to be the head guy, at which point I started to realize that church was a systems issue for me. As I reflected, I realized I was not willing to simply rearrange the deck chairs on the *Titanic*. Something more radical needed to occur, and so I turned down both salary and prestige.

I started a website, the Ooze, with Dave Trotter in 1998. The Ooze was about a conversation. It formulated thoughts—both mine and others'. Many of the contributions are just as valuable six years later, because many people are wrestling with the same questions. I later created Etrek to become an online training vehicle.

With the Ooze, I tried to create a party—a *learning* party. I started with a party mentality, not a platform party, not a product party, and not a publisher party. I connected with the underground, the alternative. Let's have a conversation in a safe place that allows for a freedom of voices. Let's move to places where the church is uncomfortable. That is the story of the Ooze.

Mal Calladine, Tribal Generation, Sheffield, U.K.

I was born in 1968 in the predominantly upper-middle-class town of Royal Tunbridge Wells in Kent. It is just within the commuter belt of London. My family was not Christian; my father was a Freemason and an alcoholic.

At age eighteen, I dated a Christian girl whose family was actually functional. This had quite an impact on me, because they loved me, as rough as I was. One day I went to an evangelistic meeting and prayed "the prayer," receiving Christ as my Savior. I started reading the Bible every day. I spent three years looking for a job and eked out a living as a tennis coach and health instructor.

At the same time, I traveled to Brixton to visit Mike Breen, who was an Anglican vicar in a tough parish in the east end of London. Brixton is like south-central Los Angeles in many ways. I loved the church's openness to prophetic leading—God was very much involved in the worship. They used to say, "God is in the house." The church was youthful, interactive, multicultural, and felt like a set of friends.

At nineteen, I went to a polytechnic school in Oxford, where I majored in town planning with a minor in sociology, law, and politics. One of my strongest desires was to show that church needn't be embarrassing; it could be cool. Our college Christian Union was the biggest in the country, with four hundred students involved. It had a great rock band, and I headed the missions stuff and later led the entire Union.

I talked to Mike Breen about going into ministry but feared it would suffocate me. I started at Brixton, moving there in 1991, just as Mike was moving to Little Rock, Arkansas. The Brixton congregation placed a strong emphasis on discipleship. There were five core components of our discipleship training that went under the name *Lifeskills* (now called *Life Shapes* and published by Cook Communications in the U.S. and by Kingsway in the U.K.). A simple shape for easy memory retention represented each of the five components. Subsequently, three others were added.

Our small groups were partially inspired by Ralph Neighbour. The groups gathered in clusters or congregations (we had five of these), a model inspired by the family, synagogue, and temple structure encountered in Scripture. The Brixton church's closest resemblance was to John Wimber's teaching in terms of worship, ecclesiology, and missiology. The small groups sought to do power evangelism. Single moms and their kids led one of the clusters, and one was led by an eight-year-old.

I moved to Merseyside in the north of the U.K. in 1992 to be with Bob and Mary Hopkins and Youth with a Mission (YWAM). I visited Sheffield quite frequently because my girlfriend, Chriscelle, was working in a hospital there. I tried to be very involved in the Nine O'clock Service (NOS). The power of God was certainly there. It was a roller coaster, technically brilliant, but something scary as well.

Soul Survivor, based in Watford, asked me to lead their church-planting movement, so I moved to Chorleywood in 1994, just as Robert Warren was leaving St. Thomas's and Mike Breen was arriving in Sheffield as his successor. I wasn't very involved in Soul Survivor. For the most part, my time was spent negotiating ministries that crossed diocesan boundaries. Soul Survivor was fairly independent, mostly running conferences rather than being a church-planting movement. Its focus was first worship and second evangelism.

In 1996, my wife, Chriscelle, and I moved to Sheffield, where I worked at the largest sports camp in the nation as the head of human resources. I told Mike Breen we were back in Sheffield, the city we had come to love. Mike gave us time to get restored and to get a rhythm back into our life. After we had been there a while, St. Thomas's Church offered me a youth pastor position, which I turned down, as I had no passion for under-eighteens. I was excited about what God was doing with the over-eighteens. I started working for twenty hours a week in 1998. My dream was to develop a new paradigm of church—a church for my generation. There was a group of people who liked what God was doing in the services but still didn't have a belonging place. Pete and Caroline Harris led an Alpha and wanted to start meeting with me and Chriscelle.

In January 1997, we started a small group with Christians who wanted Alpha. Each week we added one person, so by September we had thirty people in our group. This group consisted of a fairly specific age because, as I commented at the time, "You can't talk about masturbation and rock 'n' roll with your grandmother in the room!"

The small group split to form four groups. Every third Tuesday we met as a cluster. By 1998, we had three clusters. In 1998–99, we started a year-long training program, originally called YAPs. In our groups, 50 percent came from Christian leaders' families, and the other half had no Christian background at all. As it turned out, the Christian leaders usually converted the nonbelievers through their time at university.

The small group provided a sense of belonging, whereas cluster groups, which grew to between eighty and one hundred, provided a sense of affinity as well as the main avenue for mission. Our primary evangelistic venue was soccer. We had five teams in a league, with each team related to a cluster. The cluster was "small enough to care, and big enough to dare."

We now have a teaching service that teaches cluster gatherings. We have no prescribed vision for small groups and clusters, but because each leader has gone through *Life Skills,* we know that a certain DNA has been passed on. If someone wants to start a group, the cluster leaders bless them. No cluster lasts forever. But we don't lose people—we "reenvision" them in some other forum.

We believe that small groups can be "NGOW": Non-Guitar Oriented Worship (and teaching is optional as well). Only two times in Scripture do Christians sing, and on both occasions they are in prison! Once every three months we have roughly forty prayer stations with twenty people visiting each at a time.

Leadership both emerges from below and comes from above. A functional team handles logistics, and a pastoral team is concerned with vision and people. The cluster leaders are the key pastoral leaders. The logistics team seeks to deliver the vision, not come up with it. The vision of a cluster is service oriented. It is a place of incarnation, of establishing community. Some cluster members actually move to be nearer to one another. Right now there are fifteen clusters.

Beginning in 1998, our celebration events met in City Centre. In 2000, we moved to the Roxy, a downtown dance club that had closed. In 2002, we lost the Roxy, and in 2003, we moved to what we call the Philadelphia Campus, which used to be an electrical engineering factory.

Jonathan and Jennifer Campbell, Seattle

Our journey has taken us on many paths, but a passion for Jesus has been woven throughout. We were both raised in Christian homes with good church experiences. It was during our college years that we came to understand what it means to surrender to Jesus in radical obedience. We met at U.C. Davis, where we both were leaders in campus ministry. We graduated on the same day, married a year later, then moved to Auburn, California, in 1987, where Jonathan began to serve as associate pastor of a Baptist church.

Everything seemed to be going well. We enjoyed the people, and the church grew rapidly. We had a house in the country and helped design a new church building on the edge of town. It was a healthy church, and we never got "burned," but something wasn't right. Despite many new members and lots of baptisms, there seemed to be very little transformation of lives or impact in our community. While growing professionally, we felt we were slowly dying spiritually. We were expending more time and energy on preparing for the next Sunday to attract people than on being present and listening to the Spirit. Somehow in the course of events, it seemed like we were serving the church more than Jesus. Our life in Jesus and our position in the church blurred.

We kept asking ourselves, Do we really want to give our lives to this? Are we willing to spend the rest of our lives building the organization? What difference is all this making in society? We had to get out—into business, overseas missions, or urban church planting.

In 1992, I (Jonathan) became a church-planter strategist for the North American Mission Board (SBC) in Southern California. We moved to the rapidly growing area of the Inland Empire. I was enlisted to direct a strategy for starting one thousand churches in less than ten years. Being way in over our heads forced us to a time of radical questioning. I read everything I could get my hands on in regard to church strategies and models. I also noticed that nobody at that time was speaking of church-planting movements in the West.

I finally prayed in desperation, "Lord Jesus, I don't know what to do. Which model of church and mission do you want us to follow?" After a few moments of silence, I sensed a clear answer: "Do you want *me* or a model?" It wasn't the answer I had hoped for. It would have been so much easier if he had given me a specific blueprint or had pointed me to an expert I could follow. Then I sensed the Spirit say, "If I show you a model, you will follow it. You will seek to perfect it with the best of intentions. Instead, will you trust me? Follow me. I am the Way."

After this, our journey was guided by these questions: What is the way of Jesus? What is his Spirit saying? How will we live this out in our cultural context? We questioned everything—all the traditions and norms we had grown up with—and looked deeply into Scripture to pull out the essentials of the way of Jesus. We are grateful for the fellow pilgrims from both the United States and abroad who walked with us during this time. During these early years of church planting, we began having children and started a business. Jonathan completed his Ph.D. during our last four years in California, not for the degree but for the accountability. We were encouraged and challenged by several mentors during this period: George Patterson, Tom Wolf, and Wilbert Shenk. We were also inspired by the writings of Roland Allen.

A year after our first church start, we replaced the large weekly church celebrations with simple gatherings in homes, apartments, and businesses. We'd given up our dedicated building, all programs, preaching, professional staff, and budgets. We felt like the Spirit kept stripping stuff away from us and our concept of church and leadership. We thought that one day there would be nothing left! We slowly began to accept that Jesus was enough. Is that so bad—just Jesus and one another? Or are we too dependent on the comfort that comes with the organization? How much flexibility can we handle? Are we mature enough to hold on to Jesus and him alone? What would that mean? Could this be a test of genuine spirituality?

We wanted to experience the same vitality that the early church did. So we continued the process of simplifying our understanding and practice of church to the essence of Jesus. We got rid of stuff and structures so we could get more of Jesus and be free to move as the Spirit led us. If we were dropped in any new context, what would we bring? What we wanted was a simple, reproducible way of being church that could be planted anywhere. We would ask ourselves, Can a week-old Christian do this? Could we live this life anywhere?

We began to realize that if we were to see a movement, we would need to resign and make room for a new generation of leaders from the harvest. So in the spring of 1999, we were sent by our community to Seattle to start a business and gather together spiritual communities. This was a new beginning for our family. We were Jesus followers earning our living in the world. Through our business and community involvement, we felt "baptized back into the world," meeting "spiritual" people, not Christians. We would invite new friends over, have a meal, and share our stories with one another.

We celebrated in December of 1999 when we baptized a young couple, and then they baptized their three friends. No one had a church background, so this approach was fresh—less strategic and less method driven than our churches in Riverside. This was the beginning of a simple organic way of life in which the gospel of Jesus spreads from life to life through a network of relationships.

It hasn't been easy to learn how to let Jesus build his church. Just when we thought we were getting a handle on it, God led us to remove something else. George Patterson continually challenged us to question anything other than simple obedience to Jesus. One afternoon he told me, "Jonathan, you need to lower the bar of your standards for leadership until they are nothing but biblical."

From the beginning, we have sought to center on the life and teachings of Jesus, to practice the "one-anothers" of the New Testament, and to be led by the Spirit. We have also valued simplicity, team leadership, and reproduction in every sphere. During our past thirteen years of church planting, we have been through three main shifts in our approach to church, mission, and life:

1. reproductive cell church: We equipped and commissioned teams to make new disciples and to start new cell groups. We met during the week as cells and gathered as a large group of cells on Sunday.
2. community of churches/church-planting movements: When we realized we were leaving our primary mission context on Sunday to attend "church" outside our neighborhood, we transitioned our cells to become churches that met throughout the week. We gathered all together just once per month. Over time, these organic churches reproduced across many social, economic, and language barriers in Southern California and met in homes, apartments, parks, campuses, and businesses.
3. church as being/the way of Jesus: Since moving to the Northwest, church has become more of who we are than what we do. We are simply "people moving together under the headship of Christ," as John Dawson describes church.

Over the years, we have discovered there is an inverse relationship between Spirit (divine) and structure (human). The more structures we build, the less we need the Spirit. The more we welcome the Spirit, the less we need formal structures. Maybe we seek to solidify structures in order to hide our impoverished and uncertain spiritual state. We also realized there is a radical difference between movement leadership and institutional leadership. Whereas typical church leadership is driven to conserve and control, movement leadership is marked by equipping, empowering, and releasing people. We are encouraged by the early signs of spiritual awakening emerging in the West—but not so much in the church as in the fields.

We have told much of our journey in a book, *The Way of Jesus: A Journey of Freedom for Pilgrims and Wanderers* (Jossey-Bass, 2005), which points toward a way of living spirituality from the core of being—to the very connections that define humanity. We have been and are being transformed by the love of God, experiencing the freedom of Jesus, and growing in the power of the Holy Spirit as we journey with others along the way of Jesus.

Brad Cecil, Axxess, Arlington, Texas

I was born in 1958 in Detroit and raised in the Presbyterian Church. I lived in the inner city at a time when the city was becoming increasingly diverse. I began to use drugs and alcohol at the age of thirteen. My drug usage escalated, and I was getting into legal trouble, so my parents sent me to boarding school.

At the age of sixteen, I proudly proclaimed, "I am an atheist." While at boarding school, however, I listened to an evangelistic presentation from the Billy Graham Association. After much resistance, I capitulated and yielded my life to God. I started reading the Bible voraciously. After high school, I attended a one-year Bible institute, Word of Life in New York, a school affiliated with Dallas Theological Seminary. I then went on to college in Tennessee. I loved theology and considered going to seminary.

I took a job as a high school camp director in New York and continued to read theological books. In 1991, at the age of thirty-three, I began to attend seminary in Dallas. I became conflicted as I realized that seminary was not a place for open exploration of theological nuance but rather a place of reinforcing established theology. However, I continued to read extensively and learned about the postmodern transition we were in. I read the postmodern philosophy of Jack Caputo as well as the works of Lesslie Newbigin, Stanley Grenz, Miroslav Volf, and Walter Brueggemann. These writers had a profound influence on me.

In 1995, Pantego Bible Church asked me to start a service geared toward young adults. We launched Axxess as an exploration of ministry in a postmodern context. Our Sunday service attracted one hundred twenty-five- to forty-year-old suburban professionals, most who were lifelong Christians. After a while, we began to attract a lot of alternative people as well. It was quite an interesting mix.

Other postmodern expressions of church had sprung up across the country, but we didn't consult with them. I visited University Baptist Church in Waco, and Chris Seay and I became friends, so, of all other churches, UBC had the most influence on us. Apart from my connection with Chris Seay, we felt isolated until we went to the Gen-X 2.0 Conference in 1997 at Mt. Hermon. For the first time, I heard church Christians talking about postmodernity. I was so surprised anyone was talking about it at all.

Over time, we at Axxess changed our ecclesiology. We observed that the modern church had developed a didactic teaching model of spiritual formation (i.e., the informed teach the uninformed). It was assumed that this is how one develops spiritually. The modern quest to find a place of irreducible certainty, which the philosophers call foundationalism, caused Christians to desire this same thing—a pure foundation. For modern Christians, this is what the Bible has become. My contention is that the Bible was never intended to be a foundation built on empirical observation of Greek, Hebrew, and Aramaic words.

We studied transformation. We recognized that most of the transformative things in our lives are missing from the predominant model of spiritual formation in contemporary churches, such as permanent relationships, shared experiences, inspiring art, and self-sacrifice, among others. Relationships are perhaps the most transformative thing in our lives, especially in areas such as values and compassion. It is very hard to teach these concepts didactically. Instead, they are shaped through a long-term process of observation, understanding, and modeling. We realized that we were not transformed by listening to sermons, even when the messages were reinforced with drama, music, and PowerPoint. As a result, we placed our priority on sharing life together. At that time, we switched from a large group pattern of church to that of a network of house churches.

Steve Collins, Grace, London

I was born in 1959 in Grimsby on the east coast of the U.K. but was raised in Bristol in the west. I attended the University of Bath and then moved to Surrey to work in London, where I now live. I came to faith at the age of twenty in the charismatic wing of the Church of England. I was in a church that was "full on" charismatic like the new churches, with some seriously unsound theology! It was a time and place when anything could be justified by saying, "This is what God is telling me." To disagree was to be accused of "resisting the Spirit." So we went along with the craziest things in fearful obedience. Of course, I have learned a lot since then about abuses of power and the real workings of the Spirit. I spent the remainder of the 1980s rebuilding my faith.

In 1984, I moved to Surrey, joined a Methodist church, and participated in its leadership. In the mid-1980s, there was a good number of twentysomethings in the church. There was rock 'n' roll worship. But by the early 1990s, the average age in the church was sixty-five, and only four twentysomethings remained.

I was a clubber in the mid-1980s and saw the beginning of rave culture in 1988. Between 1988 and 1991, I became fascinated by the spirituality of club culture. I felt God on the dance floor, not in church, and at the end of the "service" I felt clean. My fellow clubbers pursued God's presence and found it in the club. A question gripped me: Why is the church not plugged into this subculture?

It is important to note that I was the "normal" person in the U.K., doing what normal young Londoners were doing, listening to that music, wearing those clothes, going to those clubs. This was not some freak underground but the creative edge of mainstream culture. But where were the Christians? How was the church engaging with this culture? I knew about the Nine O'clock Service in Sheffield, which was a sign of hope to me that some Christians somewhere were indeed engaging with club culture [which had quickly become the dominant culture of people under forty in the U.K.] and the secular world of the 1990s. I didn't know of anywhere else. The "new" Christian stuff I had come across was embarrassing, uncool, and a standing joke to non-Christians. Nerds with acoustic guitars singing "praise you Jesus" is still the dominant caricature of "modern" Christians in the U.K.

In 1990, my life consisted of church involvement at the Methodist church, participation in rave clubs, and pursuing my vocation as an architect. I had both my church life and my other life, which was the life of a typical Londoner. I considered "church" to be the odd thing in my life, not the club scene. Church was the strange little underground that hardly anyone knew about. Over 90 percent of people in the U.K. don't go to church, and their ideas of Christians mostly involve either the elderly or fundamentalists.

By 1995, I had had enough of the Methodist church I had been attending. I felt alienated. I remember addressing the church council on a property matter and thinking, "I'm the youngest person here by twenty years. None of you has the least clue about my life." When in 1995 NOS collapsed, I felt my light of hope went out. But I saw the people involved on TV and said to God, "These are my people. I have to be with them." So after that I was praying, "Get me out of here!"

In 1996, I began to attend a Christian-run nightclub in London called Abundant. Many of the members of Abundant belonged to an exciting church called St. James-the-Less, which had professional musicians, great preaching, and about four hundred people under forty years of age. A pub was open on the doorstep after the service. That was when I said good-bye to my Methodist church. After seeing a special on worship experiments on TV, I decided to check out Grace in London, led by Jonny Baker. I was immediately hooked by alternative worship.

Alan Creech, Vine and Branches, Lexington

I was born in 1966 in eastern Kentucky. I wasn't raised in the church, and even though I wasn't Catholic, I attended Catholic school and vacation Bible school in the summers. At the age of twelve, I asked others if I could go to church with them. I went to catechism through the Catholic Church and was baptized at the age of fourteen. I became a teenage Catholic apologist, going to mass every day. Sometimes it was just me, the priest, and the nuns.

Several years later, I attended East Kentucky University, where I joined the Newman Center. I became interested in charismatic gifts at that time and attended those groups as well. At one point, I considered becoming a priest, but when I met Liz it was all over! We were married in the Catholic Church in 1988. Soon thereafter, we joined a Word of Faith Pentecostal church out of Tulsa and became really involved. It was more hierarchical than the Catholic Church! We were part of that community for ten years, with one year on staff as an interim pastor. The church was big on submission and authority. I was also strongly influenced by the cell movement of Ralph Neighbour and started cell groups during our stay there.

My wife, Liz, and I planned to plant a church in another city. The more we thought about it, though, the more we became convinced we should stay in the same location but attempt something different. The church did not understand that at all. We wanted something more relational, nonhierarchical, and less structured, and I did not want to be labeled as "charismatic." I became post-charismatic at that point, which did not mean that I denied the charismatic gifts but that I doubted they should be the defining mark of my Christian life.

We did not attend a church for six months, but we began to meet with others in a small group called Vine and Branches. This group was a vision with a website before it was a church. We went down a bitter path, griping a lot about the institutional church as we moved toward being a cell church. It was cathartic for us. After six months, we stopped that meeting.

In late 2000, we began the group again. We still didn't know what we wanted it to be. We were less cell oriented, meaning we were not hierarchical or building bound, we did not rely on professional ministry, and we did not major on Sundays. Instead, we were more geared toward relational activity.

It was around this time that we made connections through the Internet with others doing similar things. We found that Jason Evans and Matthew's House in California were praying for us regularly. We found Vineyard Central's website and met Kevin Rains and others in Cincinnati from whom we learned a great deal. Lifelong relationships were developed with these and several others at that time.

In the fall of 2001, the third iteration of Vine and Branches began. It is this group that has stayed together ever since. We started with six or seven people, and now we have nine adults and four kids.

Anna Dodridge, Bournemouth, U.K.

I was born in 1980 and raised in Dorset in the U.K. I was raised in a Christian family in a kind of independent, free evangelical congregation. My parents are amazing and never forced me into their faith but were always supportive. They were a big influence on how I view evangelism, because they just lived very Christlike lives. I grew up knowing that Christ was good because my parents were so awesome.

Growing up, I enjoyed all the things I probably shouldn't have enjoyed. I think I was aware of the fact that God was there and that I liked him, but I put him off for a good while. And I am so glad I did! I realize that sounds bad, but I really believe that growing up with non-Christians and experiencing the culture of the world has been good for me. I feel better connected with the people around me because I have at least a clue about what people my age want in life, because I wanted it right along with them. Best of all, I didn't get stuck in the "black hole" of the Christian subculture. Obviously, I wouldn't recommend that people give up on Christianity in order to get trained in the way of the world, but looking back, I know it has helped me a lot. I was very lucky to have some sound Christian friends who were an influence on me too. But mostly we were bad influences on each other!

When I really moved on in any kind of faith journey was at university. I did my first degree, in music, at Southampton University from 1998 to 2001. I met a lot of Christians, and the university had a very large and well-known Christian Union. I got involved in the Christian Union and was asked to be a cell group leader. By my third year of university, I had stopped any involvement with the Christian Union and had given up attending church. I think I wanted to make sure I didn't end up resenting God because I was so frustrated by Christians. I had already begun down the road of emerging church but just hadn't realized it. I was getting together with some Christian friends and just chatting about the people around us, discussing what we could do to help them practically and spiritually. We prayed for people. We were really all about being concerned about people's everyday lives rather than anything too super-spiritual.

I then took a year off to help me decide what to do next. I went back to university in Bristol to train as a secondary school music teacher from 2002 to 2003. I lived at home, near Bournemouth, for the year between universities and then came back and moved into my current house in central Bournemouth in the summer of 2003. I spent a year when I was in Bristol not really attached to a church, although I had some Christian friends around. They were all very happy with their cell church structure, and although I could draw from them and had support from them, there was no acknowledgment of a church-type responsibility to one another. I had contact with my church community back at home, but I certainly wasn't in communication with them all that much. I am so glad, for it allowed me to seek God for myself and to work out exactly what I wanted and needed out of church. It allowed me to take responsibility for my own faith. I didn't have too much additional pressure from other people expecting things from me, and selfishly, I didn't have to put too much effort and energy into supporting others, which was helpful really.

It is odd looking back on it now, but I really couldn't see the disparity between feeling I was a strong and mature Christian who people looked up to and the fact that I was far more interested in drinking and kissing boys. Obviously, now I can see that I was clearly not happy as a Christian, at least not in the context I was in. I can see that I was good at the habit of being a Christian but not very good at loving Jesus, and no one had pointed out to me that that was the important part. I didn't like how

Christianity was being presented to me, and I didn't want to be a part of that. But what I didn't know was that this was not what Christianity had to be about. All I wanted was to love Jesus and to get on with life, not go to boring meetings.

It took me a year or so to find some Christians who were on a similar wavelength, people who were fed up with the Christian Union because it was all politics and false relationships and fake smiles. I was disillusioned by the fact that I was being told these people cared for me. They pretended to love me as family, as Christ loves the church, but they didn't have a clue about who I was. It all seemed too shallow, and everyone was far too happy with that.

So I started questioning everything that was done, every decision made. Every time we organized a mission week, I was there asking what good it would do. I was like this at my home church too, never satisfied. I couldn't understand why people were happy to accept the answers they were being given when they were so obviously unhelpful.

I was told that I had this problem and that problem. I began to ask whether people knew me at all and whether they had ever even met a non-Christian! People I had known all my life didn't trust my judgment as a Christian. I was given the same answers to questions, and the last thing I wanted to do was give those same answers to other people.

It was good to hang out with people who were attending different congregations, or none at all, and I trusted them, because they invested in me as a friend, not as someone they saw twice a week on a Sunday morning and at a cell group. This is when I realized that I could be honest with people and that they actually cared. We did some practical stuff, like playing football with some kids on the local housing estate with a reputation for violence and poverty where a few of us lived and getting together with some girls who had low self-esteem. It was practical help and evangelism the way I thought it should be.

When I moved back to Bournemouth, I hung out with some friends—some of them were Christians, some weren't. The Christians among us started getting together, mainly because we were all into music and clubbing. One of my friends worked for a charity and was paid to go into the nightclubs to be a sort of chaplain, doing pastoral care for people and talking to them and being a Christian presence. So we were part of that, clubbing and evangelizing the way we thought it should be done.

I was pretty fed up with my church congregation because they refused to support me. They couldn't see how I could possibly want to go into nightclubs, and they thought it was disgraceful that we were encouraging the culture. They were happy to support us if we stood outside nightclubs and handed out tracts, but they didn't like us going into them, getting into the culture, hanging out with clubbers. Well, I ignored them and went off to Ibiza, Spain (a magnet for clubbers from all over Europe) for a couple weeks.

So I guess that brings us to the first realization of emerging church. We met a girl who was pretty messed up but was very interested in hearing about Jesus. We hung out with her in her flat full of drugs and DJs and listened to her story, answered questions, and got to be good friends with her. She decided to become a Christian, whatever that meant in reality, and after a while so did her boyfriend (now her husband and also a bit of a crazy pastor).

We were told by those ever-so-wise Christians around us that we needed to get her into a church quickly. We said no, there was no way any of us was waking up on a Sunday morning, and there was no way that she or her boyfriend would connect with bad 1990s worship music, half hour preaching, and NIV Bibles. So some of my friends and I started hanging out with them in a more purposeful way, discipling them, learning from one another, praying together, eating together. It was great because so often we could do this with non-Christians too, so we weren't exclusive or shut off.

After this, we started talking about what church was anyway. Lots of people thought we had chucked the baby out with the bath water, but we decided that all we needed were the vital parts of church outlined in the Bible. These were first, fellowship: we hung out together and shared our lives and experiences; second, worship, teaching, learning: we talked about Jesus, talked about what we found in the Bible, talked about our lives, listened to music, thought about God, loved one another, and served one another; third, evangelism: we spent time with non-Christians. It was as simple as that.

We gradually discovered more Christians who were in the same place: fed up with traditional church, heavy-handed guidance, the abuse of authority to keep people relying on others' wisdom instead of trusting them to grow themselves, noninvolvement in people's lives, ineffectiveness in the world around them, irrelevancy, and reliance on "how we always did things."

Where are we now? We gather as people who are interested in this community. Some are still involved in congregations, but most have stopped being a part of them. We get together every month or so. In reality, people are a bit lazy, and it doesn't happen as much as it should. We communicate a lot through emails and phone calls about prayer requests, news updates, and general things or prophesies we have found interesting. We all have deeper involvement with small groups, normally those that have to do with what we do: where we work or what our interests are. For instance, I am into clubbing and DJing and promoting, so I am involved in the lives of those with similar interests. Some people are in a band; some people work in design and Internet stuff; some people are involved with the international students in town.

Our community goes away a couple times a year. We spend the weekend together, hanging out, eating, drinking, walking, talking, sharing our stories, praying, discussing the Bible. It's not often that the community gets together as a whole like this. Most of the time we are gathered in smaller groups, households, friendship groups. But when we all get together, there can be up to twenty or thirty of us.

We did not really think about creating a club culture form of church. We went clubbing together, and we often prayed before going and while we were out. But I can't see that we could have transferred our ideas all that well. It would have been too exclusive. We didn't want a community of just clubbers. We have families and people who aren't into clubbing among us, and that's great. They support what we do and vice versa. It's much better this way. We can grow up together, and if we lose interest in clubbing, we don't lose interest in one another or the community.

As a community, we are quite a large group, including people we have met through friends of friends. We are mostly people in our twenties and thirties, but there are a couple families with kids. We are on the whole pretty much white, lower-middle class English people. I guess that's because our area has that socioeconomic makeup. We are a fairly wide spectrum of people from the area, but on the whole the area has a very small spectrum of people. Some examples give a flavor of who we are: Gaz and Jeremy and their respective families are boat workers, love motorbikes, live on socially and economically deprived estates, and work with the kids there. There are a few students, some artists, some musicians, some people who work normal nine-to-five jobs, some clubbers, and some ex-junkies.

We get together in bits and pieces; some people see one another more than others. We simply live our normal everyday lives. Our community is about the relationships. We have relationships with one another and with God all the time, not just when we are together. So we can see one another in ones and twos and in larger groups. We can phone and email. We are as involved in one another's lives as we can be and support one another as much as possible, but obviously some people are closer than others.

Ben Edson, Sanctus1, Manchester, U.K.

I was born in 1973 in Barnstaple, North Devon, in the southwest of the U.K., near Cornwall. My father is an Anglican vicar, so I was raised in a Christian home. By the age of fifteen, I had tired of church and Christianity. My faith was virtually nonexistent.

When I was sixteen, my father was appointed as the warden of a Christian community in Devon called Lee Abbey. During this time, I lived a bizarre existence. I was a non-Christian living as part of a Christian community! I was going out most nights with friends from the local village, drinking and taking drugs, then returning home to a Christian community.

I continued this lifestyle into university. But after a painful breakup with my girlfriend, I gave God another chance. I cried out to God at my point of need, and God met me in a profound and life-changing way. As I reflect on it, the most important factor in my journey back to Christianity was the Lee Abbey community. I was accepted, welcomed, and loved within that community. It was not about one person; it was about the five to six hundred people who were part of the community the years I was there. They weren't perfect. They had fallings out and could be judgmental and arrogant, but they were real people who were sincere in their faith. I saw the good times and the bad, and therefore this was no rose-tinted view of community—it was the real thing.

I could contrast Lee Abbey with my community at university, which had a similar demographic but a totally different values base. These people were great friends but could at times be rather selfish and hedonistic. I saw people descend into serious drug abuse, abusive relationships, and exploitation of the vulnerable. They were crying out for purpose and meaning. At university, I joined evangelical churches, but they were never really a fit. Within me was always the feeling that there was no way my friends could come along. It would be culturally alienating to them and would sour our friendships.

I was selected to train for Church Army (an Anglican society of evangelists) in 1998, as I sensed a call to evangelism. I trained for three years at theological college, completing an M.A. in theology and religious studies. During my time at college, I became more and more frustrated with church; I struggled with certain aspects of evangelical theology and was drawn to the mystical side of Anglo-Catholicism. However, both strands of the church turned me off. I didn't want to go to church and be told what to think and believe. I wanted to discover for myself. The church I attended was intensely frustrating. I found that they had no outward focus and therefore were very insular.

My impetus to start a church came from within my own Anglican tradition. The initial drive came from the diocese of Manchester. In 1996, the IRA planted a massive bomb in the city center of Manchester that caused loads of damage. Fortunately, no one was hurt, and the bomb was the catalyst for change. The city council redeveloped the city center into a modern European regional capital. Part of this redevelopment was to encourage people to move back to live in the city center. After college, I became the city center missioner responsible for the church's outreach ministry in the diocese of Manchester.

I made contact with a number of people when I first moved to Manchester and discussed with them my job and whether they would be interested in establishing a new church in Manchester. We first met at the end of October 2001. Six people were interested in forming a church. We began to meet weekly and gradually invited new people. We decided on the name Sanctus1, aiming to increase in size and to begin having public worship events.

Our first public worship was at Manchester Cathedral on February 17, 2002. It was very experimental in content. Approximately twenty people attended. Since then we have been meeting for public worship once a month. Services have grown in popularity and reputation, with numbers varying from fifteen to sixty.

The group that forms the backbone of Sanctus1 meets weekly on Wednesday night. I have taken pastoral responsibility for this group, which has been a privilege. Currently, about forty people meet in two Wednesday night groups. The format varies: We discuss issues, read the Bible, and engage theologically with film and music. We also have services, social events, and other activities. The Wednesday night gatherings are based around discussion and adult learning techniques. Both Wednesday groups meet together once a month for a shared Eucharist.

The majority of people who attend are between twenty-five and forty and reflect the city center dynamic. Some live in the city center, while others use the city center to work and play. There are a number of recognizable groupings within Sanctus1. A large proportion is involved with the creative arts. For example, there are musicians, visual artists, arts development workers, graphic designers, and architects. We are also attracting a number of people from the gay community. This is simply due to the inclusive welcoming attitude that is fundamental to the ethos of Sanctus1.

The growth within Sanctus1 over the past year has been organic. People have shared what Sanctus1 is about with their networks of friends and contacts. We have not had evangelistic missions or events, but we are a mission-focused church. Growth and mission are part of the DNA of the church rather than an add-on annual event. We are reaching the dechurched rather than the nonchurched: people who have stopped attending church because of boredom, hurts, changes in circumstance, or a number of other reasons. Our next challenge is to attract more nonchurched people to Sanctus1. We are now running a club night in a bar in the city center that is a place for natural evangelism to take place. We are planning to open a night café in the near future and to start a third Sanctus1 group that will be more accessible to those with no church background.

Roger Ellis, Revelation Church, Chichester, U.K.

I was born in 1959 in Portsmouth, U.K., into a family that was not Christian. In my late teens, I had a dynamic experience of God, an encounter of the Spirit at a crazy charismatic church down the road. I had lots of friends who came to faith as well, but I couldn't bring long-haired metal guys to the church. They didn't fit the framework, and I didn't know what to do with them. The church didn't understand the culture I came from. As a nineteen-year-old, I did not experience a church that could relate to my friends.

At the time (1983), *youth church* was a swear word. It was later relabeled "church in emerging culture." We were doing whatever happened with no clear concepts to guide us. We realized that others were creating models of mission in other cultures around the world, so why not us?

Jason Evans, Matthew's House, Vista, California

I was born in 1975 in San Diego, where I have lived my entire life. I was raised in a Christian home and came to faith at the age of six. I attended a Free Methodist church where I grew in my faith. In high school, I took over the youth group and began to run it. I was strongly influenced by and identified with the punk scene as a musician. For the next seven years, I was part of a punk band, and yet my faith remained central to me.

In 1992, I met Brooke, and in 1997, we got married. In 1998, I began working with the youth group at a local Southern Baptist church,

Daybreak. I became church administrator and then the young adult pastor, leading small groups and getting a big service going. This was the "coffee and candles" seeker model of service, with the young people sitting on rugs and chairs. They wanted the "Starbucks feel." I found this to be an impossible model. People did not want a watered-down version of the gospel. The "five steps to freedom" style was patronizing. The first thing I was given to read was Rick Warren's *Purpose-Driven Church*, for our church was strongly committed to the models of Bill Hybels and Rick Warren.

I taught from Scripture but tried to stay topical, staying true to the seeker model. This clearly was not working, but I didn't know what else was out there. The people preferred small groups to the large gathering, which gave me a great deal of grief. In addition, singles, when married, were expected to join the main service. I felt that our small group leaders ought to be recognized by the church as leaders and be ordained, but I knew that would never happen.

In driving to church, we would pass through blighted areas with poor migrant workers, and then we would arrive at a rich church with a huge building program. I was haunted by the question What am I doing this for, when this other community could use our help? My wife and I began to meet with another couple who had recently resigned their youth pastor role at a megachurch. Each week we resonated with this couple. Matthew's House was born here. I resigned and prepared the leadership of my groups for my departure.

We began Matthew's House in the city of Vista. We brought friends to our informal meetings, where we talked about our lives and prayed together. Some of the young people asked Jesus into their lives, and it happened quite naturally. For a year, we kept thinking we were going to launch a church plant, until we realized that this was all we needed. Matthew's House is the story of Levi the tax collector. It is a place where saints and sinners can get together and party with Jesus in their midst.

Matthew's House planted four house churches and many others that subsequently folded. Lately, we have been adopting other house groups that want to connect with us. We represent a communal way of life, not a meeting.

Dwight Friesen, Quest, Seattle

I was born in 1969 in southern Manitoba, Canada. I came from a line of three generations of Mennonite pastors. My own family worshiped in the Christian and Missionary Alliance Church. However, we maintained the ethos of the Mennonites. My parents were very mission minded. In junior high, I had a "come back to Christ" experience, and I felt called into ministry at the age of thirteen.

I went to Canadian Bible College (CMA affiliated) to become a youth minister. At times I felt frustrated that I needed to go through hoops to get to where I wanted to go. After seminary, I served in Billings, Montana, as a youth pastor. At one point, sixty non-Christians showed up at the church basketball court. The church said that each church member could bring only one non-Christian. I was disillusioned by this kind of attitude. After two years, I resigned to go to seminary.

I went to Trinity Evangelical Divinity School in Chicago, not so much because of the seminary but because it was near Willow Creek Community Church. At TEDS, I received an M.A. in religion, and my wife earned an M.A. in teaching. While at Willow, I had various pastoral responsibilities. I experienced life and grace in a new way, which caused me to love people more than programs.

In 1995, my wife and I went to Latvia for the summer, where we started a seeker small group. When I returned, I realized that very little was being done to understand culture here in the U.S., to reach people like me. We then decided to plant a church in Seattle. I wanted to plant a Gen-X megachurch like Willow Creek. It would be big and media driven. It would have to be a good size if it was to work with Gen-Xers.

So in 1996, we moved to Seattle. Our first underlining principle was to engage missionally, so we listened to people as we went to clubs, coffeehouses, and art shows five nights a week. We also visited fifty churches in the first year. The most discouraging aspect was that they were all the same. Almost all had adopted a giving perspective, by which I mean "our service is our gift to you." The music was pop. The sermons were pop psychology, with the underlying message "For the most part we can help make your life better. This is a place you want to be." It felt plastic. At no point in the service did my presence matter. I felt it wouldn't make a difference whether I was there or not.

Our second principle was relational. We didn't want to do anything that would violate the nature of relationships. This principle saved us from pursuing the Gen-X megachurch model.

We both got jobs in the community and started a Bible study in our home. We thought to ourselves, "If we are going to start a church, why not just *be* one?" This felt authentic to us. So we began to act like a church. We opened our home and had a meal. Most people came through their work relationships. We began to meet at a café in 1997,

which was the beginning of a dream for us. Our band played Smash-
ing Pumpkins, REM, and U2, and black clothes were everywhere. We
had between forty and sixty people on most nights, all Caucasian, all
single, all in school. The core group, of twelve to fifteen, was made up
of married couples.

We started small groups. Then in 1998 a crisis hit. A good friend decided not to come on staff. I realized that I had been setting inappropriate
goals for him. At the same time, we lost the café. As we were meeting
in a room at Starbucks, one of our group asked, "Could it be there is
an invitation here for us? Could it be that we need to listen to what is
being said?" What had our dream been? We realized it had become all
about the video montage, following up with new people, starting new
groups. It had all become too much of a business.

So we stepped back to catch our breath. We talked about refocusing
to become a community that is intentionally missional. We created a
new monthly rhythm of gathering. One Sunday a month we met in
someone's home; another Sunday each month we had a worship gathering; on another we had a teaching time; on another we had an open mic
through which we shared what was going on in our lives. We wanted to
see Christ in one another, "storying" the gospel. Our small groups were
the main source of continuity, supplemented by occasional weekends
spent together.

I felt like I was dying, dying to the idea of the megachurch pastor,
which seemed to me now as though it would be abusive to those who
came. This was a time of serious soul searching. "If I am not that, then
who am I?" I asked myself, for now I was faced with an invitation to
labor in obscurity. I felt devastated. I would need to work bivocation-
ally. Serving people in this way would never give me the recognition I
wanted!

The church became less programmed. But it seemed to fit with who
we were. I began to develop more of my interior life by visiting local
monasteries. I felt like I needed God. I was no longer certain of my
relationship with him. Formerly, I knew the rules, followed them, and
then I was good to go. But now the dos and don'ts hold less and less
weight. I felt a loss of security in who I was in relationship to Christ. I
felt adrift. Speaking at our gatherings, I spoke more of doubt than of
certainty. But opening up with my doubts and concerns freed others
to do the same.

Our biggest ministry gives hope to those who have given up on church.
We experience divine hope in our community by "being present in one

another." We have a value that says, "We don't know for sure, but we sense God is calling us." It is an ethos we are creating.

Rob Graham, Levi's Table, St. Louis

I was born in 1961 in St. Louis. I was raised in a Christian home and became a Christian when I was six years old. I attended a Baptist church but later became involved in nondenominational churches and started church planting at the age of twenty. In addition, I learned to lead worship by playing the guitar. While I was leading worship for various churches and church plants, I always supported myself and my family through nonchurch work.

In 1995, I came in contact with the Vineyard and became an assistant pastor and worship leader in Virginia. In 1997, my family and I returned to St. Louis, where I began to lead worship for a nondenominational church, Discovery Church. Then, in 2001, I fulfilled a lifelong desire to start a church where I would be supported full-time.

We met with six others, looking to begin a church plant. As we were beginning, we did the demographics. We were going to have the church with coffee and all the trimmings. But then we started asking some disturbing questions: What is church? What is the goal? Why are we doing everything we are doing? Why do we sit in rows? Why do we have a band? What are the results? Along the way, I picked up the book *Missional Church*. In reading the chapter on "closed-sets" and "open-sets," I was jarred. Is this what I am trying to put my arms around? I struggled with this. It was a very painful and confusing time for the six of us. It was out of this community that Levi's Table was born. There are now about twenty adults and ten children at Levi's Table. No one gets paid, everyone tithes, and the bulk of our money goes to a local food pantry.

Simon Hall, Revive, Leeds, U.K.

I was born on the very day the Beatles released *Sergeant Pepper* in 1967! I was raised in Leeds, in the north of the U.K., in a lower-middle-class community. I wasn't raised in church, but the schools I attended were nominally religious. At the age of fifteen, I wanted to run away from home. My life was hellish, but hearing at a Luis Palau Mission that Jesus would forgive my sins, I thought I would go for it. I wanted to live differently from my parents as well. I went to Oxford for four years, where I participated in an alternative community, Joy, and returned to Leeds after graduating.

The most important moment in my life with Jesus, after meeting him for the first time, was meeting him in a nightclub context. Before I became a Christian, I was into heavy metal (AC/DC, Black Sabbath, Judas Priest, etc.), and afterward, I failed to like the bland music made by Christians. I fell back into the club scene in Leeds, which had turned into goth, and my last two years at school were spent living in and loving the church I was in and the goth scene.

The moment that started the journey that led to Revive took place in 1993. I had just done a week's mission at the local high school. That Sunday night, about fifteen kids filed into our church and sat in the back row. They all had made a commitment to Christ. I had prepped the minister that the service was going to be for them. But we had to start with a hymn to keep the traditionalists happy! By the time the hymn was finished, just one kid was still there. The rest never came back. The message they communicated was, "You told us being a Christian was relevant to our lives, but you lied." I wanted to tell the truth, and to do that I had to be a part of a community that was living out what I believed in a way that my friends could understand.

Revive is still going after eleven years, and it has about sixty committed members. The largest age group consists of those between twenty-one and twenty-six. Revive is mainly made up of people who didn't fit into "regular" church. They were too cynical, too rebellious, too radical, too charismatic. Our members are mainly from the charismatic spectrum, so they might have experienced Church of England (a few), Baptist (a lot), and charismatic churches, like Vineyard (a lot).

We are trying to integrate the passion and the radical discipleship (at least the intention of radical discipleship) we inherited from our charismatic parentage, with the authenticity and relevance of the alternative worship world. Two communities have helped us, namely, the Northumbria Community and Church of the Savior in Washington, DC.

Todd Hunter, Christ the Community, Yorba Linda, California

I was born in 1956 in Santa Ana, California. In 1975, at the age of nineteen, I gave my life to Christ through Greg Laurie's ministry at Calvary Chapel Riverside. I met John Wimber, at that time a Calvary Chapel pastor, who mentored me. At the age of twenty-three, I moved to Wheeling, West Virginia, to plant churches. We started various churches in that part of the country.

In 1986, I returned to Southern California and became the executive pastor of the Anaheim Vineyard. I served in that role until 1991, when I had a crisis. First, I thought I was to assume the senior pastor role at Anaheim, and second, I had serious issues with the Kansas City prophets, so I moved back to Virginia Beach and planted seven other churches. It was then that I received my M.A. in biblical studies from Regent University in Virginia Beach. In 1994, I returned to Southern California to be the national director of the Association of Vineyard Churches, in which role I served until 2000. I realized I was not a religious bureaucrat.

In 1996, because of my curiosity, I began reading extensively. I found the missiologists and the philosophical work of Dallas Willard the most helpful. I was coaching Gen-Xers at this time, while serving as national director of the Vineyard. For the last three years, I have mentored over one hundred leaders, but no more than twenty or thirty at a time. Most recently, I helped a community get started in Eagle, Idaho.

Si Johnston, Headspace, London

I was born in 1976 and raised in Bangor, Northern Ireland. Like most of my generation growing up there, I had a daily drip feed of religion of some sort. The trouble was that with each daily dose of religion came a daily dose of sadness at the conflict. After the Enniskillen bomb, when I started asking questions about the goodness of God, an elder told me, as an eleven-year-old kid, that I shouldn't ask such questions about God! Church was always there and was a part of the furniture of my life. I didn't question it, like I didn't question my dad being my father or my house being the place I lived; it just was.

I was on the receiving end of various atrocities, which in the end turned me away from my received faith traditions upon arriving at the university in Scotland. During that time, as a DJ and a club promoter, I soon discovered that this underground community was a whole lot more authentic and real about life. As my faith in God evaporated, church became increasingly irrelevant.

The point at which church died again was after a friend died from Ecstasy. Some friends and I began our own church-within-a-church at Aberdeen. Ever since then, I have always sought to be a part of an authentic Christian community.

You have to have sympathy for Gandhi when it was, as he observed, the genuine lack of love and compassion among Christians that sent him packing in other directions. I would love to be able to say that I can't understand what he was about, but that would be a lie! Since it's always helpful to declare your hand at the outset, I'm Northern Irish (and therefore white, middle class, and educated) and was, like a renowned Christian ulsterman before me, a "reluctant convert"—reluctant because I just couldn't bear playing ball with church, as I understood it, for reasons that Gandhi stated. I guess you either let that stall you or you try to do something about it. I opted for the latter.

After some years of formally studying theology, I found myself on a journey to a "merging" church. Steve Chalke put together a partnership between a large (in terms of the size of the building but not the congregation) inner-city London church and Oasis (a Christian charity focused on social engagement). On June 8, 2003, the two of us joined up, and now, to varying degrees, we are "emerging."

Upton Chapel has a significant history in social engagement. Upton Chapel was originally led by Rowland Hill; it became the birthplace of the Bible Society, the Shaftesbury Society, the Ragged School Movement, and several other significant initiatives. In fact, William Wilberforce and his crew made it their central London base from which they put an end to the transatlantic slave trade in the British Empire. Interestingly, the landmark spire was donated by Abraham Lincoln's family to thank the church for its support and inspiration in the battle for the emancipation of slaves in America. That was then. When we moved in, it contained a very small, predominantly black group of people who were trying their best to be faithful. The only service was on Sunday morning. The rest of the week the building was sublet to various groups, most notably the globally renowned Cornish Society.

We started a team that was responsible for the growth of this church, and we changed the name to Church.co.uk—Waterloo. Essentially, our DNA is about making the message of Jesus accessible to everyone by stimulating debate, resourcing experimentation, and modeling innovation in expressions of Christian faith and church for the twenty-first century.

Stripping things back, we aim to be:

- 24-7: providing a welcome to everyone whatever their situation, whatever the time, day or night
- holistic: offering support and inspiration to the whole person and the whole community
- global: serving as a hub or resourcing base for global mission

In particular, I am involved in the explorational side of the project. There was no Sunday night service, and so, having a blank sheet of paper, I and a group of six others began something. We're just not sure what! The evening is called headspace because that is often something you need if you live, work, or just exist in London. It begins at 7:00 p.m. in our café. Then there is a call to worship. For about fifty minutes, we move to the auditorium, where we lead one another in structured worship. In the final part of the evening, everyone moves next door to the pub, where the conversations continue.

Recently, inspired by the past activities of Wilberforce and others, we held a conference on the issue of human trafficking. Amazingly, as if by accident, this conference evolved into a collective of people from various emerging church groups across London responding to issues of injustice. Protest4, as the growing network is now known, is socially and politically engaged in making positive and practical steps toward justice.

Most recently, I have moved on from Church.co.uk and headspace.

Andrew Jones, Boaz, U.K.

I was born on September 7, 1963, in New Zealand. I moved to Australia when I was seventeen. My parents were not believers, but they sent me to a Presbyterian Sunday school for a few years, where I heard the gospel. My teens were interspersed with rebellious vandalism and drunken parties, as well as groovy times with Christian youth groups. Just before I turned seventeen, I decided to follow Jesus fully. I was impressed with some of the young people in the youth group I was attending. They had joy and purpose. I just had hangovers. I wanted their life. I wanted to follow Jesus like them.

Church didn't work for the people who were joining me in my faith journey. Two events come to mind. First, at seventeen, I became a fundamentalist street preacher, staying out until 2:00 a.m. with a thermos of coffee and a bag of gospel tracts. The first person who prayed with me to receive Jesus was not able to adopt my church culture. Neither were the others. Leading them to Jesus was easy compared to entrenching them in the church. I enjoyed my church and adapted to the culture, but the people I was leading to Jesus could not make the transition. I knew we needed new churches and different churches, but it was not until the 1990s that I began to start other churches.

Second, I moved to San Francisco in 1995, and God gave me a passion for the street kids and the young people among the postmodern subcultures: goth, rave, hippie, punk, metalheads. Many of them were coming into the kingdom, and the traditional churches could not hold them. I had no choice but to create new forms of church, new wineskins, so that the new wine would not leak out.

I started getting calls from around the U.S. and found myself traveling around the country to help things get started. In 1999, I put twenty-five thousand miles on our Winnebago. Then in 2000, I made the leap to Europe and have been working around the world with Europe as my base.

Right now, my family and I are starting a monastery in Orkney Islands, U.K., and I still travel one-third of the time to be with emerging church networks. I am a consultant with the Baptist General Convention of Texas and an associate of DAWN Ministries. Our ministry, called Boaz, hosts international round tables and large-scale worship installations. I have been a blogger since 1997 and am probably the world's oldest VJ (video jockey). And I *love* the church.

Billy Kennedy, Sublime, Remix, Cultural Shift, Southampton, U.K.

I was born in 1962 in Liverpool in the northwest U.K. I lived there for three years, after which time I moved to a location near Glasgow, U.K., until age eleven. Then I moved to Banbridge, Northern Ireland, until age seventeen. I was raised in church, my father being a Baptist minister. I always had faith, but when I was eighteen years old, I left home and traveled around the U.K. with my job, seeking a faith of my own. I tried a wide variety of churches. Then I moved to Southampton, where I attended Southampton Community Church. My first week there I had a significant encounter with the Holy Spirit. I was hooked!

We began Sublime for the teens in our area as a ministry of Southampton Community Church. We also started Remix, which later became Cultural Shift. The reasoning behind this development was that I desired to see young people become disciples. I had been involved in youth evangelism but was frustrated by the lack of lasting fruit. I felt we needed something different and tried a range of events and projects, but nothing quite hit the mark. I came to realize that the larger church was detached from youth culture and was trying to squeeze the next generation into its mold. Someone needed to break the mold and to focus on what Christ really wants—disciples.

The event that marked the transition for us was when we got to the end of ourselves—the end of our ideas and resources. All our youth workers resigned for one reason or another, and we stopped our youth ministry. We then decided to meet weekly to pray. This was in the middle of 1994. I had also met Martin Smith around this time, and we decided to try a monthly worship event called Cutting Edge. It was

also during this time that the church in the U.K. had begun to experience renewal coming out of Toronto Airport Vineyard. A number of
our young people were impacted. It was the convergence of these three
events that birthed Sublime.

Dan Kimball, Vintage Faith Church, Santa Cruz, California

I was born and raised in New Jersey and had no church experience
apart from my parents occasionally dropping me off at a church. I had
no concept of the teachings of Jesus or the story of the Bible from these
early church experiences. After attending Colorado State University, I
moved to London for a year with the punk/rockabilly band I was the
drummer for. There I was befriended by an eighty-three-year-old pastor
of a tiny church comprised of elderly people. But there I saw Jesus in
the people, and I committed my life to follow him through the ministry
of this tiny church.

When I returned to America, I had no concept of denominations
or what to look for. I looked up "Bible" in the yellow pages of a phone
book and ended up at a large, wonderful, contemporary Bible church.
At that church, I got involved in ministry and became the high school
pastor (even though I had never been to a youth group in my life). After
several years of following the Willow Creek model of youth ministry,
in the early 1990s, I began to notice that a change was happening in
culture and the way youth responded, the questions they were asking.
As much as I tried to help youth become a part of the main services of
the church, there was resistance and a lack of connection for most of
them (even though it is a great contemporary church). It was frustrating
seeing youth leave the high school ministry, not connect with the main
church, and drift off.

So I asked if I could experiment with the college group since the leader
was leaving. I began forming what I would call focus groups of Christian
and non-Christian teens and those who were college age. I started asking
questions and doing a lot of listening. This led to the birth of Graceland
in 1997, which started as a young adult Sunday night service in the existing church. After listening to teenagers and young adults talk about
what kind of church they would like, we changed the space and made it
more like a coffeehouse/art gallery environment. We moved the podium
from up on the stage to down among the people. We experimented with
worship using art. We brought in some liturgical elements and other
worship practices from throughout church history, not because they were
cool but because as a community we found we resonated with them as

ways to worship God. We made a lot of methodology changes. But it really was more than methodology—it was in retrospect a heart change and values change. We became more community based in decision making. We became excited about being Jesus to those in our community who normally would not be in a church. We started home groups that met midweek that older people from the main church led and through which they mentored the younger.

This slowly evolved to where we realized this was not just an age thing. It reached beyond the age parameters of eighteen to twenty-nine. That is when it became a church-within-a-church (although we didn't publicly call it that). The many people who were involved, the way we used the arts in worship, the way we approached leadership, and of course God were behind the rapid and large growth we experienced over the next several years. But that is when the trouble began.

Questions we never thought of arose. How does our church fit within the whole church? How are the elders of the main church involved in this? How is the senior pastor involved? What happens now, as people can stay here and grow older together and not have to become a part of the other church services of the main church? I was eventually told by the senior leadership of the main church that Graceland was too independent, and decisions were made to enfold Graceland into the life of the main church. Our staff was divided up into various departments, and we were told the teaching of Graceland should be the same as the rest of the church. The goal was uniformity so that things could be neater and more under control.

This deeply affected me, and although I was not asked to leave but instead to lead in making these changes, I realized I could not do that. All the changes I was being asked to make went back to the very reasons we needed to start Graceland in the first place. I was being told, "It's nothing. Just keep doing the music you are doing, but preach the messages we are preaching in the main church so that there is unity." But I began a soul search, asking, "Why does this feel wrong? Is what we were doing simply the same as the main church but with different music?" I began asking fundamental questions such as What is church? What is a pastor? I realized that what had started as a methodology issue had turned into an ecclesiology issue.

During this time of trying to explain to the senior leadership of the main church why we needed to do things differently the book *The Emerging Church* was written. It was sort of an apologetic to keep myself sane as I tried to explain why the changes involved more than just changing the music and lighting some candles. I was rethinking church as a whole, rethinking what it means to be kingdom-minded in our culture, rethinking leadership, etc. Once you go down this road and really process this, it is somewhat like being born again in terms of how you view what it means to be a church and what it means to be a Christian.

Because of the strong relationship I had with the main church, I was eventually able to launch a new church, Vintage Faith Church, with the support of the mother church. We still have a strong and healthy relationship with the mother church, and the tension is now gone since we are on our own. Graceland, after the changes were made, lost its identity and sense of community. It eventually was folded into the life of the main church, and the weekly worship service came to an end. This is why I am passionate about trying to communicate that being "emerging" is not about the style of music. It is about rethinking church as a whole in our post-Christian culture. If we aren't doing that, we are changing only the outer dressing or refluffing the pillows, not really changing. To me, that is what the emerging church must do not only to be missional but also to survive in the decades ahead in our post-Christian culture.

Chris Matthews, Extreme, Red Café, Swansea, U.K.

I was born in the early 1950s and raised in Swansea, U.K. From an early age, I attended an Open Brethren church, where I stayed until my mid-twenties. I married Barbara in my early twenties. We eventually left the church, dissatisfied with the status quo, and joined Linden Church in 1980, which was part of the new church movement (formerly known as the house church movement). In 1982, we joined the leadership team and are still on it to this day.

In the 1990s, it became increasingly clear that existing expressions of church were significantly limited in their ability to connect with the emerging generation, and through the work we were engaged in (schools and universities/colleges), we began to think about what alternative shapes of church might reach a post-Christian generation. This exploration didn't sit well with some people in the church. Even though we were considered a new church, there was quite a resistance to change. The exercise of control and the wielding of power were huge issues. A large number of people left Linden in 1997 over the issues of the form and the shape of church. It was a particularly painful experience, but for those who remained, it was a time when we were able to redefine who we were and where we wanted to go. This was when we set up Extreme and Red Café.

Extreme was Linden's expression of church in youth/emerging culture. It began in 1997 and launched Connected—a youth and community project in 1998. The purpose was to provide facilities for young people and to engage with the community in a way and at a level that the church had not previously done. The project was born out of the vision of Extreme and those at its core. Following a series of pilot events and trial approaches, and in cooperation with the local police and others, Linden purchased a building on the seafront in Mumbles in March 2000. We felt it was important to be on the main thoroughfare. We have just recently laid Extreme to rest as we feel it has run its course.

In January 2001, Red Café was opened as a point of contact with young people. It is a youth and community project and was not set up as a stand-alone church plant. We never really wanted to be separate. There would be major implications for resources and credibility. Being connected to something bigger has made a huge difference in all sorts of areas. Red Café quickly became very popular, providing a safe environment in which young people could hang out. It also offered workshops and training in a range of areas: recording, video, dance, recording studio work, DJing, etc. Personal development for young people was high on the agenda. The project looked to make connections with young people, particularly those who either were already disaffected or were in danger of becoming so. Red Café was open for young people three evenings a week and six times a week during school vacations. Red Café also became the venue where Extreme held church meetings.

We also featured small group activities. Some took place in homes and were discipleship based. Others were lunchtime events in local schools. Clearly, all were part and parcel of church, and for lots of young people, this was their only connection with church.

The Sunday evening meetings, which continued until recently, helped maintain the impetus and the energy to keep Red Café running. A lot of the focus for these times was prayer for resources, strength, inspiration, etc. What held us together was not keeping a meeting going. It was more intentional than that. We prayed for the young people and the team, and we thought about how we worshiped and how we learned. Our focus was and continues to be how we make the faith more accessible to young people who have little understanding or experience of God and church.

Even though we laid Extreme to rest, Red Café is alive and prospering and has grown and developed well. We now have two buildings and employ a number of staff part-time. We branched into alternative curriculum, working with schools and educational services to provide courses and approaches that work with disenchanted young people who are finding school a challenge for a variety of reasons. We have seen God provide for us in amazing ways.

We expect to launch a new church that will target a younger age group. We are thinking of a five- or six-year plan, and some of the people who grew up being a part of Extreme will be involved. Others who were formerly with Extreme are now in different parts of the U.K., and lots of them are involved in innovative things for God. It seems that once the mold is broken and people find life outside the confines of traditional church, it is hard to go back and settle for the restrictions again.

In the main, Linden is a place where new and creative approaches are welcomed and encouraged. It is a diverse church and quite dispersed in many ways. The relationship focus that is at its core is very strong now, and that is what holds it all together. There isn't a great deal of structure to lean on, but there is a lot of energy for seeing God's kingdom come. The founder of the church, John Sampson, has just been awarded the M.B.E. (Member of the Order of the British Empire) by the Queen for his services to the community. He is seventy-two and still going strong, although he doesn't really play a huge part in leading these days. It is a recognition that one of the values at the core of the church is to be here for the benefit of those who are not a part of us.

Joel McClure, Water's Edge, Hudsonville, Michigan

I was born in 1973 in Michigan and was raised in an independent Christian church. I was part of church life but became more serious about my faith during my sophomore year of college. During my junior year, I decided to pursue vocational ministry, so I attended Lincoln Seminary in Illinois. After graduating from seminary, I served as a pastor in rural Illinois from 1999 to 2000. I moved back to Michigan, where Randy Buist gave me a call.

Joining Randy and a group of others, we set out to begin a Willow Creek–style congregation. We had looked at a seeker church in greater Dayton, Ohio, Southbrook, which got us thinking more about the Willow model. In November 2001, I got in touch with Todd Hunter, former national director of the Association of Vineyard Churches (Yorba Linda, California), who began a mentoring relationship with us. We started to think seriously about creating missional communities as opposed to beginning a seeker church. We went to conferences throughout 2002 that helped shape for us the idea of a missional church.

I always felt dissonance in my experience of church. If it is about making disciples, why isn't discipleship happening? Why was there so little spiritual maturity in the friends I had known in church for so many years? I read Dallas Willard, and it just clicked. Now I understand. There is a radically different agenda in churches today. Discipleship is an optional thing in most churches. For Randy, his transformation came through the mentoring of Craig Van Gelder and reading Stanley Hauerwas's and Will Willimon's *Resident Aliens*. Their writings resonated with him in a way that some Reformed writers had not.

Randy and I spent 2002 trying to come to grips with the repercussions of all this new understanding. In 2003, our task was to facilitate this kind of transformation in the thinking of everyone else in the group. Water's Edge began with about fifteen people, and by 2004, it was at about thirty, of whom perhaps twenty are highly committed. We are multigenerational, with people spread out throughout the age groups.

Brian McLaren, Cedar Ridge Community Church, Cedar Ridge, Maryland

I was born in 1956 and grew up in Maryland, where I have spent my entire life. At the age of thirteen, I was convinced I was not going to make it as a Christian if it meant being part of fundamentalism in general and the Plymouth Brethren in particular. By the age of fifteen, I was struggling deeply with my faith. I was invited to a Bible study led by a fellow from Young Life who took me under his wing and mentored me. At the same time, the Jesus Movement came to Maryland, and I was attracted to the reality I sensed there. By the time I was sixteen, I had both feet on the Christian path. Looking back, it's clear that I was at heart an evangelist; in fact, I started a Bible study for my non-Christian friends while in high school.

At the University of Maryland, I majored in English, very much interested in the artistic side of philosophy. I was part of Cornerstone, a Christian community and study center near the university. I read a lot of Francis Schaeffer in those days, and his writings gave me permission to engage my intellect with my faith, as did the writings of C. S. Lewis. I now realize that for all his brilliance, Schaeffer didn't grapple with postmodern issues in ways that satisfied me. I got an M.A. in English in the early 1980s, focusing on Walker Percy, and taught at the university and a local community college until 1986.

My wife and I and another couple planted a house church in Maryland in 1982. I was spending at least twenty hours a week working with the church, along with my duties in my full-time teaching job and growing family. Eventually, we felt it was time for me to leave teaching to focus on full-time pastoring. We were not part of the house church movement that said, "This is the only way to do it." We always respected that there were many ways to be the church. We had a strong social concern through these years and helped a lot of refugees resettle. Our church was trying to be the kind of place where charismatics and non-charismatics could get along, with an openness to the Spirit of charismatics and the rootedness in Scripture of evangelicals. Because of my evangelistic gifts, I wasn't satisfied with vibrant worship and good Bible teaching, so I attempted to encourage our church to reach out to non-Christians. One Sunday, for example, I tried to encourage the congregation to reach out to their neighbors. I said, "If your neighbor comes over and smokes, put out an ashtray." You would have thought I had encouraged mass fornication based on the reaction I got from a few people!

To help us reorient around evangelism, we restarted the church in 1987 to 1988. Of the eighty adults who were a part of the original church, at least sixty stayed to help start the new one. We were positively influenced by Rick Warren and Bill Hybels, but the church did not fully participate in the seeker model. We focused on evangelism, and the change worked. We grew to two hundred adults in two years, about 55 percent of whom were previously unchurched.

Our congregation was diverse, from highly educated rocket scientists (NASA was nearby) to addicted high school dropouts. By the early 1990s, many of the new people were coming to me with questions—postmodern questions, if you will. These questions could not be solved with the answers I had learned from Josh McDowell and Francis Schaeffer. Over the next few years, their questions became my questions too.

Even with the church's new beginning, I found that by and large neither evangelicals nor charismatics liked non-Christians very much; the intolerance was real. I started to wonder if the religion we practiced was more the way of the Pharisees than the way of Jesus. I didn't know a single Christian leader I could talk to about my misgivings. I knew nobody who was struggling with these questions and misgivings, at least not with the intensity I felt. The spiritual disciplines I had learned from my evangelical and charismatic background got me through this dark night of the soul. During this time, I learned I needed to trust God more than my theology about God. I tried to imagine a faith that was not so mechanistic, simplistic, and systematic.

In 1995, I reached a low point and thought, "One year from now I will be out of the ministry; one year from now I'm not sure I will attend church anywhere." About that time, I began writing my first book—a kind of self-therapy, I guess. In 1998, I connected with the Young Leaders Network in Glorietta, New Mexico. I had a wonderful experience with them and felt I had found others who shared my misgivings and wanted to find better answers to the questions that were being raised. My book *New Kind of Christian* came out of my experience with the community I met through Young Leaders Network. I could not have written that book—or any of my recent books—without that community. Also through Todd Hunter I got to know Dallas Willard, who personally encouraged me and made a great contribution to my thinking through his writings and dialogue. It has been an incredible decade—discovering that I wasn't the only person dealing with questions and misgivings about modern Western Christianity and finding wonderful conversation partners and companions on this journey.

Mark Meardon, Eternity, Bracknell, U.K.

I was born in Oxford in 1973, the son of a vicar. From the ages of five to seven I "came forward" to make sure of my salvation. At fourteen, I was filled with the Holy Spirit for the first time, which gave me a boldness about my faith that I didn't have before. I left Bracknell to go to university in Southampton. After graduating, I returned to Bracknell at age twenty-one.

I started a mission to teenagers. I didn't desire to be a full-time youth worker to serve the kids in the church. Rather, I wanted to do mission to the young people outside the church, and the church encouraged me to pursue my heart. I brought together a small group of fifteen-, sixteen-, and seventeen-year-olds who started to ask if they could run the youth services themselves. I had never heard of a model where youth services were run by youth and owned by them. We had twelve or fifteen on our team, with maybe four leaders at the beginning. We sought to build a community where Christians and non-Christians could experience God's love. We wanted to pursue that and see where it would lead.

The Sunday night meeting, which attracted other youth groups from across the city, began to lose numbers, going from over one hundred to thirty. People left because it had changed. Young people were running it, with less quality, more experimentation, and more participation by young people. It is what we were supposed to be doing, but many weren't crazy about it. For us, the need was to be a community.

We moved the meeting to a Friday night, and instead of monthly, we met every two weeks. There were only twelve of us, but it is there that Eternity was birthed as a congregation, although we didn't know it at the time. On January 13, 1995, we had a simple service and talk, and a few came to faith. However, it was no longer a "youth service." The youth were now stakeholders, and they put their energy and effort into the meeting, convinced that the meeting "falls or stands with us."

We started a Wednesday night Bible study/cell group to disciple the people who came to faith. Everyone was attached to the cell, but some would come on Friday nights, and some would come to the all-church meeting on Sunday nights. After some became Christians, they became quite invested in the success of the group. The first cell grew, and three more cell groups started.

I used the same ministry style I had learned at university in Southampton—young people doing ministry for themselves. I didn't set out to become a congregation but to be a community, but maybe six months later, the leaders of the church thought we had a congregation. It was quite organic when it started. The leadership wanted to respond to what God was doing. Mike Pilavachi, who started Soul Survivor (Watford, U.K.) just a bit earlier, was a great help to me.

Initially, we had no titles, but after a year, the congregation became more formal. Today, it has twelve or thirteen groups. Area leaders are over three or four cell groups. There are over one hundred in cells each week. The people in the cell groups outnumber those in attendance at our Friday service. At the all-church service, Eternity is one of the four congregations that take turns leading. Our service starts at 7:30 p.m. It is relaxed. We casually interact, worship, have a talk/teaching, and have a prayer time. At times, we structure things as dialogues or as game shows.

We have a high commitment in the church. It is a real family to many. Some youth spend a year volunteering before they go to university. Our youth support the church 40 percent. The remainder comes from local sources, including businesspeople.

Every September we lose maybe 20 percent of the group, so every three years it is virtually a new congregation. The center of the church continues to be the fourteen- to eighteen-year-olds. We also have a group of people in their twenties who returned from university. Over the years, we have had several hundred people as part of our community.

We desire to be truly missional. There are no other religions in town, which is 98 percent secular in terms of religious attendance anywhere. Twenty percent of those who come to the church have had no previous church contact. We work in the schools as evangelists, we have a drop-in café and an under-eighteen club, and we have two full-time posts as well. We used a nightclub for services in the heart of town, and we hope to return there sometime soon.

Rachelle Mee-Chapman, Thursday PM, Seattle

I was born in 1969 and raised in San Francisco in a Christian family in the Lutheran tradition. I attended an Assembly of God school and then went to Seattle Pacific University. While there, I attended the Seattle Vineyard. In 1996, I moved to Vancouver, British Columbia, to attend Regent Seminary. My husband and I each received master's degrees in Christian studies. He did an M.Div., while I studied spiritual direction and art. In 1999, I returned to Seattle and joined the staff at the Vineyard, where I was ordained.

Besides overseeing the small group ministry, I took responsibility for the Lent and Advent programs, which, through art, became really moving. However, the rest of the year was flat for me. I came to realize that artists ought to function as the main leaders of the gathering, setting the tone for worship. Artists intuit the truth through their art. In 2001, the Vineyard hired a worship director who started "Prayer Infusion" and "Worship Infusion," basically alternative forms of worship. I realized that I needed to speak a different language. I could no longer sit through sermons and forty-five minutes of worship songs.

After meeting for a year with burned-out evangelicals, together we formed Thursday PM in 2003 under the Vineyard umbrella. Twenty or thirty regularly gather in a house where art plays a significant role. We throw art parties at coffeehouses as well. We have no intention of growing big.

We left the Seattle Vineyard in the fall of 2004. The multicongregational experiment wasn't functioning that well for us. Our needs as a neo-monastic community were different from the needs of a traditional Vineyard church, and we didn't have enough in common any longer. It was an amicable decision, and the Seattle Vineyard sent us off with prayers and kindness. Since that time we've moved more deeply into the neo-monastic model, and we are finding a lot of affinity with our de facto sister abbey at Church of the Apostles (Karen Ward). We are lodged under the umbrella of Vineyard Community Church in North Seattle. The pastor there is a friend and mentor (Rose Swetman). We remain connected to the Missional Cooperative, a group of like-minded missional/postmodern communities.

We are now called Monkfish Abbey. Our website is www.monkfish-abbey.org. It will be a sort of "shareware" site for similar neo-monastic groups. We'll be posting our rites, rituals, and art-based practices there and inviting others to add to the collection. Our hope is that other Monkfish-like groups will form hither and yon.

Kenny Mitchell, Tribe, New York

I was born in 1972. My dad had recently returned from Vietnam and was finishing up his time in the army. My parents grew up in Harlem, and I grew up in the projects on the east side of Brooklyn. An older missionary couple went door to door in the projects. They started a house church in the black projects. My mom began to attend this house church, where the meetings were held in the basement. My mom, a confused Catholic, became a Christian, and years later my dad became a Christian as well.

I began to pray at the age of five, and supernatural joy dropped on me. I began to do evangelism at supermarkets, telling people that God likes them. As a result of my reading the Bible, I wanted to be baptized. I was told I was too young, that I had to wait until I was ten. I was crushed! When I was ten, I immediately went and got baptized. At the age of thirteen or fourteen, I started a youth group, and ten friends of mine accepted Christ. This was in the Christian Church of North America.

I began to organize parties, and at fifteen I was DJing. Some guys who were running parties left town and asked me to take over the name of the party. At fifteen, I was promoting and DJing. God provided obvious opportunities for me. There were lots of gangs, mostly Chinese. Our area was also a mecca for transient gangsters coming out of Brooklyn. I was right in the middle of the crazy scene. I lived like this throughout high school.

During high school, I went on a summer mission trip to Japan. Re-calling a mission conference on Hudson Taylor and the China Inland Mission, I realized that this was what I wanted to do. I returned to Brooklyn to finish high school, and between 1988 and 1992, I was part of the skate revival, when hundreds of kids became Christians.

I attended Nyack College, majoring in Bible and missions from 1990 to 1995. During my college years, I was the president of the missionary society, promoting missions and preaching every Friday at the college's chapel service. I worked full-time at a radio station doing urban programming. I also was DJing.

During my senior year, when I considered serving in my school's denomination, a leader of my college said to me, "I recognize God is with you, and I encourage you to run with that. But you're like an atomic bomb—you would blow things up in our denomination, and there would be more fallout than blessing." Some time after that talk, I grew a beard and dreadlocks, which expressed the desert I was in. I also broke up with my girlfriend.

After graduation, I went to Revelation Church in Chichester, U.K. I went there because I thought they were working in the club culture. The truth was they had hopes of working in the club culture, and I became the fulfillment of those dreams. Through a prophetic prayer, I was told, "You will learn what you need to learn, but you will learn as you lead us." Within a few weeks, I found myself leading DJ worship in Chichester, U.K.

I started a cell group for the clubbers, and I worked with artists at Revelation Church. Pete Greig and I functioned as a think tank, and we had a blank check as to what we could do. We created some new rhythms with the influence of Celtic spirituality. I hosted creative parties and experimented with art, music, and dance. At this "clubby worship," musicians and fine artists explored spirituality through beats, paints, and praying. It was a cool time of experimenting—this was in 1995 and 1996.

Pete Greig and I were rethinking church, and we started Warehouse as a separate congregation within Revelation Church in Chichester. We built a leadership team. In 1997, we planted another church in Portsmouth.

From time to time, I would still get invitations to work at clubs in New York, and I would bring my team. In 1996, I toured Germany and got involved in raves. I got married in August of 1998, and I moved back to New York in September. Seven came from Revelation Church to New York with me and my wife. We started a little ministry house, a sort of halfway house, with loads of people coming through. I hooked up with the guys from my old neighborhood. A lot of the skateboard guys came back. We hosted big dinners and just hung out with people. We had conversations about God. We would just let God get involved.

We would pray and feel the presence of God. This was my scene, my culture.

On Saturday nights, we had music, praying, and creative elements. We had samplers, DJs, music, hip-hop. We also had an open mic. It was fun for some and worship for others. Some felt that "if this is a church, we need a name." We took the name Tribe.

We soon became more purposeful. We taught the values of cell groups. We used principles, but we tweaked them for Brooklyn homeboys. The group grew to twenty-five to thirty people. We had five on the core team. We split into two cells, and we made the Saturday night gathering a monthly event. Then our team leader from Revelation Church left. We stayed as a leadership team, but we did not have an official leader. Tribe dropped down until it reached seven people. It stayed at that size for a while.

Then people started coming back. We spent six months meeting in a bar on the lower east side. We would grab some tables and hang out. This was church for us—I was actually teaching at the bar—fifteen people in an alcove, trying to copy the way of Jesus. The larger group had no church background. I wanted to show that worship is not just about music and songs but the whole of life, to be a living sacrifice. How do we do that? Maybe in a bar? Three people became Christians in that bar in 2000.

At that time, I also cut a CD called *Brooklyn and Beyond*. In my day job, I served at an HIV/AIDS rehab center forty-five hours a week. Members of Tribe became buddies for my clients, as social justice was at the heart of what we did. In 2001, it was clear that mentoring was needed in Tribe, and in 2002, I began working full-time for Tribe. It was a leap of faith.

We had two big groups until 2002, and we now have four cell groups. We also meet twice a month on Saturday. We call it "big hug." We catch up with one another and have some form of worship. It is artistic with a rough element. It is not slick; it is just a way to get together. There are forty-five in the community as a core, and another thirty don't commit to a cell group but come to the "big hug."

Ian Mobsby, the Epicentre Network and Moot, London

I was born and raised in Wales and the U.K., but I have lived in sub-urban London for as long as I can remember. I am thirty-six years old and was brought up in a left-wing political family. My mother's family was communist/Marxist and very anti-Christian. My father left the household when I was ten, so I grew up in a one-parent family. Life was tough, and therefore my left political leanings took a strong root.

I was very anti-Christian until I was seventeen. I was exposed to the Christian faith through religious education in schools and TV. I think I can identify quite a deep emotional sense at Christmas and Easter, which I would now attribute to the Holy Spirit. At seventeen, I encountered Christians of a charismatic evangelical persuasion. It felt like coming home and was very emotional, and I had a profound conversion experience. I was a very mixed-up kid, and these early years helped me get my life more on track, but it took me a while to get it together. These were the starting moments that led to a huge spiritual ride.

The next important moment was going to university in York, where, in the middle of the rave scene in the north of England in the early 1990s, I experienced Visions in York and the Nine O'clock Service in Sheffield. My cultural world and religious world hit head-on. This changed my outlook, and traditional church never appeared the same way again. An incarnational approach to being church felt so right. I did not fit in that well with traditional church. I wanted a more relational approach because I understood the Trinity as the perfect expression of community. I had a desire for an inclusive church in which liberation and transformation were key expectations.

Traditional church did not relate to the world in which I lived. It appeared withdrawn, concerned about keeping holy and preventing infection, similar to the Pharisees in the Bible. To me it was obvious that such a conservative outworking of the gospel did not relate to what I believed Jesus taught about the kingdom of God. I also experienced some controlling expressions of church, with power-crazed leaders, which did not relate to my understanding of the priesthood of all believers and the body of Christ as models of faith communities.

When I finished studying in York, I returned to London, where I had lived, and renewed old friendships. I wanted to set up something similar to what I had experienced in York. The Epicentre Network started as an alternative worship service and grew into a community and then a church-within-a-church, as it was attached to a charismatic evangelical Church of England church. The church grew and did some great stuff in the areas of mission, worship, and fellowship, influenced as it was by Robert Warren's *Being Human, Being Church* and the writing of Mike Riddell. However, the church simply did not feed me, and I went through a deconstruction/reconstruction experience of faith. Those were hard and exciting days. Alternative worship communities such as the

Epicentre Network in the 1990s and more recently Moot became places of questing for being authentically Christian and being the church in a postmodern world.

Aaron Norwood, the Bridge, Phoenix

I was born in Oklahoma in 1973, and I grew up in Arizona. My family was Southern Baptist, and I accepted Christ at a young age. I followed Christ in high school, but I became more serious about my faith in college and felt called to be a youth pastor. After graduation, I attended Southwestern Baptist Theological Seminary, where I received my M.A. in religion.

I worked as a youth pastor for four years. In 2000, I got fired as a result of philosophical differences with the senior pastor, who wanted me to adopt an entertainment style of ministry because the church was in decline. I thought we should address real needs, helping kids live a life of mission. I felt that the message "Jesus can save your soul and take you to heaven" was trite. It was far removed from the world of jail and drugs that I had experienced in my first youth pastor position. Even with the suburban job, I felt that the kids didn't want to be entertained. We couldn't do it as well as the world could anyway. However, I could help them live a missional way, through serving instead of bowling, or through mowing people's lawns.

I liked what I heard Tony and Bart Campolo talking about. They were kingdom minded, and that was what I wanted to be. After leaving the church, I thought that if I were to do ministry again, it would have to be different and real. I was fine with never being paid in ministry again. I worked in a group home, which was very hands-on because I was meeting kids' needs.

The Bridge had already started and didn't have a pastor. They called me in January 2000, a real answer to prayer. It was exciting and hands-on as well. We had ten or twelve people who were all students. It was just a service with no building, but the focus was to get people to serve. We had small groups in homes. We had worship services, but I didn't want the focus to be worship. Our perspective—our "community feel"—was the house church model while remaining Southern Baptist.

On the first anniversary, we began meeting in a nightclub on Sunday nights, and that defined our identity in the wider community, declaring, "We are open to pagans and non-Christians and everybody." The format consisted of a full band with lights, and I would give a talk. In the spring of 2004, we moved into a bar, and we really like the context there. The bar stays open while we meet upstairs. The Sunday night church is a group of people who understand that they are part of God's movement in the world. There is a strong sense of calling to the university. The students are the church.

The morning service has about forty-five people who come for a full brunch. We modeled this after the House of Blues gospel lunch in Hollywood. We have done this since August of 2003. This crowd is different from the one that meets on Sunday nights. We meet at Rio Vista in a poorer part of town. The church service attracts between thirty-five and fifty people. Half of the people are Caucasian, and the other half is divided equally between Hispanics and blacks. Five to ten homeless people also attend.

Rio Vista is the local food and clothes distribution center for the Southern Baptists. It serves 1,300 people a month, offering food and clothing to 350 families. We built a computer lab and provide after-school tutoring and ESL classes. To the Rio Vista residents, we offer the opportunity to learn and to worship on Sunday mornings. We have four small groups, which total around forty people. Rio Vista residents are represented in the volunteer base as well. People in the community come to the church and start volunteering, getting involved in the mission of Jesus. To the residents of Rio Vista, serving makes sense.

The leadership team is set right now. The main focus of the small groups is living like Jesus by participating in the mission of God to bring people back to God through serving. We are kingdom minded. If someone wants to start something, I approve it, providing the person is a part of the community and it doesn't go against Scripture. We encourage people to be creative.

I see us as an emerging church because our focus is on serving. The Christians who live outside Rio Vista must be converted to serving. They believe in it, but they don't understand how to connect to it.

Doug Pagitt, Solomon's Porch, Minneapolis

I was born in 1966 and came to faith through a friend. I was discipled through Student Venture, a Campus Crusade affiliated high school ministry. Before that time I was completely ignorant of Christianity, having been raised outside the church. I lived my whole life in the Twin Cities, with the exception of two years, 1997 to 1999, when I worked with Leadership Network in Dallas.

For eleven years, I worked at Wooddale Church, a large megachurch known for its innovative methods where Leith Anderson was the senior pastor. I served as high school pastor there, and I also graduated from Bethel Seminary during that time. Wooddale had a megachurch mentality with a CEO and staff. It was a great time of growth for me, with many people who loved me deeply. It was my first and primary church. I was supported and cared for in this church and on the staff.

In the midst of this environment, I began to wonder about the kind of Christianity I was propagating and if it could be sustainable long-term. In the midst of the caring community, I was troubled by my thought that it was too much work and too corporate. I had issues with the corporate, business nature of the church. I also had issues with the evangelical nature of the church and how limited it was in regard to the gospel. Much later, I would be able to give words to this. At that time, I felt I needed to learn more, that I must be missing something. I realized that maybe my struggle was a valid one, that there really was something wrong. I felt pressure to apply Christian, well-grounded answers to the world. Instead, I wanted to explore questions, such as what kind of Christianity I was a part of. However, I was not being paid to pursue answers to questions. I needed to do that on my own.

It was then that I joined the staff of the Young Leaders Network in Texas. At Solomon's Porch, which we started in 2000, we asked, "How do we need to live in the world in order to pursue the agenda of God in the way of Jesus?"

Mark Palmer, Landing Place, Columbus, Ohio

I was born and raised in rural Pennsylvania in a fundamentalist Baptist church. I raised my hand at six years of age, but it was not until my sophomore year of college that my faith began to make sense. I felt I had to decide whether I was going to continue in my faith or give it up. I needed to decide once and for all if Jesus was real, if there was something about Jesus that I could not walk away from.

I continued at the fundamentalist Bible college, receiving my bachelor's degree in youth ministry in 1996. I was a punk, and I liked to have fun. I had a gut feeling that I might want to start a church, but who was I? I was twenty-one years old!

I couldn't do anything else, so I decided to be a youth pastor. I got a good setup with a decent salary. I could do basically whatever I wanted, as long as it didn't affect the big people's church. But I knew taking the job would be a big mistake.

My experience of church was a very broken one. I knew it wasn't going to be a good ending. My only hope for sanity was to find some people to gather with who felt the same. After five months, I left the church and passed up two other jobs because I just couldn't do it anymore. I passed a point of no return. I needed to explore what was in my heart. I truly believed that Jesus and his followers and the church are the hope of the world and that we are to extend the rule and reign of God in the world. I felt it intensely. I spent two years searching in what was a crazy time for me. I had no one with whom I could process my suspicions about church.

Two years later, in 1998, my wife and I invited a few others to our house for breakfast. We broke out the Bible and listened to some music. The group stuck. There were nine of us who were bitter, confused, and close to walking away from church. It was a time of deconstruction for us all. We called ourselves Veritas Community Church and met Sunday mornings. Up to that time I had not found anyone outside our community who shared our thoughts, so we were putting the pieces together on our own.

After meeting for a while, our group decided to have an outreach. At a nearby deli, we met in the back room. We bought food and invited friends who asked questions about spirituality and Jesus. We did this for thirteen weeks, until our credit cards were maxed out. Our group was made up of those who had never followed Jesus or felt burned by the church. Our living room could no longer hold the group, so we looked into renting a facility. But as we couldn't afford any, we decided to close the group after two years of meeting.

Later on, a few of us wanted to create a rock 'n' roll venue. A store-front church agreed to give us space to do this. It turned out to be a step backward into church for the sake of having space for rock 'n' roll. We had heard of a church-within-a-church, where you could have a separate Gen-X service with a different name but still be connected. However, we were so far apart from the church theologically that it wasn't healthy. The group quickly stopped again.

In January 2001, my wife, Jennifer, and I felt we were supposed to start churches and to rethink what they are about, but we were burned out and poor. My wife gave me permission to give it one more shot. That fall Jennifer and I started Landing Place with two others. One year later, in 2002, we had eight people. The next year we grew to fifteen, and the third year to anywhere between thirty and forty-five.

In 2002, we started a second church, and now we have three churches. Each group that meets is its own church. The realization was slow, for it was a slow, dying process going from one model of church to another.

The typical age of members is twenty-four. The youngest is eighteen, and the oldest is thirty-five. Ninety percent of the members are in their mid-twenties. Most are single or married without kids.

Pip Piper, Maji, Birmingham, U.K.

I was born in 1964 and grew up in the Midlands. I was raised in the Church of England, beginning as an altar boy at the age of eleven. In my teen years, I participated in the music and drug culture. At the age of eighteen, I had a conversion experience. The following morning I woke up and went outside. While I stood gazing at a tree, somehow it all fell into place. I knew how the world worked and my place in it. That mysterious connection with God has never left me despite many sojourns into questioning and disconnected feelings toward the church.

There have been times when I have flowed in the mainstream of church expression, but I have always at some point come away dissatisfied or disillusioned with what I eventually discovered. Like many, I have a love/hate relationship with mainstream church, the corporate expressions of the way of Jesus. I know it's necessary, but I'm just not sure why anymore.

Maji was an informal gathering with no membership. It wasn't a church, but for some people it was a spiritual collective gathering point. People came from a variety of backgrounds and faith perspectives as well as church bases. Maji went on for about eighteen months with five or six key people and about twenty to fifty attending.

I'm simply trying to follow Jesus as a twenty-first-century husband and father who works in the creative media world. I'm struggling, truth be told, but a lot of that has to do with life's pressures as much as getting my head around theology today. I know I just need to focus on Christ's life and what made him tick and do the same things. That's how it all began for me, and that's how I want it to end. Whether I clap and sing a lot in that pursuit or sit cross-legged and hum, the test is in the life lived.

Kevin Rains, Vineyard Central, Cincinnati

I was born in Cincinnati in the summer of 1969 and was raised in a middle-class suburb near woods and creeks that were full of adventure. I went to church often. My family was conservative Baptist and significantly involved at the church. My teen years were a bit uneven. I was mostly a good boy, with brief forays into partying and deep spirituality, sometimes on the same weekend.

In my late teen years, I was deeply impacted by reading *Shadow of the Almighty* by Elisabeth Elliot. This book was the sounding of a call for me in terms of consecration and life direction. I got serious about my faith and sensed a desire to serve in a daring, enduring, deep way. My sanctification had not reached my need for adventure and excitement, but it was a start.

In my college years, I got involved in cross-cultural ministry and theology. I traveled quite extensively throughout Europe and Africa on mission trips and worked for a year with Floyd McClung, international director of Youth with a Mission (YWAM), putting together a one-year mentoring process for leaders. I also looked at urban ministry in Amsterdam. When I returned to the United States in 1993, I started an alternative dance club downtown, which later became a Vineyard church.

I married Tracy, and we began attending Vineyard Central in Cincinnati in 1994. At the time I was a social worker. After a short while, VC made the journey to home-based churches. For me, this signaled the shift from being an attendee to being a leader/pastor, as I was assigned the leadership of the downtown church. That little core grew from eight to thirty pretty quickly and eventually spawned several groups. They didn't all survive very long.

We were still very new and green at this mode of church life, and mistakes were made along the way. But God was gracious and patient, and we were bent on learning. For me, this model—and I'm reluctant now to call it that—was the culmination and logical conclusion to some shifts in my own ecclesiology and practice that were being deeply influenced by the cell church movement. I loved and admired the cell church movement but just didn't think it took things far enough, at least for what I sensed I was called to.

Paul Roberts, Third Sunday Service, Resonance, Bristol, U.K.

I was born in 1960 in Swansea, U.K., and raised in the high church tradition of the Anglican Church in Wales. I dropped out of church at the age of twelve or thirteen but returned in my later teens, partly for the girls in the church youth group, partly because of the young evangelical assistant minister who helped me make sense of Christianity as relevant and vibrant. I recommitted my life at that age, but I definitely had faith as a child. Charismatic renewal hit just before I went off to university in 1978, but it was a solitary experience, and as the church I attended wasn't charismatic, I had difficulty understanding what had happened to me until I joined the Christian Union at Manchester University. This student Christian scene was my first experience of full-on Christian culture, and while I appreciated much of the content it gave my young faith, I was rather concerned about its otherworldliness and isolation from the culture of our peers. As a part-time DJ, I was at home in the culture of the clubs, but the Christian circles I then moved in were either uninterested in this or even antagonistic toward it. I was the only one in the student Christian Union to celebrate openly my love of funk, soul, and (what was then) hip-hop—and me a white boy from south Wales!

After one year at university, I changed course from my childhood career route of electronic engineering to theology. After university, I was accepted to train for the Anglican ministry and went to St. John's College in Nottingham, U.K. During this time, I began my doctoral studies, which looked at the way a nineteenth-century church (the Catholic Apostolics) moved from a charismatic understanding of the church and Christian initiation to developing one of the most ornate baptismal liturgies of recent centuries. I guess I was trying to make sense of the link between a sacramental approach to Christianity and charismatic experience. I completed the Ph.D. by 1990, working part-time through my first two posts. After three years as an assistant minister in Manchester, U.K., I was appointed to teach worship and doctrine at Trinity College in Bristol. After many years working within charismatic and evangelical church settings, I found myself reevaluating more positively the sacramental and catholic roots in which I had been brought up. But more than one link was missing between the charismatic mission-focused church of my peers and the often rather effete, cultured catholicism found in the Church of England.

In 1991, I visited the Nine O'clock Service mass and found charismatic, sacramental, and mission-focused Christianity fused in a form that was radically connected to contemporary club culture. Not only were my Christian roots connected for the first time, but my cultural roots were too. It was a life-changing moment for me. On the train back from Sheffield the next day, I scribbled down all my recollections of the service before the memory started to fade. I wrote to Chris Brain shortly afterward but received no prompt reply—I did eventually, months later, by which time I had started making plans of my own. Several evenings during those years I went out on my bike, cycled around the center of Bristol, watched all the young people clustering around clubs, pubs, and cafés, and prayed that God would do something in the city in which I lived.

In 1993, after several more visits to NOS, I took a sabbatical to study all I could find on postmodernism and to make contacts with a number of alternative worship groups (including Visions, the Late Late Service, and Joy, then in Oxford). Following the Glasgow trip, Doug Gay put me in touch with a few people who'd recently moved to Bristol. Eventually, it seemed as though there were enough of us wanting to do something and that the time had arrived. My wife, Sharon, and I persuaded our church, St. Matthew's, to allow us to run monthly experimental services with these people, almost none of whom at that time were church members. The Third Sunday Service was an accidental name, as that was the Sunday we met each month. It ran at St. Matthew's from 1993 to 1999, when I moved to become vicar of a couple of neighboring churches.

In 1997, we found that a number of other small groups, with histories linked to Harry and Greenbelt but without a church connection, were coming each month, so we changed to become a collective comprising a monthly alternative worship service and three weekly groups. In addition, we began a monthly discussion meeting at a pub along the lines of Holy Joes. A smaller, low-tech Sunday evening service took place in the intervening weeks. At our peak, we had about twenty-five to thirty "full" members and a monthly service with about one hundred attendees, many of whom were members of other churches in the area but were coming to us for a dose of something different. These days it would be called a network church. In those days, it didn't have a name in Christian parlance, and I was a bit concerned that the local Anglican hierarchy would be bemused, if not suspicious, if they knew the sort of things we were doing. The lesson of NOS was the importance of accountability of ministry and leadership, so our isolation in those days bothered me.

The service declined following my relocation and the change of name to Resonance. A new job brought a considerable increase in my workload (I found myself the leader of two independently operating churches). I could no longer put in the time, nor did I have the energy, to stimulate initiatives. Key leaders had either left or taken on new job and family responsibilities. Eventually, it was clear we had to take a break, as the big services were becoming a burden rather than a blessing. We continued with the low-tech weekly services, which became very small. However, in the past year, we have recommenced quarterly services, which are well attended, with a growing group of new people working together. We are somewhere between a service and a church at the moment. I'm currently praying and thinking hard about what to do next.

Peter Rollins, Ikon, Belfast, U.K.

I don't have a strong religious background and didn't really come into contact with people who took their faith seriously until I was seventeen, when I came across a highly motivated group on the street representing the charismatic movement. About a week after my initial encounter, I was getting ready to go out for a night with some friends when, for no apparent reason, I had a temporary mental breakdown. It all literally happened in the space of a minute. Only seconds before I had been absolutely fine. Then I was a mess.

I ran out of the house in tears and sprinted about a mile and a half to the church where I had initially met the group. Because it was a Saturday night, no one was around, but the church was open. I went inside and looked around in a dazed kind of way. After a few moments, I saw a light emanating from a room at the bottom of a long staircase. I went down the stairs and walked straight into a prayer meeting. Of course, they all stopped and looked in a somewhat bemused way at this disheveled stranger in their midst. Shortly after this I made a commitment to enter the faith community. About a month later, I found out that the prayer meeting I ran into was one in which they were praying for me! I quickly began working for my church and helped found a church plant in Carrickfergus, outside of Belfast, Northern Ireland. I was even a full-time evangelist for a year.

I founded ikon when I was twenty-eight, but it was not out of dislike for the established evangelical tradition. There is a parable about a man who took two camels to a market; one was laden with cotton, the other with salt. On the way they had to pass through a river. The camel with the salt felt great when he got to the other side because all the salt had melted, while the camel with the cotton drowned because it had become so heavy. One river, but very different results. I was like the camel with the salt. My church actually proved to be a liberating place that helped to transform my life in a good way, while for others, well, they drowned. That sounds a little strange, and you could easily ask me why, if the church was so liberating, did I leave and set up ikon? As liberating as it was for me, I began to find the evangelical theological discourse slightly violent. By this I mean that I began to sense that it did an injustice to my concrete religious experience and the idea of God.

I always had the feeling that the faith language I had been given didn't do justice to my experience of faith. This was not itself a problem, as I don't actually believe that any discourse can. The problem was that the discourse I had been given didn't seem able to recognize this insufficiency. So I decided to find some people who would disciple me in a more liberating way of thinking. Unfortunately, when I looked around, I could find only the dead, so I listened to them. I read some of the mystics, like Pseudo-Dionysius and Meister Eckhart. I delved deeply into philosophy and theology (eventually being drawn to a phenomenology), and I traveled to see other groups. In the midst of this, I began to find a language that I believed could prove liberating to the Christian community, a language that had been excluded and silenced by the dominant Western theological tradition.

The whole ikon project represented the culmination of these thoughts; it was designed as a means to explore this new (and very ancient) language. What I found was that there were countless people who felt as I had, people whose religious discourse was doing violence to their religious experience, and ikon became a place of liberation to those people.

Ikon was never intended to be a home, but then it was never expected to last this long. I, like many, have my doubts as to whether the transition is possible, yet I am no longer the principal person behind this community. The longer it has gone on the more it has outgrown my petty visions and been revolutionized by those who have come on board. While I hesitate about the future, there are others who believe it is possible, and I am also slowly daring to believe. We shall see.

Nanette Sawyer, Wicker Park Grace, Chicago

I was born in 1961 and raised in rural Upstate New York. My family sporadically attended a small Baptist church there, but we never were really part of that community. It was a church that presented a very shame-based theology. When I asked the minister what I "had to believe" to be a Christian, he gave me a simple "Jesus died on the cross for your sins" answer, which made no sense to me. I made a conscious decision at that time that I was not a Christian.

After many years of seeking, I took up meditation with an Indian meditation master who taught me two things that Christians never had: that God loves me, and how to be still and listen for God. In some ways, I am a Christian today because of this great Hindu woman. She inspired me to study comparative world religions, and so I went to Harvard Divinity School and received a master's in theological studies in 1997.

Around that time, a friend of mine invited me to his church in south Boston. I was nervous and *very* hesitant. I went to a small evening prayer service and received communion with an intimate circle of people, and a transformation began in me. I felt as though Jesus himself was welcoming me at the communion table.

I started showing up at that church on Sundays. This church was so different from the church of my childhood, because they welcomed me without asking for my Christian ID card, so to speak. They just welcomed me, pure and simple. They preached and lived a message of grace, emphasizing that we are all beloved children of God. Eventually, I was baptized in that church and felt my call to the ministry of Word and sacrament in that church.

I went to Chicago in 1999 to attend a Presbyterian seminary in Hyde Park (McCormick) and got a master of divinity degree in 2002. I never expected that my first call would be a new church development. Wicker Park Grace was the brain child of the Presbytery, which imagined a new church development that would strive to be in relationship with the unchurched and especially the dechurched, those who, like me, had had negative experiences with the church and had left it.

I was hired in 2002 to do a two-year feasibility study with pilot programs and to develop a vision that might lead to a sustainable new church community. Wicker Park, on the northwest side of Chicago, is a quickly growing, artsy, and hip neighborhood with cafés, tea houses, art studies, lots of music venues, and lots of people who've been burned by the church.

In January 2004, we officially became a new church development of the Presbyterian Church (USA). I think our project is exciting because it represents an effort of the mainline church to explore emerging church concepts. This is not to say we don't experience some resistance. After all, what will church be if it's not church as church has always been? At Wicker Park Grace, we're really working to get beyond church as institution and delve into the experience of church as people, church as spiritual journey, and church as community. We strive to be centered in a dynamic and generous Christianity, embodying a grace-based theology and living out a loving relationship with a pluralistic world.

Mark Scandrette, ReIMAGINE! San Francisco

Conceived in Pamplona, Spain, and born in Heidelberg, Germany, I spent my childhood in Minneapolis and graduated from high school in rural Alabama. During our time in Germany with the U.S. military, my parents were influenced by Navigator missionaries, and my father spent a brief time with Francis and Edith Schaeffer at L'Abri in Switzerland. When I was in preschool, we moved to an urban neighborhood in

Minneapolis to participate in a church community that was exploring racial reconciliation and connection with marginalized neighborhood residents. My family practiced a vibrant spirituality at home with singing, Scripture reading, memorization, and daily prayer. We visited people in prison, welcomed strangers, and offered hospitality and friendship to many people in our neighborhood. I had an early sensitivity to spiritual realities and made a primitive declaration of faith.

When I was in sixth grade, I heard the Creator inviting me to search for a way of life guided by revelation. I began reading the Bible and sharing my discoveries with friends. In junior high and high school, I traveled in the city and suburbs teaching children the Bible with an organization called Child Evangelism Fellowship. In the churches I was a part of, Jesus was significant primarily as a Savior from eternal punishment and guilt, and right doctrinal beliefs and knowledge of Scripture and their inerrancy were emphasized. In those communities, there was often fear and paranoia about contemporary culture, concerns about liberalism, and an emphasis on reclaiming the territory of the Christian roots of American democracy. My family and our church communities were influenced by the teachings of people like Bill Gothard and James Dobson.

In high school, I lived as a voluntary ascetic. I did not watch television, saw few movies, and listened only to Christian music. I protested abortion clinics, studied apologetics, led youth activities in my church, taught the Bible to children, and spoke at meetings for people my age. I spent much of my spare time studying the Bible and reading theology.

I began to feel a growing dissonance between what I knew of the life and teachings of Jesus and the church and evangelical subculture I was a part of. In the Gospels, I saw Jesus inviting people to be his followers, adopt his practices and way of life, and live communally. The way of life our family practiced stood in contrast to my institutional church experiences. My dad and I had many conversations wrestling through the differences between the way Christianity is practiced in American culture and the vision of life described in the New Testament. Jesus seemed concerned about the present and the future, addressed people's needs holistically, and connected with religious and nonreligious people. I was equally impressed with the quality of community and sacrifice among the followers of Jesus recorded in the book of Acts.

During my first year of college, I left my parents' church and joined a multicultural church in Tuscaloosa, Alabama. The church emphasized community, and we met primarily in homes and shared life together.

I spent time volunteering at an Alabama state mental hospital, a state prison, and inner-city boys and girls clubs. I also became involved in the art and music scene at my university.

Inspired by the missionary biographies that were read at the dinner table when I was growing up, I took a break from college, made a vow of simplicity, and moved to the inner city to love people and to share the good news. Eventually, my wife and I worked for the children's organization we had both volunteered with as teenagers. We spent four years organizing Bible clubs for kids in public housing projects and other at-risk communities. We learned a lot from the poor and disenfranchised people we served. They invited us into their families, and we spent many late nights talking and playing cards in smoke-filled apartments with kids running around us.

We traveled around the region where we lived, telling stories about the children and families we knew from our work in the housing projects and inviting churches to care for the at-risk kids who lived in proximity to their meeting places. We were saddened by the fact that the kids and families from the housing projects could not find a place in local churches, and we wished that the churches had been more excited about connecting with people from the trailer parks and housing projects. Gradually, we started a Sunday night gathering that was a mix of public housing families and middle-class professionals. Our lofty ambition was to imitate the picture of church from Acts 2:42–47. We shared a meal and the Eucharist, had an informal discussion about how we were experiencing God in our lives, and planned how we could serve one another during the following week.

Eventually, the large church we attended on Sunday mornings asked me to go on staff as an associate pastor. I had declined this invitation several times before, but this time I agreed, with the hope of helping the church become more externally focused. It also provided us with greater financial stability and an opportunity to go to seminary. The three years I spent in seminary and working at this church were quite challenging for me. I was surprised by how much my work at the church dominated my time and relationships. I lost the connections and relationships I felt energized by in the community because I was spending so much time preparing for events and teaching within the church. In addition, most of the congregation was over thirty-five, and nearly all the students left the church after high school. This made me wonder about the structure and sociology of church institutions.

We were recruited for church planting and went through a rigorous assessment process. I attended a lot of conferences and read many books on generational dynamics, postmodernism, missiology, and relationally based ecclesiology and strategy. I explained to denominational leaders that people my age and younger in urban areas required a different kind of church that was more relational and tribal. It was difficult for them to reconcile my description of church with a product-oriented vision for suburban church planting. A denomination agreed to support our relational church-planting efforts in San Francisco as an experiment in urban Gen-X church planting.

We moved to San Francisco in 1998 and began networking with young adults in local churches and sharing our vision. About twenty-five people committed to our vision of a way of being the church similar to the book of Acts. We met in apartments, shared a meal and the Eucharist, held a discussion, and sang together. Most of the life of our groups was outside our formal gatherings. We went on prayer walks together, met people in bars and clubs, and found ways to serve the poor and the homeless as well as friends and extended family members.

The church that "released" its young people to our experiment anticipated that the young adults would eventually return to the mother church. When the church leadership realized that we viewed our gatherings and network of relationships as a valid alternative to an institutional church, they withdrew their endorsement and asked the young adults to leave our groups. Many of the people who stayed with us were living with mental disorders, recovery issues, and authority problems and hoped our group could be the family they never had. I spent a lot of my time counseling group members, managing conflicts between people, and struggling to develop a vision with seminary interns. Some of us wanted an alternative kinship network. Others among us were rethinking what it means to be Christian and how to seek the kingdom of God in the here and now. Some of us had foundationalist and literalistic approaches to Scripture, while others were more open to exegeting culture and examining the lenses through which we see Scripture. After two years of gathering and sharing a lot of life and ourselves, it was clear that the vision that originally united us was no longer our common denominator. We were all in different places as people with varying expectations of what it means to be the people of God in community. My retrospective assessment is that it is hard to create something healthy and sustainable during a personally deconstructive phase. I had come to San Francisco with such high hopes and denominational backing. The end of our initial church-planting efforts was devastating to my identity as a leader.

During this same period, we were networking in our inner-city neighborhood, hosting parties with neighbors, volunteering, and building connections. I joined a local arts collective, and we became involved in a family education network. We developed a more missiological approach to our work, learning to read the cultures of our community and rereading Scripture while asking, "What does the gospel of the kingdom of God that Jesus proclaimed mean here and now?" We connected consistently with a few friends, also from evangelical traditions, who had moved to the city to seek the way of Jesus in the unique context of San Francisco. Eventually, this group of friends became the founders of ReIMAGINE!

Once a week, six of us met for a formal process of deconstructing our understanding and practice of Christian faith formed by evangelicalism and reconstructing a way of seeing and practicing the way of Jesus that seemed more consistent with our present cultural context. We found that our neighbors and friends were hostile to their perception of Christians but ambivalent or positive about Jesus and his teachings. Our assessment was that our culture tends to polarize between transcendent and immanent awareness. We saw many irreligious people concerned about social justice, earth keeping and aesthetics, and personal spirituality, while many devout Christians seemed consumed only with personal piety and the afterlife. We asked ourselves, "What kind of person was Jesus? Which dimensions of life do his life, work, and teachings relate to?" Our conclusion was that Jesus was equally concerned with the here and now and the afterlife and that he was inviting us to be not only believers but also followers of his way of life. The concept of the kingdom of God became important to us because it presents a picture of good news that is holistic and integrative. Together we wrote an initial identity statement: "We are a movement of people, living in San Francisco, who, believing that our city is loved by God, seek a way of life that reverberates with the goodness and beauty of the kingdom of God."

For our first ReIMAGINE! project we gathered seventy-five people for a twelve-week orientation to a kingdom perspective on the way of Jesus. We met on Sunday evenings for a meal, teaching, and integrative exercises. Many of the people who participated were having a difficult time reconciling their faith with life in a post-Christendom context. We nicknamed the project "City Christianity 101." It was a liberating and painful process. From this initial gathering, we launched a network of neighborhood-based faith communities, an arts collective and arts center, and various community development initiatives. Faith communities met in homes for a meal, the Eucharist, and practical discussion about the New Testament teachings of Jesus and the kingdom. The arts collective, called the BOON Project, did a series of experiential weekends, gallery exhibitions, workshops, and creativity recovery salons. The work of ReIMAGINE! continues to evolve with the ebb and flow of people due to the economy and the transitory nature of San Francisco. We find ourselves working closely with a few other families who have committed to live in San Francisco long-term. Together we serve a constantly changing cast of characters and communities.

Only recently, ReIMAGINE! became a legally recognized organization that fuels initiatives integrating spiritual formation, community building, the arts, and social action. My role transitioned from church planter to director of a nonprofit organization. This freed us to be much more experimental in our approach to our work and gave me a more credible role in the community.

There was a period of several years when our personal formation was much more significant than our programs or initiatives. We have had a lot to learn about inhabiting the ways of the kingdom. For some of us, the process of rebirthing into a more holistic understanding and praxis has been painful and has included episodes of depression, doubt, and a significant reordering of our lives. We have had to learn a path of faith that emphasizes faithfulness over success.

We are in the process of developing a Center for Spiritual Formation in San Francisco. Our hope is to proclaim publicly the availability of a new way of life and to design a body of learning and practices that will help people be formed in the way of Jesus over a two-year period. We hope to teach people to obey everything Jesus commanded and in the process to create a society of new monastic people who are released and empowered to live the way of Jesus in their vocations and relationships, wherever their journeys take them.

Dan Slatter, Warehouse, Chichester, U.K.

I was born in 1974 in north London and grew up there. My family did not attend church, but my mother's parents were involved at an Anglican church. I attended a church youth group, but there was no real content there. I had my first encounter with Jesus at age sixteen at a camp. When I went to university in the south, I was invited to Revelation Church.

Chichester is a city by virtue of having a cathedral, but it is only the size of a town. One Sunday a month many of the young people started going to the city-center congregation (Revelation Church is made up of separate congregations). The older people moved out, and it became a youth congregation by default in the summer of 1995. In 1996, Warehouse emerged, and the group was commissioned and officially sent out to form its own congregation, leadership team, teaching program, and pastoral setup. Revelation Church as a whole, consisting of about five hundred people, still met together monthly.

We moved out of the city center when we outgrew our location with sixty people. When we grew to one hundred in 1998, we began to meet at the technical college. We had pool tables and a bar, and sometimes the bar was open. We ranged in age from fifteen to twenty-two. There were six house groups, and we moved to cells by 2000, with 150 young people involved.

Our big issue was what to do with young people when they hit twenty-two, as the younger teens were too scared to be with this group. In 2000, we moved the older people out, and it worked badly. We lost a lot of people who wanted to know why they had to leave. We then put a process in place to help people transition to another group at age twenty-three and to shift to the main congregation. I admit that we still haven't cracked it. It is a weakness of the youth congregation model. Hundreds get saved, but how do they stick with church and become a disciple? Those are the outstanding questions.

We have ages twelve to twenty-two in Warehouse, and we have reached the one-hundred attendance mark again. We go to the cinema together; we have a "year out" (the year between high school and college/work) team that lives together; we meet with young people banned from school; we have a drop-in café on Thursdays. We built a community because we needed to be "branded." By that we mean being shaped and discipled. We teach a couple themes: salvation by accepting Jesus as Savior and the kingdom.

We run a nightclub for teens once a month that is widely regarded as the best party in town. It is funded by the police and local government fund because we give a positive message warning about the dangers of drugs. We teach a lot about life issues: drugs, sex, relating to parents, how the Bible is relevant, materialism and simplicity of life, and care of the environment. We try to be creative in all that we do. The cells really nail what the young people hear on Sunday. We ask them, "How did Sunday change you?" The student cells are peer led, but adults lead youth cells.

Sean Stillman, Zac's Place, Swansea, U.K.

I was born in 1967 in Reading, west of London. My mom and dad are Christians, and my dad is an evangelist. I made a decision for Christ when I was ten, but my mom and dad didn't force their faith on me. In 1996, I moved to Swansea, the hometown of my wife, Jane.

By the time I was twenty-four, my faith was bigger than church. If church didn't connect for me, it didn't matter. I had other circles of fellowship outside church. As much as I dislike much of the stuff happening in church, I wanted to plug in somewhere. So in the fall of 1998, we started Zac's Place. We started Zac's Place for two reasons. The first arose out of my observations that there was a huge gap between those I was meeting in the church and my biking mates. There was no way they would fit into the shapes of church I was familiar with. Second, I knew two guys who wanted more but couldn't stomach church. So the thought was already there, coming from the mission field.

We meet at 8:00 p.m. Sunday nights in a public bar. We do the service in the main part of the pub. Sunday night is Jesus night. I give a thought for the day, and a live band plays for a while. We struggle to attract live quality bands with a good stage presence. The whole pub goes quiet out of a healthy respect for what is said, although someone may heckle now and again. It goes down well, and the management is really happy. I find it to be the best place to meet people, but since coming to the new venue, we have lost some of our Christian tourists, because it is no longer nice and comfortable. It is a rough-and-ready pub. We have to be aware that not everyone who comes is coming to Zac's Place; they are simply coming to spend time at the pub. So we cannot assume they understand what we are about, and we have to explain who we are and what is going on.

If people don't want to be involved, they play pool around the corner. We've gained in numbers because all sorts of people come because they hear the music. On a typical Sunday, 40 to 140 people, on average 50 to 60, attend Zac's Place, a fair few because they are at the pub every night. We have through-traffic and a healthy relationship with the pub community. Zac's Place does not have clear boundaries. It is not an "us" and "them" thing. I use the analogy of Zac's Place being a scrambled egg. It is definitely a cooked egg with white bits and yellow bits, but it is hard to define where the edges are. It is difficult to discern who is in and who is out.

The pub has me as its own chaplain, and the staff see me in that role. I am the main person who has contact with the pub community, and we have a core group of twelve people who consider the community their home. I am the only paid member, but ideas are openly shared by anyone.

We have a charity and have set up a trust fund. I gave my worldly wealth to a trust to provide a support base. Individuals and a couple churches support this. We need £30,000 ($60,000) a year to cover everything, including buying the premises. We have managed to achieve a remarkable amount.

Recently, we bought a city center chapel that had closed down. It is open everyday, except Sundays, which is the day when we all go to the pub! At the chapel, we have regular Bible teaching, run a soup kitchen, help with a local drug project, and serve the poor. It would be easy to pull out of the pub, but I am keen not to. The pub is our mission focus. At the chapel, we want to have a sacred space, a more personal space where we can deal with more long-term work, such as alcohol problems. It also provides a good space for art. We have sculptures and paintings. Some are from Christians, and some are not.

With the chapel, we resist doing the 11:00 a.m. Sunday morning thing. We are really keen to see if we can make it work, taking the emphasis away from a weekly meeting and developing an ongoing community. We want to take Jesus seriously, and I hope that the community's new building will cross over with the pub and be used by a lot of people.

We are a work in progress and still in our early days. It could all still fall flat on its face. If I wasn't so convinced that I was called to do what I do, I would have given up before now. It is a hard slog, and I don't have the encouragement and support that one has from traditional sources.

Dave Sutton, New Duffryn Community Church, Newport, U.K.

I was born in 1949 in Leeds. After twenty years as a Buddhist and in martial arts, I became a Christian in the 1980s. I joined the Church Army (an evangelistic and social outreach agency of the Anglican Church) in 1986 and was commissioned in 1989. The ministry of John Wimber and the Vineyard deeply impacted my life. In addition, the social action messages of Tony Campolo and John Smith and the writings of Henri Nouwen on spirituality deeply influenced me as well.

In 1987, I heard from Campolo that God has a bias to the poor. If God has a bias, then that is where I should be working. I began to work with the lowest in society, primarily with drug addicts and young people. My direction within Church Army was in the area of social responsibility, working in poor areas.

Working with heroin addicts in Chester, I realized the church couldn't handle them. The church people were kind but couldn't understand. I experienced great feelings of rejection when those I worked with were rejected. I looked at the gospel message, and I realized we got it dramatically wrong. I felt that something was missing in the church. It was then that I began to look at new ways of being church.

I read Bishop Peter Price's *Kingdom and the Church*, which helped me realize that through planting base communities everything was to be different—including our theology. I struggled with evangelical theology, and I looked for another method to get the message across. I needed to find a totally different theology. I began to look deeper.

I read Tom Wright on the gospel, that it is not about getting people to heaven but about bringing heaven to earth. The gospel is not just about people but also about places. The gospel is a liberating thing; it doesn't just liberate people but also communities. The base community idea brings about achievable change. I looked for a method of church after my understanding of Jesus changed. I am convinced that this is what the gospel is about and that my right-wing evangelical past was wrong. I began to work in Wales, as part of New Duffryn Community Church, in an estate that had the highest child poverty in the U.K. I worked with groups of people in a small locality, with maybe twenty or thirty households working together for the transformation of their community. It makes things achievable as we ask, "What can we do for our street?"

Barry Taylor, Sanctuary and New Ground, Santa Monica, California

From the time I was eighteen, I traveled with rock bands all over the world. I became uncomfortable with the person I was becoming. I became interested in Jung, regarding my shadow side. In the late 1970s, I found Buddhism very attractive and read through other major religious works, including the Bible (my last choice). When it came to the Gospels, I felt further away experientially from Jesus than I did from Buddhism—that Jesus was more "other"; for example, in Jesus' encounters with women.

In the end, I didn't pick Christianity. I picked Jesus instead, because Jesus seemed cool and treated people kindly. From that time I sought to follow Jesus. I came to faith as I was traveling with the rock band AC/DC in the years 1976 to 1981. I trusted them more than I trusted most people, including Christians. From day one of my life as a follower of Jesus, I attacked naive demonizing. I was never part of a church in the U.K. or the U.S. When I came to faith, it was apart from any church involvement at all.

I've grown through churches, meaning that I have moved on and grown in my faith as I have moved past particular churches and what they stand for. From the very beginning of my relationship with church, I was conflicted. The church has continually affirmed its divine role in mediating God, whereas I have always had difficulty with that. I gravitated toward the nondenominational church, thinking that it would be less structured, that there would be more freedom. Actually, it was quite deceptive. The structure is still there, but it is more web-like, and one gets wrapped around in it.

In the early 1980s, I had a network of friends who led me to an independent charismatic church in Glendale, California. The church was fairly open to artists and their faith. It was part of a post–Calvary Chapel, pre-Vineyard church and was fairly white and middle class. About two hundred attended weekly. I met cool people there, although I had to battle an anti-intellectualism as well. I fought against an absolutizing of life and world that I found within the church. I was never an absolutist. This was my first encounter with church. I had no real theological mentors in the faith. I didn't like C. S. Lewis because of the social class he represented. I primarily read outside the fold of Christian authors, such as Thomas Mann and Herman Hesse, whom I then recontextualized.

Years later, I attended Lake Arrowhead Christian Center, an independent charismatic church of about 350 white, middle-class Christians. After a few years, I came on as pastor and began to do some traveling, going on a missionary bandwagon. I served at the church for a total of ten years, five as senior pastor (1987 to 1992).

I felt conflicted about the expectations and structures of church life. Churches keep doing structures whether they work or not and are preoccupied with the business of church, not living the life of Jesus in the world. At Lake Arrowhead Christian Center, I was consumed with the business of Christianity and didn't live the life of Jesus all that much. Other influences in Lake Arrowhead included reading Karl Barth's *Church Dogmatics*, a biography of John Wesley, and the works of Henri Nouwen and Fredrich Buechner. I met the Aussie John Smith at a conference in Europe, the first person I met in my entire Christian experience who served as a mentor. He encouraged me in great ways.

In 1992, I left Lake Arrowhead and moved back to the city to co-pastor the Hiding Place, which had fifteen hundred to two thousand young adults in a multicultural setting. It had been going on for about ten years. From 1992 to 1994, I served as pastor, beginning as co-pastor. It was Calvary Chapel in style but charismatic in name only. The church had definitely reached its peak years ago. It was now populated by young marrieds with kids. I was far from the other pastor theologically.

In late 1995, I left the church. I started to talk to others about the deconstruction of church as we knew it, of reincarnating life and faith in God in a communal environment. Like myself, they wanted to see something different. We conversed about faith in an environment where exclusivity was dominant. We desired to be integrated. For the first time, I had my communal expression of church in sync with my individual leanings. My desire, at least from 1990, was not to be a Christian but to be a follower of Jesus. I had difficulty trying to get people on the same page, but in 1995, I began to have some like-minded conversation partners. We called our group Sanctuary.

For the first five years at Sanctuary, we were always defending, answering questions. The question that gripped us has been, What next? We have become more relaxed about who we are. Over the years, we averaged around two hundred in Sanctuary, reaching a high of four hundred at one point. Twenty-five or so people did most of the stuff, but the "who" of that twenty-five often changed. Most regular attendees had popular culture/entertainment connections. We are not wrestling anymore with the question of will we stay Christians. Now we have finished deconstructing, and we are more focused on what it means to engage our Christian faith in broader culture.

Incarnational living is less about deconstructing, more about constructing. We are now building toward something. Sanctuary represented a deconstruction of institutional Christianity while appropriating culture. New Ground is building and embracing the whole of life. At New Ground, we have sixty to ninety in conversation. We lost people who were hoping it would become a church and because we moved to a small venue to keep it fairly small. At this point, it is a conversation about where to go next.

Andy Thornton, Late Late Service, Glasgow, U.K.

I was born in Yorkshire in 1958. My dad was a churchwarden in an Anglican church. I went to church where there were sometimes only three to five people and up to twenty on other Sundays. When I was eleven years old, I joined the choir, although I didn't really have any sort of faith commitment then. I dated a girl who went to David Watson's church, St. Michael-le-Belfry in York, when I was seventeen. I prayed a prayer, which was not a problem, because I didn't really see myself as an unbeliever. I did feel that, strangely, something changed inside me. I felt something warm and affirming and quite energizing. Because I was unchurched by this time, this was completely unexpected. I began to evangelize others.

At university, I met a very rigid and judgmental friend in a Brethren church and jumped into that group. I became the youth leader, and the youth group grew from twelve to forty-five kids. I played guitar for them. One day I introduced the wrong kind of chorus and was asked not to do that again. I thought enough of that.

I moved to Dundee, Scotland, to join a renewed church where the minister was liberating people to get on with their own thing. At twenty-two, I started a festival, and by 1985, I was running it for all of Scotland. This minister was a spiritual entrepreneur and a hugely transforming influence. He asked what your vision was and how he could support it. He would come up with the money the next week. During those years, 1983 to 1985, I was the Presbyterian youth organizer for two hundred churches in the Presbytery.

A lot of people were starting bands at the time. Some were making it in the music industry. Many had a strong sense of incarnational ministry. Christians found a prophetic and insightful voice that was heard by many people in the regular culture. We found our way into the culture of our contemporaries with a voice that was creative. U2 appeared at Greenbelt at the time, a venue that has maintained a prophetic voice. The festival I ran was called Street Level, and it ran for five years.

When the Late Late Service was developing, a few of us got together to try for a time of worship. We met at a nightclub in town and had twenty to thirty people, but it was uncomfortable for the people who came. It was not enough like a nightclub for those in that scene, and it was not churchy enough for the churched, so we moved it to the church. One hundred and fifty came to our early events, and then the crowd slowly started to decrease during the year. After a year, up to forty attended regularly.

There was a huge range of people interested in alternative worship, from those who wanted to use modern media to proclaim the gospel to those who wanted to communicate their journey through what they understood God to be. We found ourselves in the middle of this wide spectrum representing experiential spirituality. Christian spirituality felt more real to us than paternalistic Christianity. Early on we saw ourselves as gatherings of Christians from around the city. Our ages were twenty-five to forty, and we related to a certain element of culture. Our congregational premise was that we represented a segment of society, not a geographical one but a geographically mobile group able to find one another in the urban setting. We were church for a certain kind of taste, yet we networked with an all-age church. We joined a local ecumenical community of seven or eight churches and asked to be one of the congregations.

We were extremely experimental and pushed boundaries. After a year, we lost our novelty. Fifty people joined our community. Membership meant broadly, "I stand with you as an intentional community." We sought to achieve fairly similar aims and to commune with God. We were orthodox Christians rooted in the orthodoxy of church trying to reembody faith in creative ways with the gifts given us. We identified ourselves as both orthodox and freedom loving. We wanted three-dimensional worship: upward, inward, and outward. We sought to assimilate different traditions and forms into a coherent Christian expression.

We had four meetings a month. One night was education night, where we covered a biblical theme. Another night was a quiet service in which we met in small groups. One night was personal growth night, where we took what we had learned that month and applied it. The final meeting was a celebration with dance music, video loops, and teams of people involved.

In 1996, I moved to London to manage the Greenbelt Festival. I visited Doug Gay, who had started an experimental evening service called Host. Host had about twenty-five people and was much less high-tech than the Late Late Service. Host was more relational than anything. The services were low on production. A worship environment should be uplifting in which we are taken out of ourselves, but there was less energy for that at Host. The encounter with God was mediated through language and simple visuals led from the front. It was still alternative worship in the sense that there was a broader set of references. It was meditative, eclectic, and experimental in grappling with contemporary culture. Like the Late Late Service, it was highly participative, with groups of three producing the events.

I attended Vaux for six to nine months. It had been going on for a year or so, was experimental and avant-garde, and met at a huge church. There I became great friends with Nic and Sooz. Nic was one of the lead graphic designers in London and looked, with high ideals, to immerse his faith through graphic design. Vaux had a lot of high art, which was one of its strongest values.

Vaux was quite anarchic; there was no designated leader figure. People from all sorts of angles came together, but nobody was ascribed an overall production role to produce coherent outputs. "Vaux is beyond hope," I laughed at the time. "They are singing out of different hymn sheets. But who am I to say that's not what some people need to escape the timeless ecclesiastical vice that has left many who love God standing outside the doors of Christian faith."

Dave Tomlinson, Holy Joes, London

I was born and raised in Liverpool and grew up in a Brethren church. My parents were Brethren, and my uncle was one of the elders. As a not very enthusiastic teenage Christian, I read *The Cross and the Switchblade* and became interested in speaking in tongues. I went to a house church in Liverpool, where, in 1966, people prayed for me to be filled with the Spirit. However far I may now be from the charismatic/Pentecostal world, this was a life-changing experience. Needless to say, my Brethren elders, including my uncle, weren't too pleased and asked me to renounce my experience or leave the assembly. I left and joined the house church.

Throughout the 1970s, I developed a public ministry and was recognized as an apostle (church planter) among the fast-growing house church movement. By the mid-1980s, I was the leader of a team of fifteen people who were responsible for planting and supervising around fifty churches. But I increasingly felt like a round peg in a square hole. I was less and less enamored with the charismatic scene and by 1988 decided to jump ship. It was a big deal. I had no idea where I belonged. I just knew I had to take a radical step.

Harry overlapped slightly with this. I found myself a bit of a magnet for artists of one sort or another who seemed to be on the fringes of the church. A lot of my connections came through being a speaker at Greenbelt. Harry was offering a mini-Greenbelt, which was able to be more edgy than Greenbelt and much more of an arts festival. It's an event that has now attained legendary status in some circles. I look back on Harry with great affection.

Holy Joes sprang out of Harry. We needed a year-round community based on the same values and theological posture. In the early days, we met in a basement in Brixton, where we had regular gigs for alternative musicians, comedians, actors, etc. It was a small, sweaty venue (fifty people and we couldn't move) but very exciting. Then we developed the open forum that became the mainstay of Holy Joes.

We knew of Nine O'clock Service in those days and greatly admired what they were doing, though none of us had ever been there. But they were an inspiration. Alternative worship, for us, began as we provided room for artists to express their art as worship. Later, we instigated a monthly worship service, and some of the same people now organize a monthly alternative service called soul space at St. Luke's, where I am the vicar. What I like about these services is that they involve people who otherwise would never be involved in organizing worship.

Harry and Holy Joes were initially gathering points for dropouts from house churches and charismatic fellowships, but they soon opened to other sorts of people, churched and unchurched. St. Luke's is a regular Anglican parish church, but in many ways it is a gathering of the same kinds of people who came to Harry and Holy Joes. Until three years ago, it was the church where Greenbelt was based, with its offices situated in the former south aisle. This has shaped the ethos of the church.

Rebecca Ver Straten McSparran, Tribe, Hollywood

I was born in the 1950s and was raised near Fuller Theological Seminary in Pasadena. As a pastor's kid, I traveled all over the Midwest. I met my husband at sixteen, and we were married four years later. We moved to Germany for three years, and we had three children. We moved to El Monte when we returned to the States and lived there for seven years.

We lived in Altadena for a few years while I attended Fuller Theological Seminary. During my studies, in 1993, I began an internship at Wilshire Presbyterian Church in Hollywood, where I did art and urban sorts of projects. I always desired to do urban ministry and graduated from Fuller in 1996. After graduating from Fuller, I became a pastor at First Congregational Church of Los Angeles, although I had gone through the ordination process of the Presbyterian Church. I really wanted to turn around an aging urban church, but that wasn't working out. I developed an art gallery, curated it, and invited local artists. I created writers groups, artists groups, and Sunday nights at the movies and thrived in this environment for several years.

I realized Dave and I were not relating to the church as it was. I felt called to bring Christ to people, to draw them in. It couldn't be a traditional church. Most of the people we knew were spiritually intelligent. They fasted, prayed, and meditated, but they were non-Christians. For me, people on the edge, in the rock 'n' roll and artistic life, were more natural for me to minister to.

In 2000, I felt God was calling me to plant a church. I realized that I lived in the nexus of art and film, the Miracle Mile in Hollywood. I felt God was calling me to begin something in that area with the connections he had given me. We don't know how to take people by the hand and help them to listen to God. That is the purpose of church. I wanted to help people hear God speak to them. In the fall of 2000, we gathered a group of five or six people to pray to see what God would do.

Our meetings began in September 2000, with the group meeting informally. In the fall of 2001, the meetings became more formal. To this day, the Tribe community is tightly connected to the art and film industry.

Sue Wallace, Visions, York, U.K.

I was born in 1967 near Stafford in the U.K. and was raised as a Christian. My mother is Anglican, and my dad is Catholic, and between them they gave me two very different perspectives on Christianity. Dad was the one who knew a lot about church traditions, but Mom was the one who knew what to do in a crisis. I was mostly raised Roman Catholic and moved around a lot as a child before settling in York when I was eleven (apart from four years in college at Canterbury and a year in North Africa).

I remember having what some would call a conversion experience quite early in life, at the age of four, in response to a talk about God needing laborers for the harvest. I remember praying something along the lines of, "Okay. I'll help if you need people." Of course, as I grew up, my faith went through all sorts of changes and fluctuations, ups and downs. I suppose the most radical change was becoming an Anglican when I was seventeen. After experiencing the missionary church in North Africa, with its vibrancy and deep sense of community, I missed the community feeling in my church back home but found something of that community love in a local Anglican church.

My dissatisfaction with the breadth of the diet being offered by the church was a gradual process. As I got more involved in the dance culture in York in the early 1990s and saw where the culture of society in general was at, the more alien and strange the normal church experiences became. It wasn't unbearable, but it was divorced from real life, sometimes to the point of seeming like we were on a different planet. I remember seeing

Graham Cray (our vicar at the time) in 1990, and when I expressed my frustration with this duality, instead of telling me off, he said something along the lines of, "Great! Now you are starting to think the same way that someone visiting the church from outside feels. And I predict that in six month's time the rest of your group will feel the same. Then you will have to start a service of your own." He was right.

There came a time when we were ready to start our own experiments at producing worship that was more culturally relevant. What marked the transition for me and a couple other people was seeing the Nine O'clock Service at Greenbelt in 1988. It was an inspiring and life-changing moment. Our ideas of what worship should look, sound, and feel like were turned on their heads when we saw this amazing, loud, multimedia service that at the same time was deeply worshipful. I remember thinking that it was really interesting but that I could never do it in a million years.

Some people think I started Visions, but actually the truth is much more complex than that. I came on board almost by accident, by being a student with nothing to do one summer holiday. In 1989, there was an ecumenical mission in the city of York, and as part of this a bunch of people got together to open a warehouse for a month as a nightclub and band venue. Someone suggested that I might like to help. Although there were lots of people involved in this initial project, it forged links between a few like-minded people who were interested in mission and culture, where society was going, and how we as a church could respond to this. A small group of around fifteen met together regularly after that for about two years, and it was out of that group that the warehouse service, which was later named Visions, was formed.

The first service was in 1991. We started with three experimental services held every three months. These then became monthly services. After a couple years, we realized we missed having communion, and so a communion service was started to meet our needs. We continued having services every two weeks for around ten years or so, when something wonderful happened. A few creative people moved to York and got involved with the group. Suddenly, we had enough people to form two teams (in effect, two Visions rather than one), which finally meant it was possible to have weekly services without the same bunch of people running them every week. In many ways we still feel fragile and vulnerable and small, but God has given us so much inspiration and so many creative people. I have the chance of being surprised and amazed in worship by the creativity of our other team.

Karen Ward, Church of the Apostles, Seattle

I was born in the early sixties and raised in Ohio. I grew up in the Lutheran Church, Missouri Synod, and attended a Lutheran parochial school, after which I went to a small, private Methodist college in Ohio. There I majored in political science, psychology, and business. I ran the Lutheran group on campus but never thought of ministry, as the Missouri Synod Lutherans never ordained women. The only church in Columbus was an Evangelical Lutheran Church of America (ELCA) church, and there I was encouraged to attend seminary. I felt called into ministry at that time, at the age of twenty-one, and attended Trinity Seminary in Columbus for the next three years. I performed my internship as a college minister in St. Olaf, Minnesota.

I was assigned, as my first call, to an African American Lutheran church in downtown Philadelphia. I had never been a part of a black church before, so this was a bit of a culture shock for me. When the lady in the big hat interrupted my three points, I didn't know what to do! After two years there, I applied to a church in the Twin Cities and was heartbroken when I didn't get it. I do believe it was because I was young, black, and a woman.

In 1994, at the age of twenty-nine, I was called by the headquarters of the ELCA in Chicago to work with them, and for the next seven years, I was assistant to the director. During that time, I traveled extensively and focused on the policies of the bureaucracy. Several times I went to the world headquarters in Geneva, Switzerland. At the headquarters, everything was upside down, while I was walking right side up. It was a machine in which I felt like a gnat on an elephant and that whatever I said would be swished away.

After five years, I began to read about postmodernity on the Internet. It gave me a language for the constant struggles I faced in the bureaucracy. Their plans to reach out to Gen-Xers seemed ridiculous to me. At that time, I was in the middle of my doctoral work. I also pastored a group of forty twenty-five- to forty-year-olds that met regularly. There was no official duty; we just liked to get together. These people thought that the idea of seeker-sensitive was really weird. They called it the "vampire church." Come and be grabbed! Like everything else, they liked storefront, organic, homegrown churches that operated with integrity and authenticity.

In 1999, I was reading the "Post-Boomer Generation" on an Episcopal website when I realized it was describing my situation exactly. In 2000, I came up with my own website to help me work out my frustrations and questions about church. I named the website EmergingChurch. com, without any idea that my name would become the name of a movement. The emerging church is what is coming to the surface. It is new, unformed, still happening, emerging. This is similar to other fields that are emerging, such as in technologies.

In 2000, my mom died. The worst thing that could happen in my life had happened, so what did I have to fear? This gave me the courage to start what I had only been dreaming of up to that point: an emerging church. I began informally discussing my idea with bishops to see who would be supportive of my plans. I did not think in denominational terms, as I always thought of myself as postdenominational. On the other hand, as a lifelong Lutheran, I saw no immediate reason to leave.

Before moving to Seattle, I visited a part of Seattle that I knew would be just right. It was the kind of community I knew in Chicago where the artists hang out, with lots of singles, art, and cafés. I knew the church needed to be right there. There were no churches in the area. The cultural resonance was Eastern, without the direct contact with religion.

Before getting funding from the ELCA, I moved to Seattle and began working at a wealthy suburban Lutheran church that paid for my move in the fall of 2001, and I worked there until the following summer.

In 2001, I pursued my vision of a church in Seattle. I wanted to plant a church among the postmoderns. I desired a church plant that would be creative and urban, as I was myself a city person. I started Church of the Apostles in 2002 with eight people who weren't relating anywhere. The biggest hindrance I have is my denomination. It is a weight around my neck. They are a mainframe; instead, they should be a hub and a router. They see themselves as having the source and the content.

Church of the Apostles is both Lutheran and Episcopal. From the Lutherans, I received a three-year salary guarantee. I wanted it all in one lump sum so I could buy $25,000 of multimedia equipment. I have my eye on an old Lutheran church right in the middle of our community in Seattle that I am petitioning for.

Andrew Jones (Boaz, U.K.) encouraged me to start a blog in early 2002. He influenced me greatly. Jonny Baker and Andrew Jones are my two mentors.

Holly Ann Rankin Zaher, Three Nails, Pittsburgh

I was born in 1972 in Florida and spent my growing-up years there and in South Carolina. Baptized Roman Catholic, I remember my mother talking to me about Jesus at an early age. We attended Anglican churches while I was growing up, and then when I was eleven years of age, we joined an intentional community in which 90 percent of the people were Roman Catholic. It was also highly charismatic. I worked in youth ministry and youth camps. In my junior year of high school, I decided to become more serious about faith issues.

I love teaching math, and that is what I began to do after college. However, I really wanted to see lives changed and desired to be trained in youth ministry. Therefore, I went to Trinity School for Ministry in Ambridge, Pittsburgh, where I got an M.A. in youth ministry. I had been with Rock the World, an Episcopal youth ministry, since my college days, specifically working with the Josiah Project. I lived in community with three others in urban settings. Beginning in 1997, I began to read whatever I could. In 2002, I attended Search Party, an early gathering in St. Louis of emerging church leaders, and that is where I met Doug Pagitt and Brian McLaren. Later they asked me to join them.

I had worked with Don Cox since 1993, and in the fall of 2002, the diocese of Pittsburgh supported Don and Shannon Cox, in coordination with Rock the World, to plant a church in emerging culture. We looked around and saw that a majority of people couldn't connect with the current structure of church. We came to realize that we were worshiping the actual form of church. We wanted to create something that would be Anglican in its ethos and identity but more fluid in its form. At first, it was a generational church plant. Then we found that it was much more about a cultural shift as people of all ages, rather than just a specific generation, began to identify with us. There were many people who felt disconnected.

From the outset, we wanted to be a church movement, not just a church plant. We wanted to be missional and not steal young people from existing Anglican churches. The diocese approved of the church and gave it tons of support and latitude. We met for the first time as a group in February 2003. There are ten people in the core group, with most of us having formed relationships through Rock the World.

In the fall of 2003, we launched six cell groups that meet during the week. They function as churches. In fact, less than half of the cell participants come to the monthly gathering. The combined attendance of the cells might number sixty, while the monthly gathering numbers about thirty. The typical members of the core of the church are twenty-somethings, followed by thirtysomethings, and a few teens and a few fortysomethings.

Three Nails has been alive for eighteen months, and amazing things are going on. We are asking, "What does it mean to be Anglican without imposing stuff on our community?" since half of the core leadership is not Anglican, and these people react against the liturgical emphasis.

I'm part of a creative expression group that takes responsibility for the monthly gathering. Different groups do the monthly event, and so it is different each month. It is quite a challenge, because there are those who believe that any musical worship is manipulative, and there are those who believe that the only way to hear God is through music. We are creating a space where both interests can be heard. We are starting to listen to one another.

Dieter Zander, Quest, Novato, California

I was born in 1960 in Portland, Oregon, and raised in an unbelieving family. I came to faith through contact with my aunt and began to attend Trinity Baptist Church in Portland, a conservative Baptist denomination. After high school, I attended Lewis and Clark College, where I graduated with a degree in music. After college, I served at an internship, and there I understood that I was called into ministry. In 1984, I moved to Southern California to attend seminary at International School of Theology (ISOT), a Campus Crusade affiliated seminary that no longer exists. I still understood that I was going to be a choral director of some kind.

As part of my internship for ISOT, I attended Alta Loma Conservative Baptist, where Bob Logan served as pastor. After I shared my dream about starting a church, Bob encouraged me to do just that. I received a vision in the fall of 1984 of young people worshiping in an auditorium with a rock band and drama. This picture was burned in my brain. I shared this vision with Bob the next Monday, and Bob challenged me to start it. He informed me that their church had been praying for someone to lead a ministry like this for the past two and a half years. At around the same time, I met a Campus Crusade for Christ staff member, Val, whom I married in December 1985. Val was an essential part of the church start.

For a year and a half, I researched surrounding churches, examining their character. I informally began NewSong in 1984 in Covina. My vision was to create a church for both the unchurched and those disillusioned with church. In March of 1986, we began to have meetings in our home, and in June, we held our first public meeting.

In 1986, the church went public, and forty-two punk rockers attended the first service. We didn't set out to start the first Gen-X church; rather, we were looking to create a church for the people in between, those too old for youth groups and those too young for, or culturally distant from, the Boomer style of church. We began with fifty punk rockers, but when I rebuked one, all but nine left. I wanted to leave too, but that September we started over again, this time with fifteen to twenty people. Between 1986 and 1988, I finished my M.Div. at the International School of Theology.

Our music was not very polished. We gave greater access to the front than seeker churches or Calvary Chapels and Vineyards did. Our talks were raw and not very deep, and we allowed questions from people, even non-Christians. The Boomer ethos was the good-looking, superman pastor. Gen-Xers felt excluded by this. We wanted to show dirt, and we included many types of people, not just professionals. We liked to celebrate. We were authentic but safe as well. We were rousing, real, relevant, and relational.

We spent the 1980s finding our voice. In 1989, we moved to Cal Poly (University of Cal State, Pomona), where we grew from one hundred to four hundred. Bob Logan joined us at this time. He was my balance and my ballast. We then had to leave Cal Poly and went to Mt. San Antonio, where we grew to eight hundred. Our next move was to Royal Oaks, where we grew to twelve hundred (from one hundred to twelve hundred in three years!). Eventually, we found a permanent home on a business site in San Dimas.

Our church was comprised mainly of dissatisfied churchgoers. Attendance was primarily at the large gathering, as we had only twelve small groups. By the time we had grown to twelve hundred, we had thirty small groups. My role was to coordinate the service, at which I led worship and preached. Bill Hybels was my model of preaching. Our services at this time were highly experiential, as I felt I needed to go with the visions people had. We were 70 percent single, and the average age was twenty-five in 1992. We were running one Saturday night and two Sunday services.

My philosophy throughout this period included church as family, as small groups, as quality programming, as servant leadership, and as a place to tell your story. At the services, we featured twenty to twenty-five minutes of rock 'n' roll praise, a time for announcements, a sermon, and a drama. My preaching style was distinct in the following ways: I did not use points, I did not give answers, I stayed in story, I avoided political issues, and I was honest in a vulnerable way. I believed in the three Rs: real, relevant, and relational.

In 1992, we tried to become a seeker church. We described the difference as showing a person a brochure about a place compared to actually going there; talking about a relationship with God versus actually having one; telling them about an experience instead of facilitating the experience. We wanted to be distinctive, to give seekers something different from what they knew. Gen-Xers wanted to experience community, not watch a documentary about it.

This seeker venture disoriented NewSong and was a massive failure. The church did not want to reach anyone. Instead, they wanted to worship God. In 1993, we gave up on the experiment and returned to the more authentic style of worship. At this time, God released me; I knew I did not have another vision or perspective to lead the church into.

It was then that I had my first conversations at Willow Creek, and for the next year or so, Bill Hybels wanted me to come. In January 1994, I decided to leave NewSong, and I departed in May of that year to start a church-within-a-church for the Gen-Xers at Willow Creek. Both Bill Hybels and I bristled at the term *church-within-a-church,* because our goal was to build a bridge to the next generation. I led a well-funded program, which we called Axis. For this ministry, we created thirty-five small groups. From 1994 to 1995, I was a teaching pastor, and in the fall of 1995, I began to try working out Gen-X forms of church. In the spring of 1996, we began a full set of services.

That same year, Hybels began a process of "alignment," meaning ministries needed to be more in sync with one another. However, this cut the legs from beneath what I was doing. I felt that Willow Creek was promoting one way of doing ministry, while I was promoting an entirely new way. I had assumed I could do NewSong in Illinois and was ignorant of the strong culture of Willow Creek.

For example, anonymity is key for Willow Creek, but Gen-Xers hate that. Not having worship is key for Willow Creek, whereas experiential worship is key for Gen-Xers. The people at Axis were from Willow Creek and had grown up with these ideas, so they weren't convinced my way was the right way. These believers didn't believe in the kind of service I was doing, so they weren't bringing their seeker friends. At that point, I took a couple steps back, and the services began to resemble Willow Creek more, except for faster and louder music. But I wanted to be an advocate for Gen-Xers, to give them a voice for how church is done. I saw that Boomers couldn't coexist with other groups as one congregation among others.

Another dynamic at Willow Creek was that some seekers were coming to the believers' meetings and not the Sundays because they wanted to experience what we were talking about. Axis had about six hundred to eight hundred people as part of the community. Hybels expected faster growth and was disappointed. I had sufficient staff, but I just didn't lead them for growth. I believed that Axis was to be experimental and that we were not to evaluate it for several years. This was part of my understanding in coming to Willow Creek in the first place. It was a bit of a surprise to me when the focus became numbers and not experimentation.

I advocated for the Gen-X generation. Although I was a "tweener," I wanted Boomers to understand the Gen-Xers and to provide them space to lead a church. Much of my work at the time was looking to give leadership opportunities where there were none. There was a general dismissal of the difference. "When they grow up and get on with the main church, Axis probably won't be necessary. This Gen-X ministry will help them stick around until they grow up," Hybels said. I thought I was forming the next thing the church would become, but Hybels thought it was a sub-ministry, like a high school ministry. Boomers went through their antiestablishment phase and eventually returned to church, and they expected Gen-Xers to do the same. However, Gen-Xers never knew Ward and June Cleaver, and they never wanted to return to that.

When I found out that Axis was a holding tank, a place to let the disgruntled hang out until they were ready for real church, I knew it would be just a matter of time until I left. Ultimately, I didn't believe that Axis needed to fold into the rest of the church, and Hybels did. Even though church-within-a-church did not work in this case, I am still hopeful about that model.

In 1997, I received a manuscript of Dallas Willard's forthcoming book. It changed my life. It was as profound an experience as when I first came to Christ. I never really understood how Jesus could be the teacher of my life. He is the Lord of life, the one who could show me how to live. I felt that I never really got the gospel. It was so powerful that it took me about a year to get my head around it. That's when the hunger began. What would happen if we tried to live this out? I saw the gospel as an invitation into kingdom life. As they were with Jesus, would people be drawn to life through people who lived the kingdom?

My wife, Val, and I took a five-month sabbatical in 1998. We desired to move to an urban setting because of the diversity of ideas, people, and religions. Part of this was a reaction to suburban northwest Chicago, which was so mono-cultural. What would happen if we lived around non-Christians? Would they be drawn to Christ? In 1998, Carol Davis encouraged me to think about San Francisco. When we moved there, we found that every window faces our neighbors. Our lives were lived in front of others. We asked ourselves, "What would living the kingdom look like in San Francisco? How do we get people to consider Christ when they are anti-Christ? This is a future city, a postmodern city. Can we figure out how to live the gospel in this context?"

My wife and I lived in San Francisco for five years in a two-bedroom, twelve-hundred-square-foot flat with our three boys. When we moved in, we asked, "God, why are we here?" We got to know our neighbors. We discovered that loving our neighbors meant getting to know them, serving them, and helping them know one another. One of our neighbors commented, "I don't know what you guys have, but an enzyme has been added. Once there was no life; now there is life."

We encouraged people to realize that everything counts, that life-giving events manifest God's kingdom. We sought to pull together what the gospel was. We contacted Dallas Willard, who counseled us that the key thing is asking the right questions. "What question are you seeking to answer?" Willard asked. I responded that we wanted to ask and answer the question What is the gospel? We got a group of Christians together to share our thoughts. They thought the question was ludicrous. "Everybody knows what the gospel is," they said. However, we realized they were mistaken.

We started a little nonprofit organization. We didn't want to tell others we were ministers or missionaries. We wanted to reimagine what a life with God might look like in real, practical terms. We recontextualized ourselves in order to have conversations with people.

Each one in ReIMAGINE! has a different emphasis: Mark Scandrette with art, Linda with social action, myself with neighborhood-based faith communities. We gather to do good news to the neighborhood. The groups meet to be servant-oriented to the neighborhood. We meet, first, to be with other Christians and, second, to reimagine life with God, rethink the gospel, and reapply it as a practical outworking of doing good in the world in Jesus' name. Each of us seeks to be a coworker with Jesus, flowing from the gospel.

For a while, I worked at two churches. At Quest, a church plant in Novato, California, I worked with community groups. At the other, BayMarin (San Rafael, CA), I worked as a worship leader on Sunday mornings. We moved to Novato, which is still in the Bay area, as we couldn't afford to live in the city. In February of 2005, I made the decision to work solely with BayMarin as the pastor of arts and spiritual formation.

Research Methodology

Our approach to this study was exploratory. As opposed to testing a particular thesis, we investigated the nature of emerging churches and movements. Through our first set of questions, we sought simply to better understand these communities. Who participates in these innovative forms of church? How different are these churches and leaders from one another? To what extent do they differ significantly from their predecessors and prevailing models of church? Will they play a significant role in the future of the Western church? Are they groundbreaking frontiers, or are they diversionary fringes?

Primarily, we chose an interview approach supplemented by case studies for our research methodology, giving those involved the opportunity to tell their stories as well as to respond to the questions that emerged, which we used in subsequent interviews to facilitate comparisons. We employed interviews, observations, and document analysis to achieve our aims.[1] In designing our research, we hoped to locate some of the most vital new forms of church in the West. Through our research, we aimed to discover why these churches are so vibrant and alive and why those creatively immersed in popular culture gather at these sites, especially when there are so many options for spirituality outside the church.

---

1. We triangulated our research using multiple methods (interviews, observations, document analysis, video, and personal experience). Triangulation involves using more than one research method in a study. This is done to minimize the weaknesses in any one particular approach and to provide a more comprehensive picture.

Through both interviews and case studies, we sought examples that illustrated the wide range of significantly innovative approaches to church. Our use of extensive interviews was designed to identify common characteristics as well as to isolate individual insights and variables. We noticed similarities among emerging churches and leaders as a whole. Our research was designed to ensure that we identified the right patterns, that we heard the many voices, and that we adequately represented them through our interview choices and open-ended approach.

The first task was to cast the net broadly to identify the churches that appeared to meet the following criteria:

- They are located in the Western world—those countries that fully experienced modernity and are now embroiled in a cultural transition.
- They consider themselves Christians or Christ followers.
- They consider themselves a congregation or a mission. We did not want a small group of an existing church. Rather, we wanted a group that had its own leaders and performed all the functions of a church.
- They meet at least monthly. We did not want an occasional grouping of individuals.
- They are still meeting. Many groups are now defunct, but we wanted groups that are exhibiting influence now.
- Their group or movement is less than twenty years old. We sought groups that connected to contemporary culture with a fresh vision.

Of those that met the above criteria, we specifically focused on those communities that most often expressed the following characteristics:

- They maintain a strong corporate expression outside the church walls through the forms of popular culture, such as club culture with DJs, dance, imagery, pub culture, artistic communities, or youth culture. We wanted to identify the groups that are strongly committed to engaging the outside culture rather than confining themselves to evangelical, contemporary Christian subcultures.
- Their gatherings employ a multisensory communication approach, utilizing visual arts, movement, symbols, incense, icons, candles, DJ music, etc.

Beginning in the year 2000, we conducted a snowball[2] search for anyone and everything associated with innovative churches. We searched the Internet using the keywords *postmodern* and *church*; *postmodern* and *worship*; *Gen-X* and *church*; *Gen-X* and *worship*; *buster* and *church*; *buster* and *worship*. We conducted searches on spirituality, alternative worship, and postmodern religion, to name but a few. We visited all the e-zines, blogs, and chat rooms that discussed new forms of church. We explored books written by church consultants. We visited the most frequented websites among emerging church leaders. In all these cases, if any of the churches met the requirements listed above, we included them in our database. Admittedly, we cast the net pretty wide.

Next, with each church in the database, we followed its recommended links and added those churches that met the criteria. We repeated this process until we found no new names. At several points in the study, we emailed various experts and church leaders and asked them for a list of emerging churches. If these churches met our requirements, we added their names as well.

Our preliminary research in the spring of 2000 revealed approximately two hundred churches and communities that fit our criteria. At the same time, we recognized that we could not ascertain the nature of these initial communities without a visit. As we plotted their locations, we discovered that they were often clustered around centers of technology and within world-class cities that were making a global cultural impact, which meant that they were also centers of mass media. Our assumption was that these new churches would be both multicultural and urban in ethos, because such was the cultural environment of the emerging generation. It should be noted that such churches need not necessarily be located in a city to have an urban culture, because it has spilled over into suburbia, small towns, and even villages. Urban no longer describes a location but a way of thinking and a lifestyle.

Following the initial data selection, we contacted many of the sites we had identified. Some of these websites referred to meetings and groups that no longer existed. We continued to modify our search until we had verified the groups that seemed to meet our criteria. These churches responded to our inquiries, confirming that we were accurate in our understanding of what they were doing. They, in

2. One person leads to another and to another, and the sample continues to grow and grow. Hence the term snowball.

turn, referred us to other communities and leaders we might want to include.

We ranked the groups based on the number of recommendations by others. We noted where they were located and what they were doing. We contacted many of their websites and received responses from most. We found that groups of churches tended to reference only those within their particular network. Patterns of relationships emerged that enabled us to separate our rankings by network.

Is it possible that we missed an entire movement? We may have missed a small group here or there, but we followed every group that had any sort of Internet presence or relationship with those who had an Internet presence. For us to have missed a church group, it would need to have had little or no influence or contacts outside its particular small group, and, ultimately, these groups were not part of who we were interested in talking to anyway.

We identified leaders we could consult regarding the churches we had identified in our search. We ascertained from them which of the churches were the most significant in terms of our criteria, and thus excellent candidates for a more in-depth case study, and whether there were others we had failed to identify. This helped narrow down our case study selection to no more than forty to fifty churches in the United Kingdom that met our criteria.[3] The number was similar in the United States.[4] During the course of the study, we became aware of the evolving and expanding nature of the movement in both countries.

We visited a number of these churches to interview their key leaders. We visited the U.K. in April and May of 2001, and we interviewed the leaders of U.S. emerging churches beginning in the fall of 2002. Our primary pursuit during this time was to see the big picture by mapping the movement as a whole. During 2002 and 2003, we studied these movements to ascertain the patterns within emerging churches and to develop criteria by which they could be recognized.

During our four-week visit to the U.K. in April–May 2001, interviews were the primary method for our study. We heard the stories of

3. In a way, our method resembled respondent-driven sampling, except for the fact that more often than not the information we received came from websites.

4. In the United States, we paid closer attention to the issue of cultural forms. Because of the large amount of funds available to purchase high-tech media, churches in the United States could on the surface appear to have made the necessary cultural transitions to engage in mission. On closer inspection, however, they have remained profoundly modern in their underlying cultural assumptions. In the United Kingdom, the church has neither the resources nor the church-related constituencies to replicate the North American experience.

these groups, their histories, and their varied approaches. We scheduled interviews with church leaders who were starting and/or leading churches and movements. For two weeks in April, Gibbs interviewed young people at the annual spring harvest gathering in the U.K.[5] As a speaker at the spring harvest conference in April, he interviewed those who seemed to be participating in a ministry that met our criteria. At the same time, Bolger traveled around the south of the U.K. and Wales, visiting church leaders and querying them about their ministries. We joined efforts as we went to the middle and the north of the U.K. to conduct additional interviews.

Beginning in the fall of 2002, we interviewed emerging church leaders in the U.S. We interviewed at the Ooze annual gathering in Minneapolis during October of that year, at the Emergent/Youth Specialties event in San Diego in 2004, and through extensive phone conversations beginning in May 2004.

In our initial face-to-face, email, and telephone interviews, we used a semi-structured approach. We wanted general impressions of their stories, journeys to that point, and impressions of other groups. We asked the following questions: What are your subsequent reflections as you look back on your journey, and where do you see yourself heading in the future? What is your relationship to other movements? What books do you consider significant? What is particularly different about your meetings, inside and outside the church? During our visit to the U.K., we endeavored to attend as many meetings as time permitted.

We tailored each interview to the level of expertise of the leader. We asked leaders who led the various movements questions in their domain of understanding. In regard to those leaders whose interest was primarily in the local group, we limited our questions to that particular group. For every group we selected, we identified and spoke to its key leaders. We were particularly sensitive to avoid letting our presuppositions intrude into the discussions and influence the responses.

Some of the leaders' interviews we conducted together so as to be informed about each other's interview techniques. This enabled us to arrive at a common style that allowed closer correspondence in the information gleaned separately. After each interview, as soon as we were able, we transcribed our recordings as fully as possible but not necessarily verbatim. We then worked through the transcripts, assigning paragraph headings to indicate major topics. Finally, at

5. In 2001, sixty-four thousand people gathered, distributed between two locations and over three weeks (approximately ten thousand people were present for each of the weeks at each location).

the end of each interview, we listed the key topics that emerged for easier referencing.

Budget and time restrictions prohibited us from making participant observation a key part of the study, as many meetings are held monthly and, because of the size of the study, we were limited to attending meetings only when possible. Instead of observation, we determined that we would support our interview research with document analysis, primarily through websites. For the most part, then, our limited participant observation served as a foil to confirm or deny other aspects of our research. Document analysis played a large role in our research, as some of these emerging communities have prolific writers, comprehensive websites, and blogs. We studied their important texts as a method of triangulation in order to discover powerful themes and narratives.

In May of 2004, in response to four years of collecting data, we created nine characteristics that seemed to capture the missiological insights of emerging churches. At that point, we again went back to interviewing to receive fresh stories and insights based on these categories. We interviewed over fifty key leaders from one to six hours via telephone or up to five extensive emails. The questions were as follows:

When and where were you born and raised?

What is your faith journey? Were you raised in the church, or did you come to faith later? Did it become more real at some point?

What led you to start this service/ministry? What was it about church that made it no longer satisfying for you? Was there a particular event that marked this transition?

Do you see yourself as postevangelical, post-Protestant? Are those categorizations a help or a hindrance?

Do you see yourself as missional? Do you stress living in the kingdom of God, living like Jesus, in terms of your faith being a way of life as opposed to a set of meetings?

Is church equated with a meeting, a place, or a way of life? How so?

Do the members of your group have any sort of commitment to one another?

How do you interact with other faiths, religions? What role does evangelism play? Does apologetics play a role?

What role does social service play in your group?

What does participation look like in your group? Do all participate at the meeting?

How important is creativity to what you do? Do you embrace material forms of culture? Why?

How does leadership work in your community?

What do you think of vision/mission statements?

What historic (e.g., ancient) aspects of spirituality does your group participate in, both in and out of the worship service?

What are the greatest realizations that have occurred since you began ministry in this way?

For some individuals, we added, changed, or deleted some of the questions based on their relative level of expertise in given areas.

After these interviews were completed in the summer of 2004, they were analyzed and compiled, and we began the process of book writing. That effort went full steam from September 2004 through July 2005, resulting in the work you are reading now.

Index

337